**FOR ORGANS, PIANOS & ELECTRONIC KEYBOARDS**

BE MY VALENTINE

384

ISBN 0-634-01466-8

7777 W. BLUEMOUND RD. P.O. BOX 13819 MILWAUKEE, WI 53213

For all works contained herein:
Unauthorized copying, arranging, adapting, recording or public performance is an infringement of copyright.
Infringers are liable under the law.

E-Z PLAY® TODAY Music Notation © 1975 by HAL LEONARD CORPORATION
E-Z PLAY and EASY ELECTRONIC KEYBOARD MUSIC are registered trademarks of HAL LEONARD CORPORATION.

Visit Hal Leonard Online at
www.halleonard.com

BE MY VALENTINE

CONTENTS

12	ALL I ASK OF YOU	90	JUST THE WAY YOU ARE
9	BEAUTIFUL IN MY EYES	94	THE KEEPER OF THE STARS
16	CAN YOU FEEL THE LOVE TONIGHT	98	LOVE ME TENDER
22	CAN'T HELP FALLING IN LOVE	100	MY CHERIE AMOUR
19	(THEY LONG TO BE) CLOSE TO YOU	102	MY FUNNY VALENTINE
24	COULD I HAVE THIS DANCE	104	MY HEART WILL GO ON (LOVE THEME FROM 'TITANIC')
27	DON'T KNOW MUCH		
32	ENDLESS LOVE	108	RIBBON IN THE SKY
36	FIELDS OF GOLD	87	SAVE THE BEST FOR LAST
40	THE GIFT	112	SAVING ALL MY LOVE FOR YOU
45	A GROOVY KIND OF LOVE	116	TO LOVE YOU MORE
48	GROW OLD WITH ME	120	UNCHAINED MELODY
50	HERE AND NOW	122	VALENTINE
60	HERE, THERE AND EVERYWHERE	130	WHEN I FALL IN LOVE
55	I FINALLY FOUND SOMEONE	125	A WHOLE NEW WORLD
62	I JUST CALLED TO SAY I LOVE YOU	132	A WINK AND A SMILE
66	I WILL	146	WONDERFUL TONIGHT
68	I WILL BE HERE	136	YOU AND I
73	I'LL BE	138	YOU ARE THE SUNSHINE OF MY LIFE
78	IF	140	YOU'LL BE IN MY HEART (POP VERSION)
80	IT'S YOUR LOVE		

BE MY VALENTINE

Valentine's Day conjures images of flowers, cards, candy and cupids as it inspires declarations of undying love. Although the trappings have changed over the years, as well as the name of day, the middle of February has been associated with affairs of the heart for centuries. Some of the details about this holiday's history are well-documented fact, other bits of information are little more than hazy tales, but all are tied to the idea of romance.

As far back as the fourth century B.C., the fifteenth of February was a feast day called Lupercalia, celebrating the protector of crops and livestock. The evening before the feast day was a celebration honoring Juno, the Roman goddess of love and marriage. Part of the two-day celebration required that all unmarried, young women place their names in a jar. Every unmarried, young man would then pick a name, and the pair would celebrate the feasts of Juno and Lupercalia as a couple. Some descriptions of the feast explain that the couple would be paired for a year. In the course of that year, many of these couples would fall in love and eventually marry.

The man for whom the holiday is named is a bit of a mysterious character. In one version of the story, a Roman priest named Valentine was imprisoned during the third century for marrying couples against the edict of Emperor Claudius II. Claudius had nothing against marriage itself, he simply believed his soldiers should remain single. Claudius was afraid that marriage would distract the soldiers from their duties, thus weakening his army. While Valentine was in prison, or so the legend goes, he fell in love with the jailer's blind daughter. Her sight was miraculously restored. When Valentine was eventually beheaded for his crime, in about 270, he left a farewell message for the jailer's daughter. He signed it "From Your Valentine."

In another version of the legend, Valentine is a doctor who was imprisoned and sentenced to death for his Christian beliefs. In this legend too, Valentine falls in love with the jailer's blind daughter, curing her of her blindness. When he is eventually beheaded for his beliefs, on February 14, he leaves her a note signed "From Your Valentine." Yet another version has Valentine not a Christian, but someone who was jailed and martyred for helping Christians escape persecution. The imprisonment, blind daughter of the jailer, eventual martyrdom and signed note appear in this story as well.

Although the facts are cloudy, someone named Valentine certainly lived and was martyred for some act of faith. In 496, Pope Gelasius declared February 14 the day to honor St. Valentine, hoping to turn attention from the pagan holidays to the Christian remembrance of the saint. St. Valentine soon became the patron saint of lovers. In 1969 Pope Paul VI removed the observance from the church calendar, but there was no removing Valentine's name from the mid-February celebration of romance.

When the feasts of Juno and Lupercalia became the Christian observance of St. Valentine's day, many of the traditions of the pagan holiday simply continued under a new banner. The holiday became the time for Roman men to state their affection for a woman. It became a tradition for Roman men to give a written declaration of affection to a woman, including Valentine's name in the note.

References to writing love letters and sending tokens of affection on Valentine's Day turn up frequently in English and French literature of the fourteenth and fifteenth centuries. Legend has it that the first valentine card was sent in 1415 by Charles, Duke of Orleans. He was imprisoned in the Tower of London at the time and sent the card to his wife in France. He sent many such cards during his imprisonment, some 60 of which have survived to the present day. The cards are filled with loving poems he wrote for her. These "valentines" are held in the British Museum.

Some two hundred years later, flowers began to appear as Valentine's Day declarations. At a valentine party given by the daughter of Henry IV of France, each young man in attendance was instructed to give a particularly beautiful bouquet of flowers to the young woman he had chosen as his valentine. Cupid began to appear on Valentine's Day cards during the sixteenth century. Carrying arrows dipped in love potions, he became tied to the day because he is the son of Venus, known in Roman mythology as the goddess of love and beauty. Valentine's Day cards were becoming more ornately decorated with each passing year.

During the seventeenth century, commercial Valentine's Day cards were available, although many people preferred to make their own over-sized, elaborately decorated cards by hand. In 1797 a booklet appeared in Britain entitled *The Young Man's Valentine Writer*. The booklet provided verses for a young man to write in the card he sent to a young lady. Soon other such "valentine writers" began to appear, as did books of responses that a young lady might choose to send back after receiving a valentine. In about 1823, "valentine writers" began appearing in the United States, where the valentine tradition had followed immigrants from Europe.

In time, Valentine's Day greetings became a huge commercial enterprise. Three dimensional valentines, constructed of pasteboard, caught on in Europe and quickly gained popularity in America as well. In 1830, a Mount Holyoke College student named Esther Howland began creating the first commercial valentines made in America. Her father, a Worcester, Massachusetts stationer, had imported large numbers of valentines from England every year. Importing lace and fine papers herself, Miss Howland employed her brothers and several others to create domestic valentines, which became known as "Worcester Valentines." The cards were priced in the five to ten dollar range, with some selling for as much as thirty-five dollars. Miss Howland is remembered as one of America's first successful business women, selling some $100,000 in valentines annually — quite a sum in the 1830's.

During the nineteenth century, Valentine's Day cards began to appear as gestures of friendship as well as declarations of affection. Falling postal rates in Europe and America allowed people of all income levels to indulge in the tradition of sending cards. Part of the tradition included sending an elaborate card that bore no signature other than "From your valentine." With the increased popularity of valentines, spoofs began to appear on the market. John McLaughlin, a New York printer, launched a line of cheap, garish, comic valentines that were dubbed "vinegar valentines." In 1870, comedic valentines designed by American cartoonist Charles Howard became quite popular. They were dubbed "penny dreadfuls" because they sold for a penny and were quite dreadful.

By the Gay Nineties, the Victorian spirit of elaborate ornamentation and mawkish sentimentality could be found oozing from valentines. Valentines from that era were festooned with spun glass, mother-of-pearl, faux jewels, ornate lace and fussy fringe. What had started as simple notes expressing affection were now enormous, bulky, three-fold constructions that had to be hand delivered because they were too large and fragile to send by post. In the later decades of the century, albums were sold for preserving and displaying valentines. These elaborate Victorian valentines, and the books that held them, are quite popular with collectors today.

Flowers have long been associated with Valentine's Day, both in the decoration of cards and as gifts. An entire language of flowers has grown up with the tradition of sending blossoms on Valentine's Day. The red rose, of course, is the flower that symbolizes love. The yellow rose is said by some to indicate jealousy, while others use them to denote friendship. The red tulip also symbolizes love, although the yellow tulip indicates hopeless love. The white lily is a symbol of purity and the forget-me-not is a symbol of true love. In America and Britain, an old tradition says that a young woman can determine what sort of man she will marry by the first bird she spots on Valentine's Day. If she sees a robin she will marry a sailor but if she spots a goldfinch, her husband will be a rich man. A dove indicates a good man and a bluebird indicates a happy man. If she sees a sparrow she will marry a farmer but if she sees a woodpecker she will never marry.

Valentine's Day has survived the twentieth century, with the holiday coming in second only to Christmas in the number of cards sold. Over one billion valentines are delivered by mail in the U.S. each year. Many Americans attempt to have their valentines postmarked by the post office in Loveland, Colorado, creating a flood of mail there every year. Some 85 percent of the valentines sold each year in the U.S. are purchased by women. The fourteenth of February remains a popular day for weddings, elopements, marriage proposals, second honeymoons and romantic dinners. Florists, candy shops and jewelry stores do a booming business during the first two weeks of the month. The day has also become a popular children's holiday, celebrated with classroom parties and valentine exchanges.

Beautiful in My Eyes

Registration 7
Rhythm: Pop Ballad or 8 Beat

Words and Music by
Joshua Kadison

© 1993 JOSHUASONGS, EMI BLACKWOOD MUSIC INC. and SEYMOUR GLASS MUSIC
All Rights Controlled and Administered by EMI BLACKWOOD MUSIC INC.
All Rights Reserved   International Copyright Secured   Used by Permission

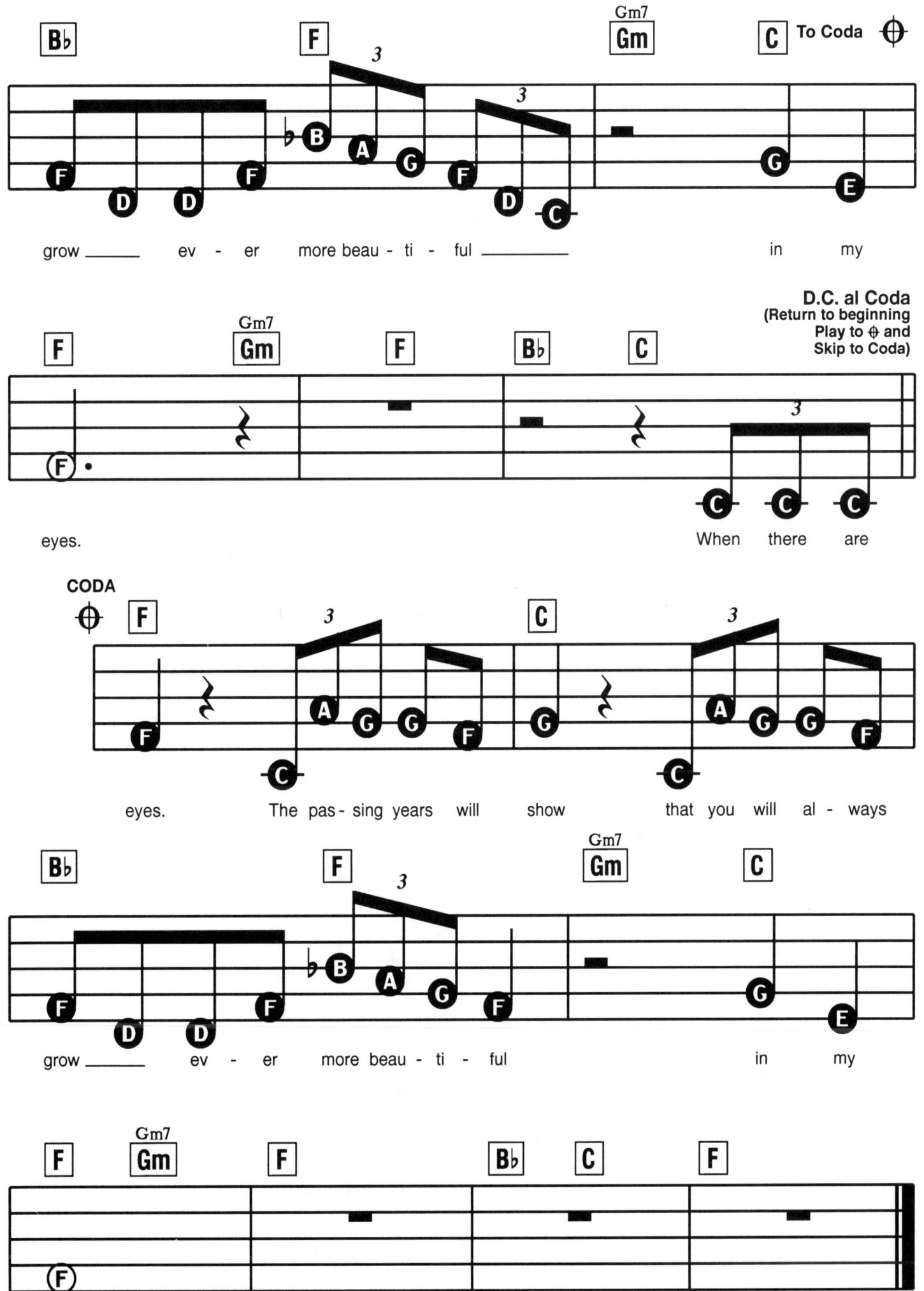

All I Ask of You
from THE PHANTOM OF THE OPERA

Registration 8 *Ballad*
Rhythm: 8 Beat or Rock

Music by Andrew Lloyd Webber
Lyrics by Charles Hart
Additional Lyrics by Richard Stilgoe

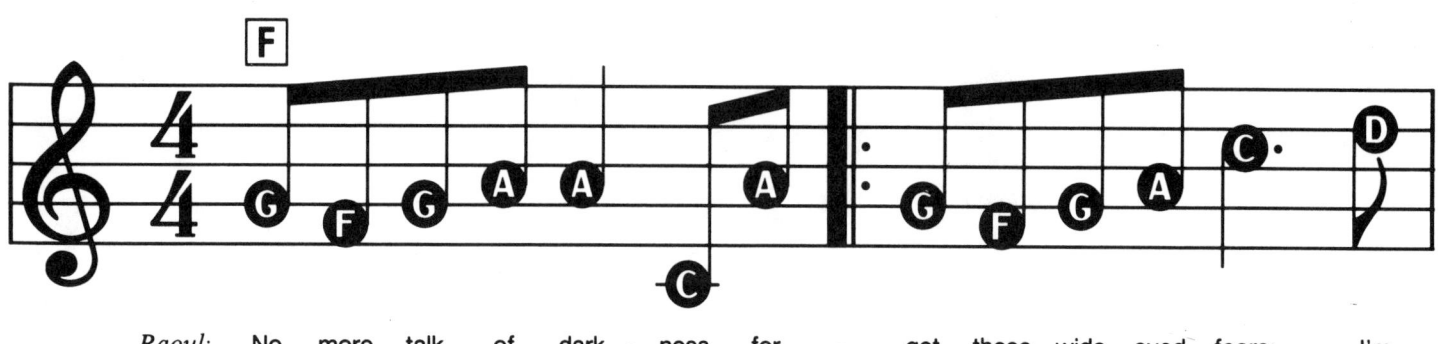

Raoul: No more talk of dark - ness, for - get these wide - eyed fears: I'm
let me be your light; you're

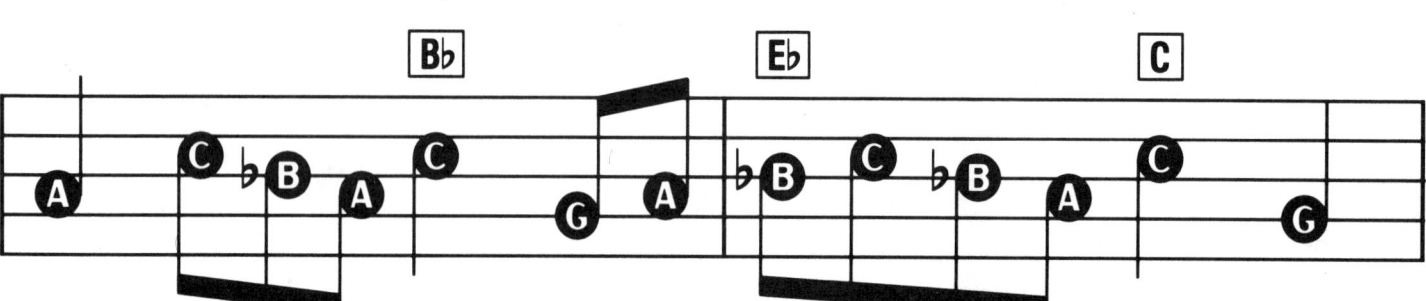

here, noth - ing can harm you, my words will warm and calm you.
safe, no one will harm find you, your fears are warm far be - hind you.

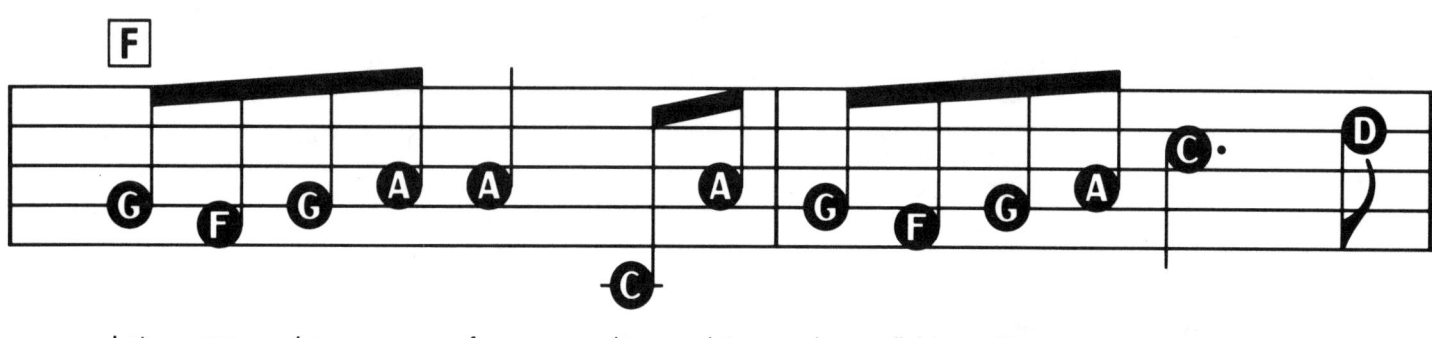

Let me be your free - dom, let day - light dry your tears; I'm
Christine: All I want is free - dom, a world with no more night; and

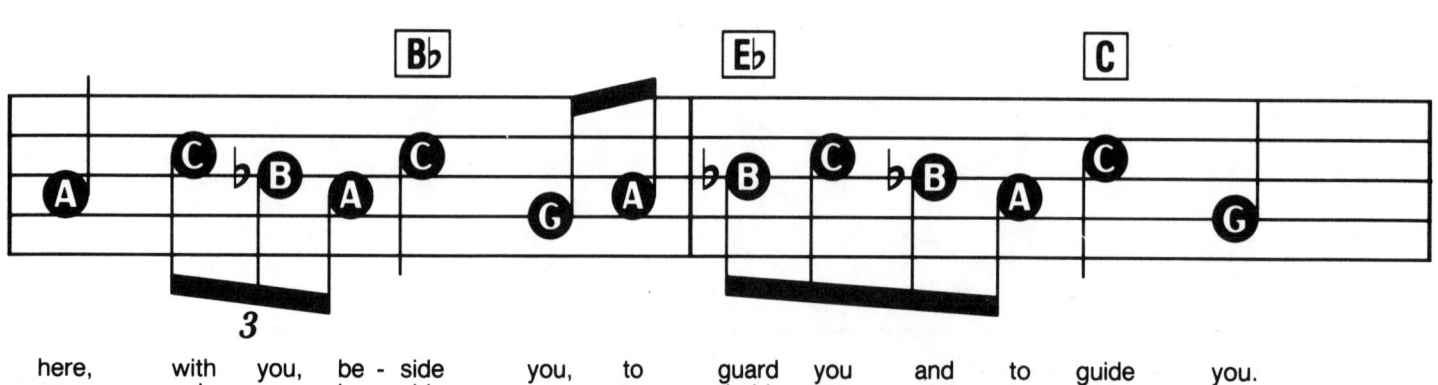

here, with you, be - side you, to guard you and to guide you.
you, al - ways be - side me, to hold me and to hide me. *Raoul:* Then

© Copyright 1986 The Really Useful Group Ltd.
All Rights for the United States and Canada Administered by Universal – PolyGram International Publishing, Inc.
International Copyright Secured   All Rights Reserved

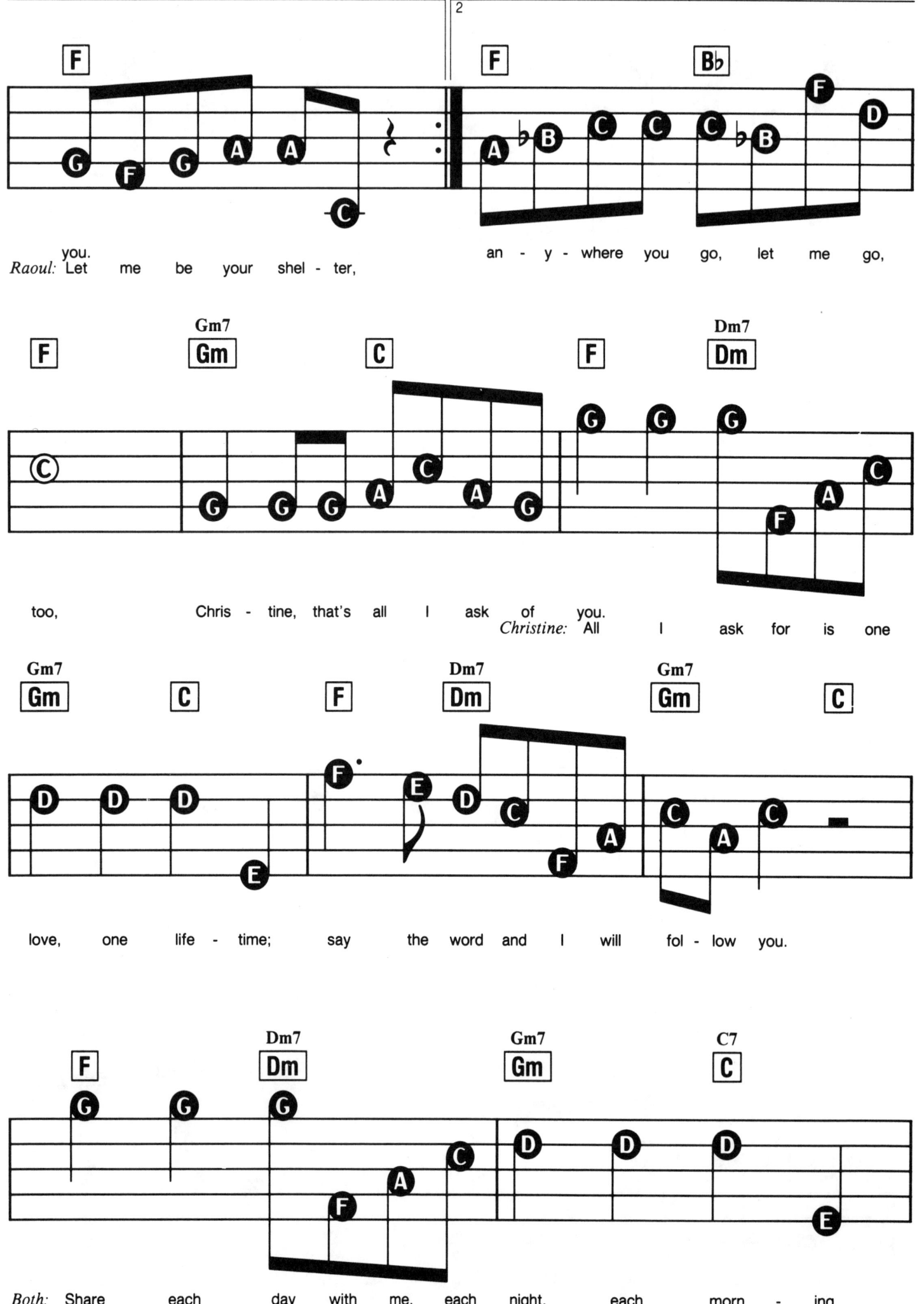

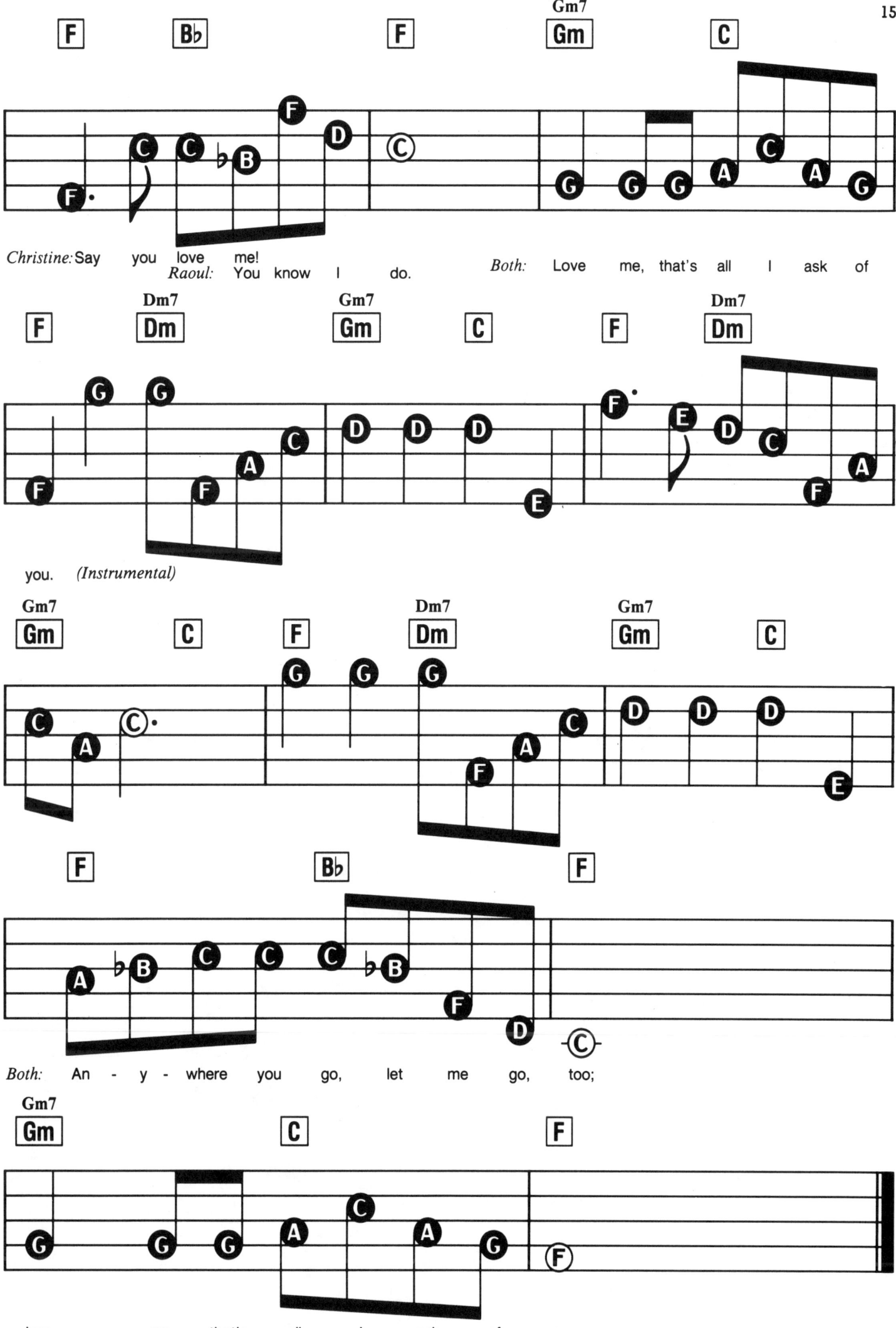

Can You Feel the Love Tonight
from Walt Disney Pictures' THE LION KING

Registration 2
Rhythm: Rock or 8 Beat

Music by Elton John
Lyrics by Tim Rice

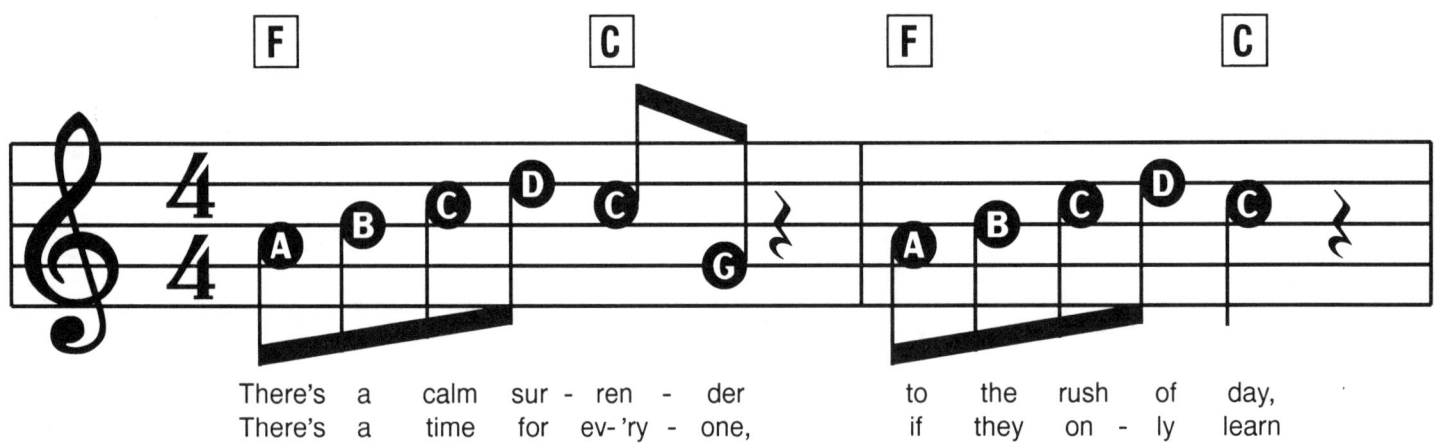

There's a calm sur-ren-der to the rush of day,
There's a time for ev-'ry-one, if they on-ly learn

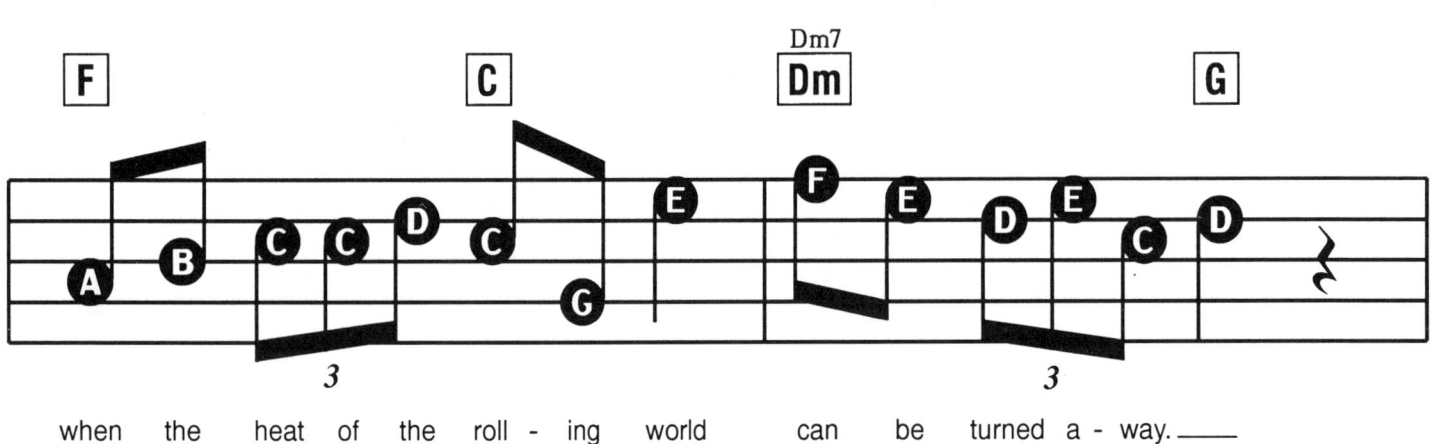

when the heat of the roll-ing world can be turned a-way.
that the twist-ing ka-lei-do-scope moves us all in turn.

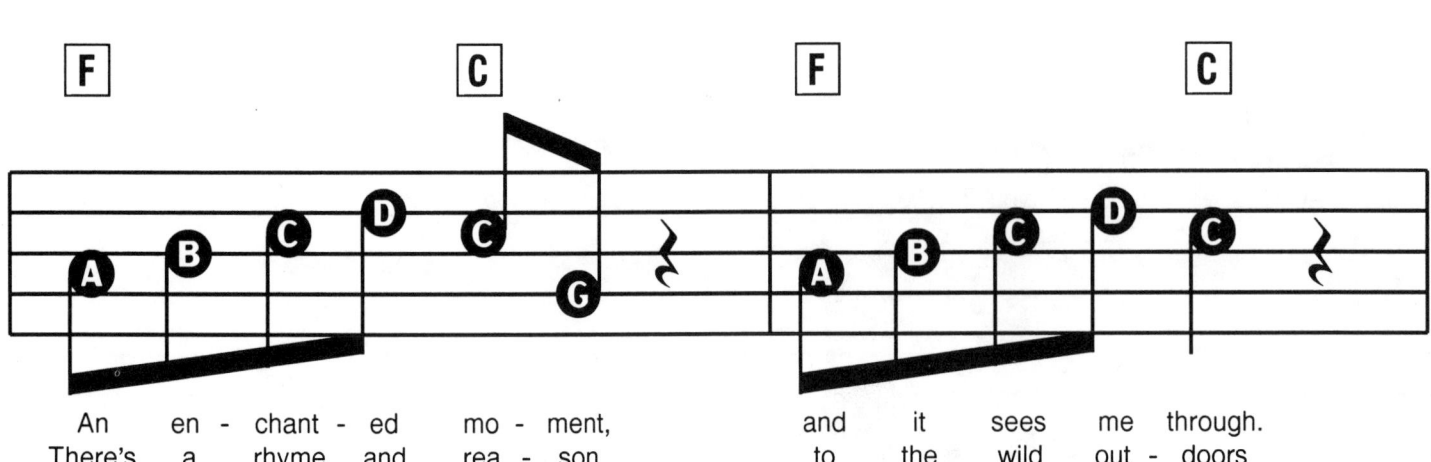

An en-chant-ed mo-ment, and it sees me through.
There's a rhyme and rea-son to the wild out-doors

© 1994 Wonderland Music Company, Inc.
All Rights Reserved   Used by Permission

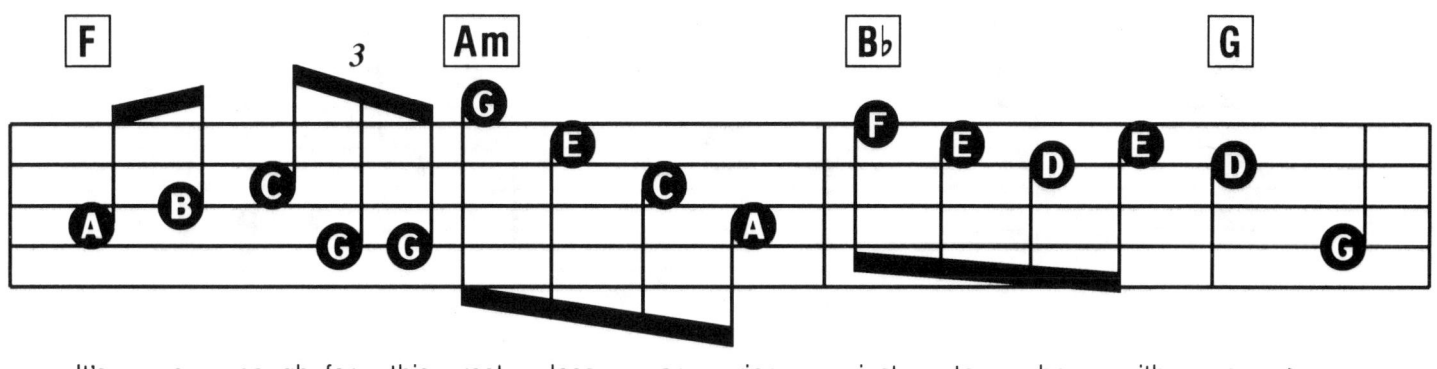
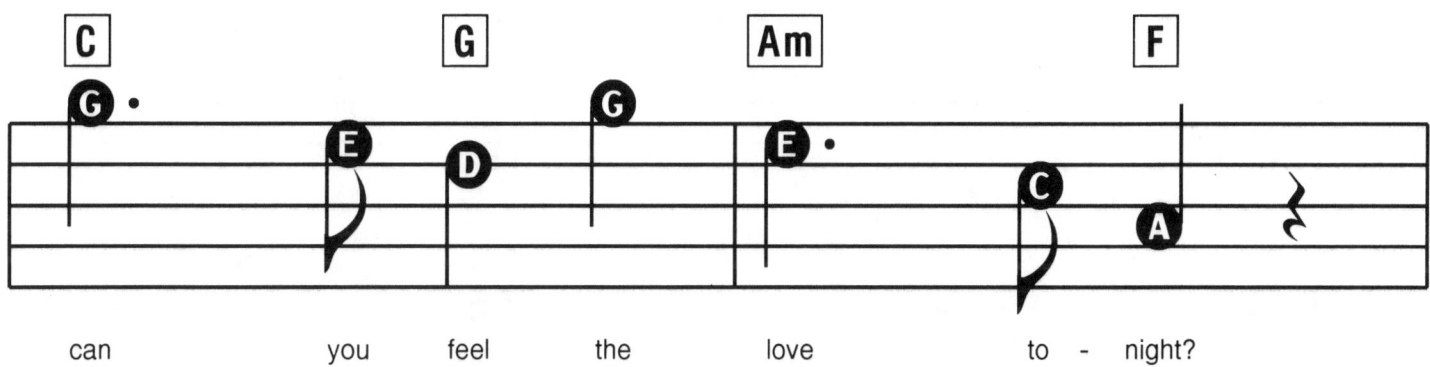
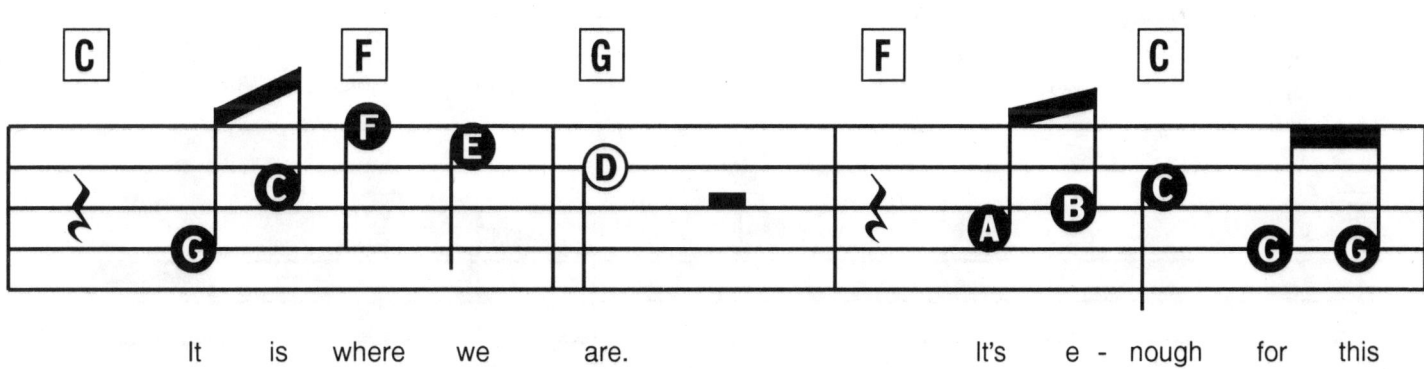
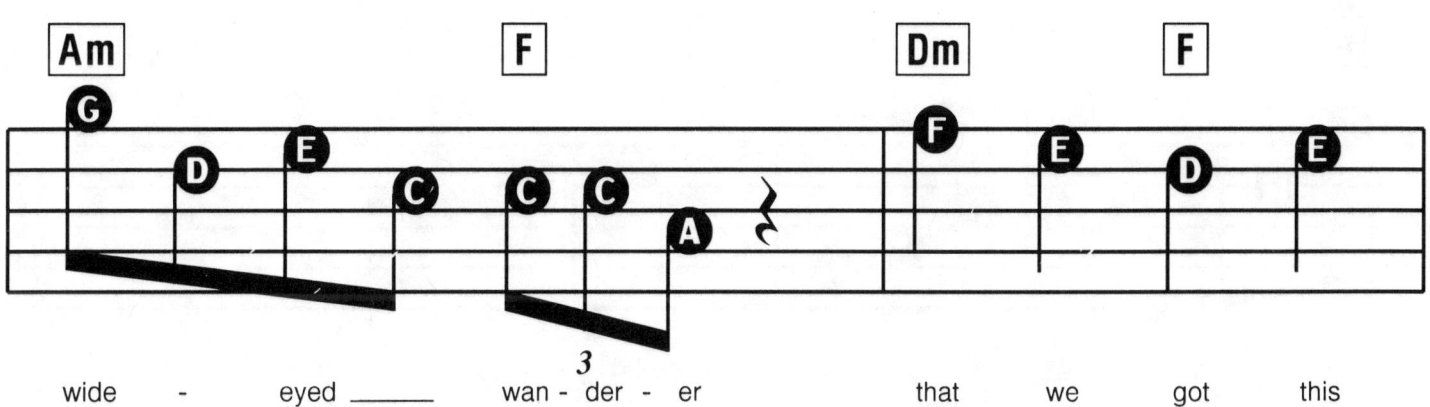

(They Long to Be) Close to You

Registration 2
Rhythm: Slow Rock

Lyric by Hal David
Music by Burt Bacharach

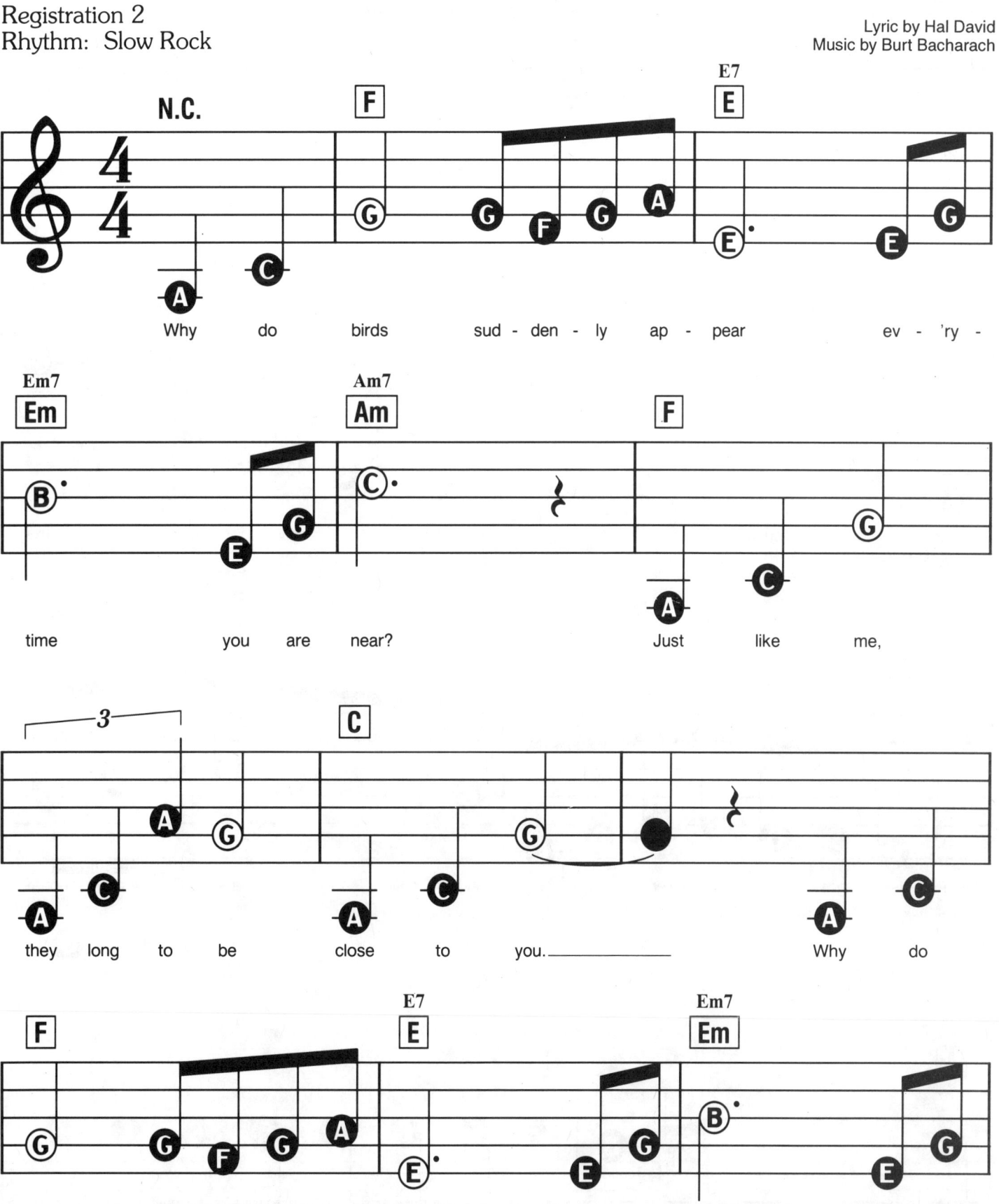

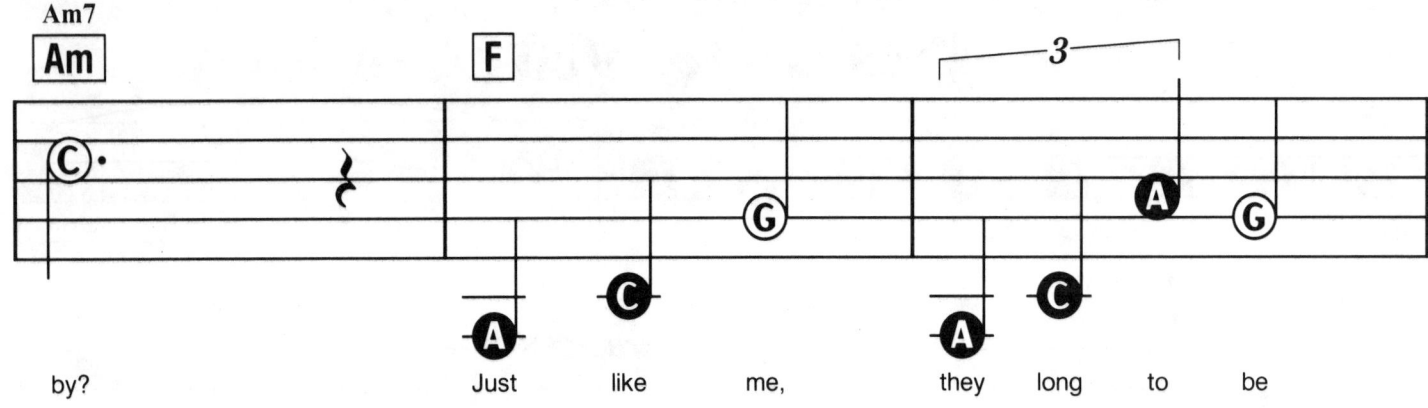
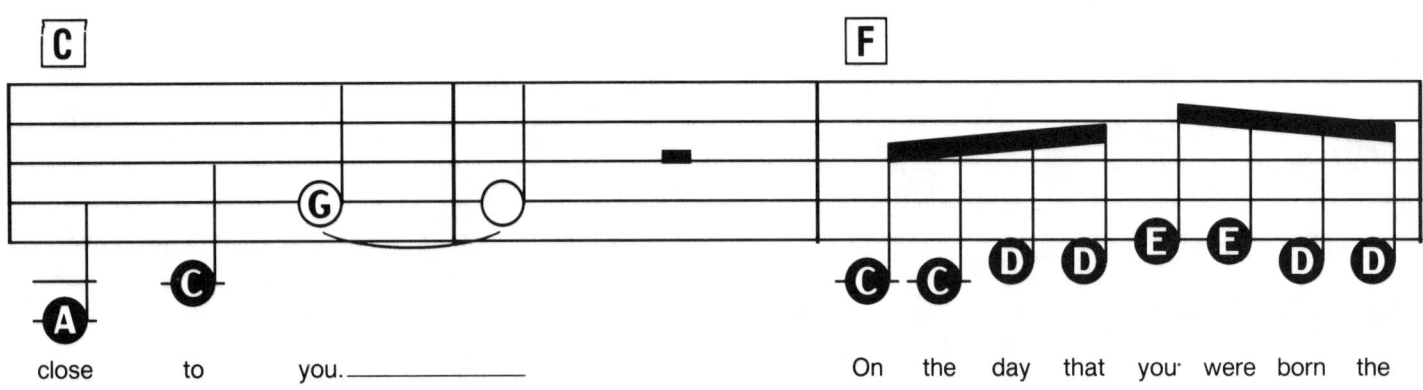
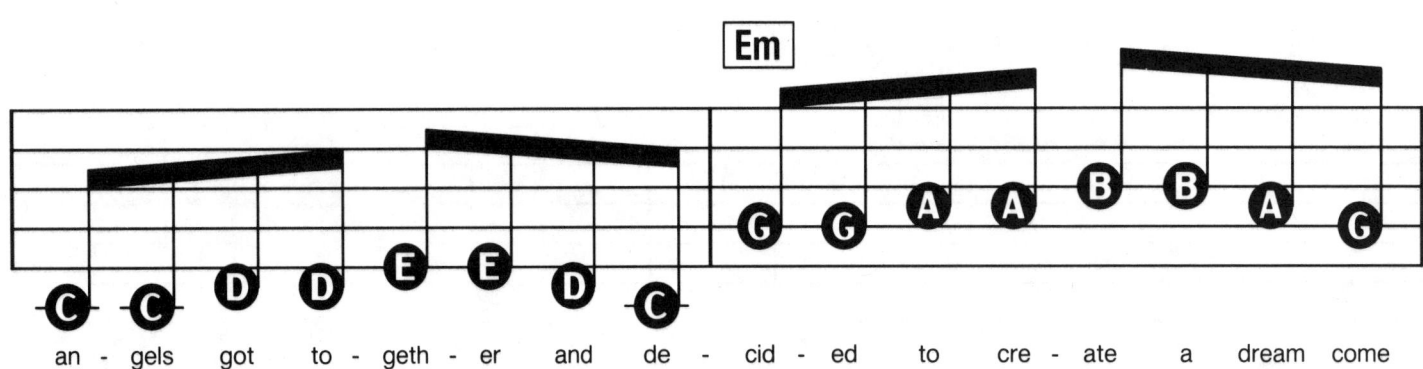
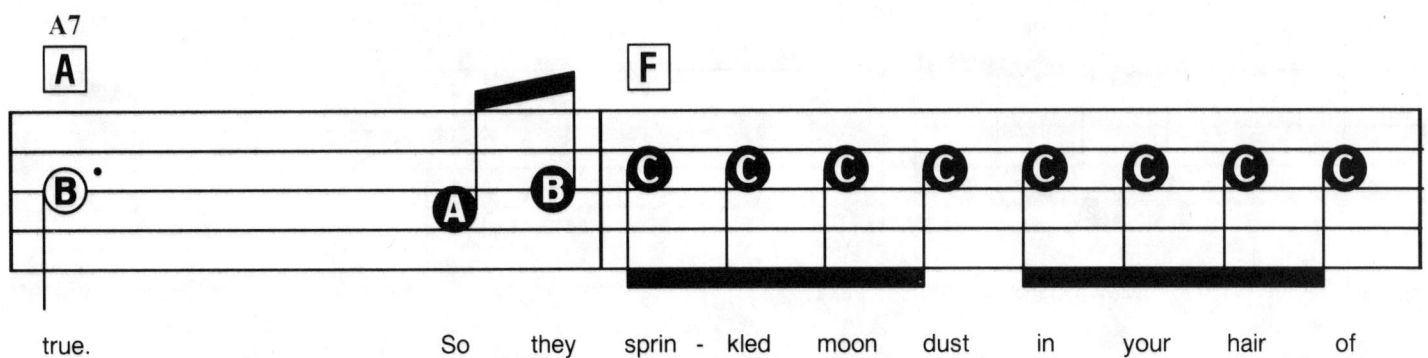

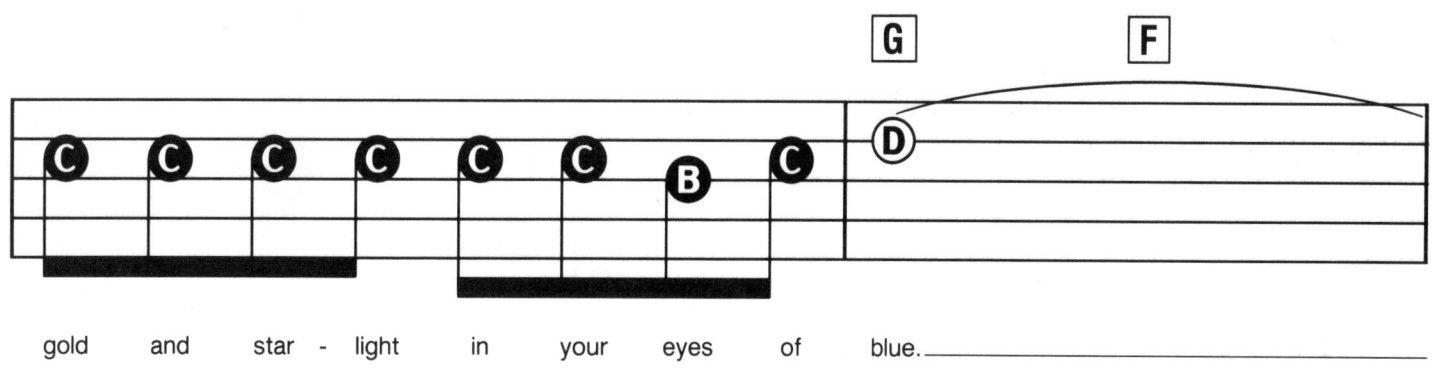
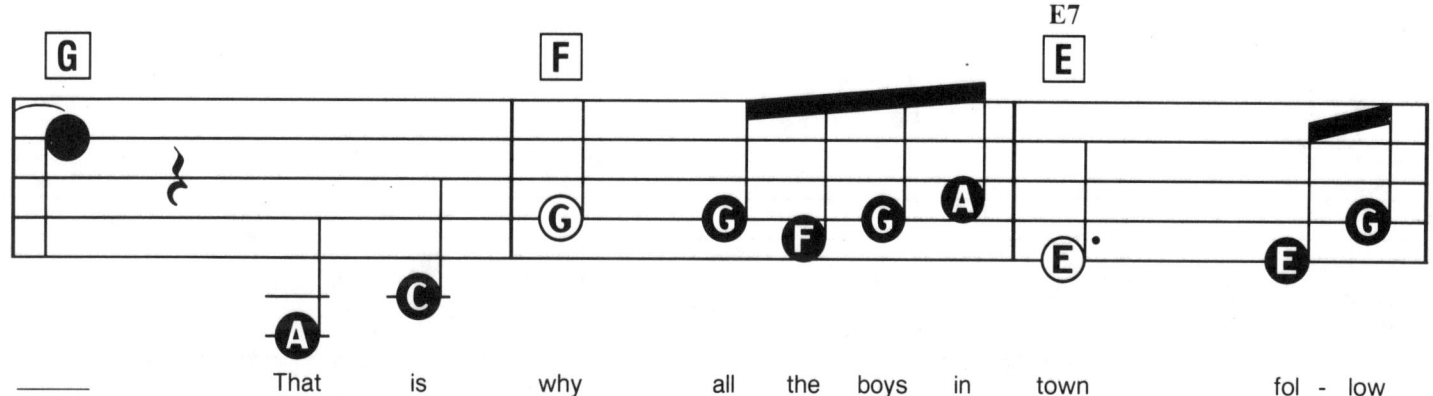
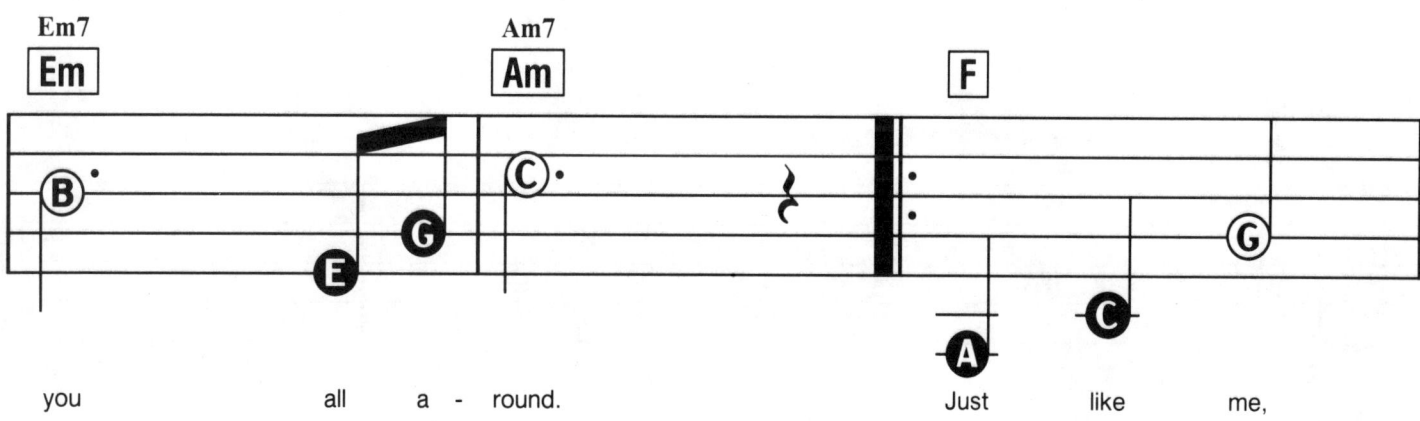
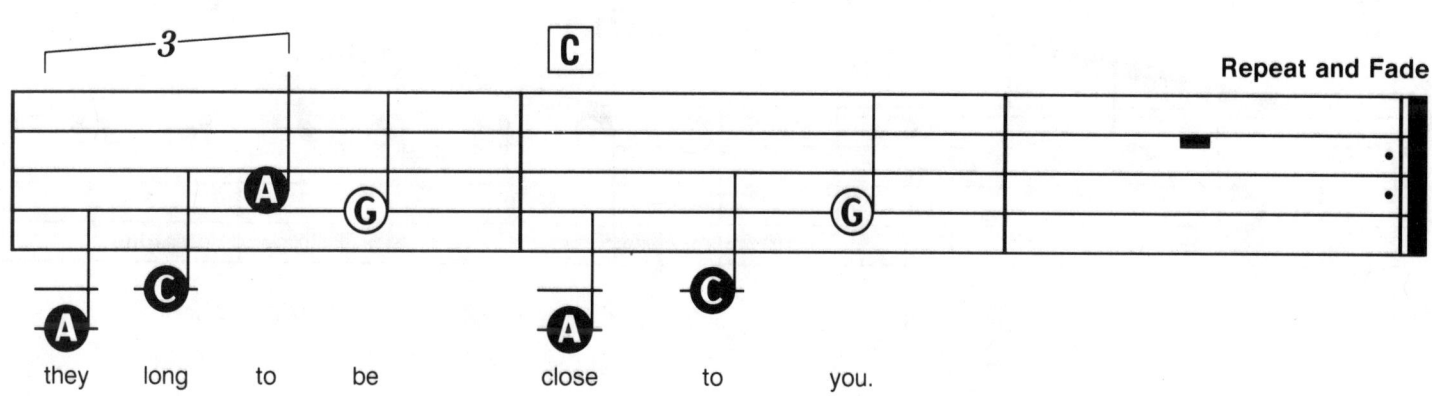

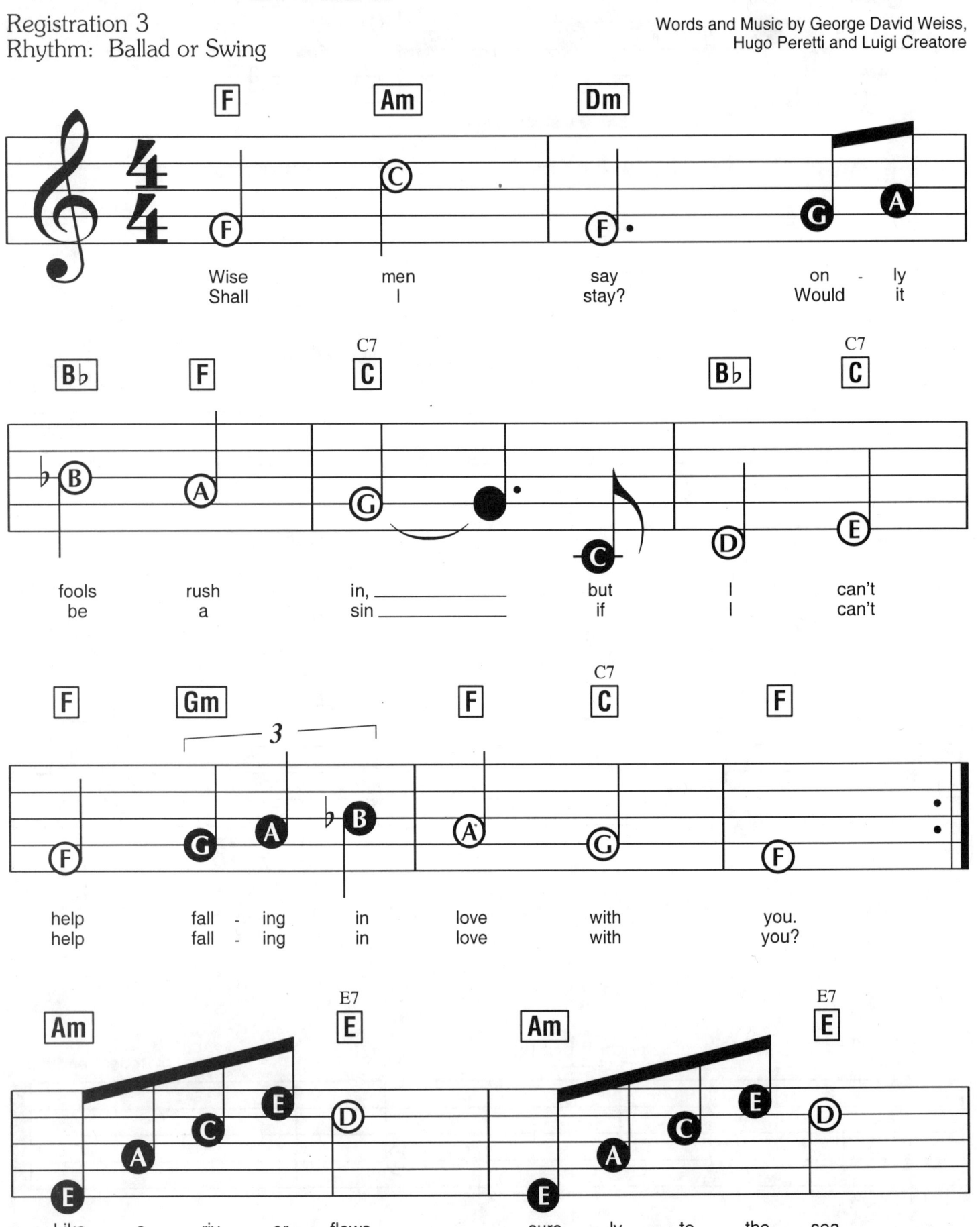

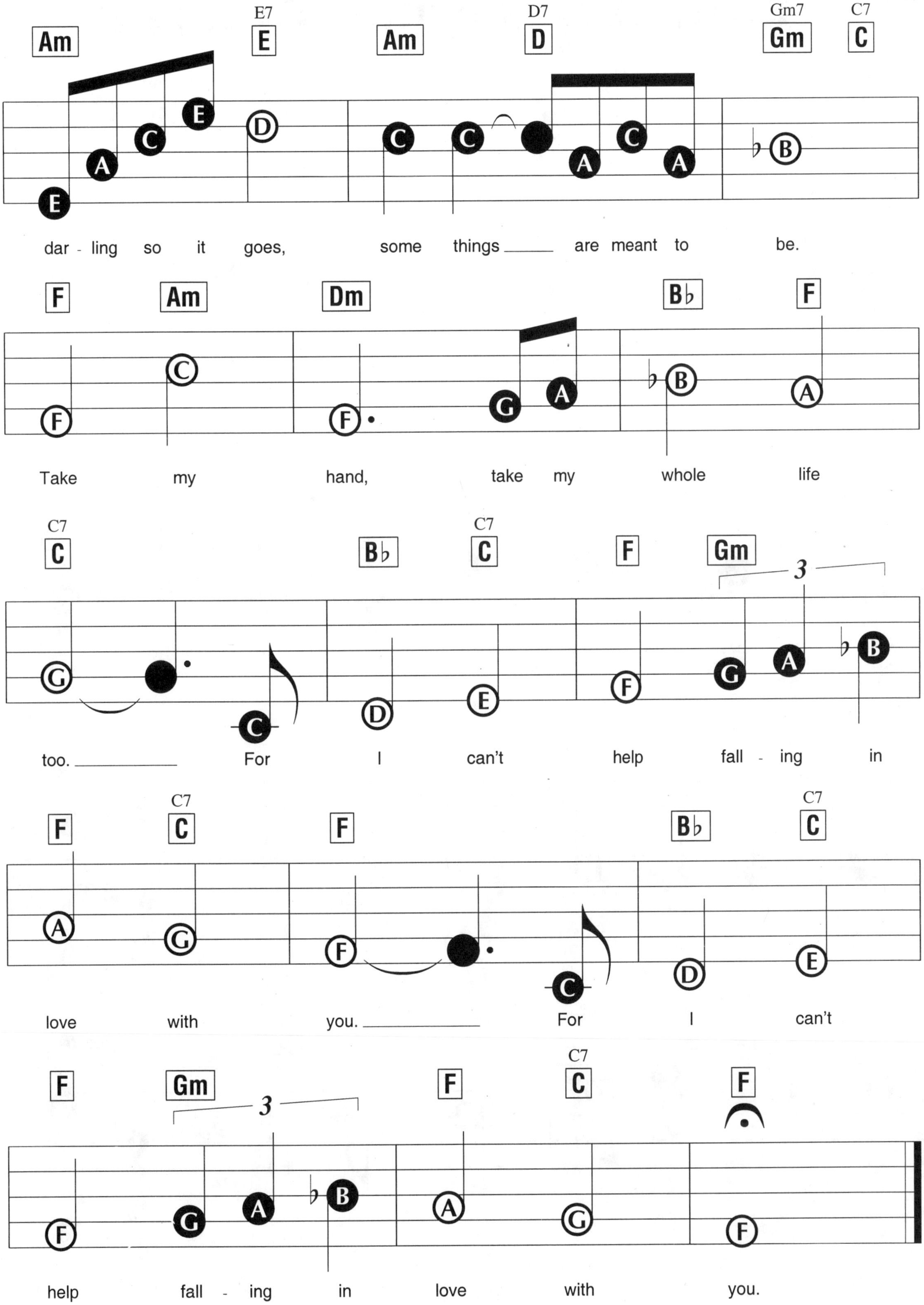

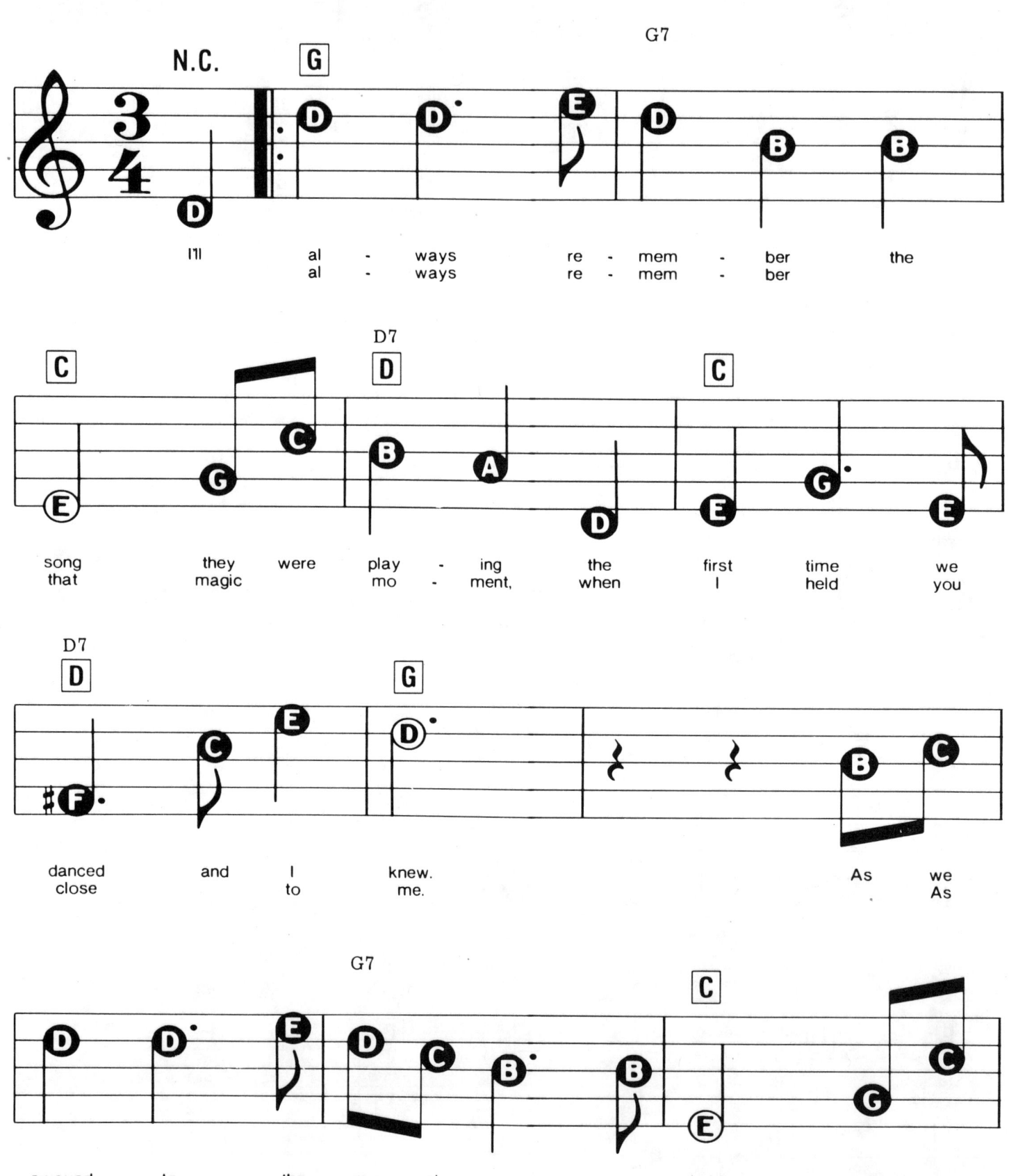

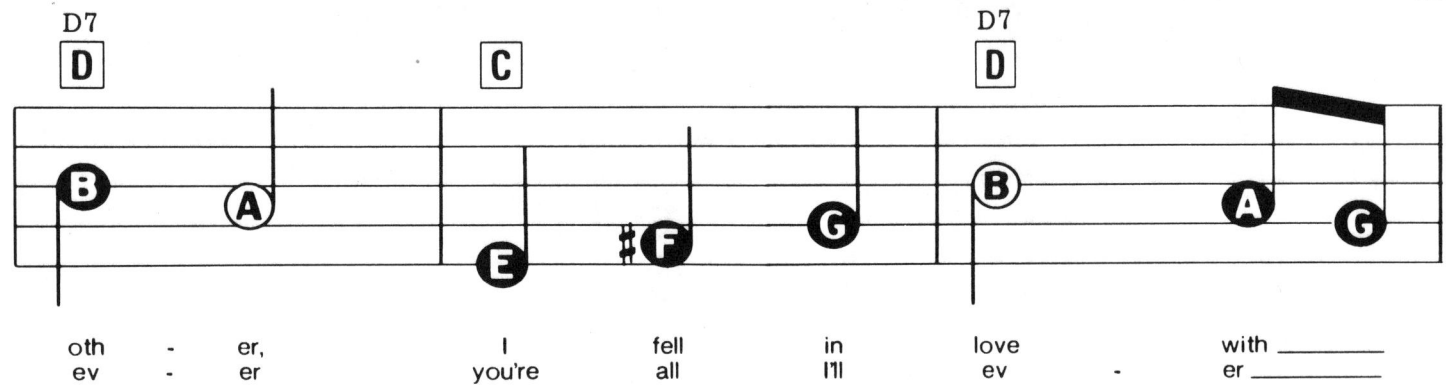
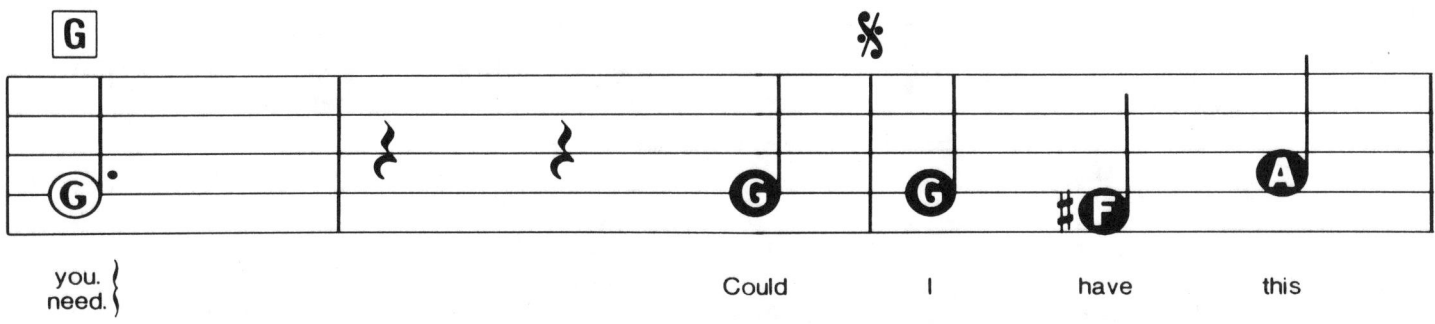
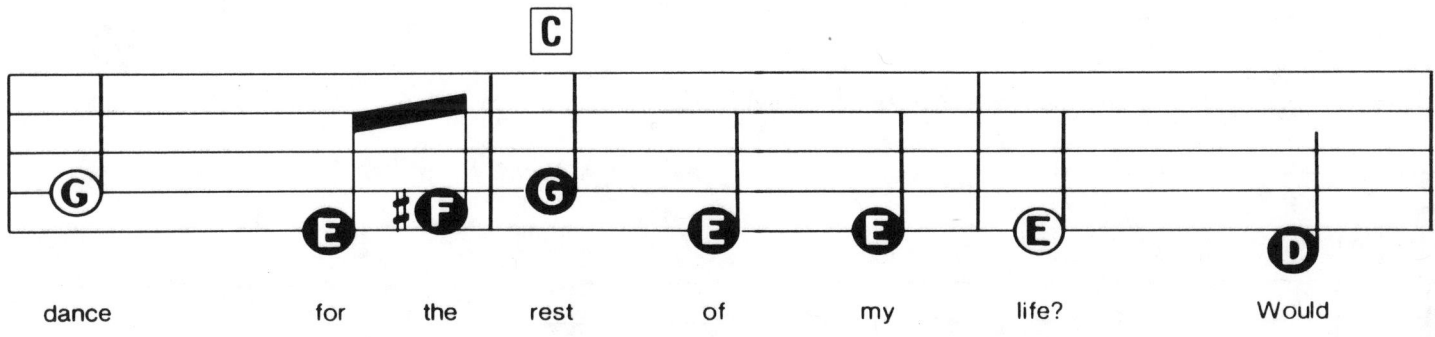
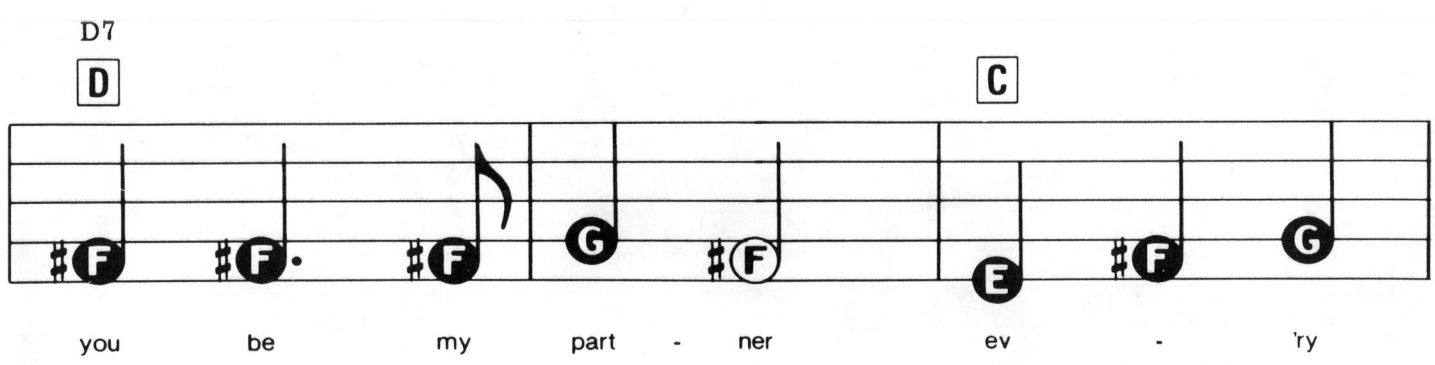

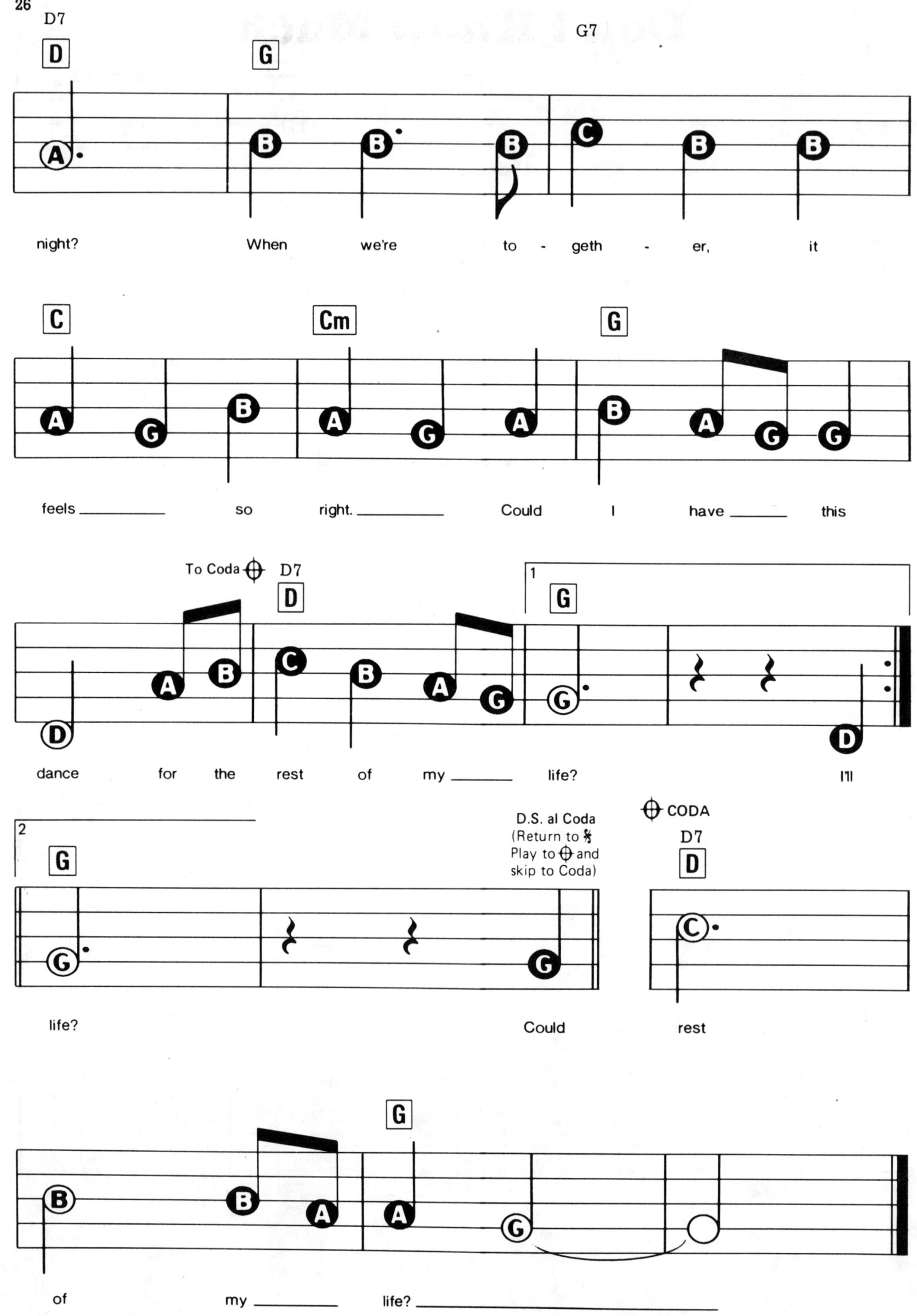

Don't Know Much

Registration 7
Rhythm: Pops or 8 Beat

Words and Music by Barry Mann,
Cynthia Weil and Tom Snow

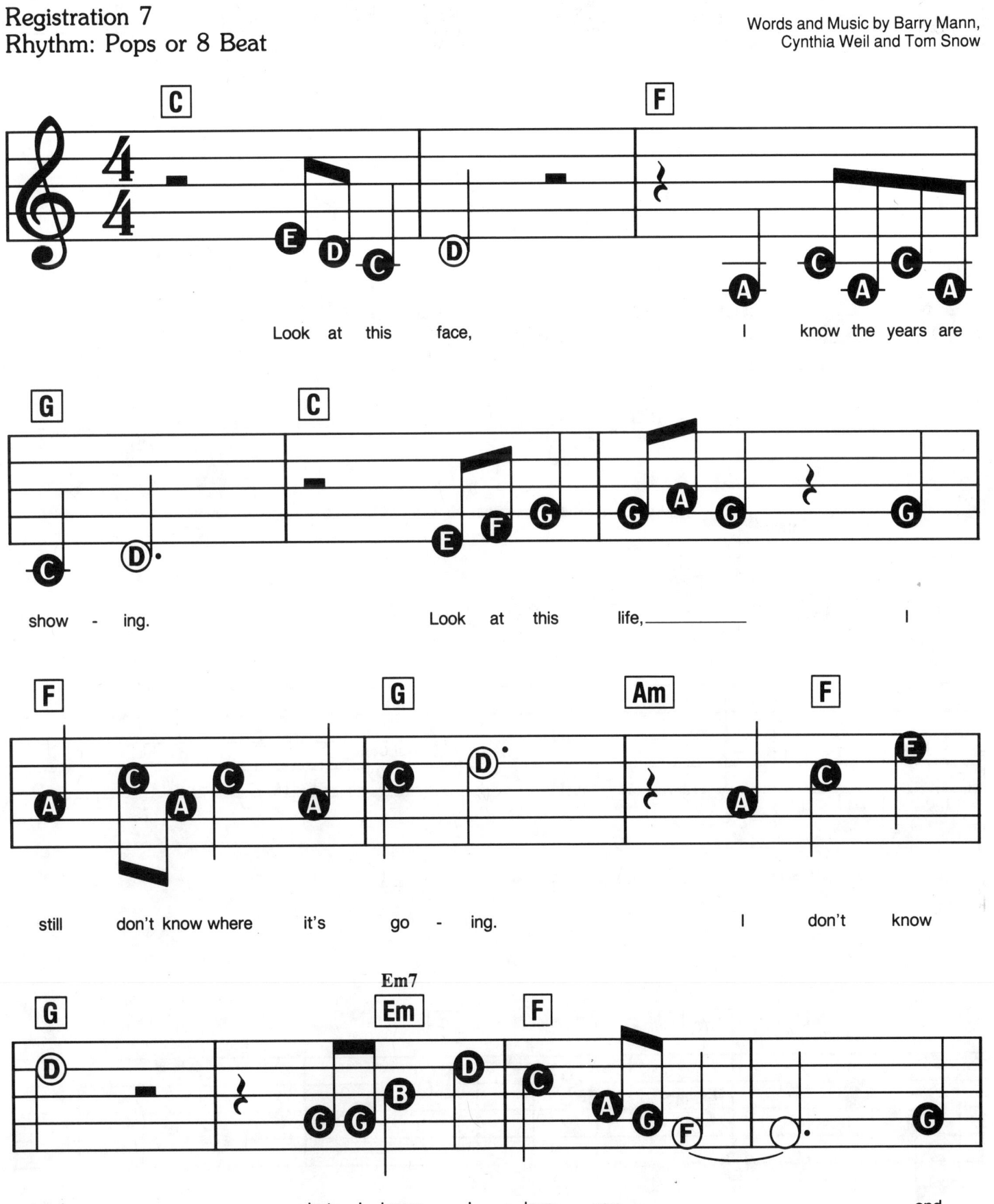

Copyright © 1980 Sony/ATV Songs LLC, Mann & Weil Songs, Inc., EMI Blackwood Music Inc. and Snow Music
All Rights on behalf of Sony/ATV Songs LLC and Mann & Weil Songs, Inc.
 Administered by Sony/ATV Music Publishing, 8 Music Square West, Nashville, TN 37203
International Copyright Secured   All Rights Reserved

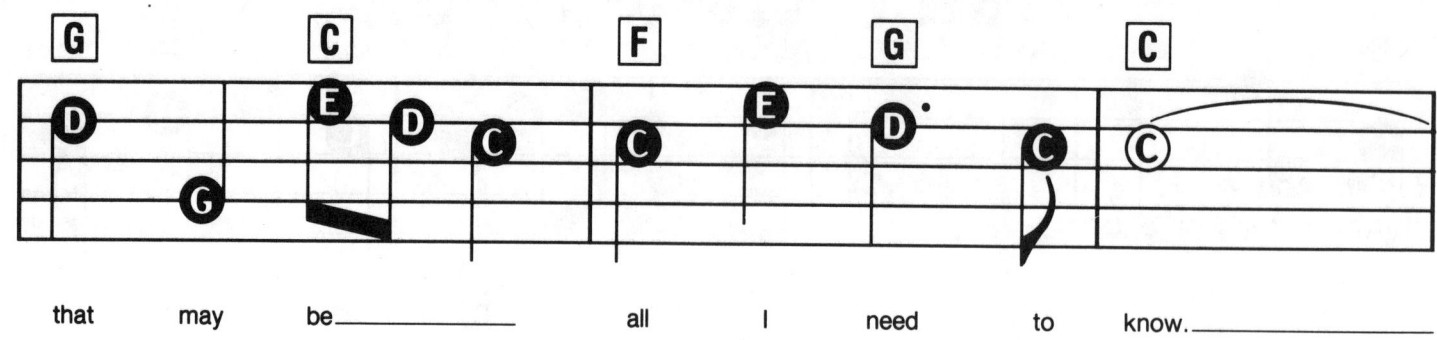
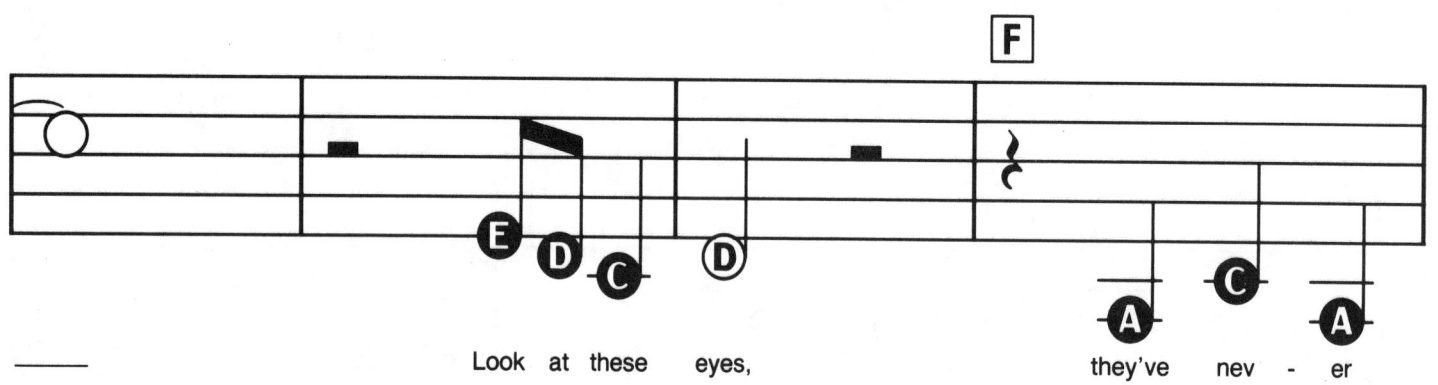
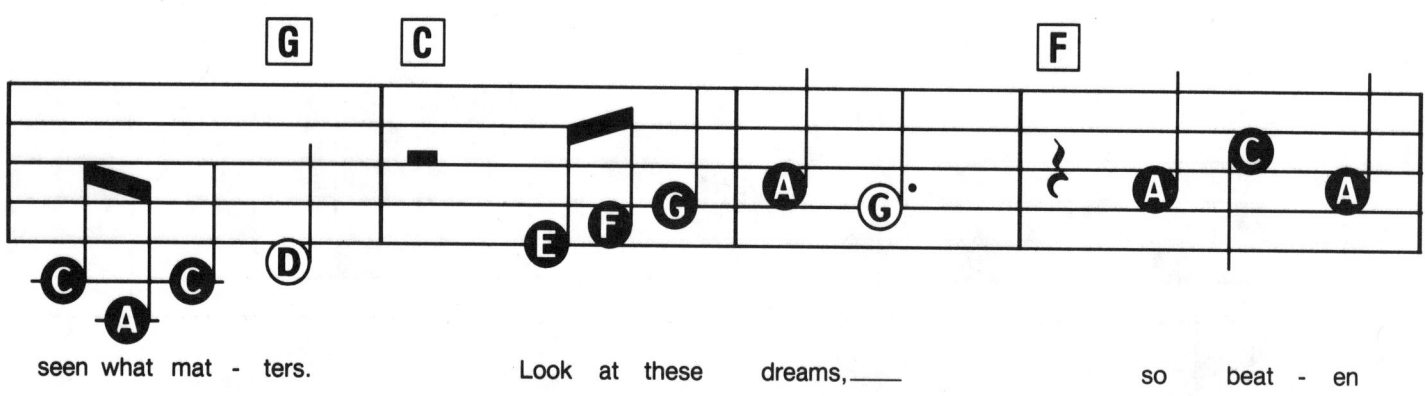
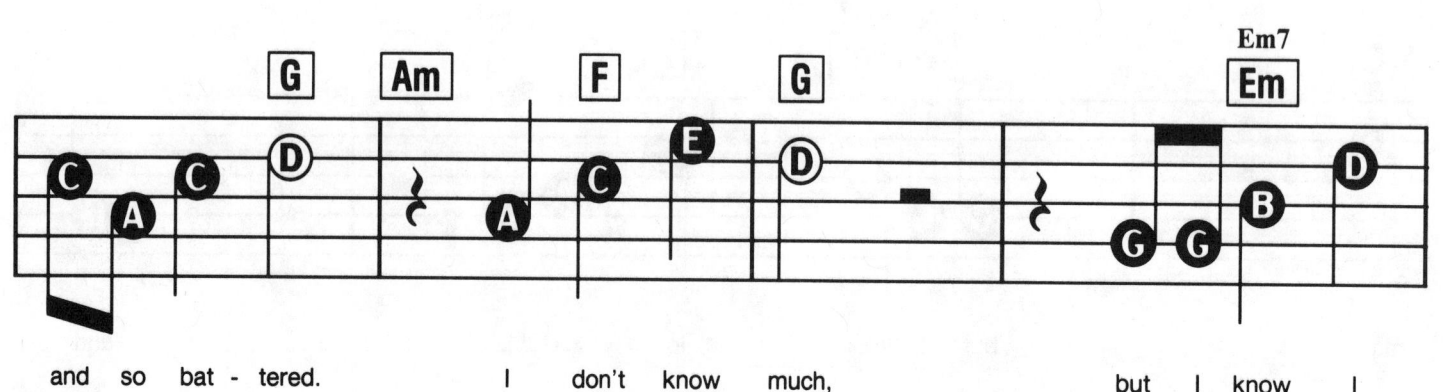

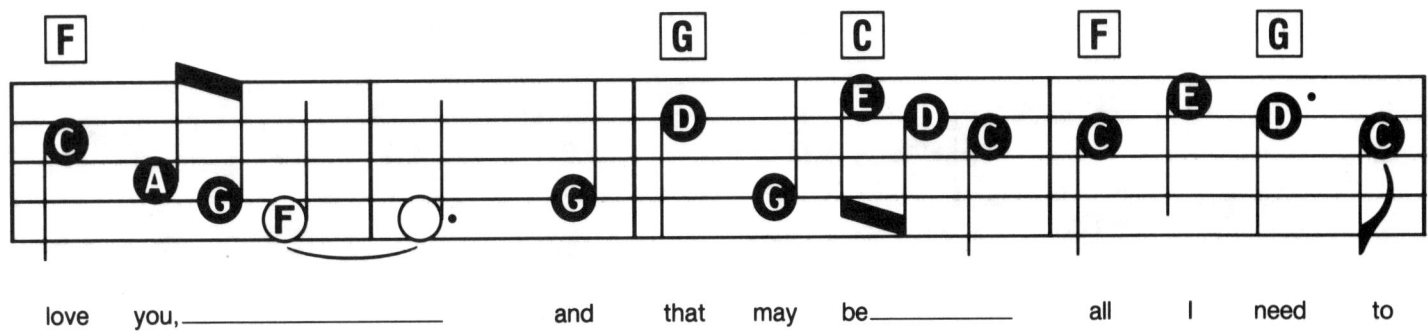
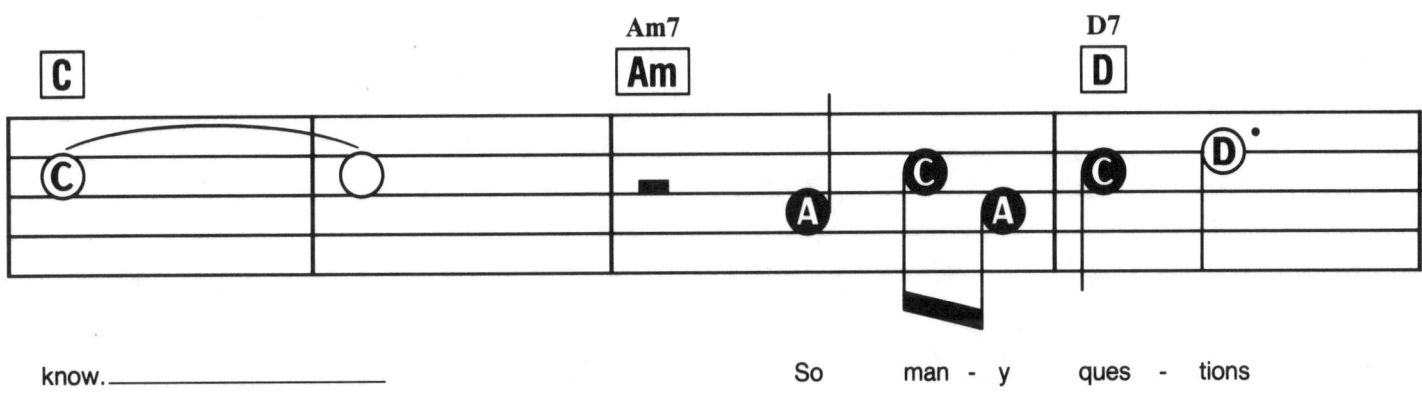
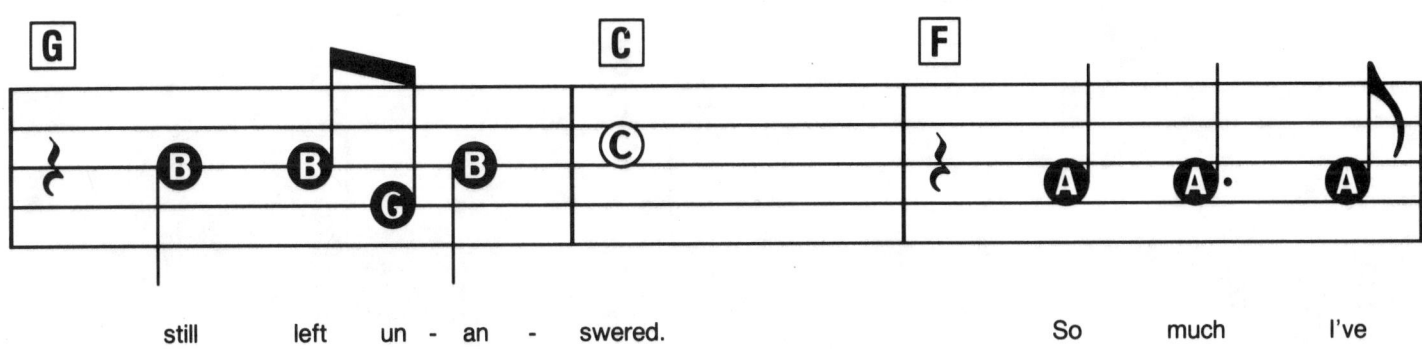
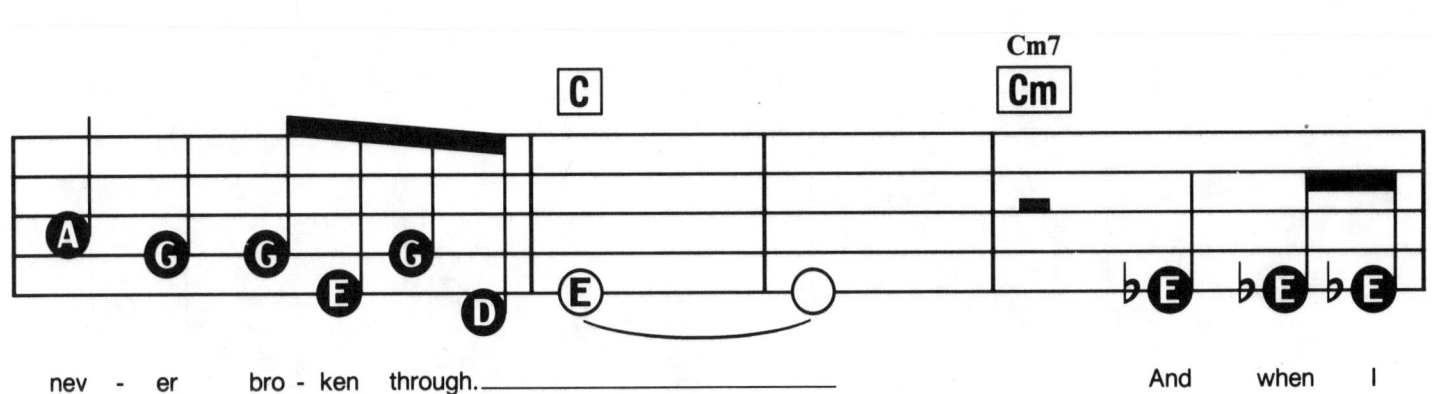

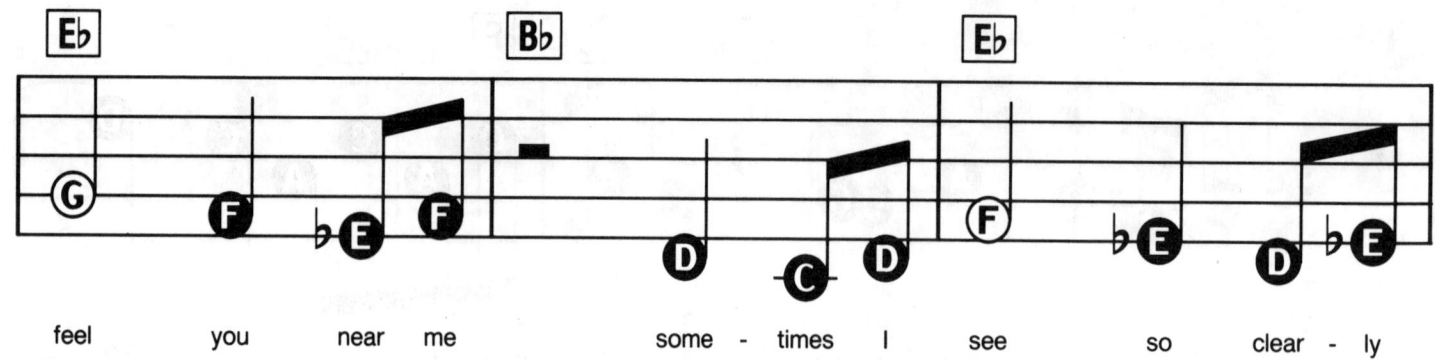
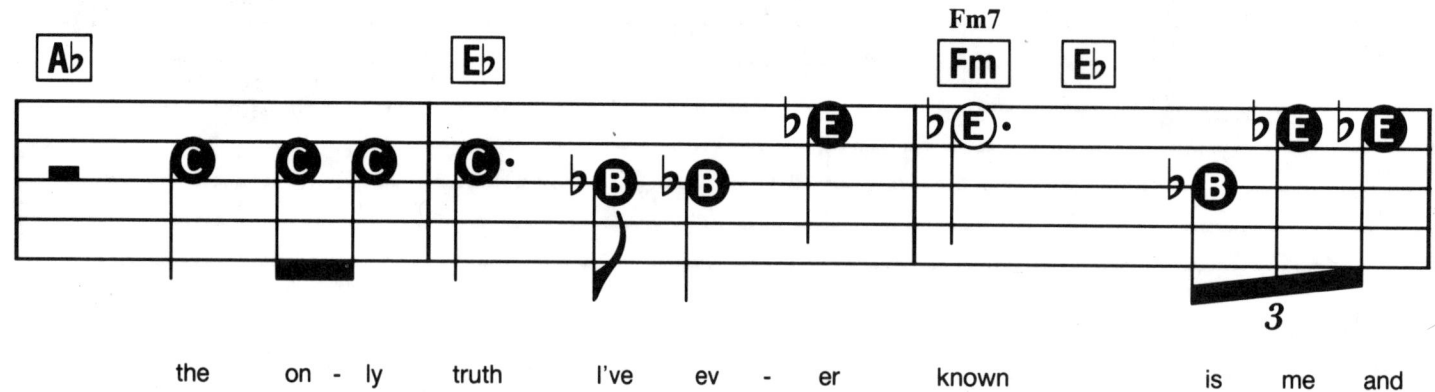
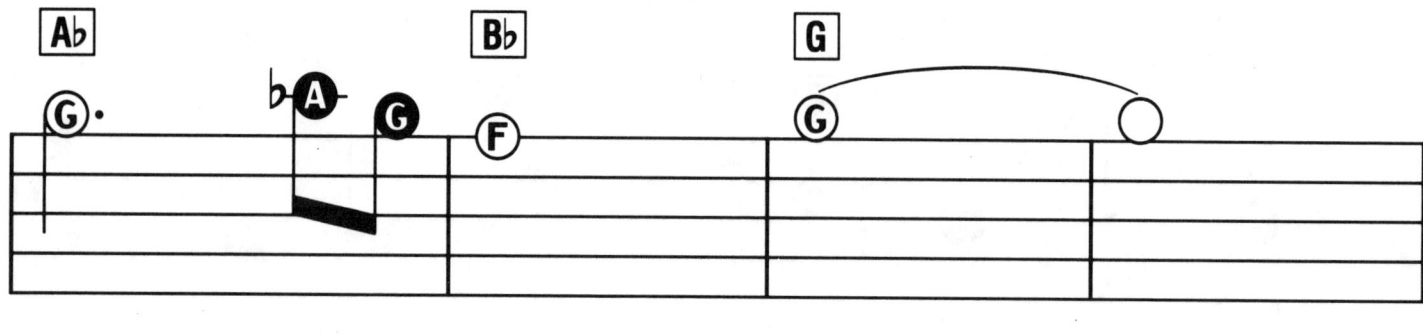
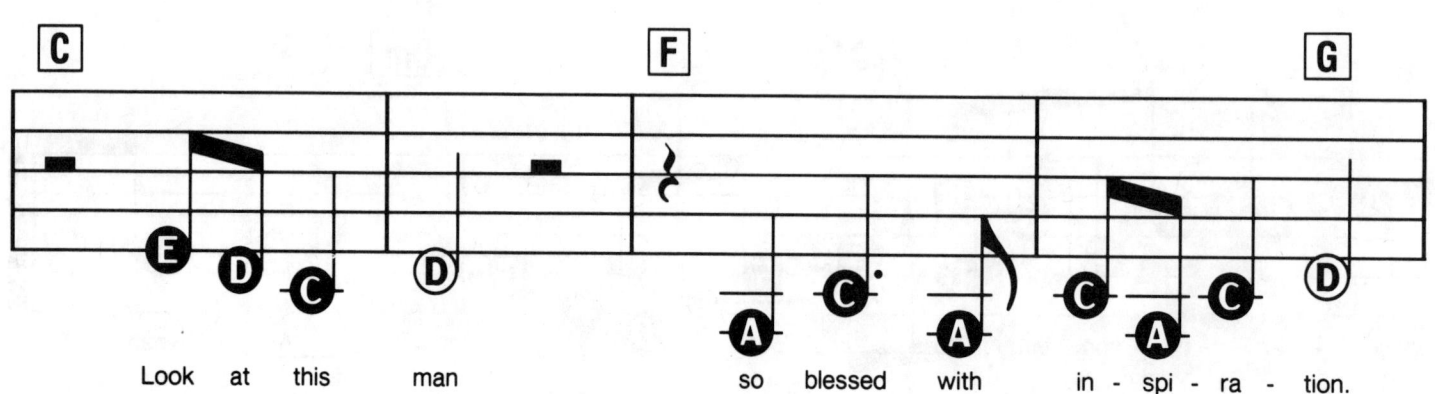

C F
Look at this soul, still searching for sal - va - tion.
G Am F G Em7 Em
I don't know much, but I know I
F G C
love you, and that may be
F G 1,2 C 3 C
all I need to know. know.
Woh.

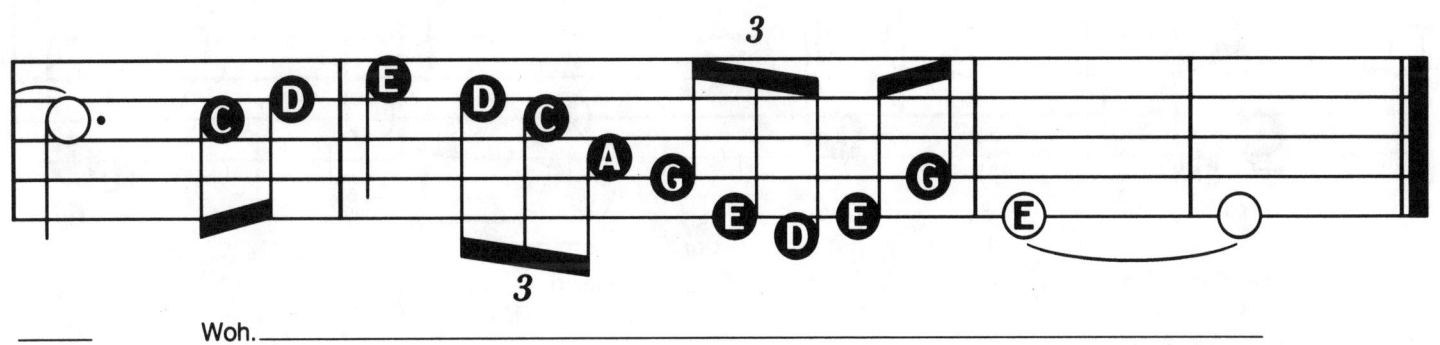

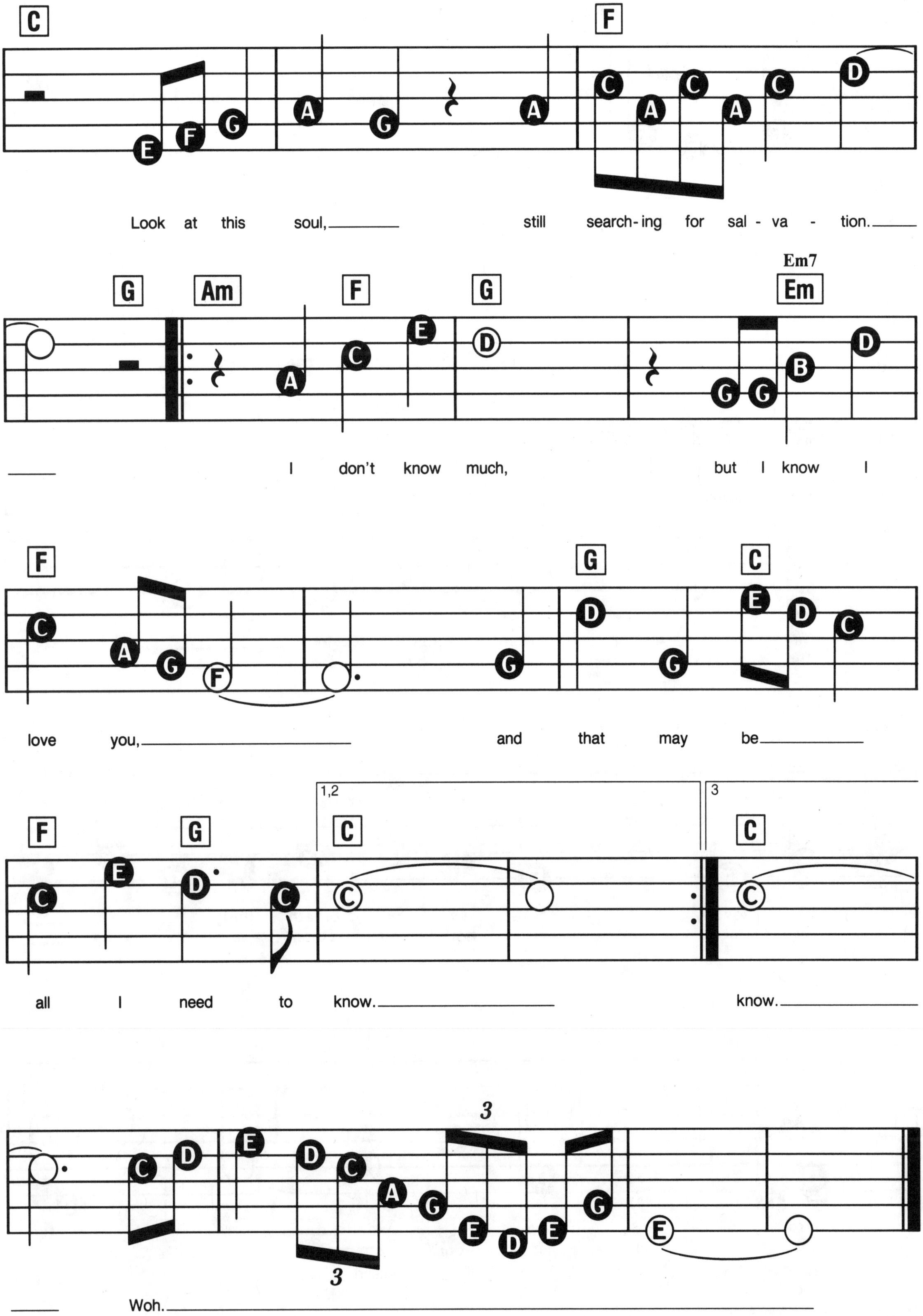

Endless Love

Registration 1
Rhythm: Rock or 8 Beat

Words and Music by
Lionel Richie

My love / Two hearts — There's only you in my life / Two hearts that beat as one

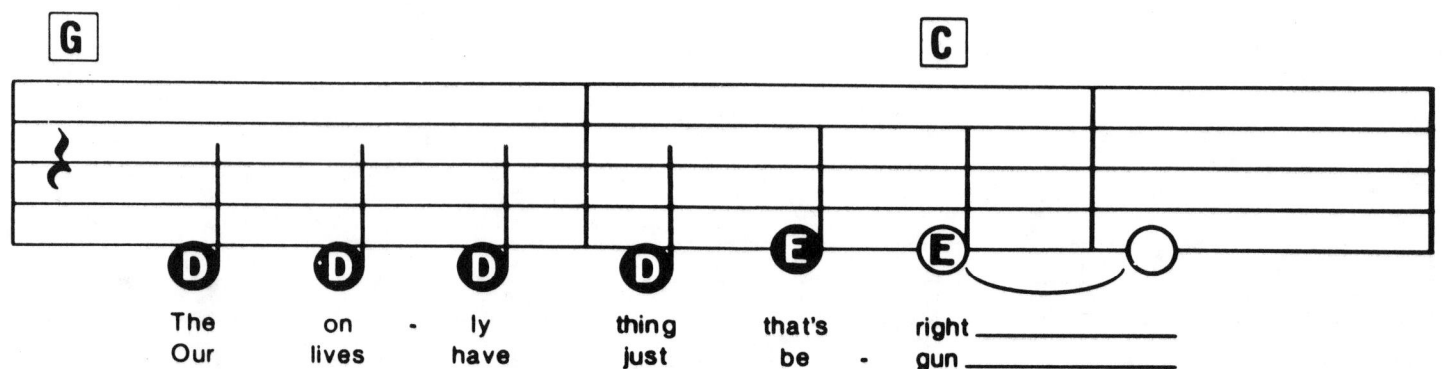

The only thing that's right / Our lives have just be-gun

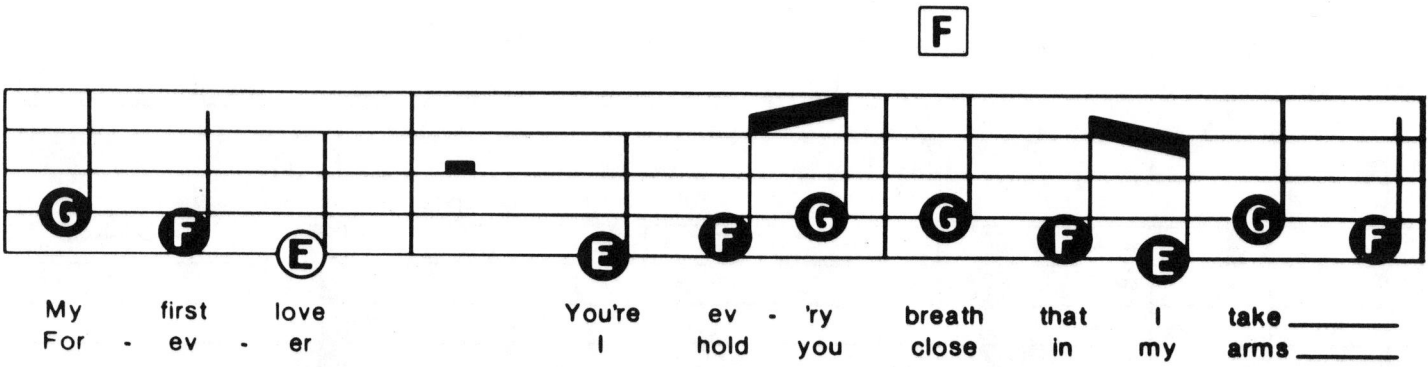

My first love / For-ev-er — You're ev-'ry breath that I take / I hold you close in my arms

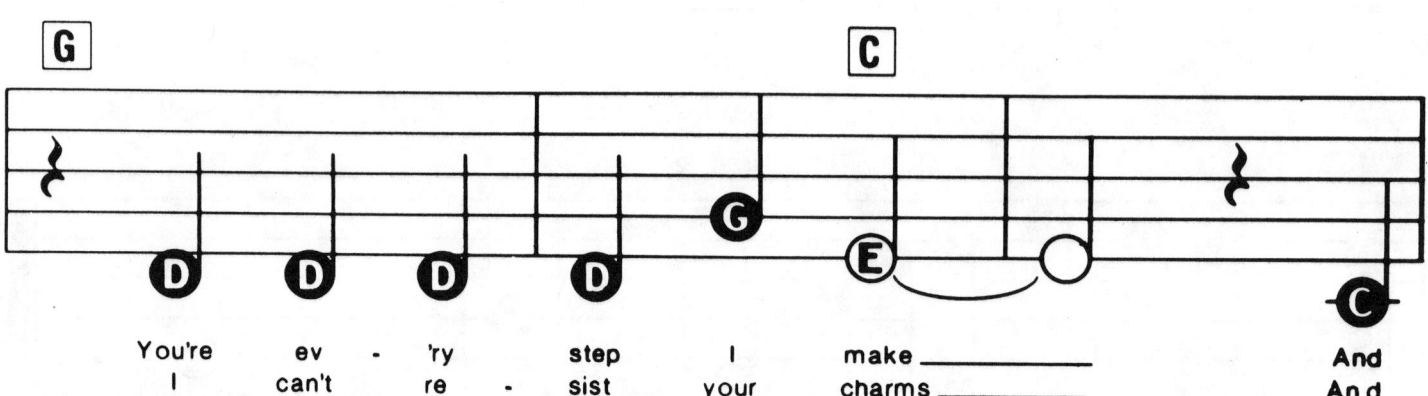

You're ev-'ry step I make / I can't re-sist your charms — And / And

Copyright © 1981 by PGP Music and Brockman Music
All Rights Administered by Intersong U.S.A., Inc.
International Copyright Secured   All Rights Reserved

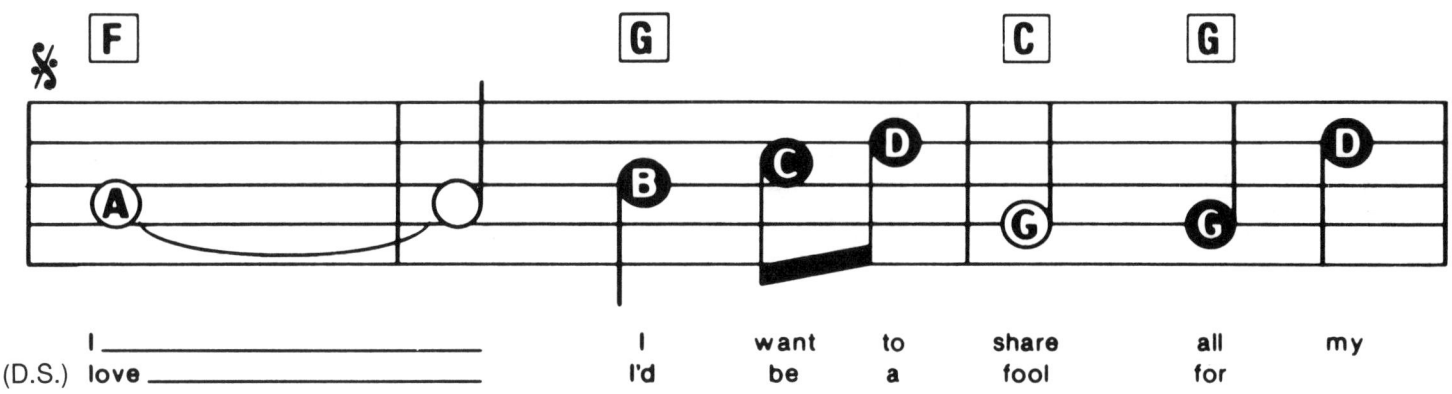
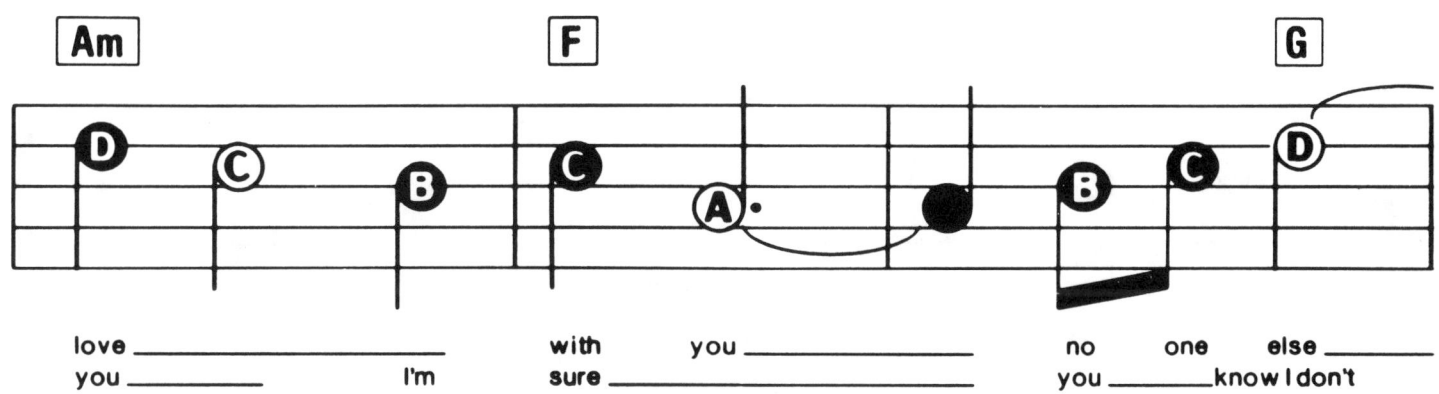
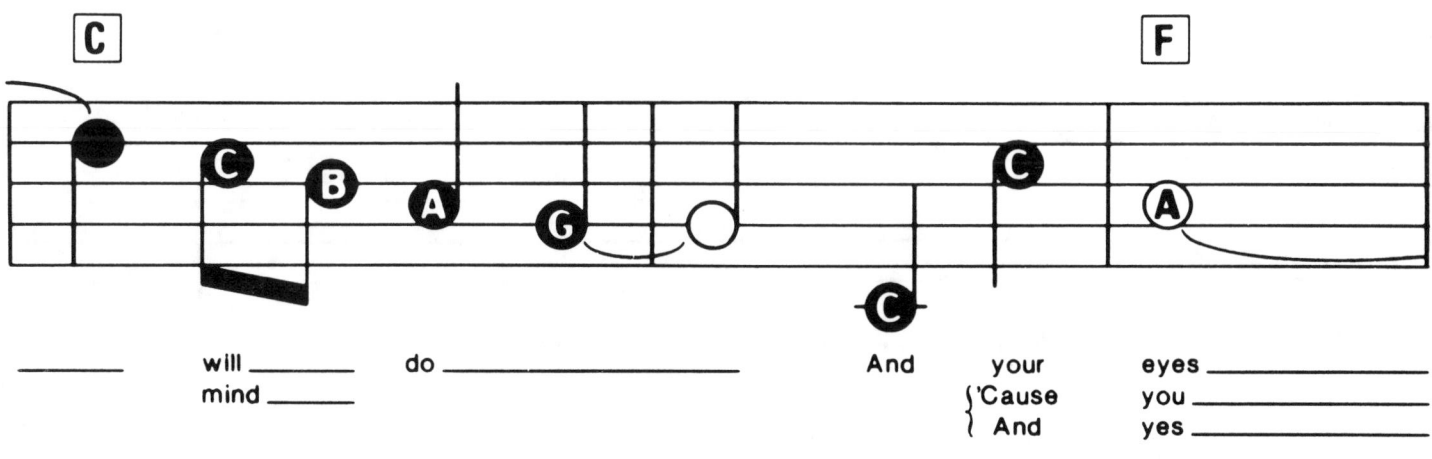
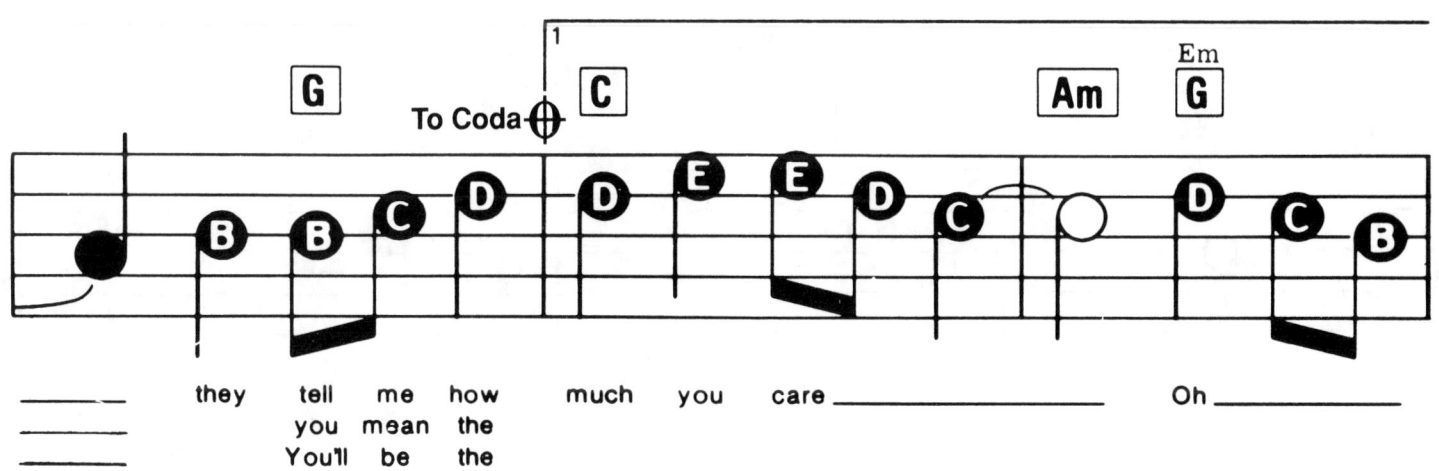

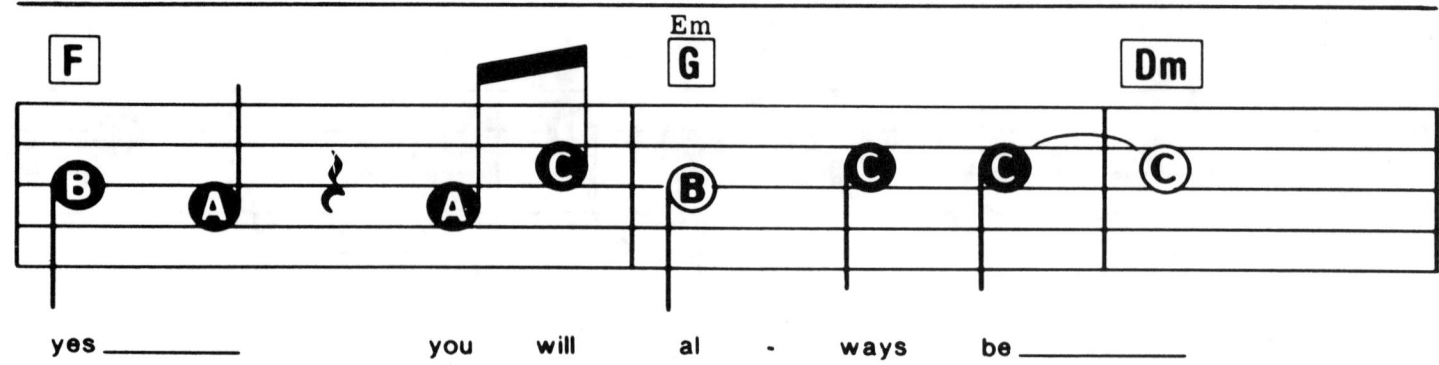
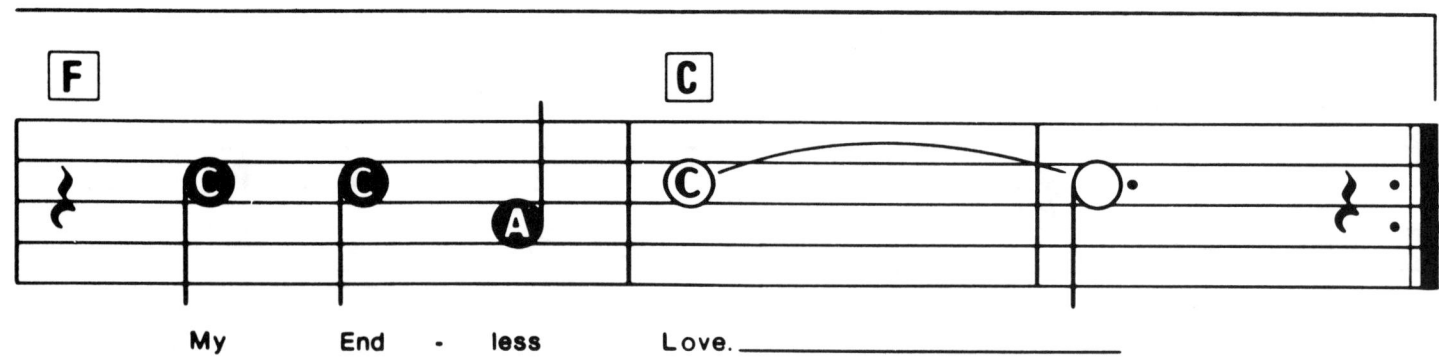
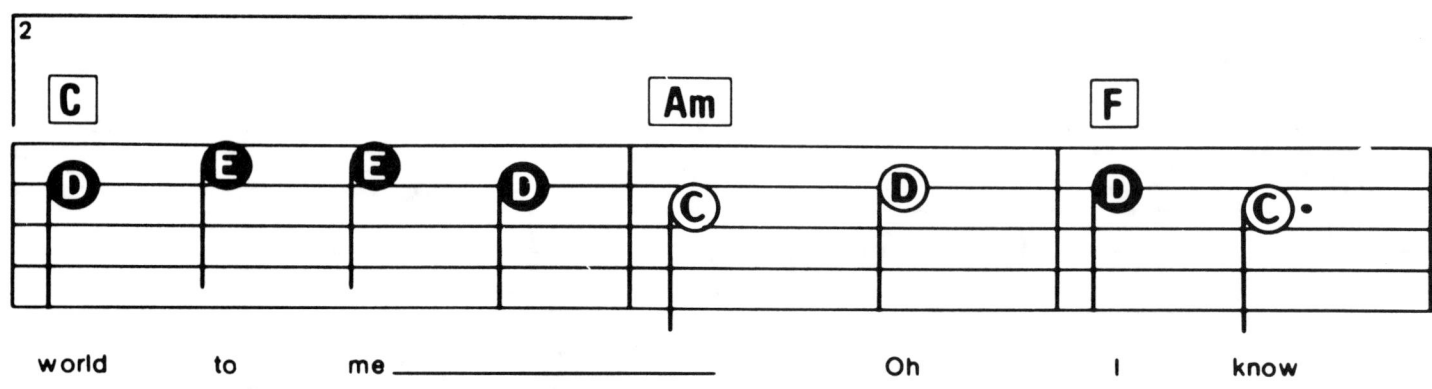
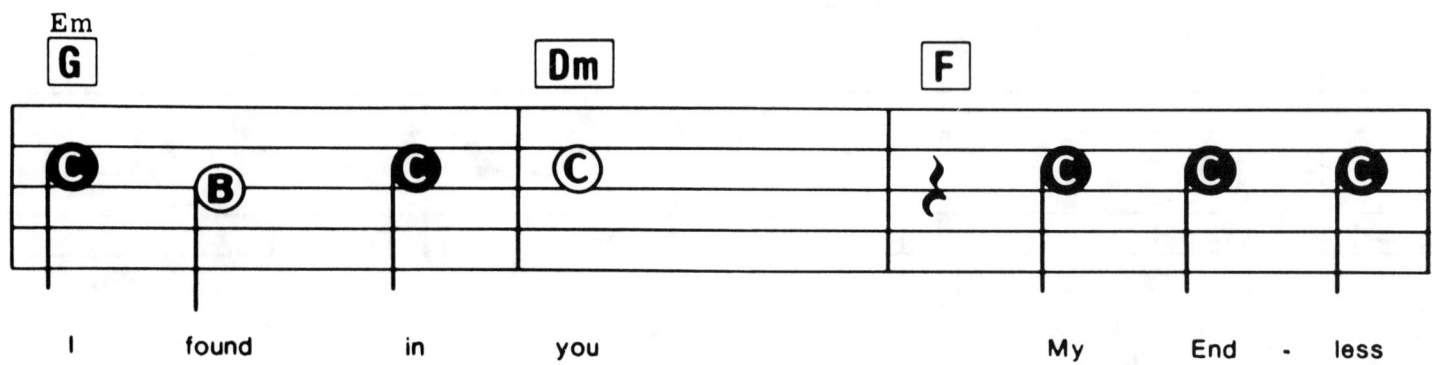

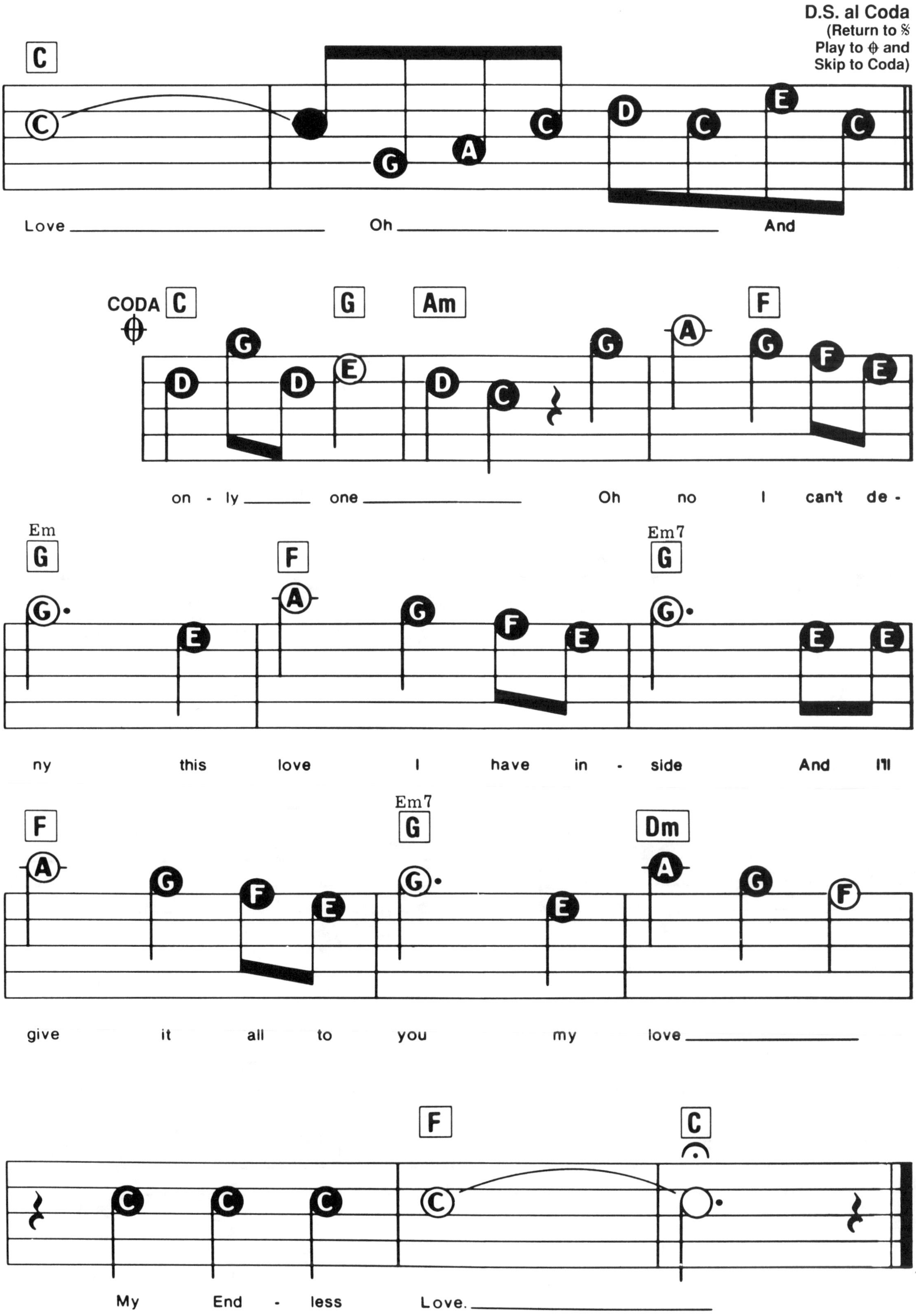

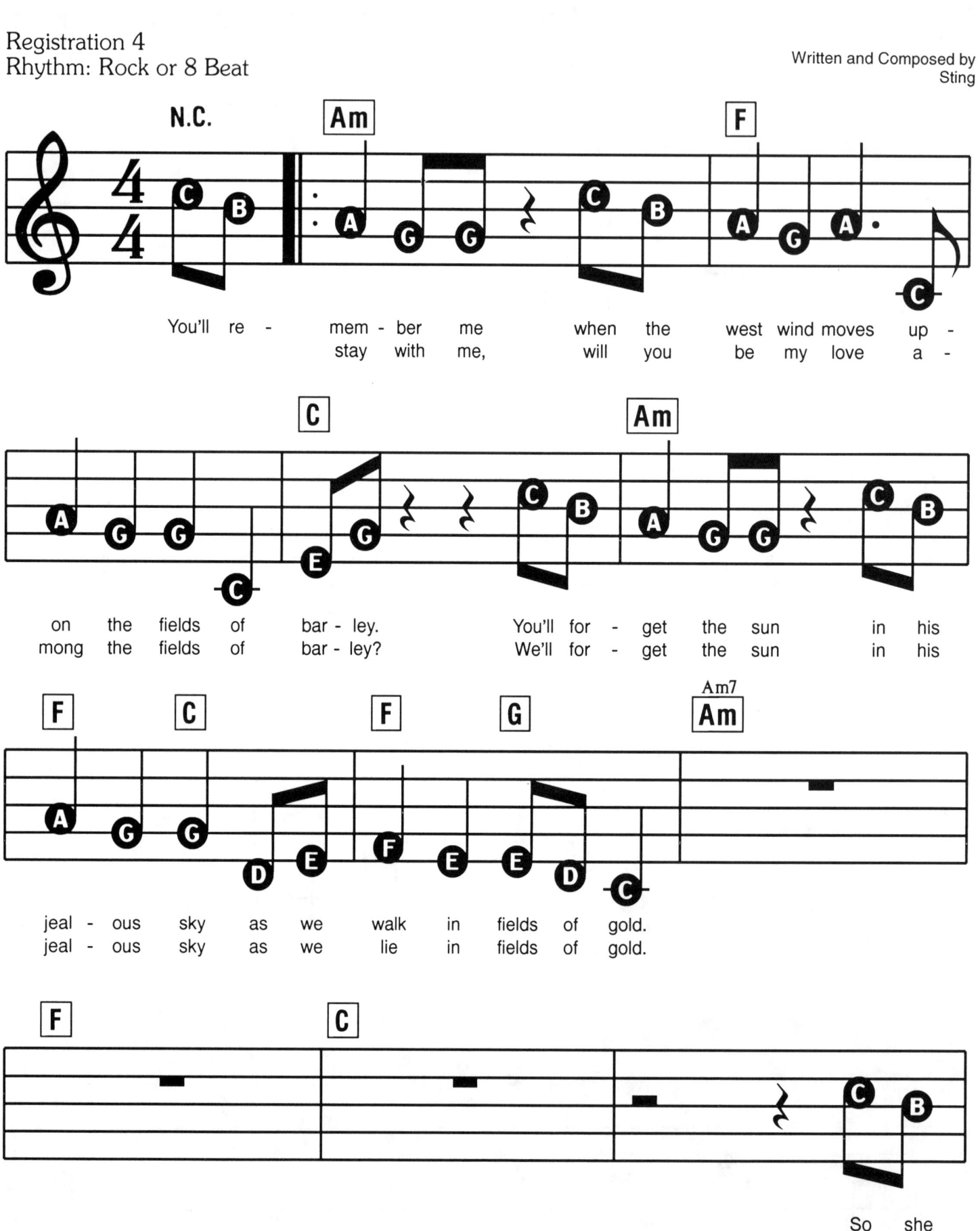

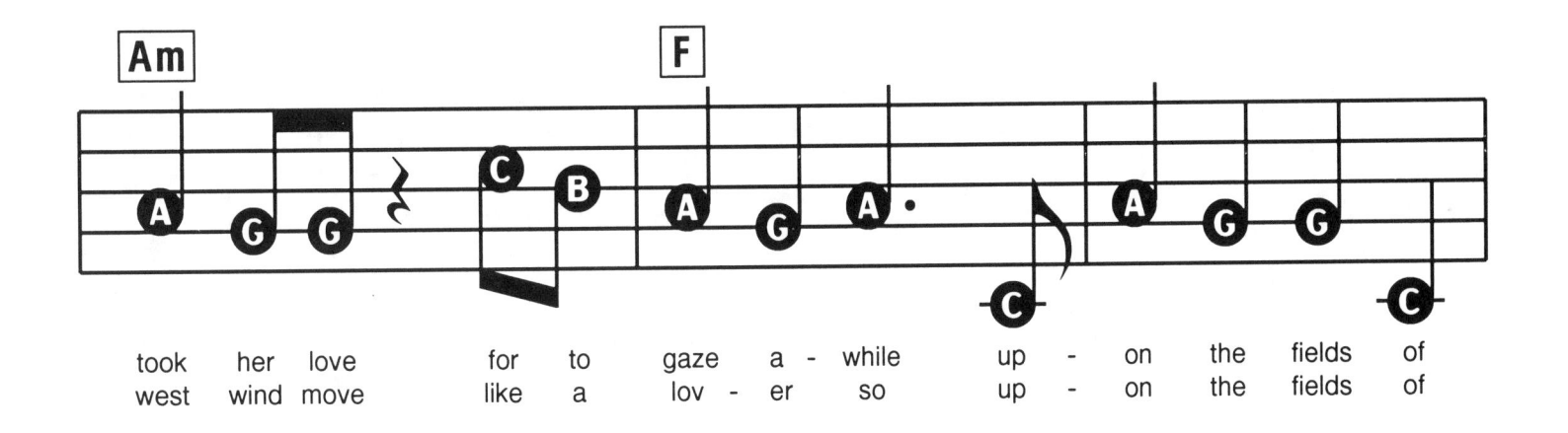

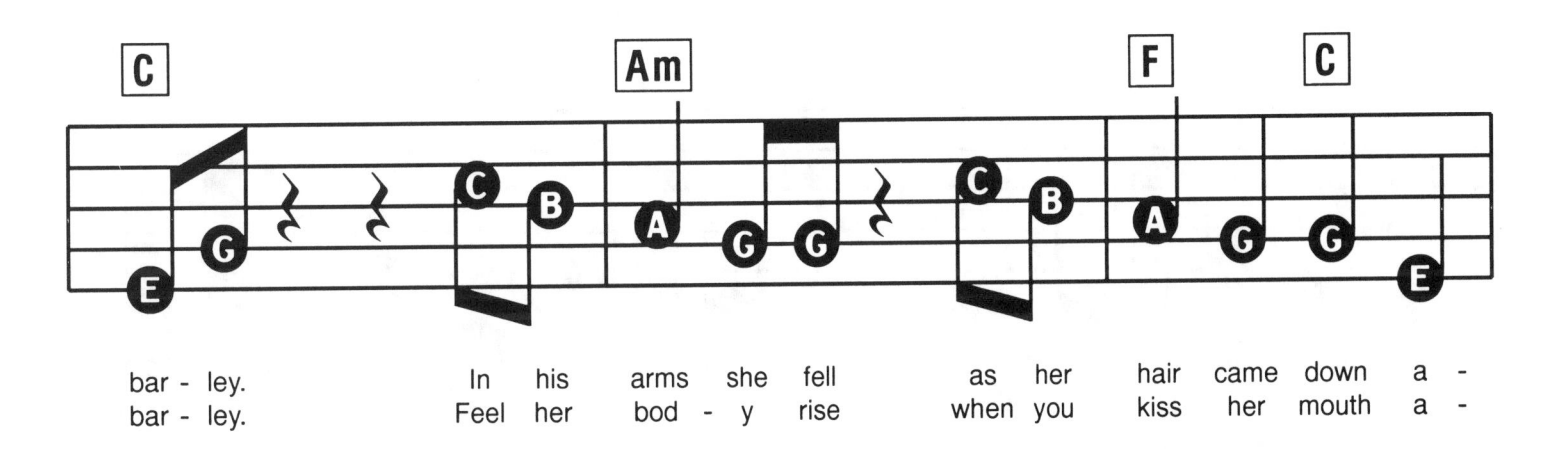

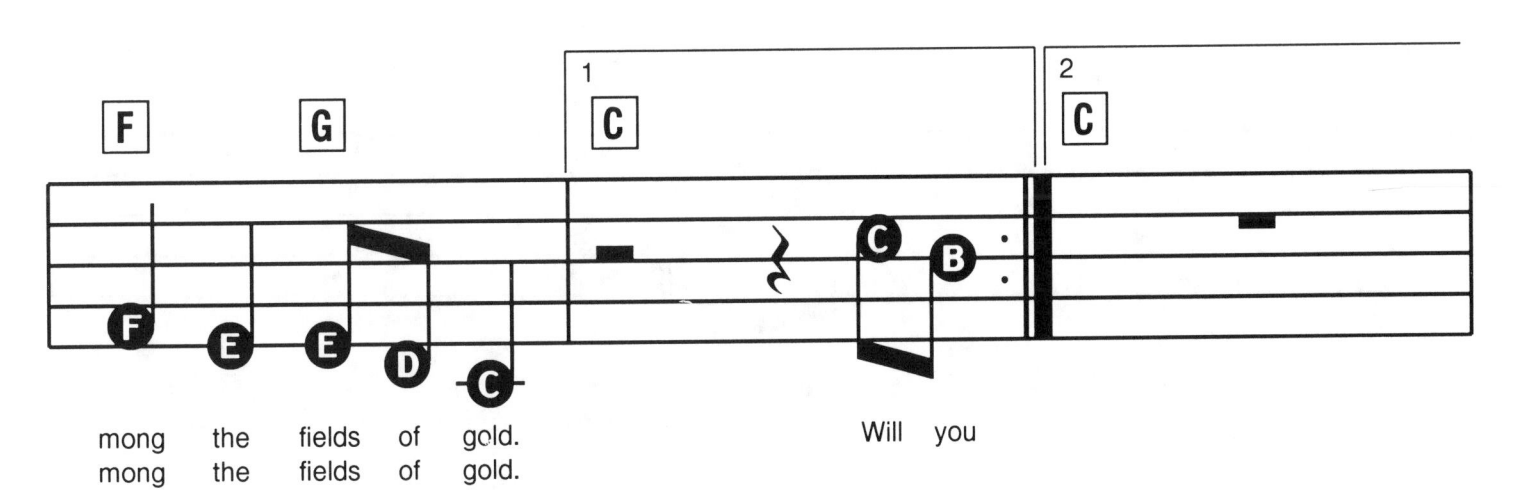

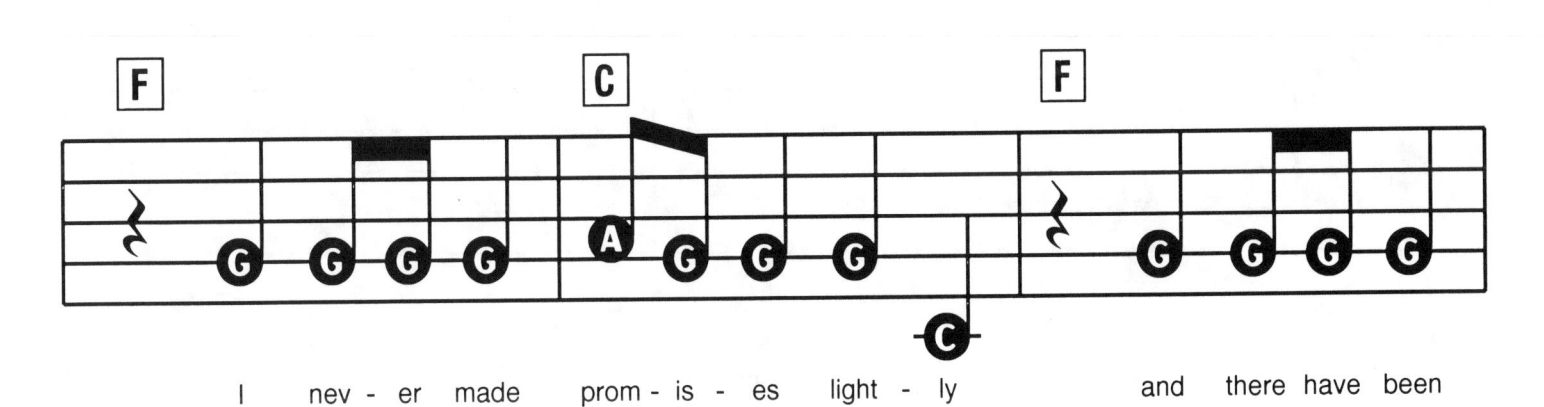

took her love for to gaze a-while up-on the fields of
west wind move like a lov-er so up-on the fields of
bar-ley. In his arms she fell as her hair came down a-
bar-ley. Feel her bod-y rise when you kiss her mouth a-
mong the fields of gold.
mong the fields of gold. Will you
I nev-er made prom-is-es light-ly and there have been

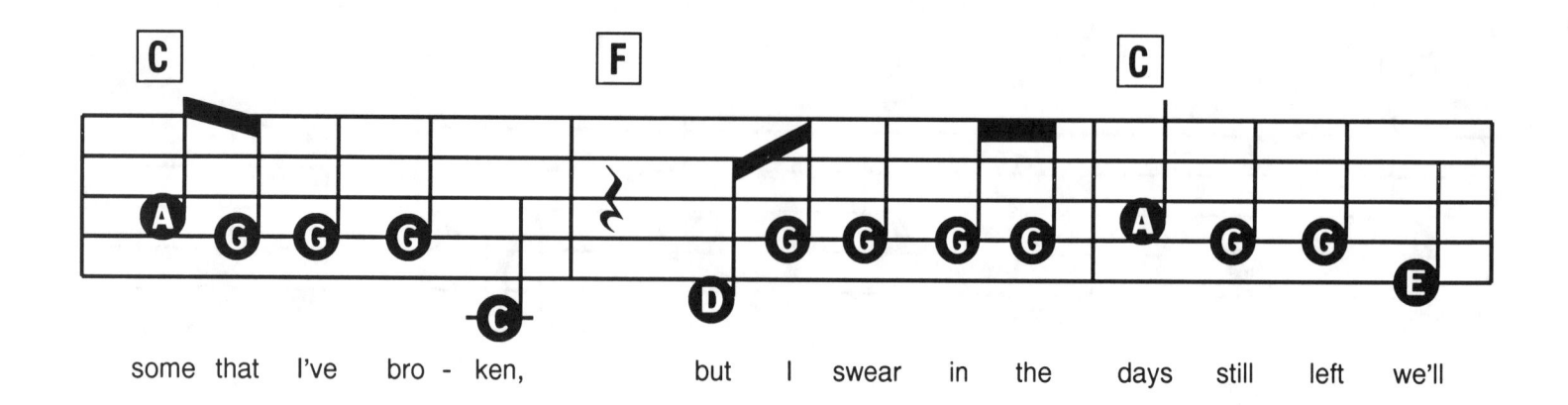

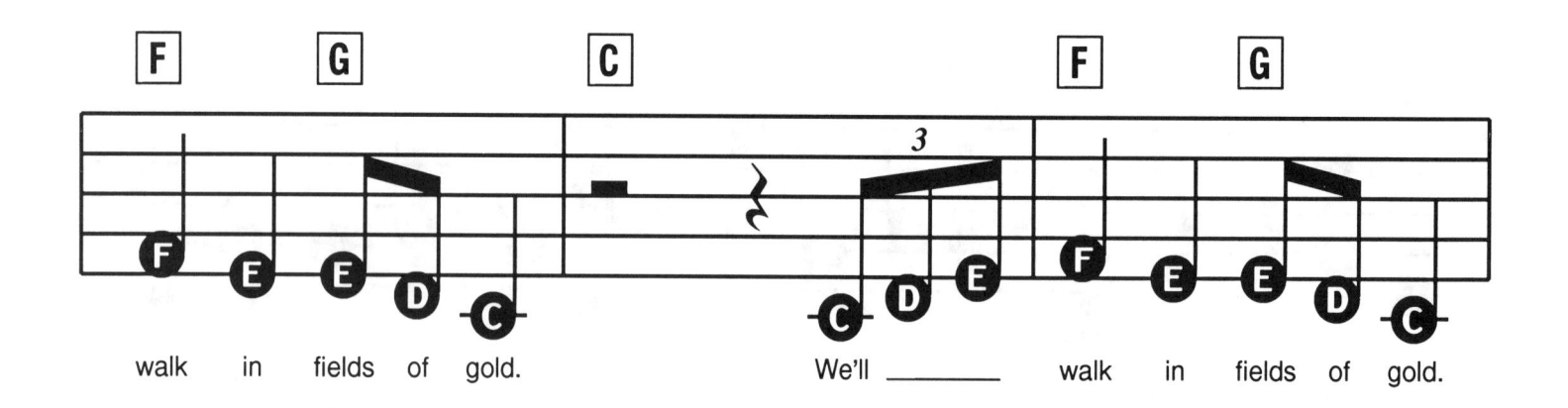

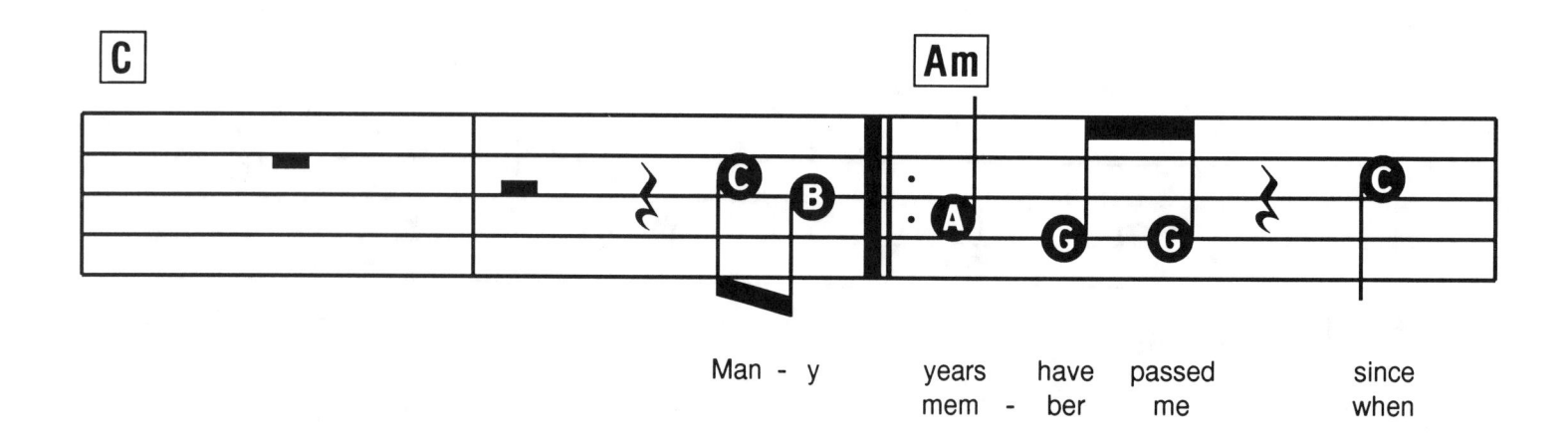

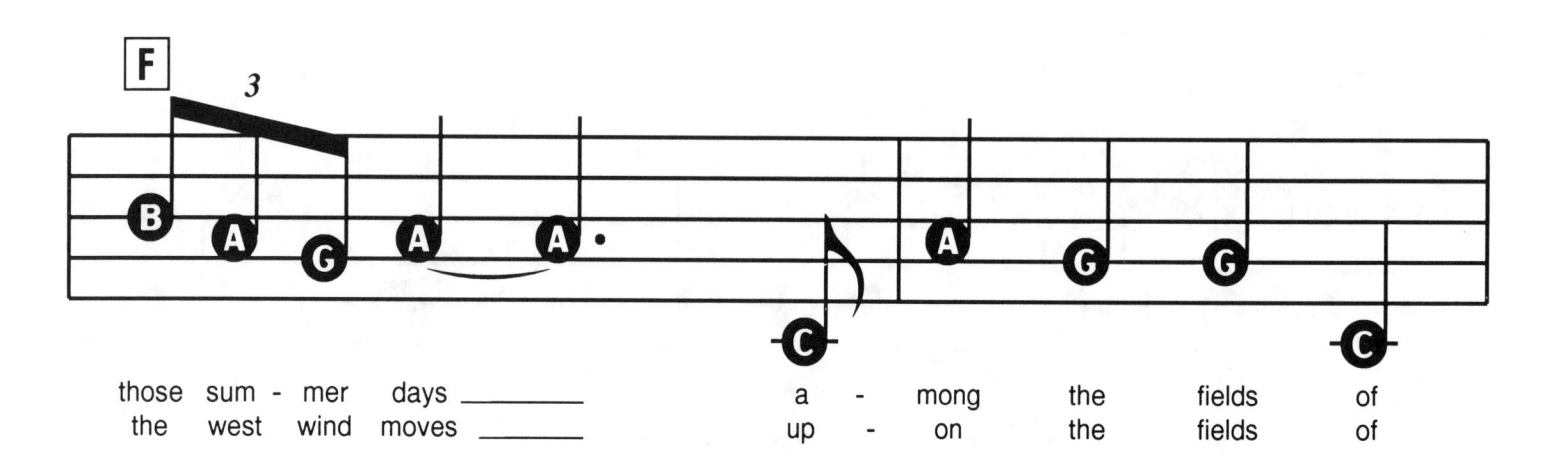

some that I've bro - ken, but I swear in the days still left we'll

walk in fields of gold. We'll _____ walk in fields of gold.

Man - y years have passed since
mem - ber me when

those sum - mer days _____ a - mong the fields of
the west wind moves _____ up - on the fields of

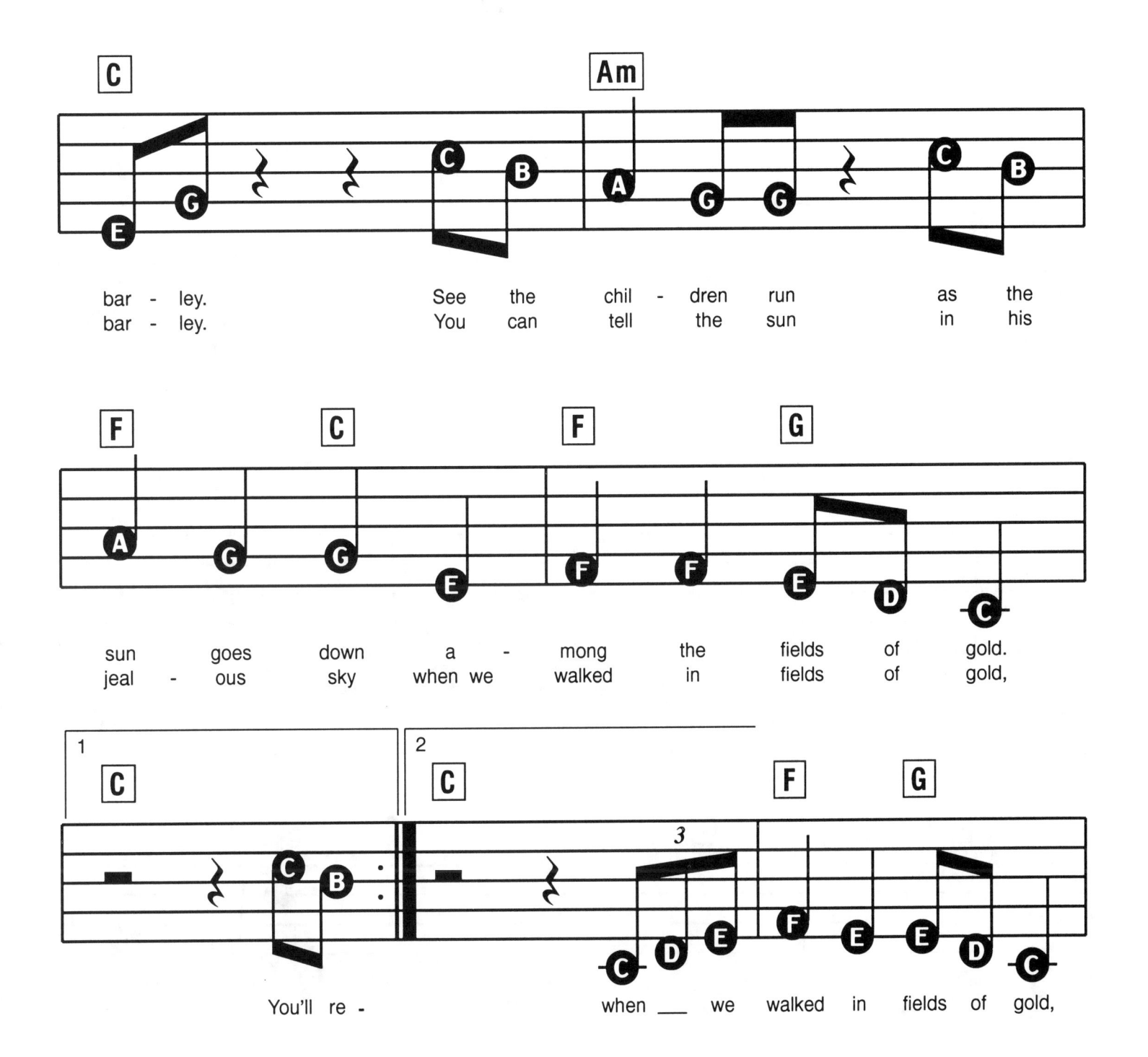

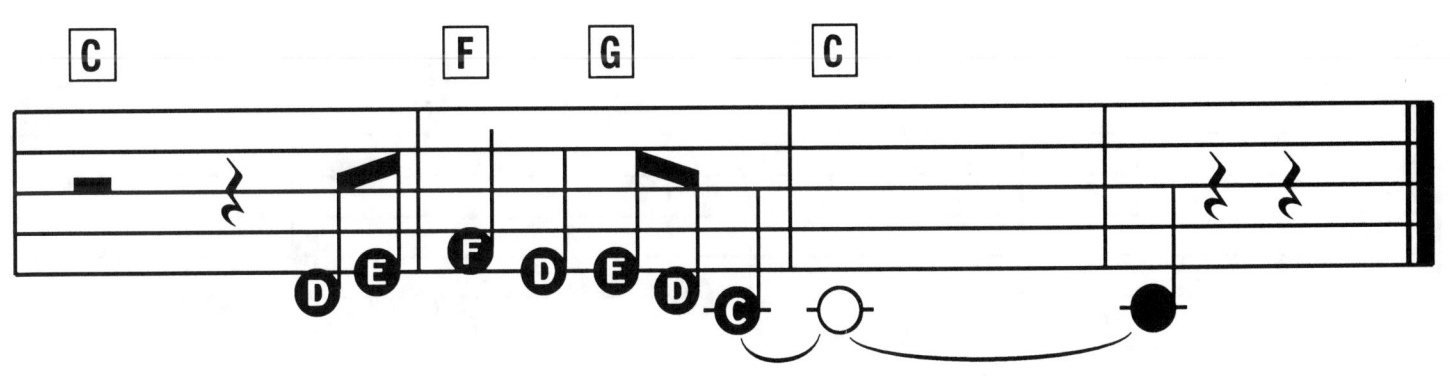

bar - ley. See the chil - dren run as the
bar - ley. You can tell the sun in his

sun goes down a - mong the fields of gold.
jeal - ous sky when we walked in fields of gold,

You'll re-

when ___ we walked in fields of gold,

when we walked in fields of gold.

The Gift

Registration 9
Rhythm: Ballad

Words and Music by Tom Douglas
and Jim Brickman

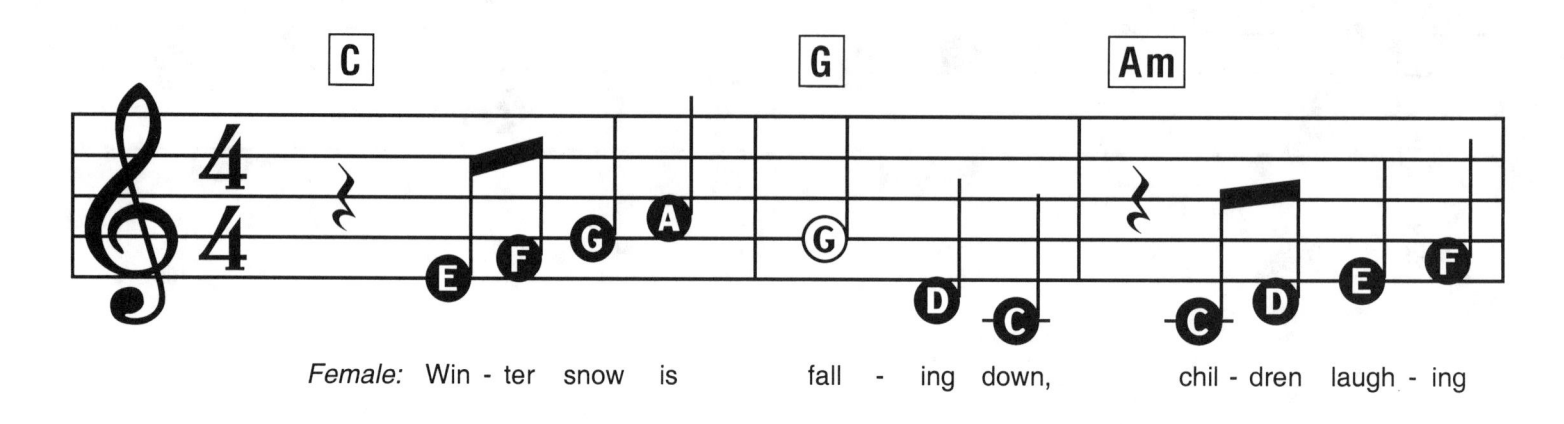

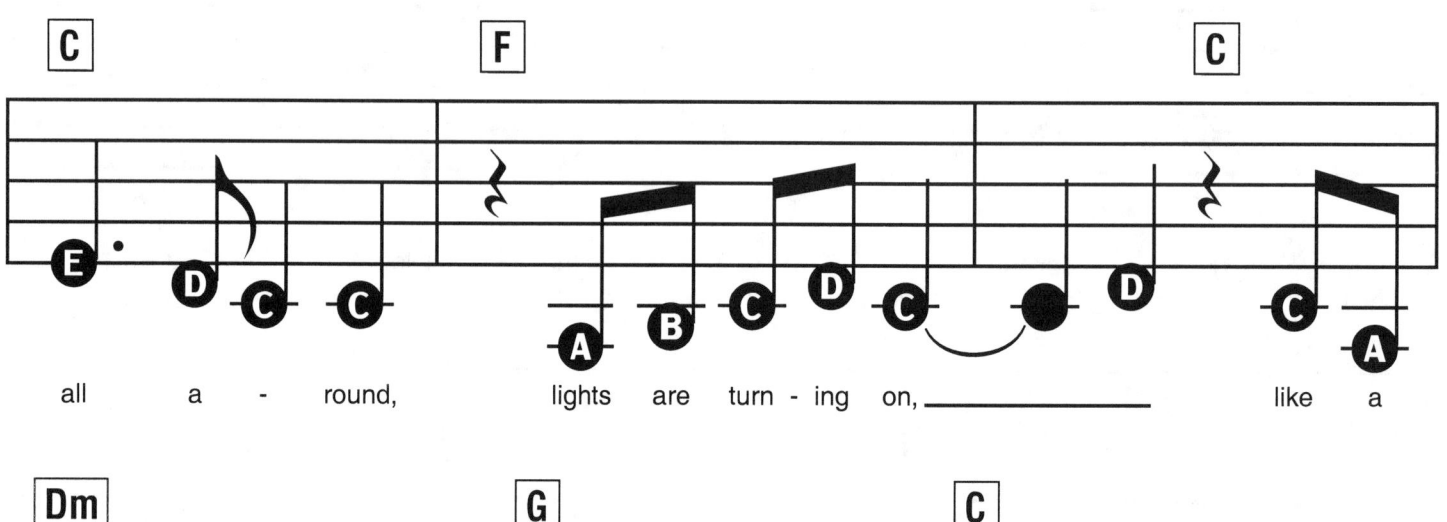

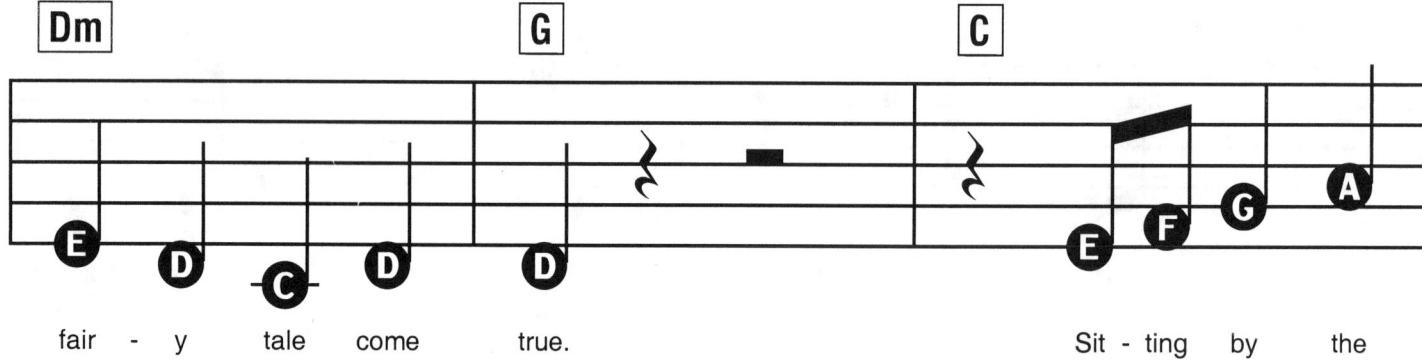

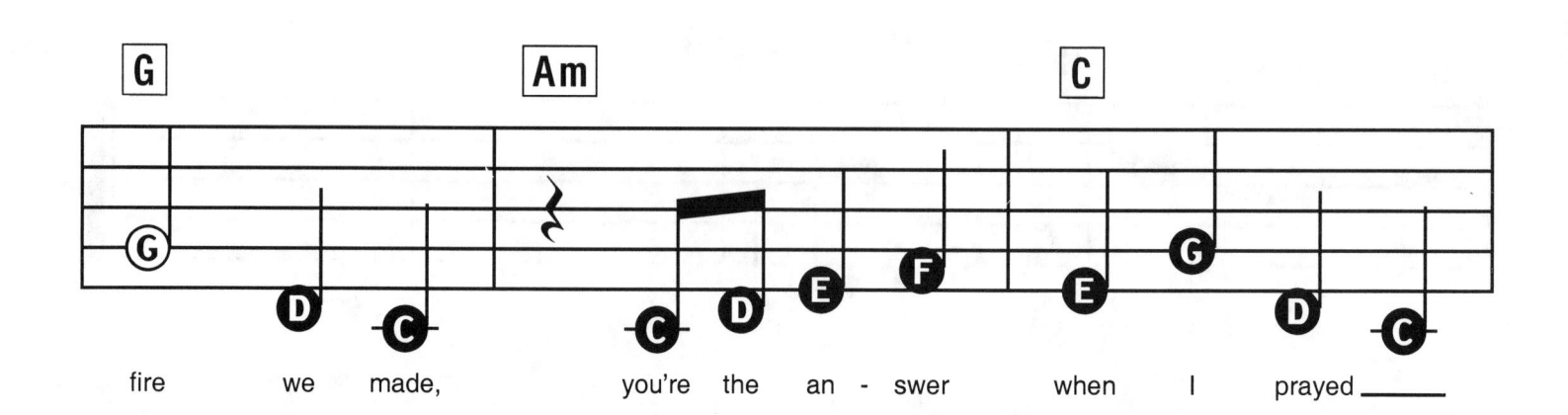

Female: Win - ter snow is fall - ing down, chil - dren laugh - ing all a - round, lights are turn - ing on, like a fair - y tale come true. Sit - ting by the fire we made, you're the an - swer when I prayed

Copyright © 1997 Sony/ATV Songs LLC, Multisongs, Inc., A Division of Careers-BMG Music Publishing, Inc. and Brickman Arrangement
All Rights on behalf of Sony/ATV Songs LLC Administered by Sony/ATV Music Publishing, 8 Music Square West, Nashville, TN 37203
All Rights on behalf of Brickman Arrangement Administered by Multisongs, Inc., A Division of Careers-BMG Music Publishing, Inc.
International Copyright Secured   All Rights Reserved

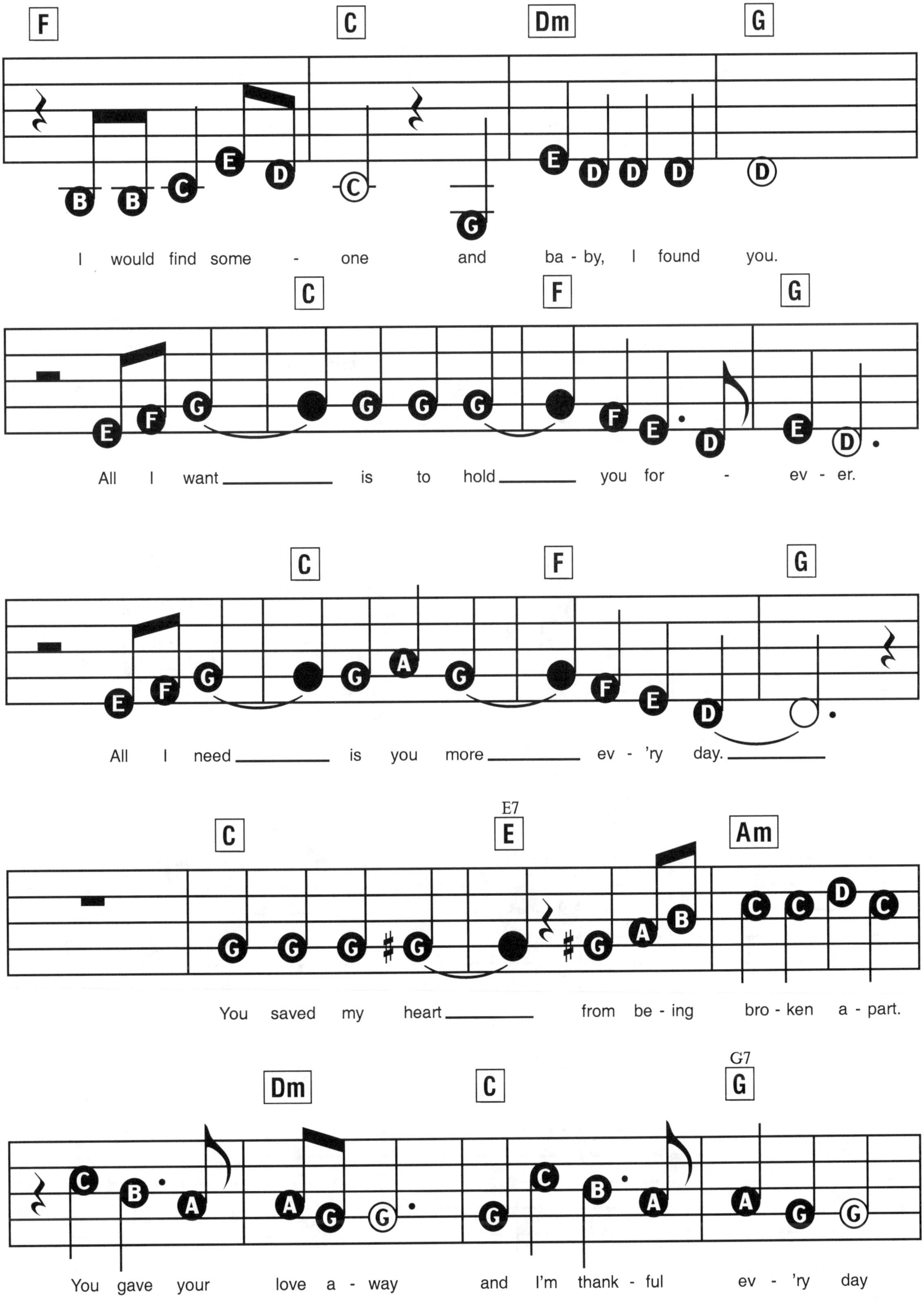
F C Dm G
I would find some - one and ba - by, I found you.
C F G
All I want is to hold you for - ev - er.
C F G
All I need is you more ev - 'ry day.
C E7 E Am
You saved my heart from be - ing bro - ken a - part.
Dm C G7 G
You gave your love a - way and I'm thank - ful ev - 'ry day

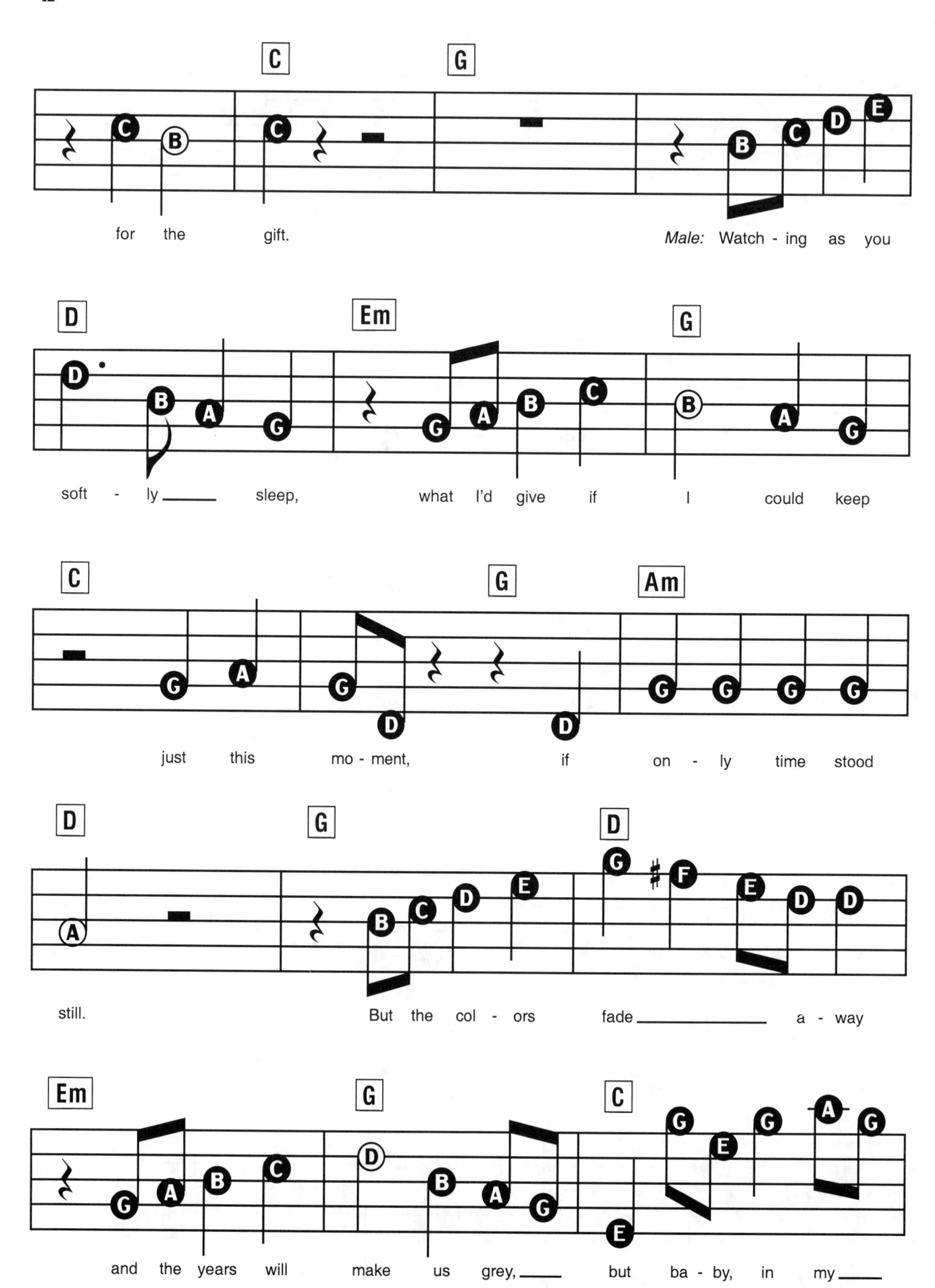

for the gift. *Male:* Watch-ing as you soft-ly ___ sleep, what I'd give if I could keep just this mo-ment, if on-ly time stood still. But the col-ors fade ___ a-way and the years will make us grey, ___ but ba-by, in my ___ eyes, _____ you'll still be beau - ti - ful. _____

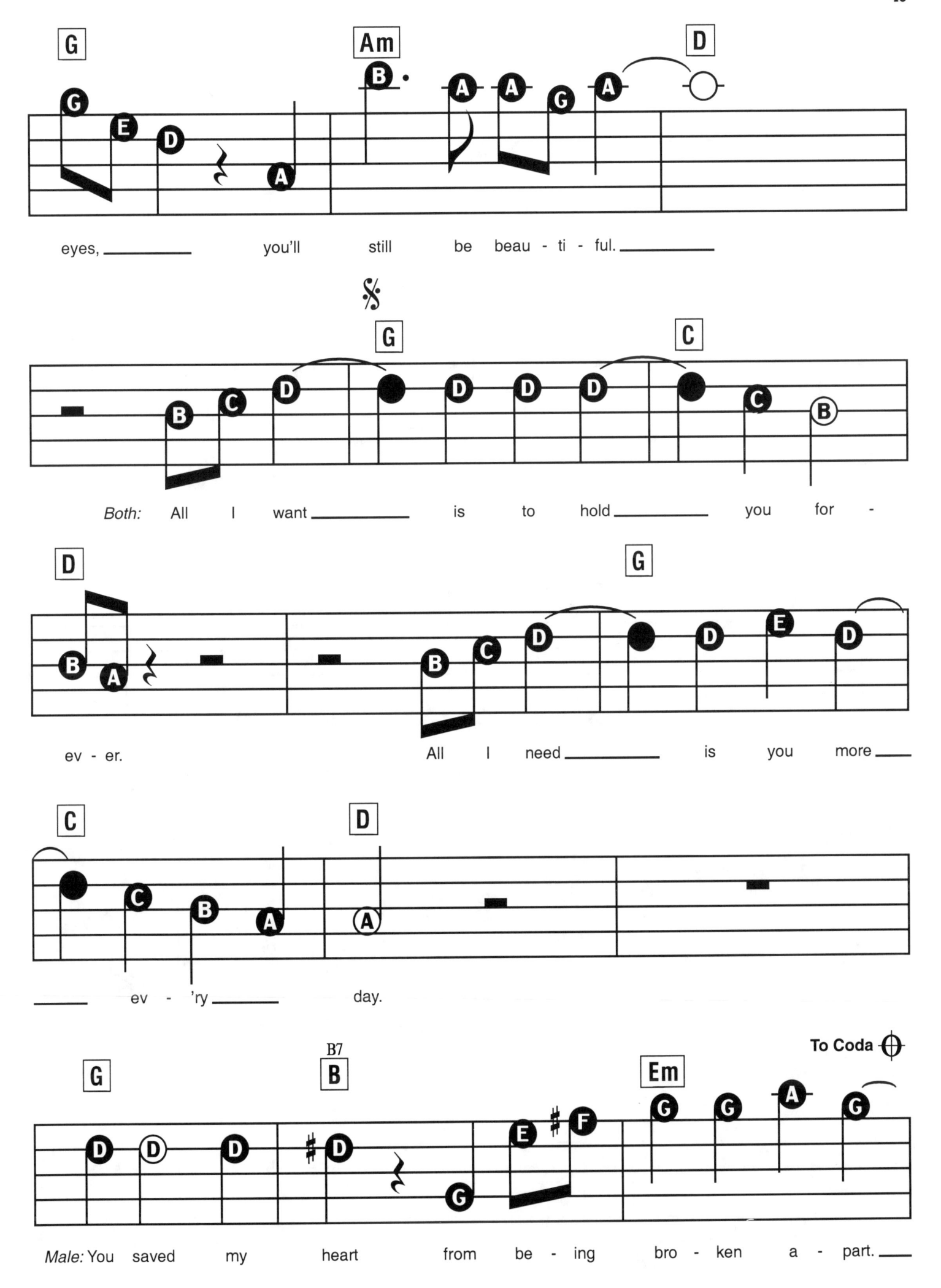

Both: All I want _____ is to hold _____ you for -

ev - er. All I need _____ is you more _____

_____ ev - 'ry _____ day.

Male: You saved my heart from be - ing bro - ken a - part. _____

To Coda ⊕

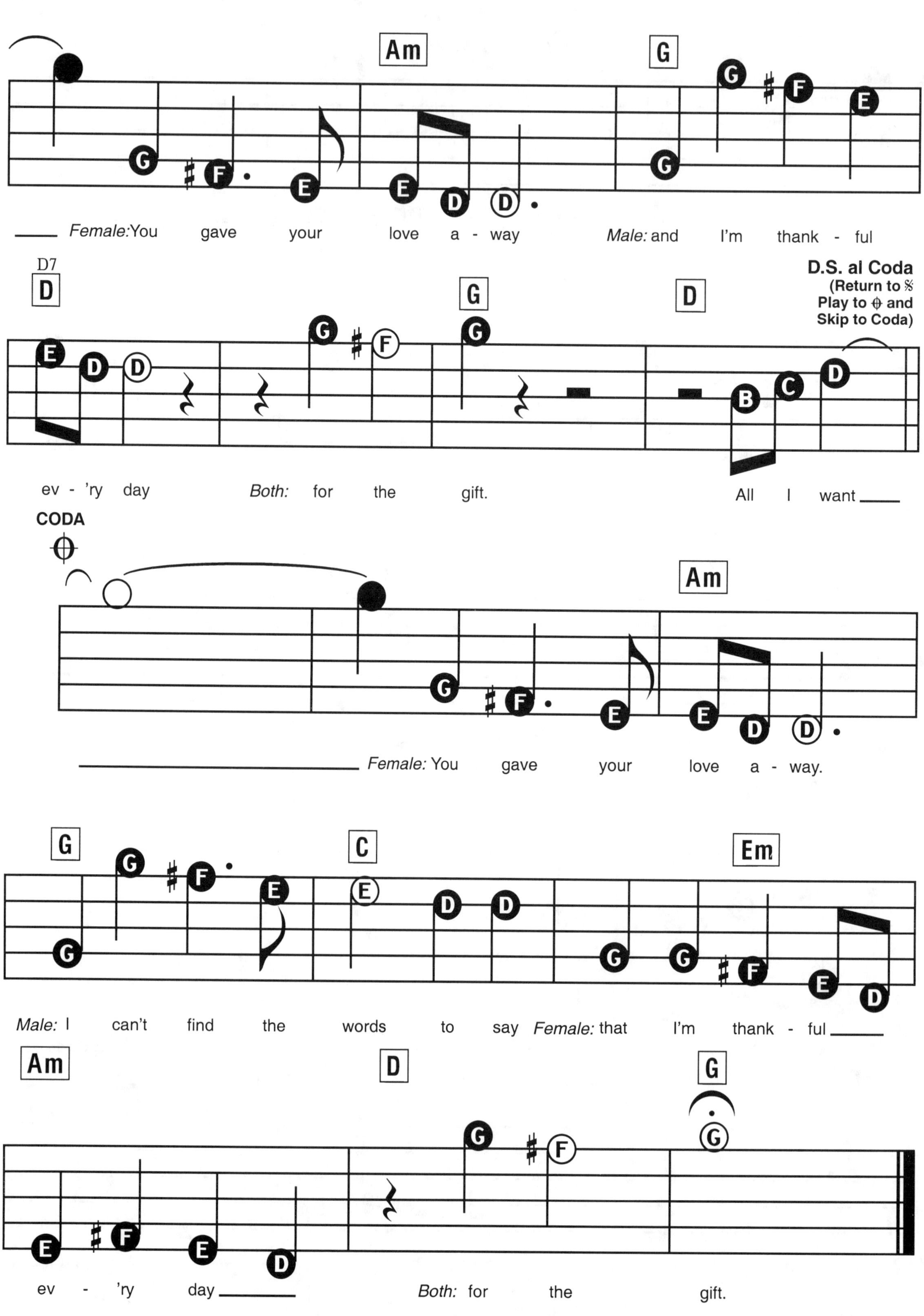
Am
G
Female: You gave your love a - way
Male: and I'm thank - ful
D7
D
G
D
D.S. al Coda
(Return to 𝄋
Play to ⊕ and
Skip to Coda)
ev - 'ry day
Both: for the gift.
All I want
CODA
Am
Female: You gave your love a - way.
G
C
Em
Male: I can't find the words to say
Female: that I'm thank - ful
Am
D
G
ev - 'ry day
Both: for the gift.

A Groovy Kind of Love

Comtempo @100

Registration 5
Rhythm: 8 Beat or Rock

Words and Music by Toni Wine
and Carole Bayer Sager

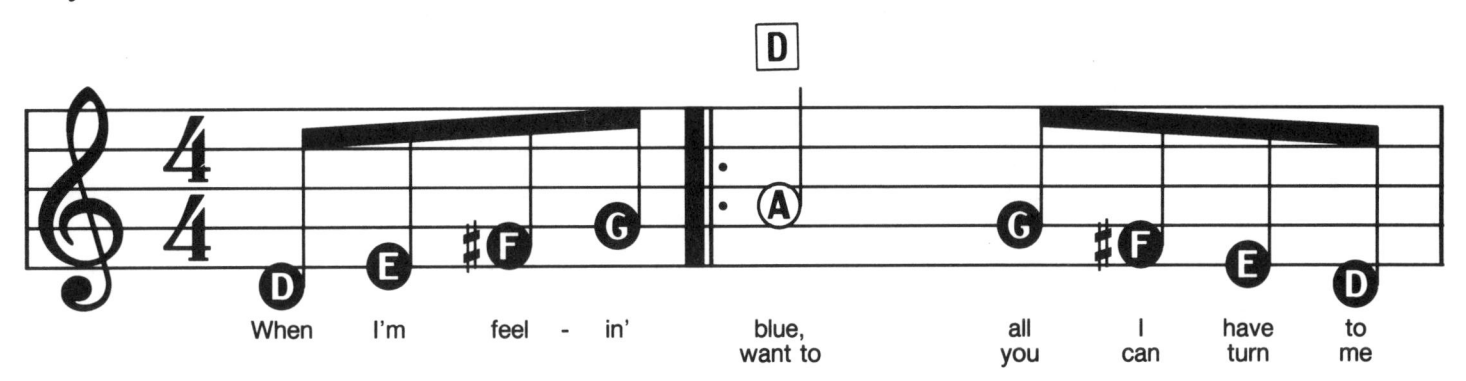

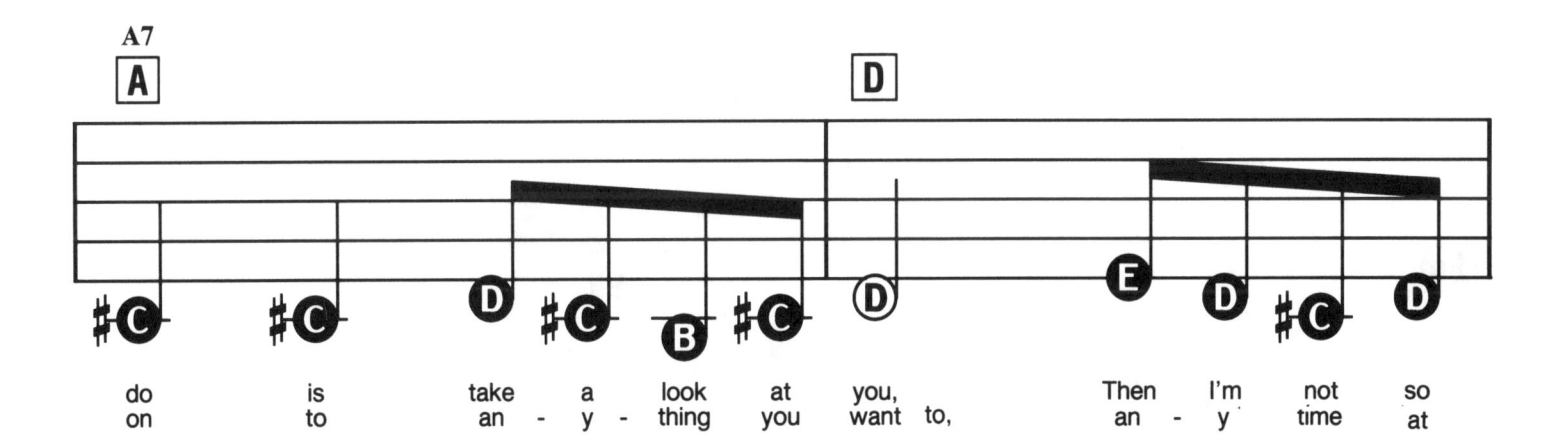

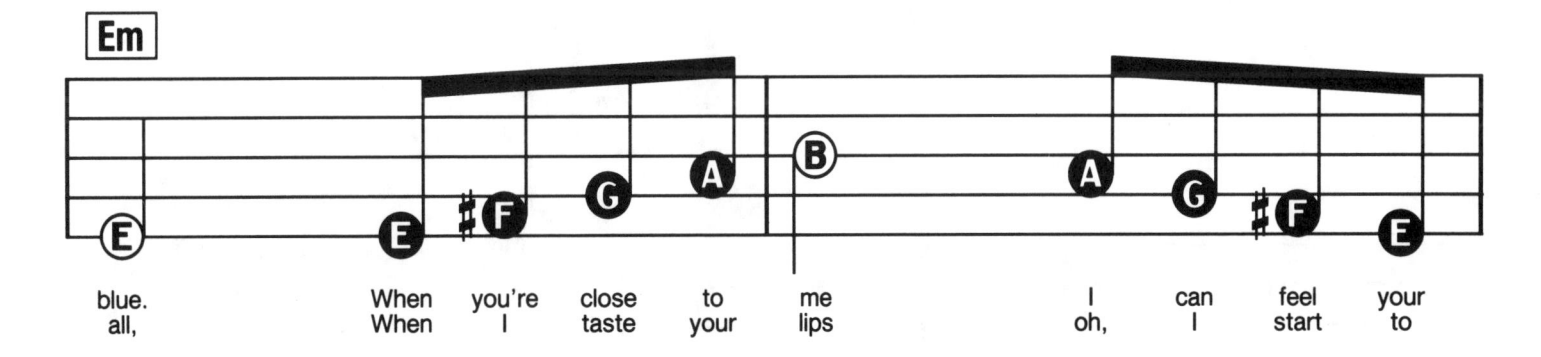

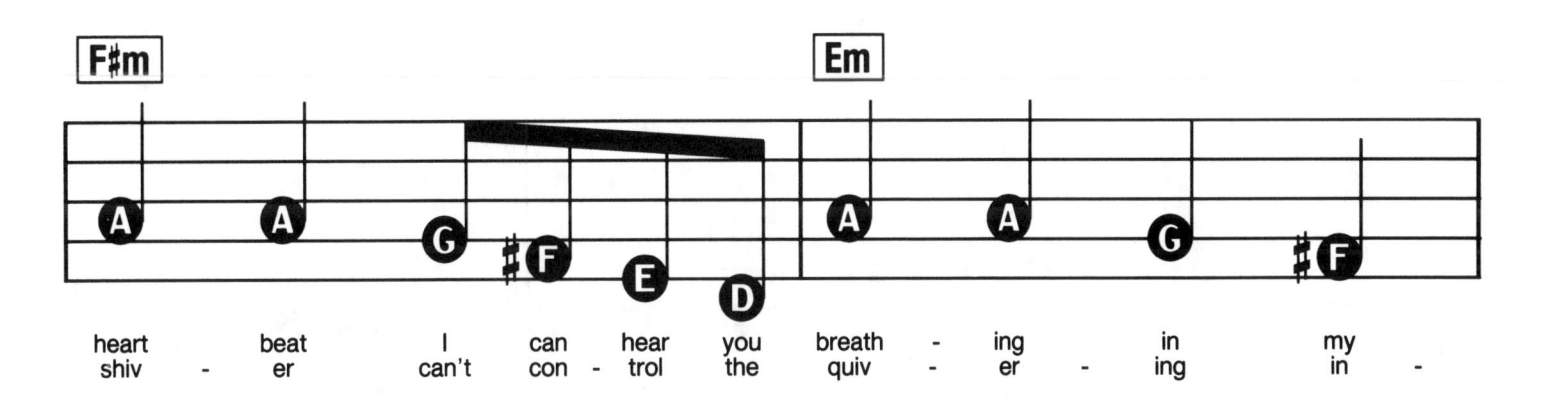

When I'm feel-in' blue, all I have to
want to, you can turn to me

do is take a look at you, Then I'm not so
on to an-y-thing you want to, an-y time at

blue. When you're close to me I can feel your
all, When I taste your lips oh, I start to

heart beat I can hear you breath-ing in my
shiv-er can't con-trol the quiv-er-ing in -

© 1966 (Renewed 1994) SCREEN GEMS-EMI MUSIC INC.
All Rights Reserved   International Copyright Secured   Used by Permission

46

Eb Fm
When I'm in your
Gm
arms noth - ing seems to mat - ter, if the world would
Fm Bb7 Bb
shat - ter I don't care. Would - n't you a -
Eb Bb
gree, ba - by, you and me got a groov - y kind of
Eb Fm7 Fm Bb7 Bb
Repeat and Fade
love. We got a groov - y kind of

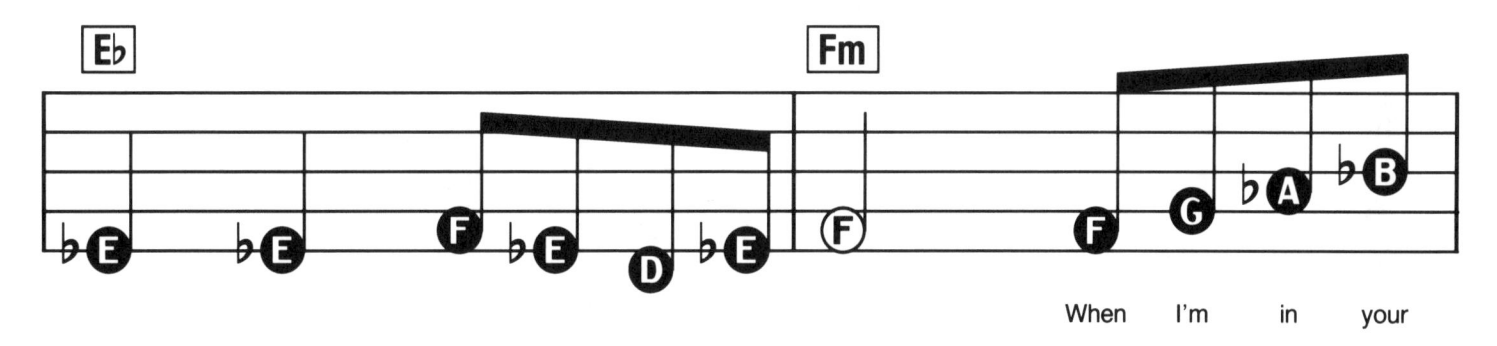

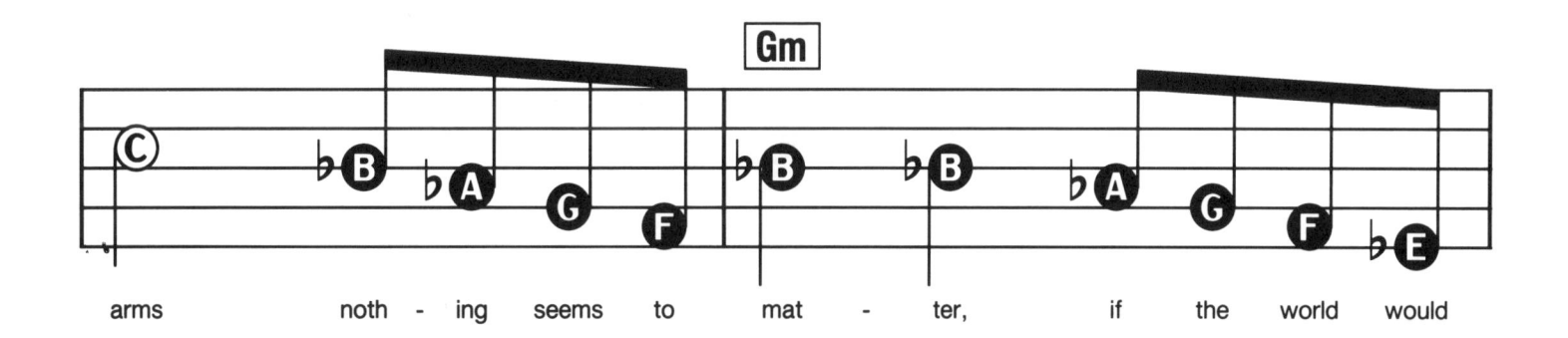

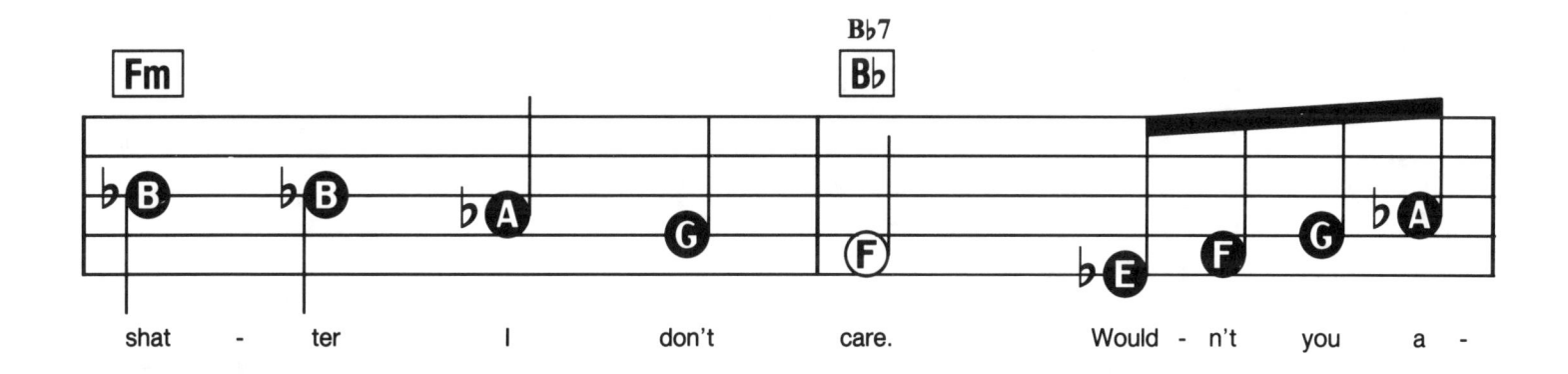

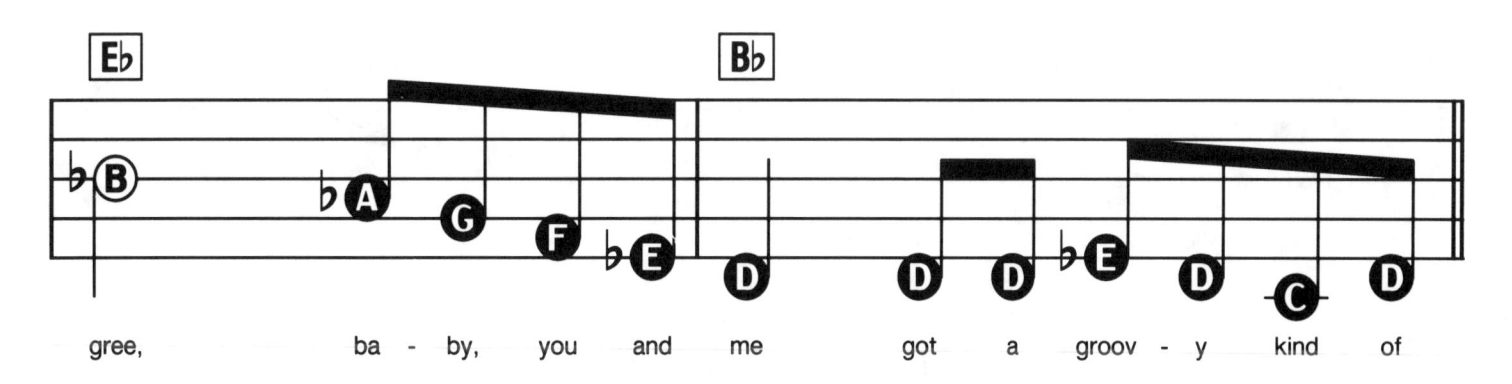

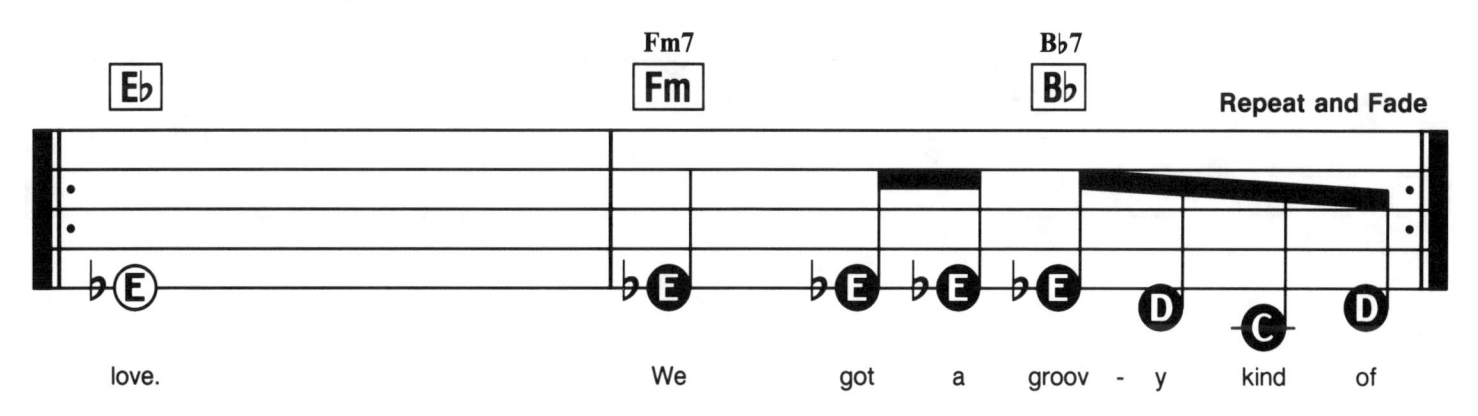

Grow Old With Me

Registration 7
Rhythm: Country Ballad

Words and Music by
John Lennon

Grow old a-long with me, the
old a-long with me, two
old a-long with me, what-

best is yet to be.
branch - es of one tree.
ev - er fate de - crees.

When our time has come we will be as
Face the set - ting sun when the day is
We will see it through for our love is

one.
done.
true.

God bless our love.

© 1982 LENONO MUSIC
All Rights Controlled and Administered by EMI BLACKWOOD MUSIC INC.
All Rights Reserved   International Copyright Secured   Used by Permission

49

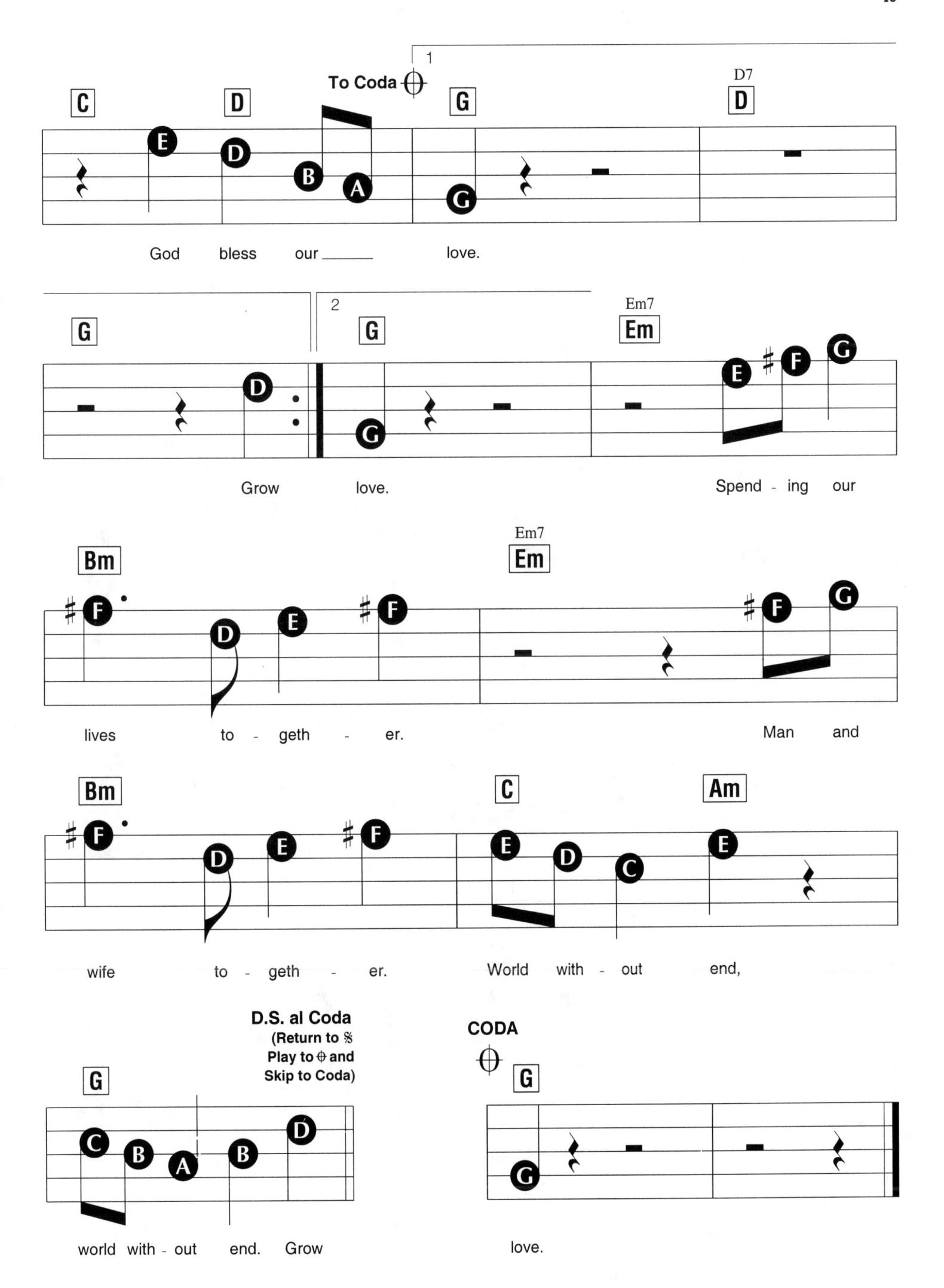

Here and Now

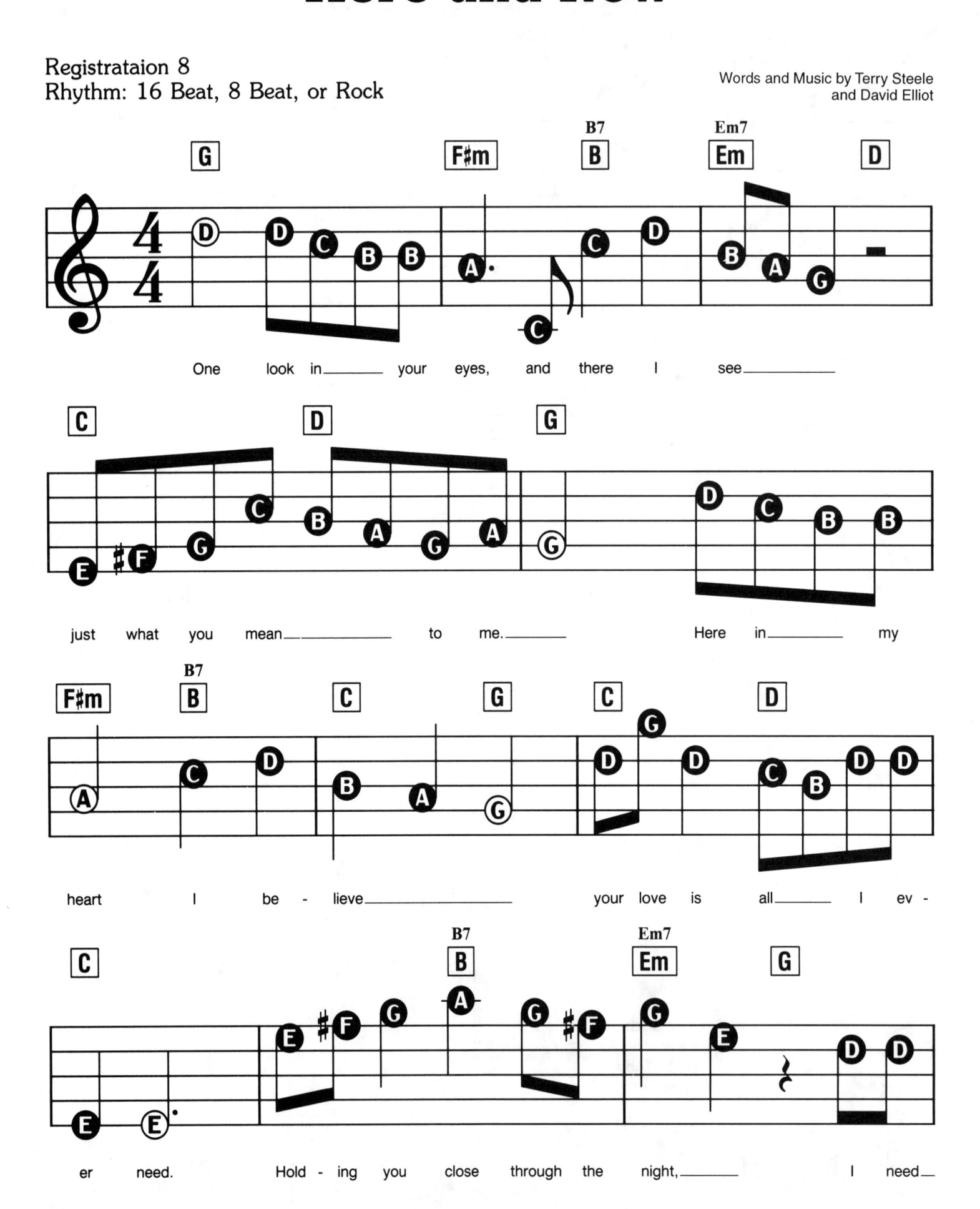

Registrataion 8
Rhythm: 16 Beat, 8 Beat, or Rock

Words and Music by Terry Steele
and David Elliot

One look in your eyes, and there I see just what you mean to me. Here in my heart I be - lieve your love is all I ev - er need. Hold - ing you close through the night, I need

© 1989 EMI APRIL MUSIC INC., OLLIE BROWN SUGAR MUSIC,
UNIVERSAL - MCA MUSIC PUBLISHING, A Division of UNIVERSAL STUDIOS, INC. and D.L.E. MUSIC
All Rights for OLLIE BROWN SUGAR MUSIC throughout the World Controlled and Administered by EMI APRIL MUSIC INC.
All Rights for D.L.E. MUSIC in the U.S. and Canada
Controlled and Administered by UNIVERSAL - MCA MUSIC PUBLISHING, A Division of UNIVERSAL STUDIOS, INC.
All Rights for D.L.E. MUSIC in the World excluding the U.S. and Canada Controlled and Administered by EMI APRIL MUSIC INC.
All Rights Reserved   International Copyright Secured   Used by Permission

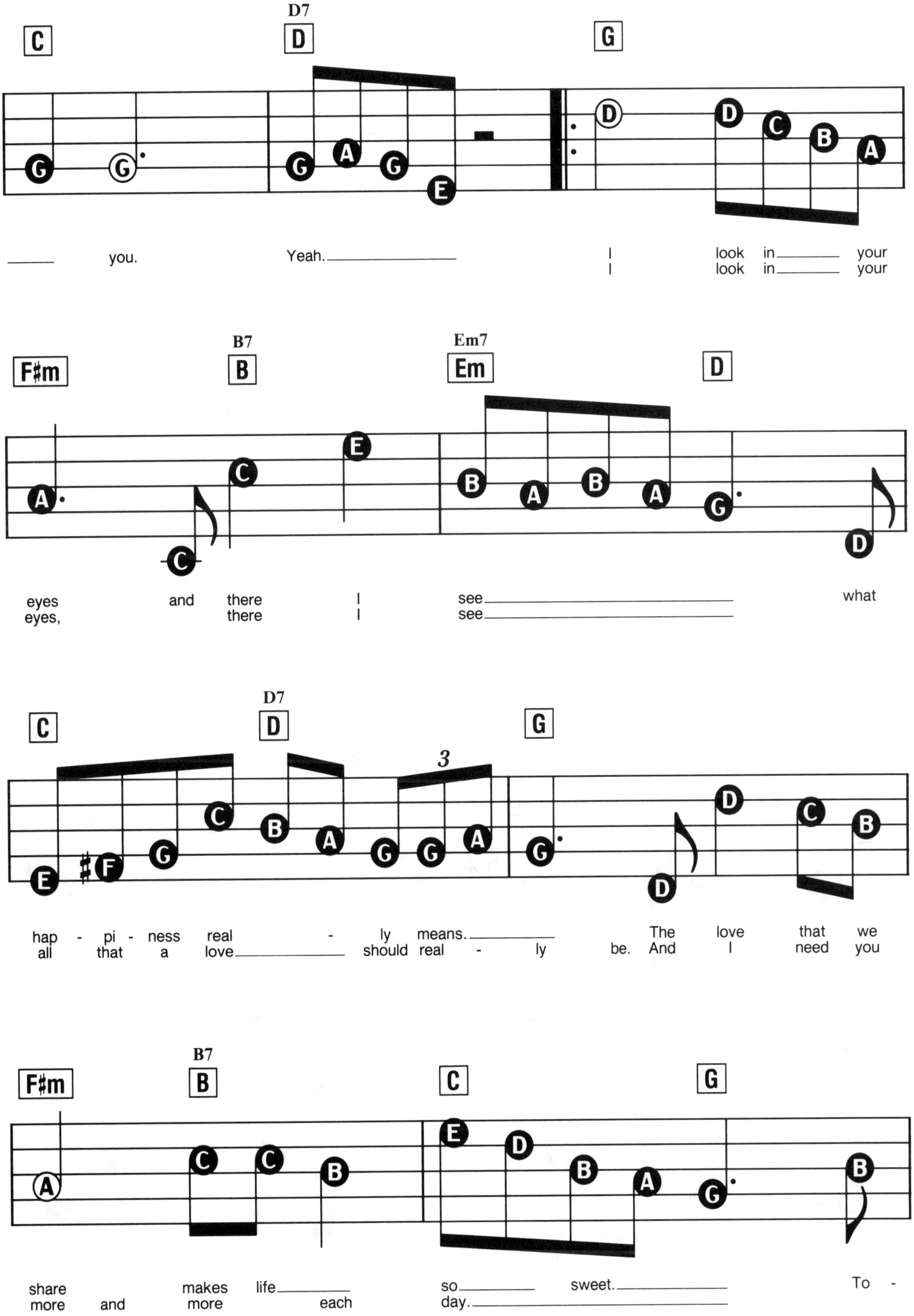
D7
C
D
G
you.
Yeah.
I look in your
I look in your
B7
Em7
F♯m
B
Em
D
eyes and there I see what
eyes, there I see
D7
C
D
G
3
hap - pi - ness real - ly means. The love that we
all that a love should real - ly be. And I need you
B7
F♯m
B
C
G
share makes life so sweet. To -
more and more each day.

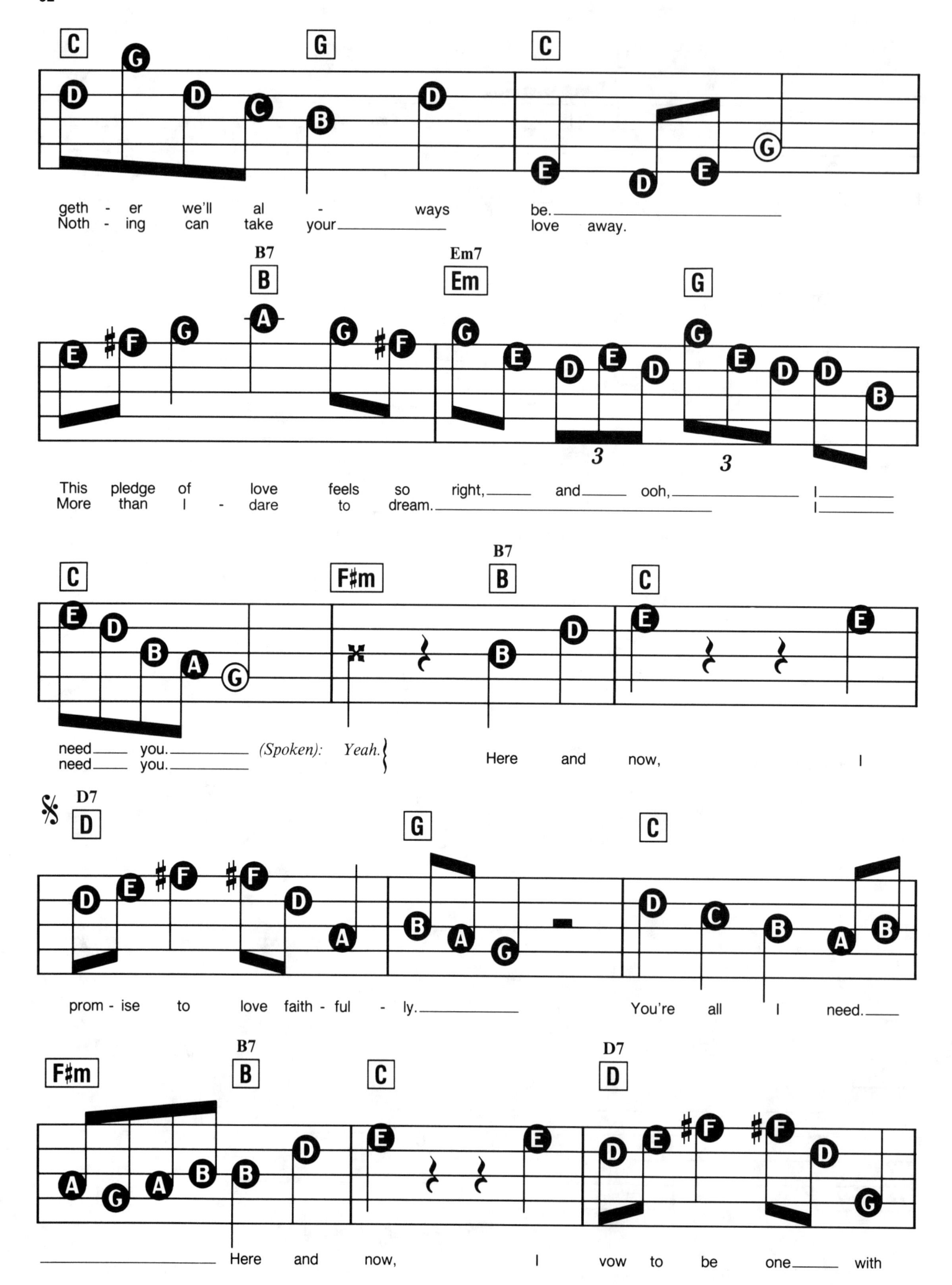

geth - er we'll al - ways be.
Noth - ing can take your love away.

This pledge of love feels so right,___ and___ ooh,___ I___
More than I - dare to dream.___ I___

need___ you.___ *(Spoken): Yeah.* Here and now, I
need___ you.___

prom - ise to love faith - ful - ly.___ You're all I need.___

___ Here and now, I vow to be one___ with

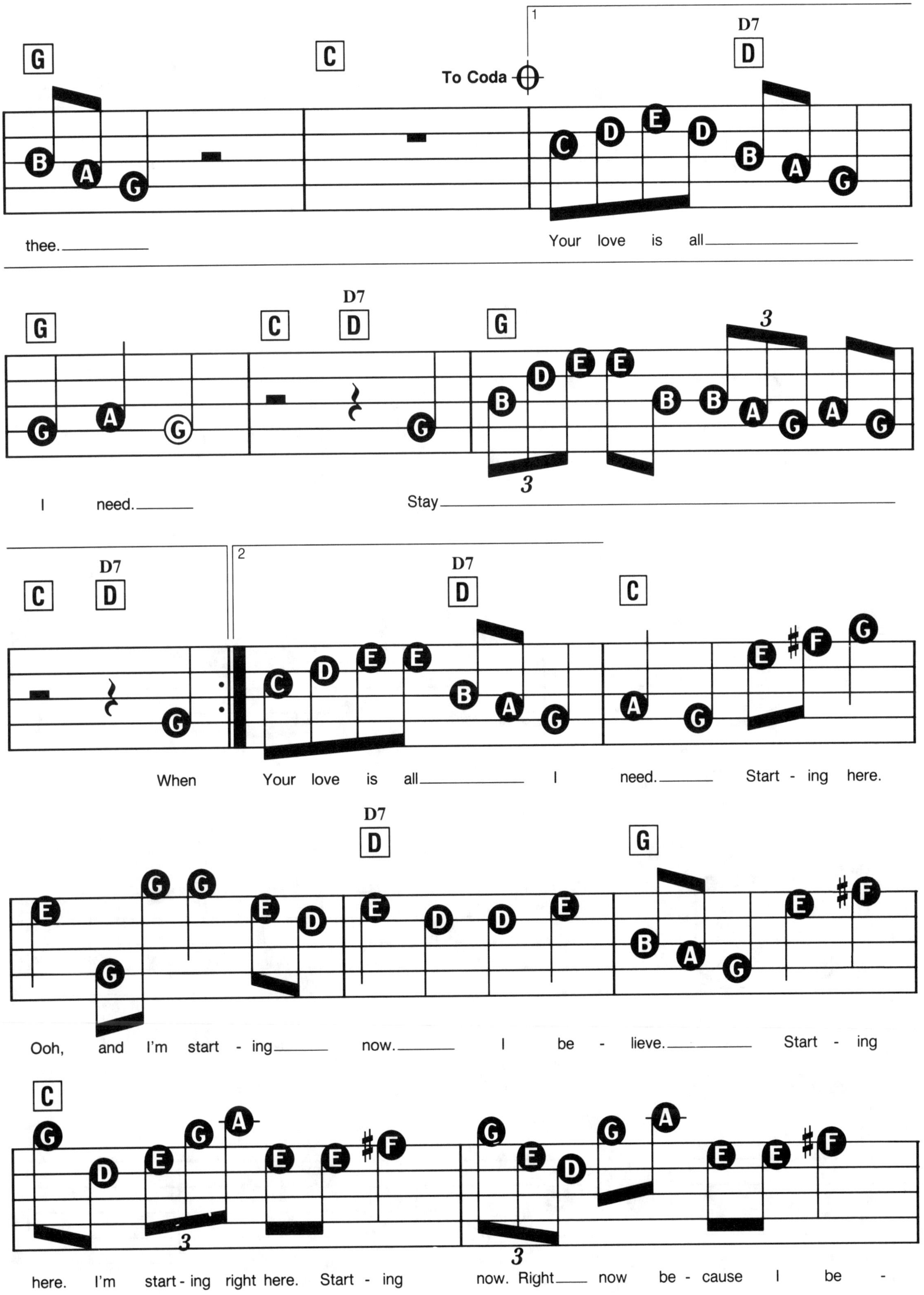

G
C
To Coda
1
D7
D
thee.
Your love is all
G
C
D7
D
G
3
3
I need.
Stay
C
D7
D
2
D7
D
C
When
Your love is all
I need.
Start - ing here.
D7
D
G
Ooh, and I'm start - ing now.
I be - lieve.
Start - ing
C
3
3
here. I'm start - ing right here. Start - ing
now. Right now be - cause I be -

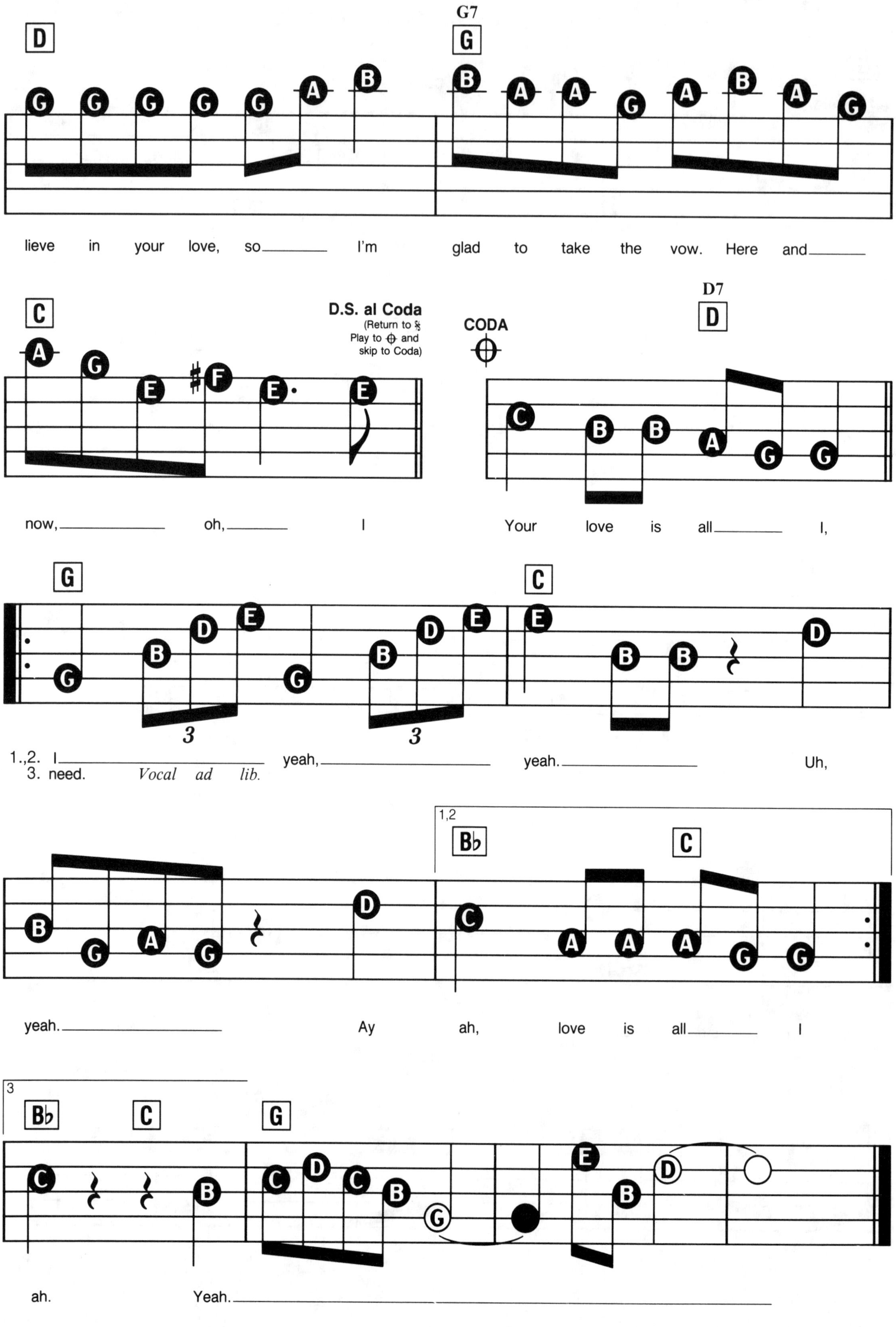
D
G7
G
lieve in your love, so I'm glad to take the vow. Here and
C
D.S. al Coda
(Return to 𝄋 Play to ⊕ and skip to Coda)
now, oh, I
CODA
D7
D
Your love is all I,
G
C
1.,2. I yeah, yeah. Uh,
3. need. Vocal ad lib.
1,2
B♭
C
yeah. Ay ah, love is all I
3
B♭
C
G
ah. Yeah.

I Finally Found Someone
from THE MIRROR HAS TWO FACES

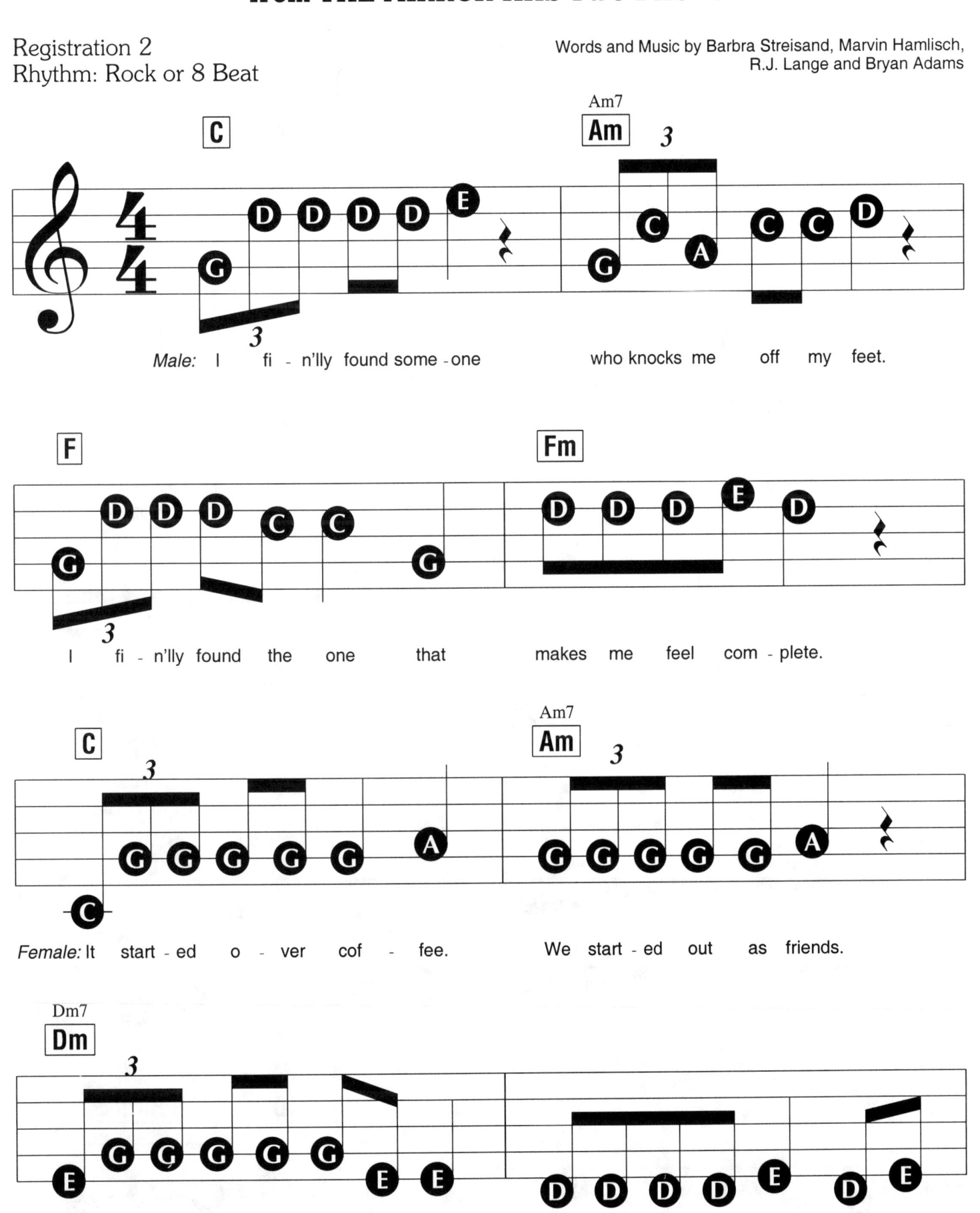

Registration 2
Rhythm: Rock or 8 Beat

Words and Music by Barbra Streisand, Marvin Hamlisch,
R.J. Lange and Bryan Adams

Male: I fi - n'lly found some - one who knocks me off my feet.

I fi - n'lly found the one that makes me feel com - plete.

Female: It start - ed o - ver cof - fee. We start - ed out as friends.

It's fun - ny how from sim - ple things the best things be - gin. _____

Copyright © 1996 Emanuel Music, TSP Music, Inc., Badams Music Ltd. and Out Of Pocket Productions Ltd.
All Rights on behalf of TSP Music, Inc. and Badams Music Ltd. Administered by
Sony/ATV Music Publishing, 8 Music Square West, Nashville, TN 37203
All Rights on behalf of Out Of Pocket Productions Ltd. Controlled by
Zomba Enterprises Inc. for the U.S. and Canada
International Copyright Secured   All Rights Reserved

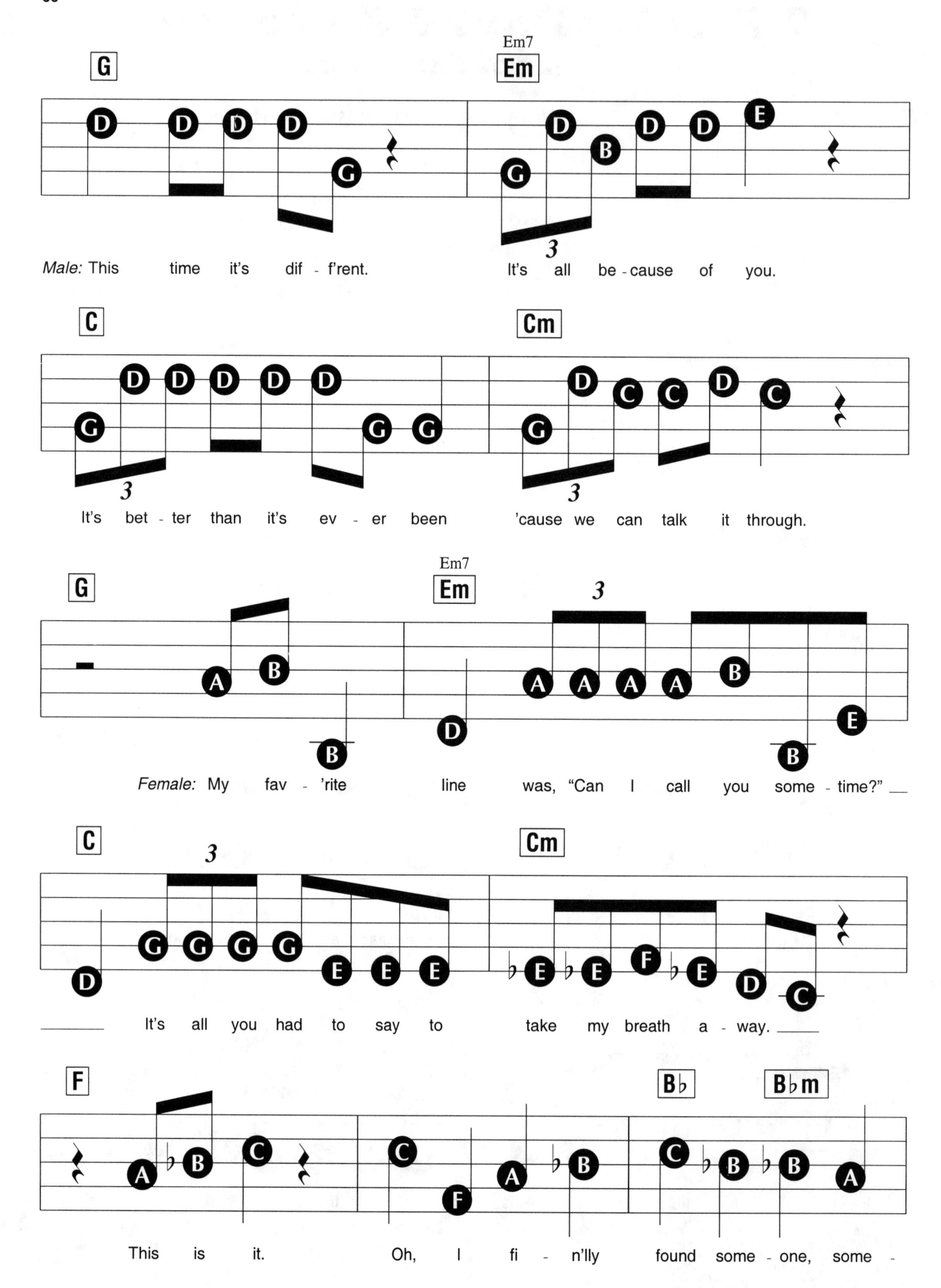

Male: This time it's dif-f'rent. It's all be-cause of you. It's bet-ter than it's ev-er been 'cause we can talk it through.

Female: My fav-'rite line was, "Can I call you some-time?" It's all you had to say to take my breath a-way. This is it. Oh, I fi-n'lly found some-one, some-

F								Bb			Bbm	
C	C	C	B♭	B♭	A	C	C	C	B♭	B♭	A	

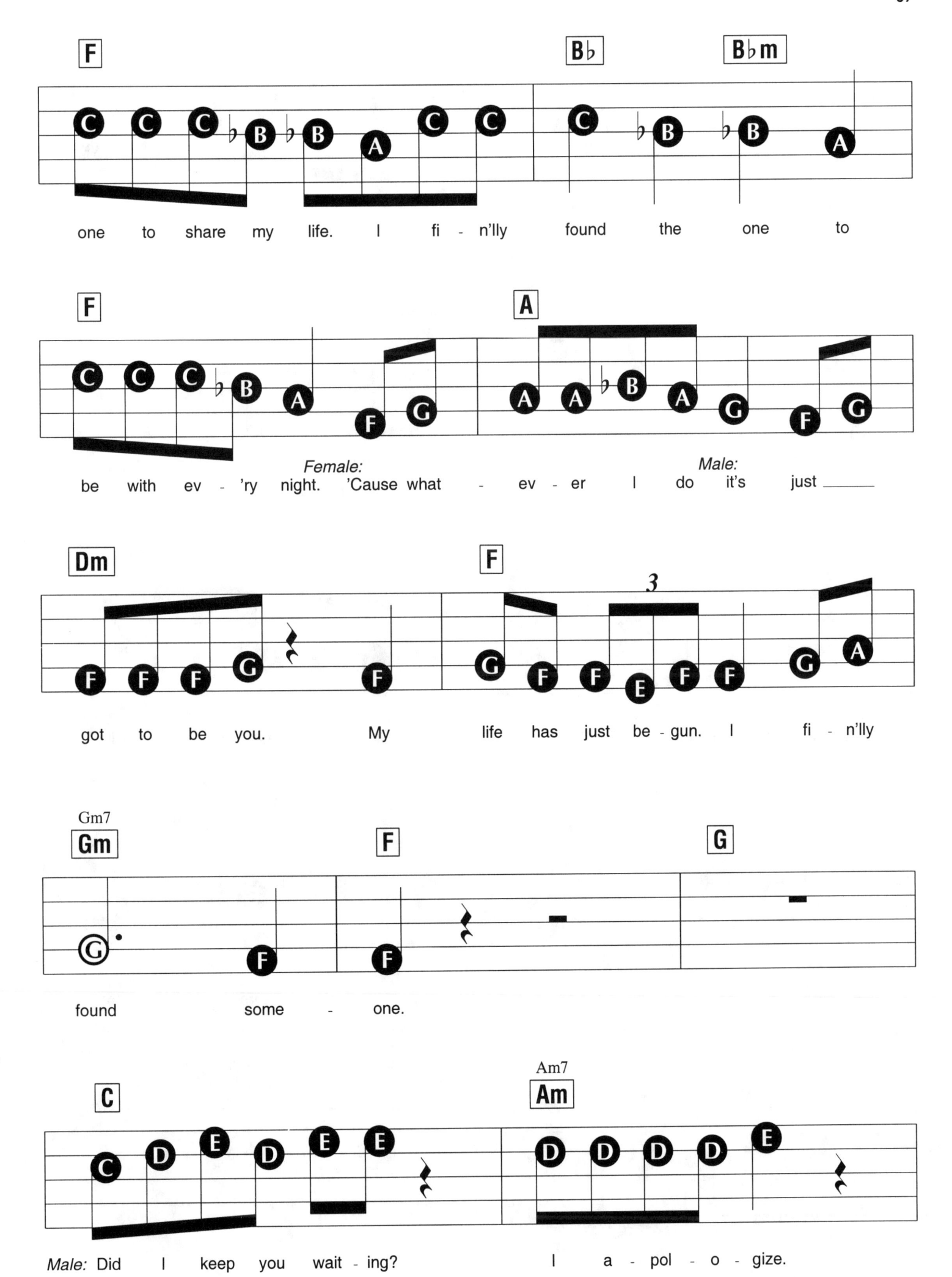

one to share my life. I fi-n'lly found the one to

F						A						
C	C	C	B♭	A	F	G	A	A	B♭	A	G	F G

be with ev-'ry night. *Female:* 'Cause what-ev-er I *Male:* do it's just ___

Dm						F				3		
F	F	F	G		F	G	F	F	E	F	F	G A

got to be you. My life has just be-gun. I fi-n'lly

Gm (Gm7)		F		G	
G.	F	F			

found some-one.

C						Am (Am7)					
C	D	E	D	E	E	D	D	D	D	E	

Male: Did I keep you wait-ing? I a-pol-o-gize.

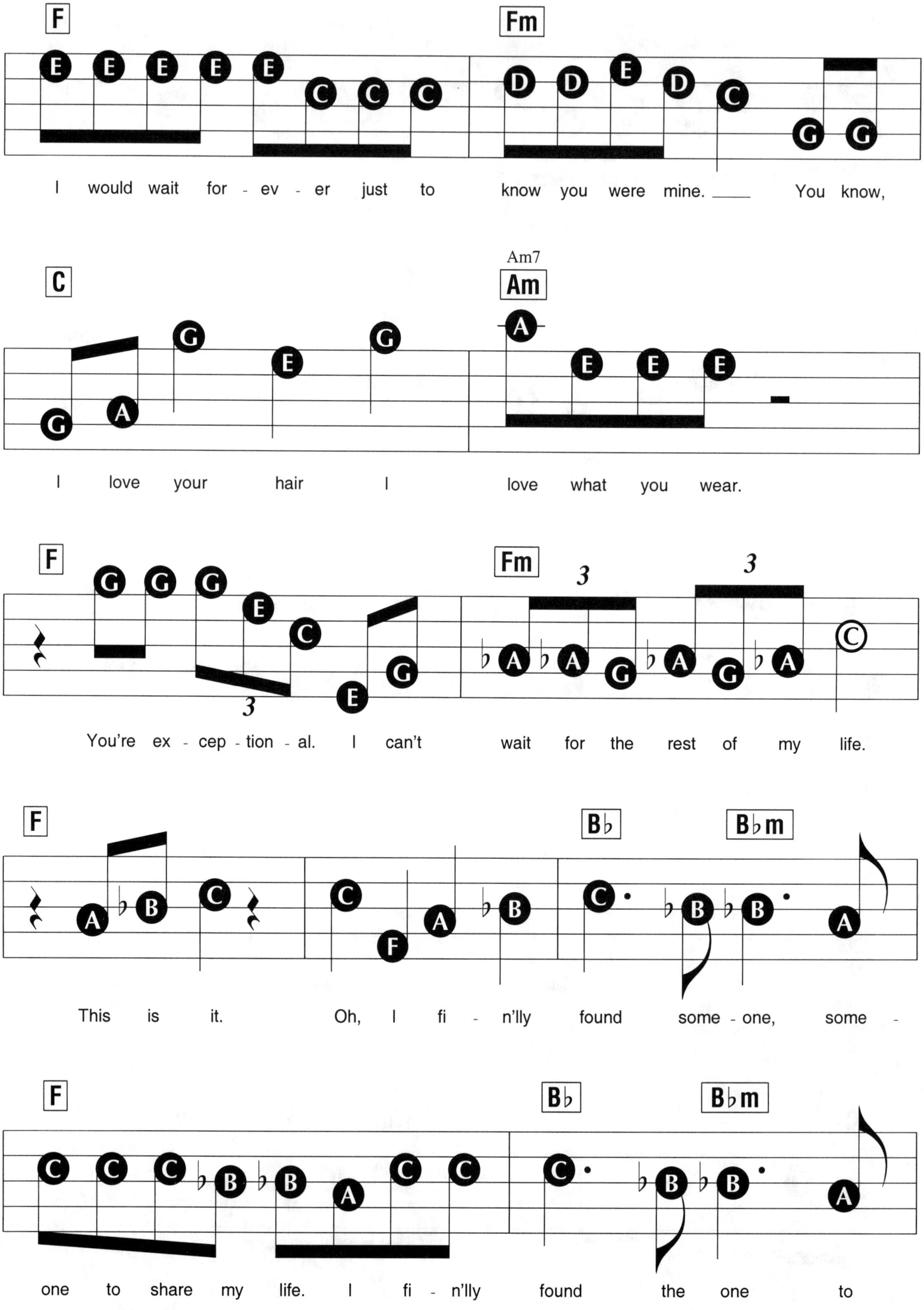
F
Fm
I would wait for - ev - er just to know you were mine. ___ You know,
C
Am7
Am
I love your hair I love what you wear.
F
Fm
3
You're ex - cep - tion - al. I can't wait for the rest of my life.
F
B♭
B♭m
This is it. Oh, I fi - n'lly found some - one, some -
F
B♭
B♭m
one to share my life. I fi - n'lly found the one to

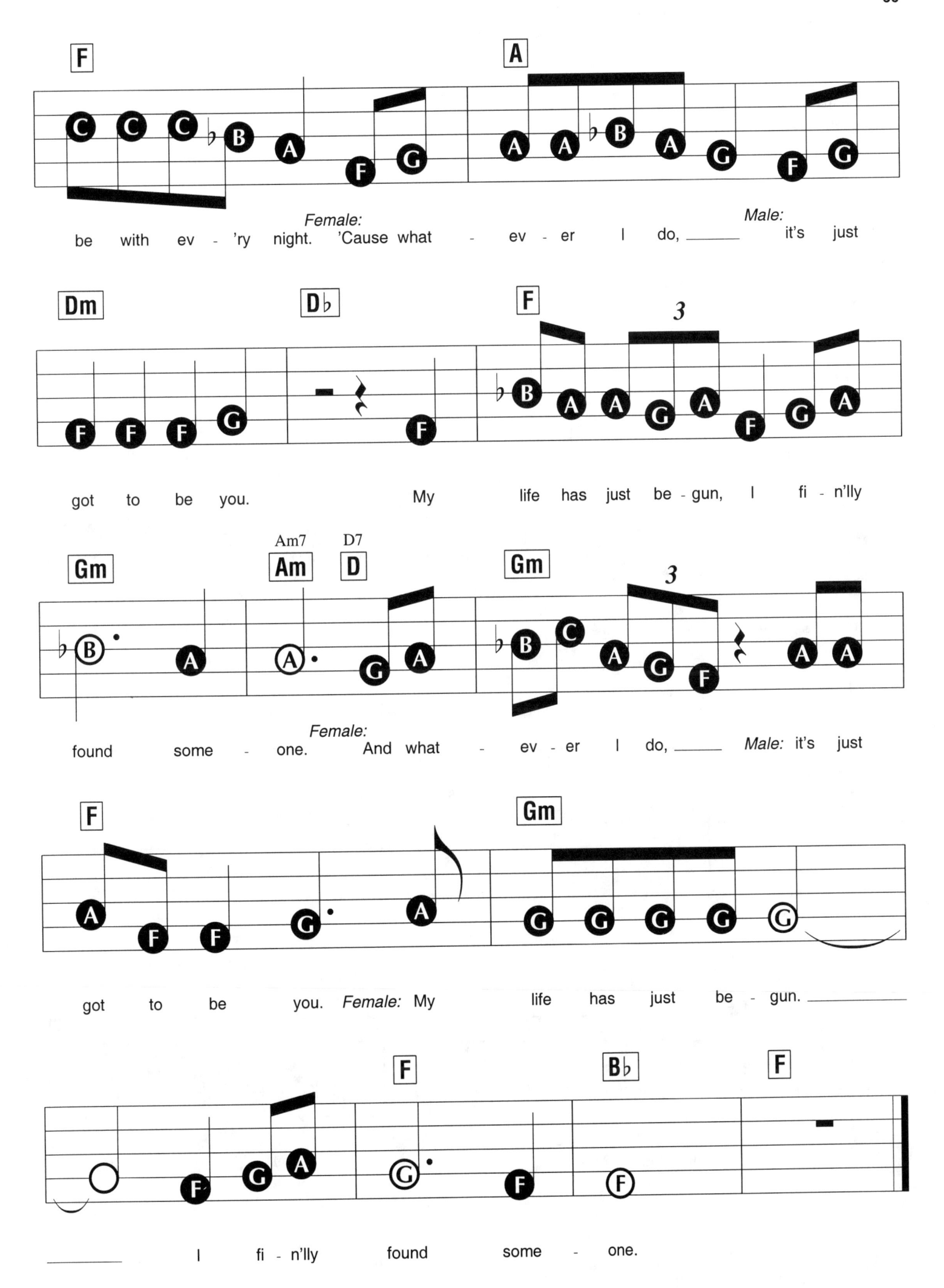

be with ev-'ry night. 'Cause what-ev-er I do, *Female:* *Male:* it's just

got to be you. My life has just be-gun, I fi-n'lly

found some-one. *Female:* And what-ev-er I do, *Male:* it's just

got to be you. *Female:* My life has just be-gun.

I fi-n'lly found some-one.

Here, There and Everywhere

Registration 2
Rhythm: Rock or Jazz Rock

Words and Music by John Lennon
and Paul McCartney

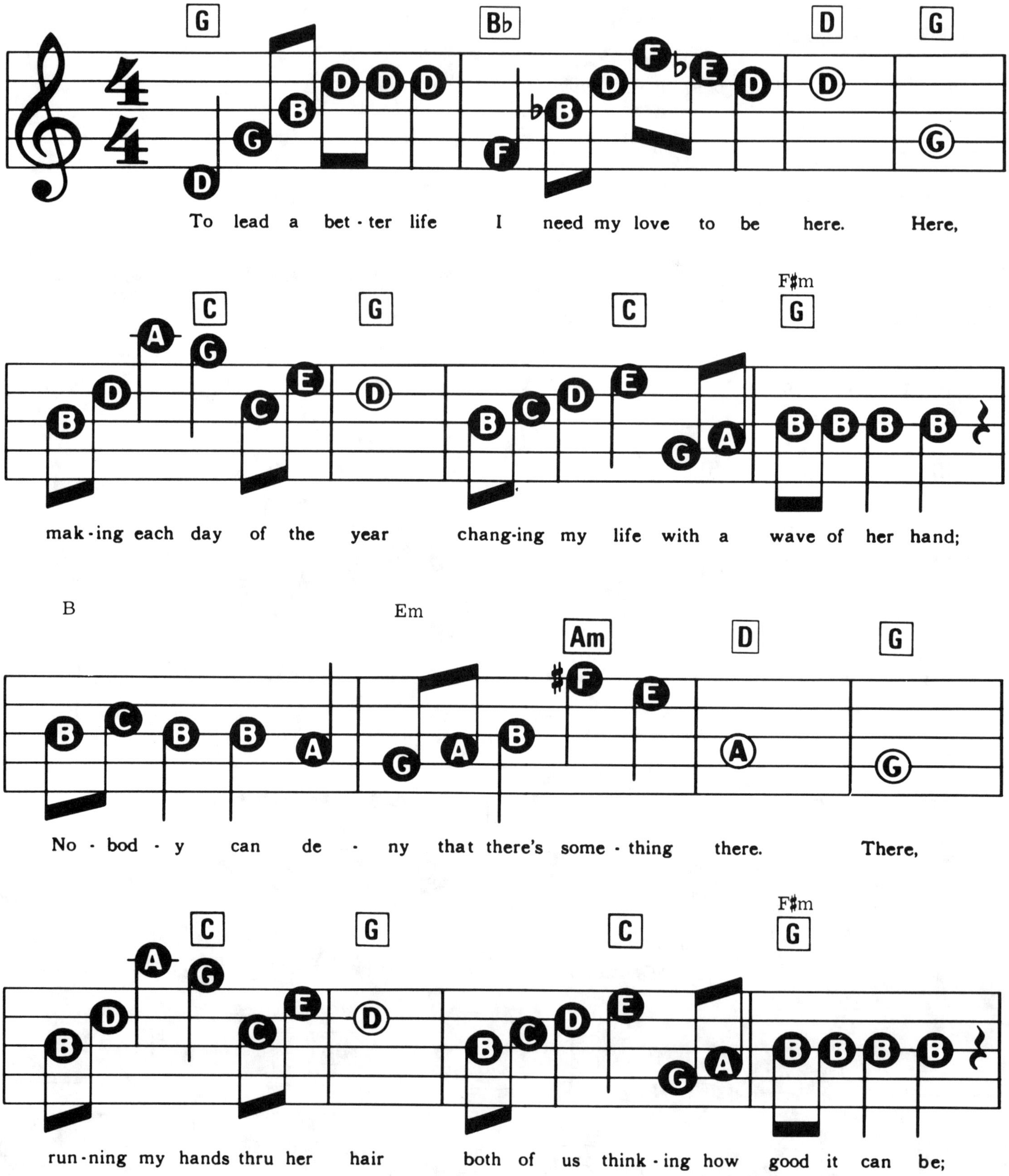

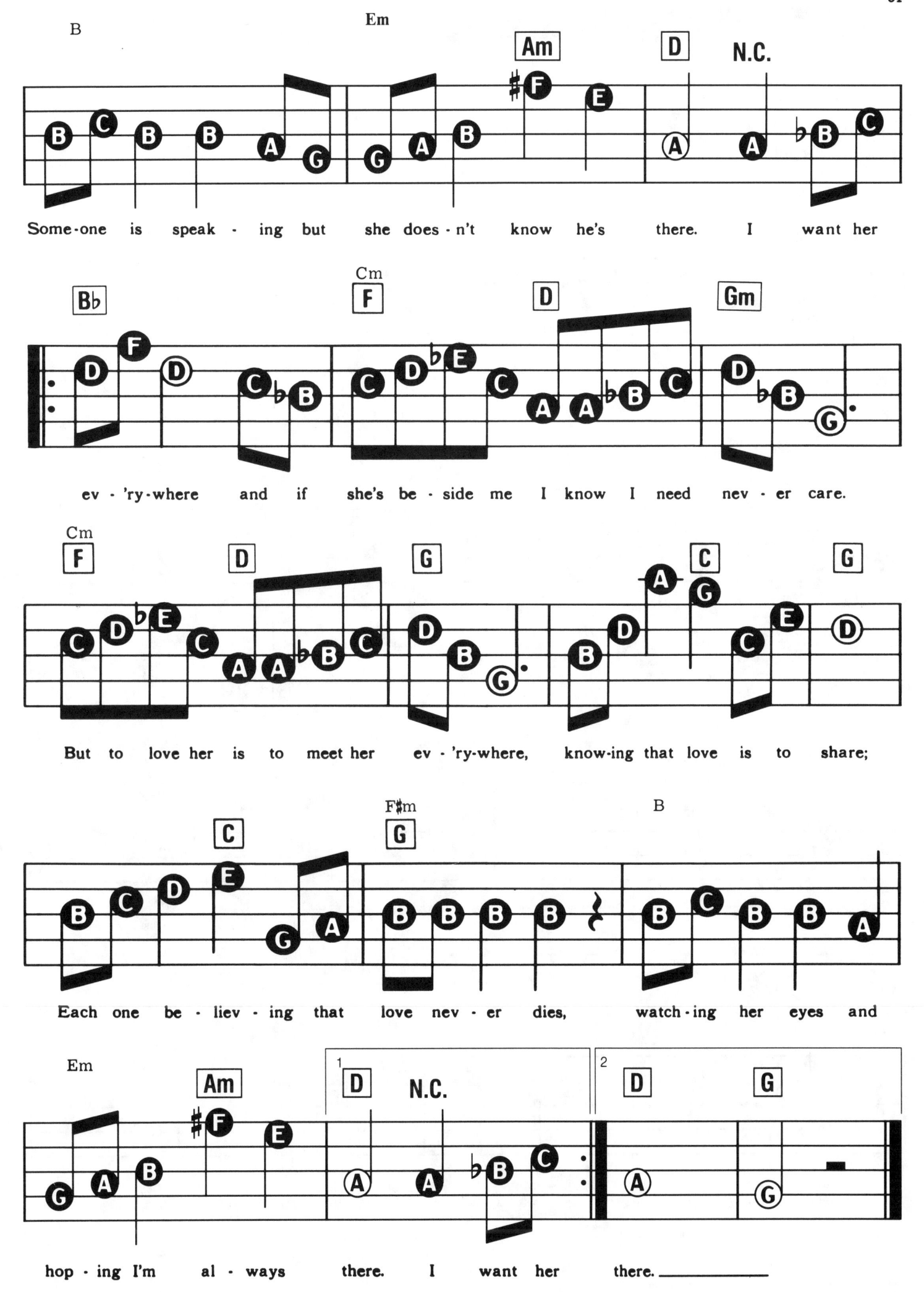

Some-one is speak-ing but she does-n't know he's there. I want her ev-'ry-where and if she's be-side me I know I need nev-er care. But to love her is to meet her ev-'ry-where, know-ing that love is to share; Each one be-liev-ing that love nev-er dies, watch-ing her eyes and hop-ing I'm al-ways there. I want her there.

I Just Called to Say I Love You

Registration 2
Rhythm: Rock

Words and Music by
Stevie Wonder

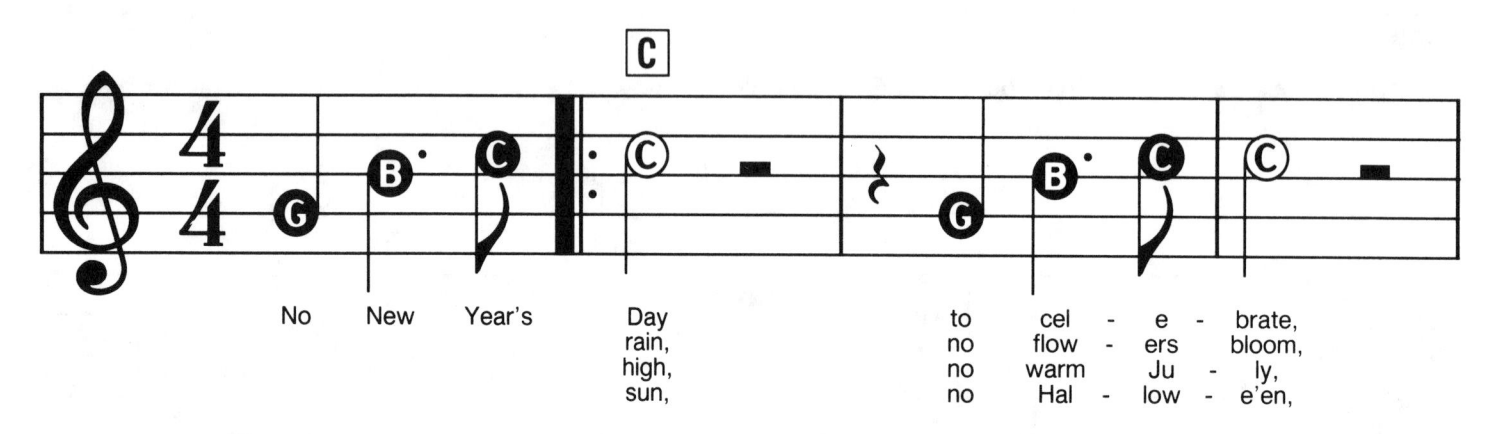

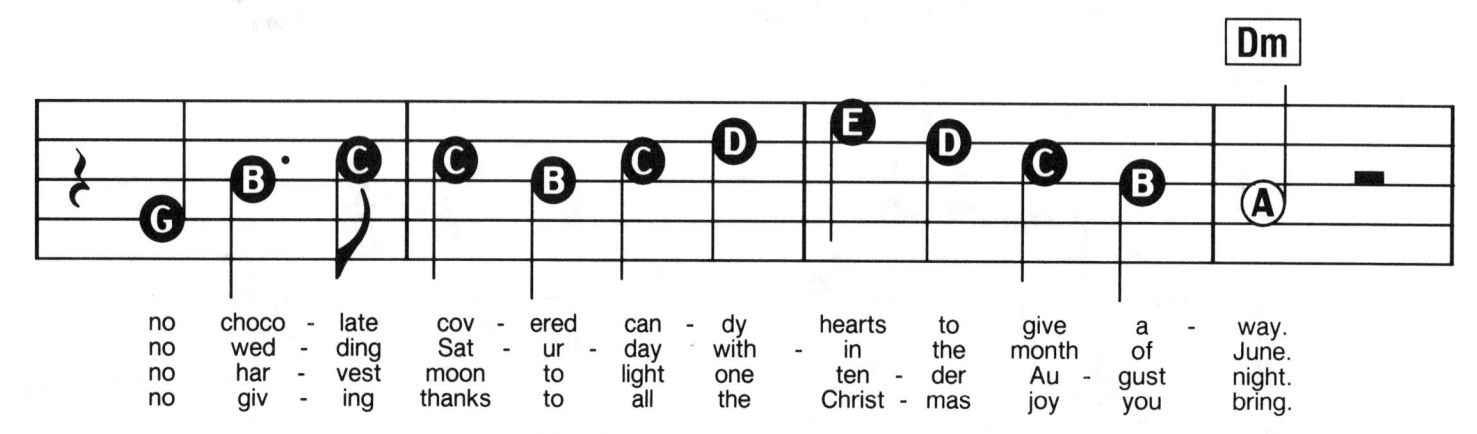

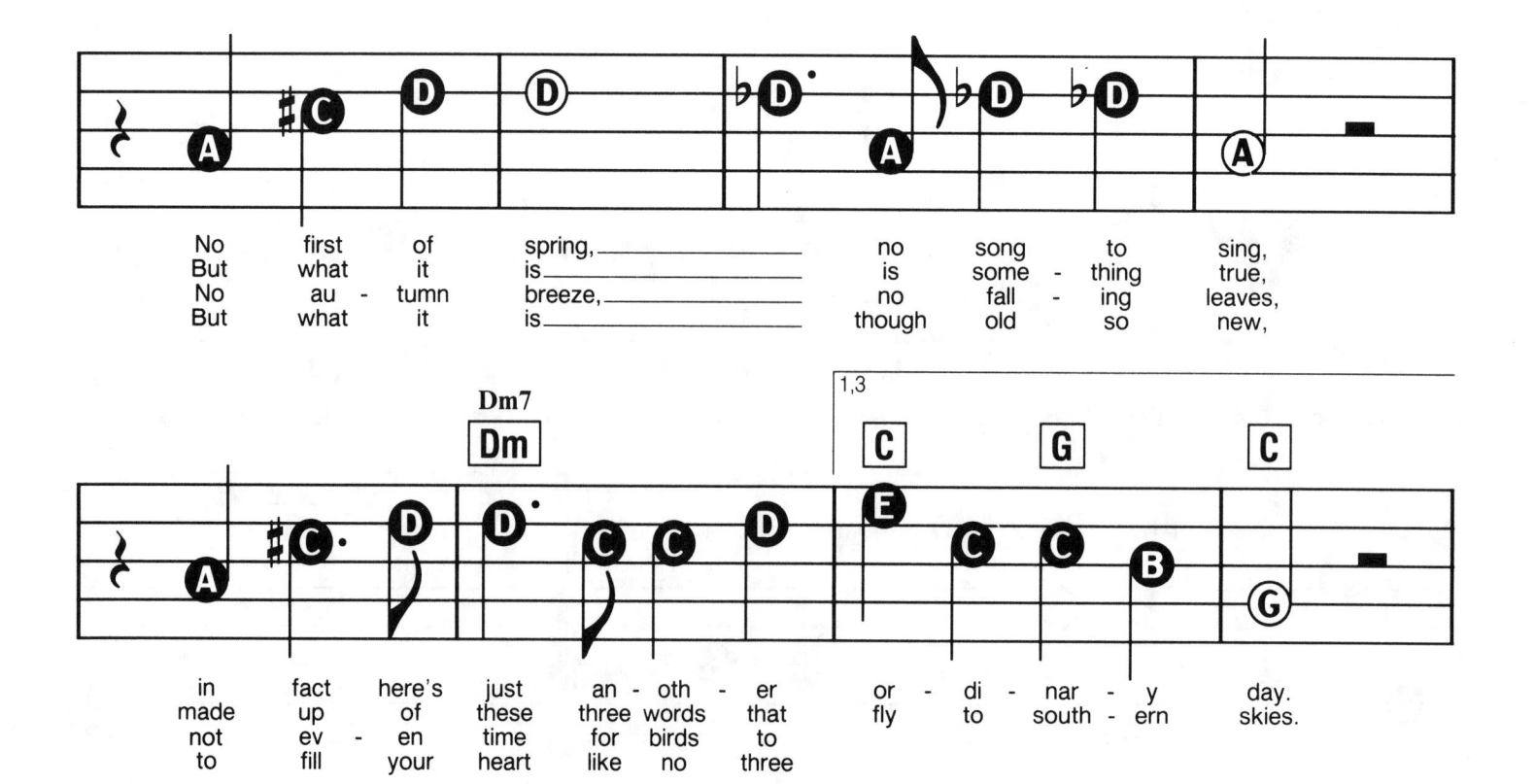

No New Year's Day to cel - e - brate,
rain, no flow - ers bloom,
high, no warm Ju - ly,
sun, no Hal - low - e'en,

no choc - o - late cov - ered can - dy hearts to give a - way.
no wed - ding Sat - ur - day with - in the month of June.
no har - vest moon to light one ten - der Au - gust night.
no giv - ing thanks to all the Christ - mas joy you bring.

No first of spring, no song to sing,
But what it is
No au - tumn breeze, no fall - ing leaves,
But what it is though old so new,

in fact here's just an - oth - er or - di - nar - y day.
made up of these three words for birds that fly to south - ern skies.
not ev - en time
to fill your heart like no three

© 1984 JOBETE MUSIC CO., INC. and Black Bull Music
c/o EMI APRIL MUSIC INC.
All Rights Reserved International Copyright Secured Used by Permission

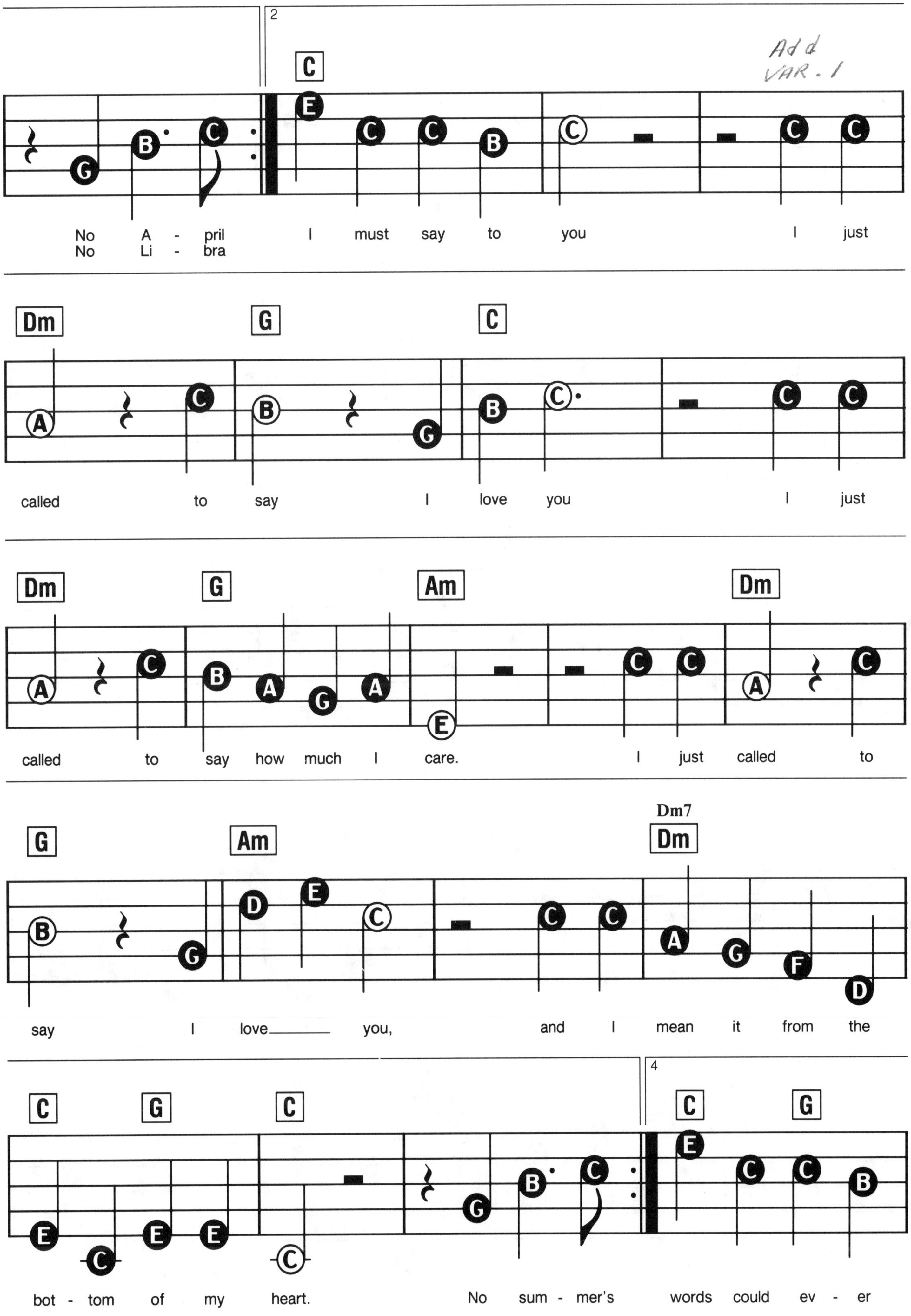
2
Add VAR. 1
C
No A - pril I must say to you I just
No Li - bra
Dm G C
called to say I love you I just
Dm G Am Dm
called to say how much I care. I just called to
G Am Dm7 Dm
say I love you, and I mean it from the
C G C
bot - tom of my heart.
4
C G
No sum - mer's words could ev - er

| C | | Dm | G |

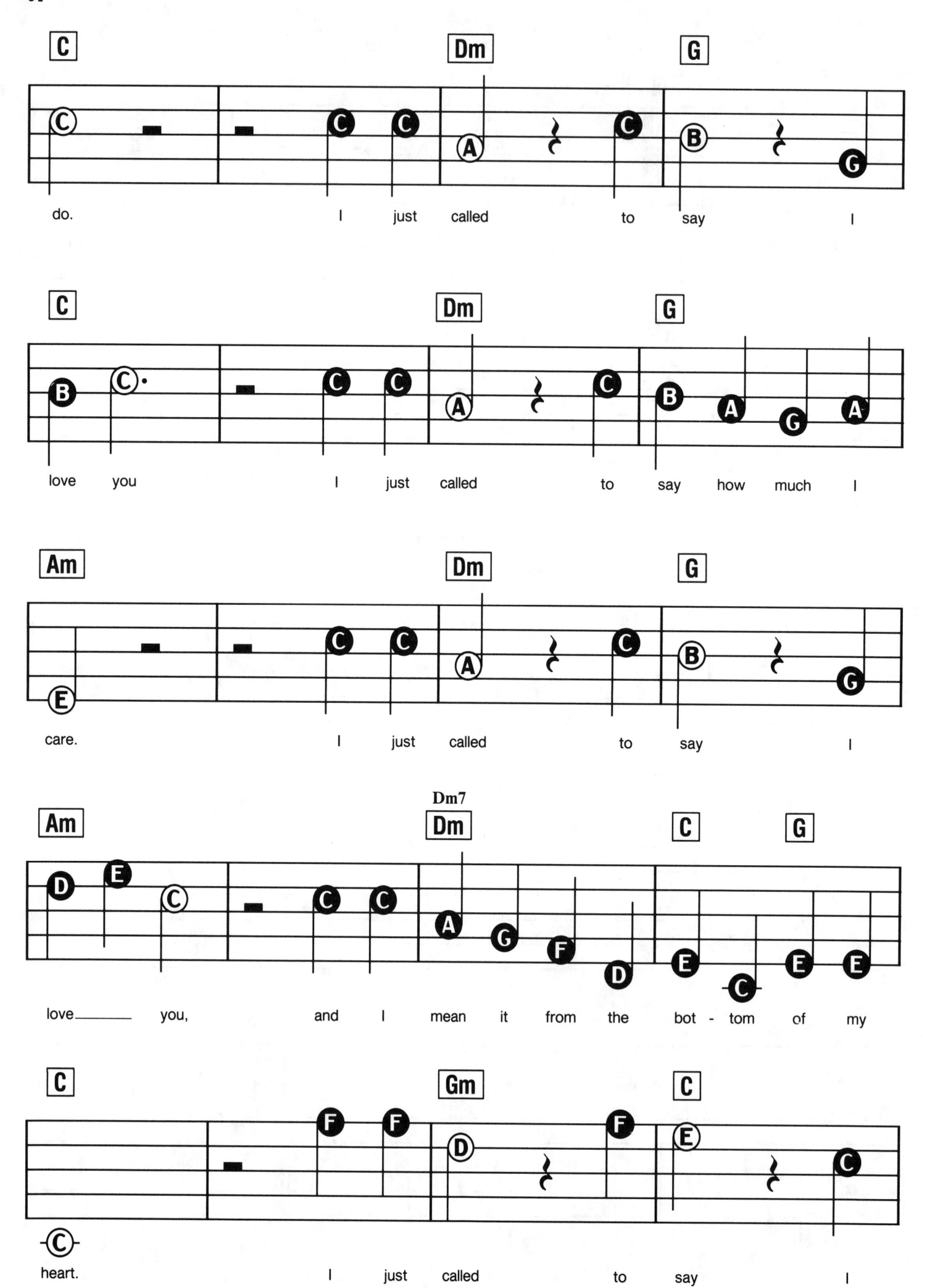

do.   I just called   to say   I

| C | | Dm | G |

love you   I just called   to say how much I

| Am | | Dm | G |

care.   I just called   to say   I

| Am | | Dm (Dm7) | C   G |

love———— you,   and I mean it from the bot-tom of my

| C | | Gm | C |

heart.   I just called   to say   I

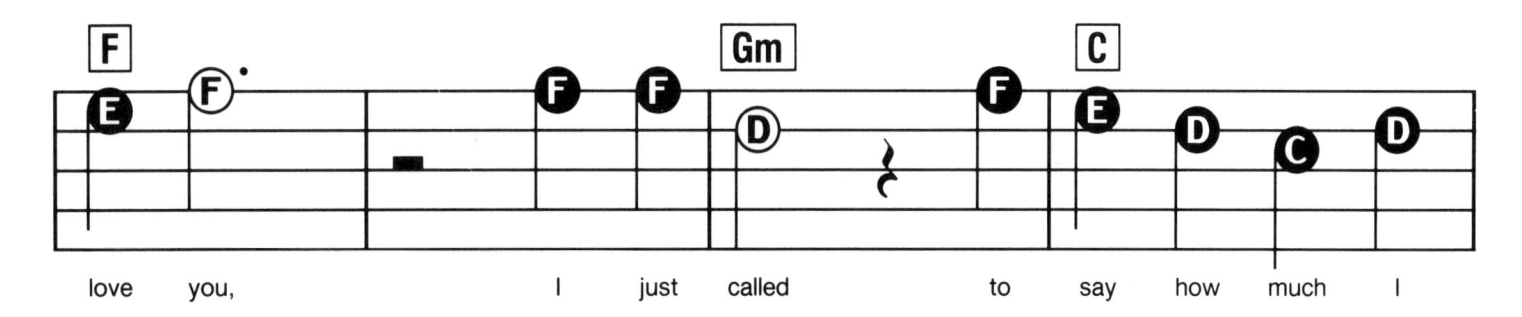

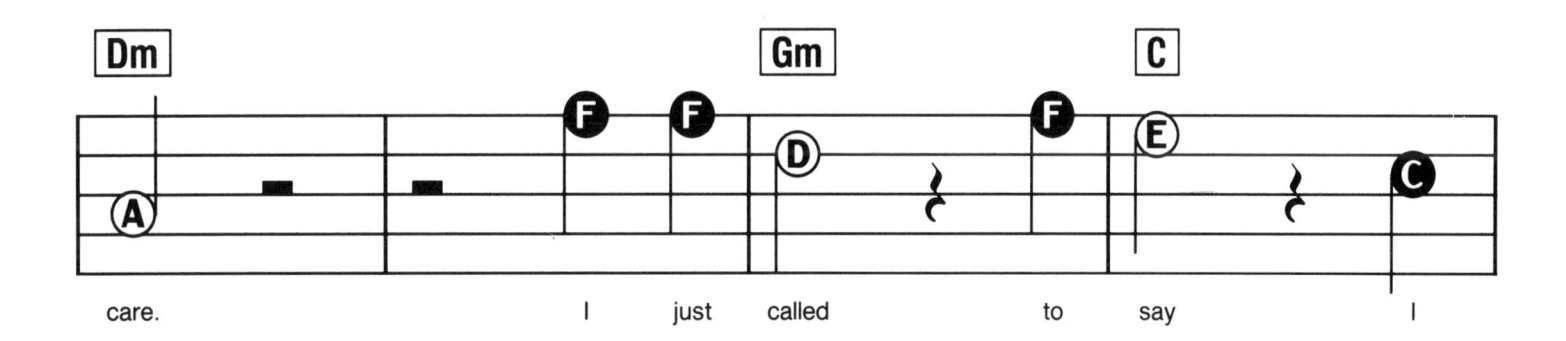

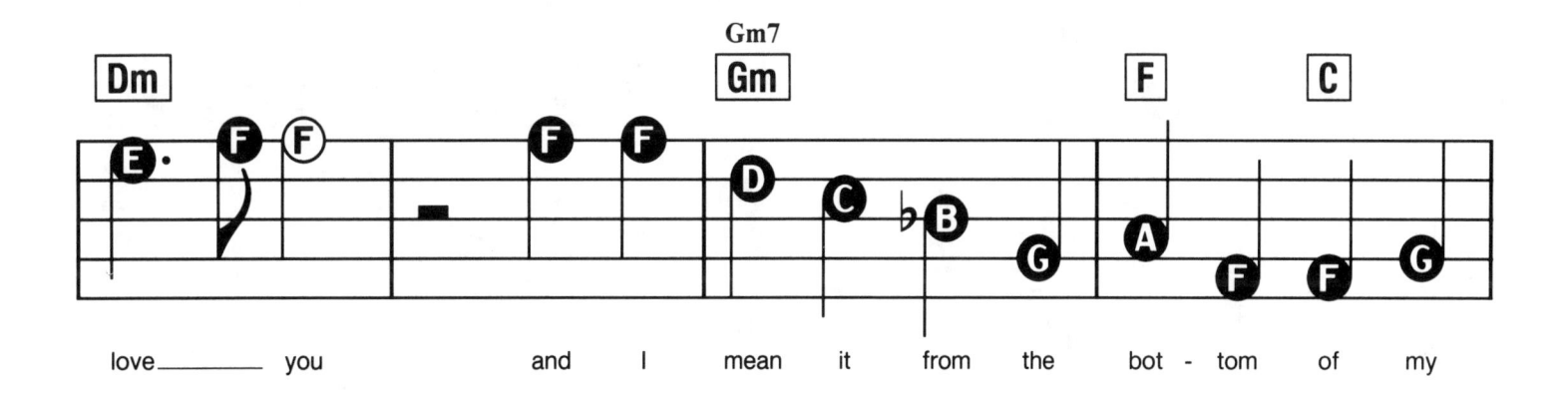

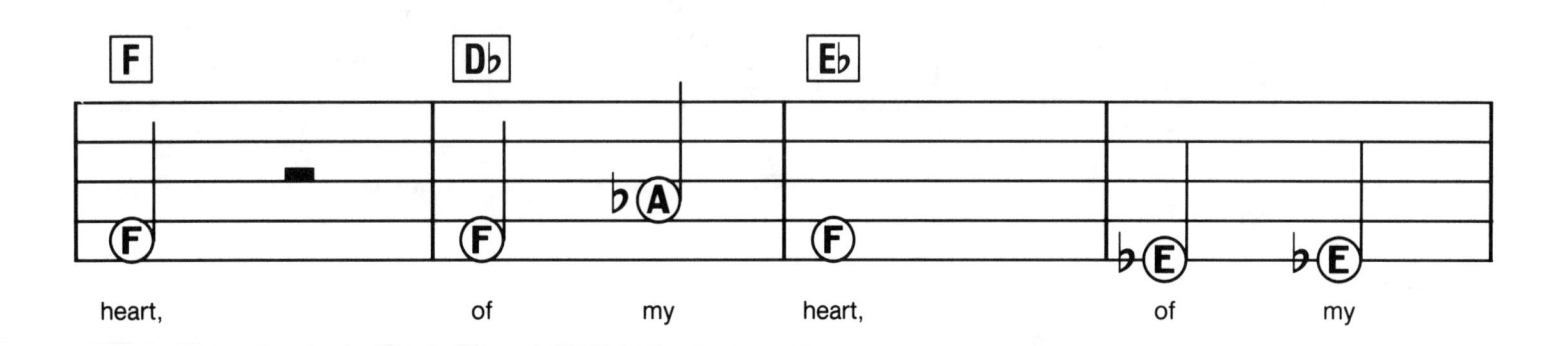

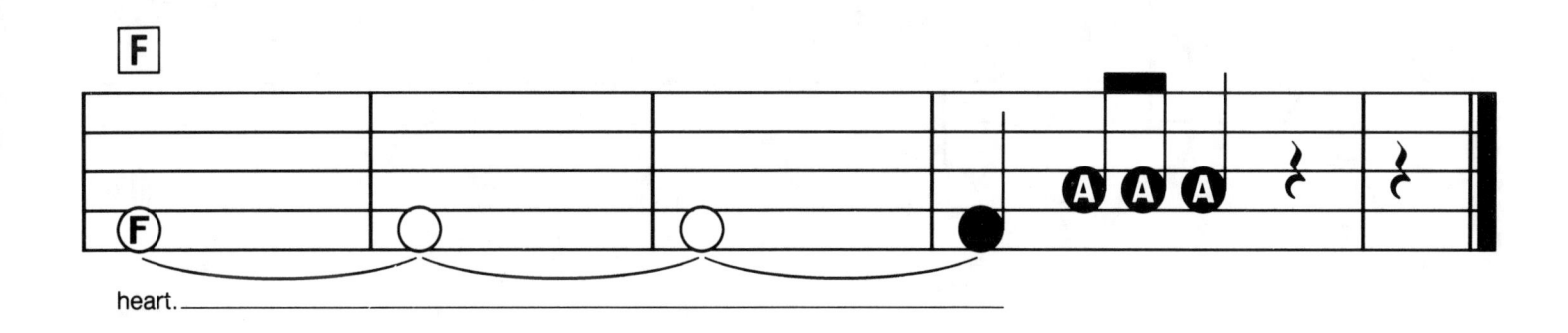

love you, I just called to say how much I care. I just called to say I love you and I mean it from the bot-tom of my heart, of my heart, of my heart.

I Will

Registration 4
Rhythm: Rock or Slow Rock

Words and Music by John Lennon
and Paul McCartney

Who knows how long I've loved you, You
if I ever saw you, I

know I love you still, Will I wait a lone - ly life - time, If you
did - n't catch your name, But it nev - er real - ly mat - tered, I will

want me to I will. For
al - ways feel the same. Love you for - ev - er

and for - ev - er, Love you with all my heart; Love you when - ev - er

Copyright © 1968 Sony/ATV Songs LLC
Copyright Renewed
All Rights Administered by Sony/ATV Music Publishing, 8 Music Square West, Nashville, TN 37203
International Copyright Secured   All Rights Reserved

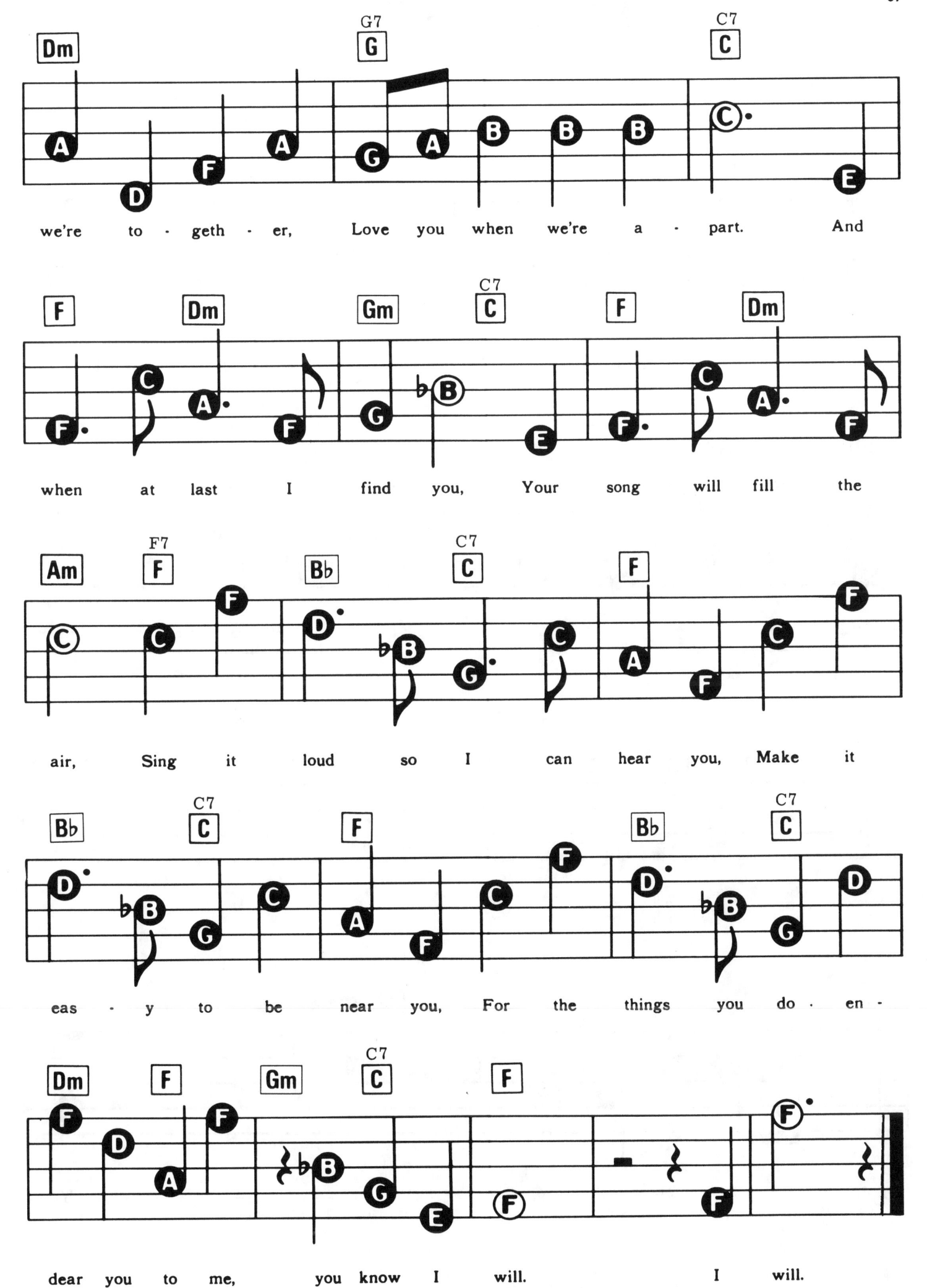

we're to-geth-er, Love you when we're a-part. And when at last I find you, Your song will fill the air, Sing it loud so I can hear you, Make it eas-y to be near you, For the things you do en- dear you to me, you know I will. I will.

I Will Be Here

Registration 8
Rhythm: Ballad

Words and Music by
Steven Curtis Chapman

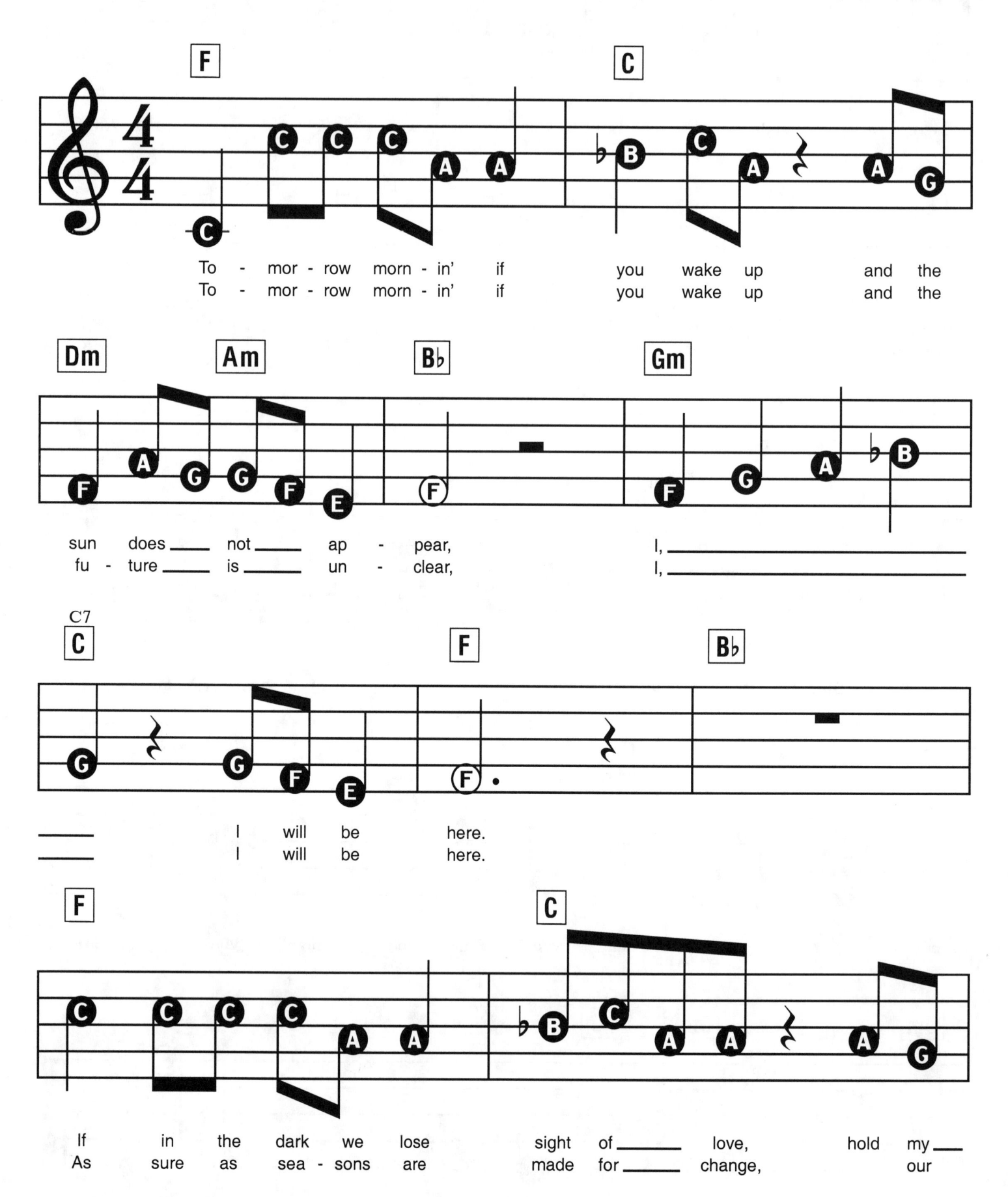

To-mor-row morn-in' if you wake up and the
To-mor-row morn-in' if you wake up and the

sun does ___ not ___ ap - pear, I, ___
fu - ture ___ is ___ un - clear, I, ___

___ I will be here.
___ I will be here.

If in the dark we lose sight of ___ love, hold my ___
As sure as sea - sons are made for ___ change, our

© 1989, 1990 SPARROW SONG, GREG NELSON MUSIC and CAREERS-BMG MUSIC PUBLISHING, INC.
SPARROW SONG and GREG NELSON MUSIC Admin. by EMI CHRISTIAN MUSIC PUBLISHING
All Rights Reserved Used by Permission

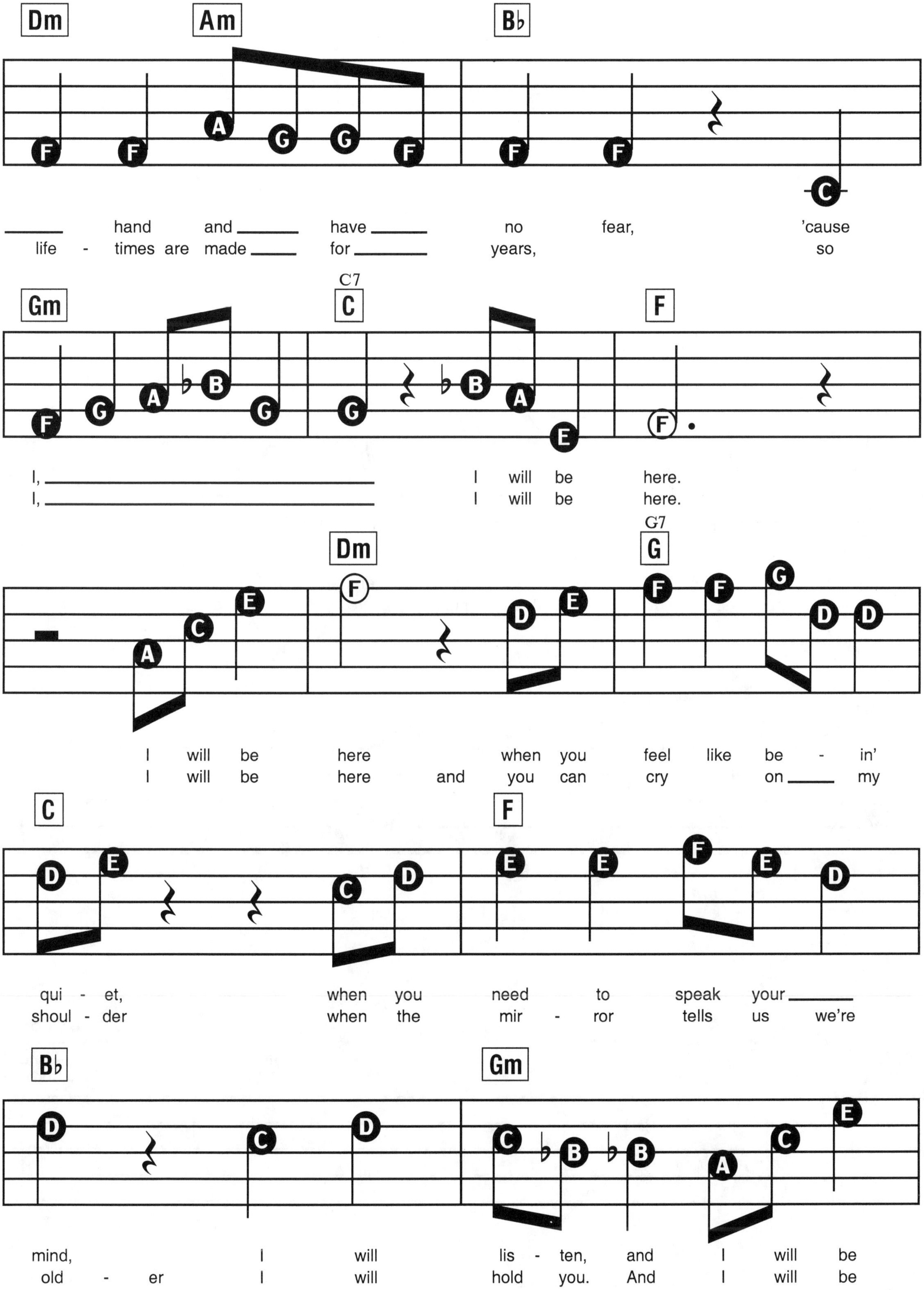
Dm Am Bb
hand and have no fear, 'cause
life - times are made for years, so
Gm C7 C F
I, I will be here.
I, I will be here.
Dm G7 G
I will be here when you feel like be - in'
I will be here and you can cry on my
C F
qui - et, when you need to speak your
shoul - der when the mir - ror tells us we're
Bb Gm
mind, I will lis - ten, and I will be
old - er I will hold you. And I will be

70

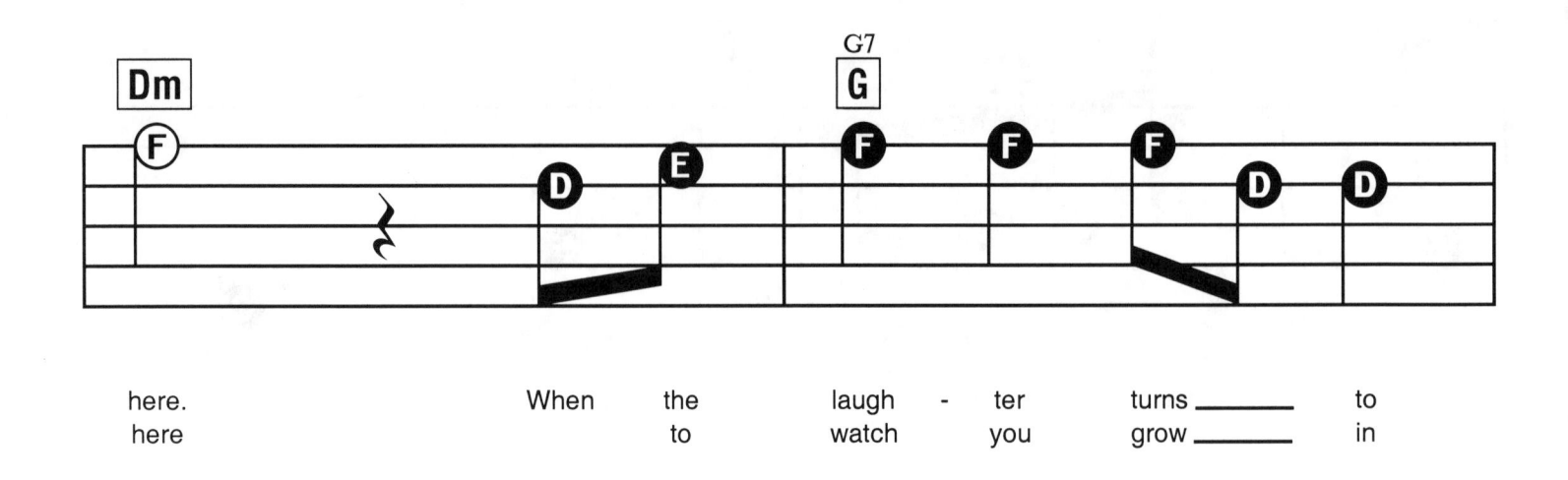

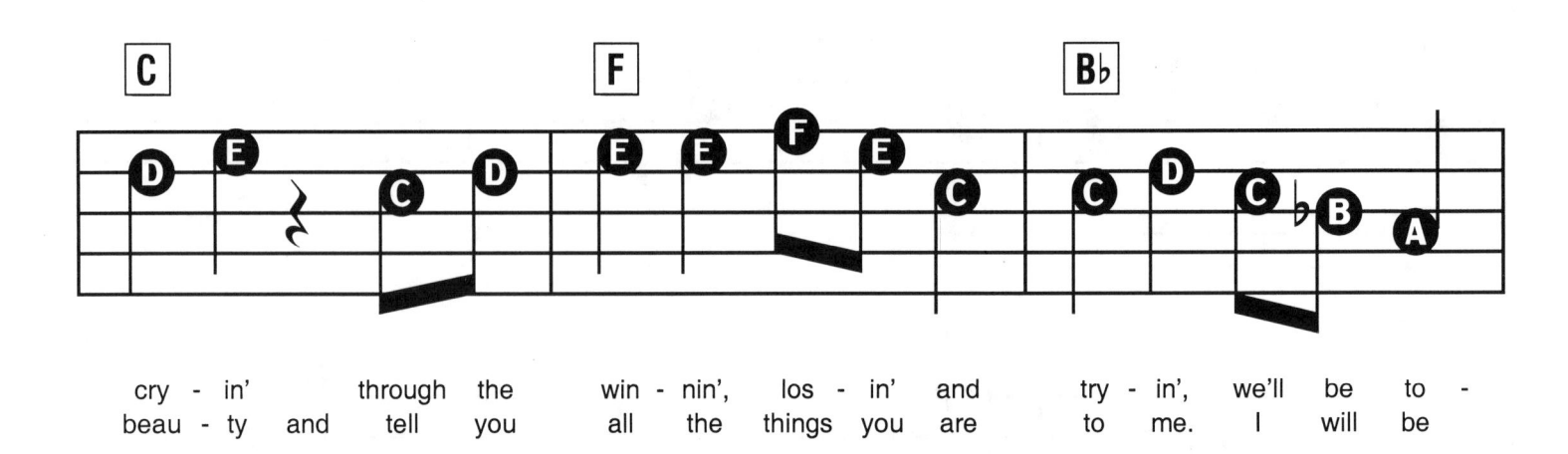

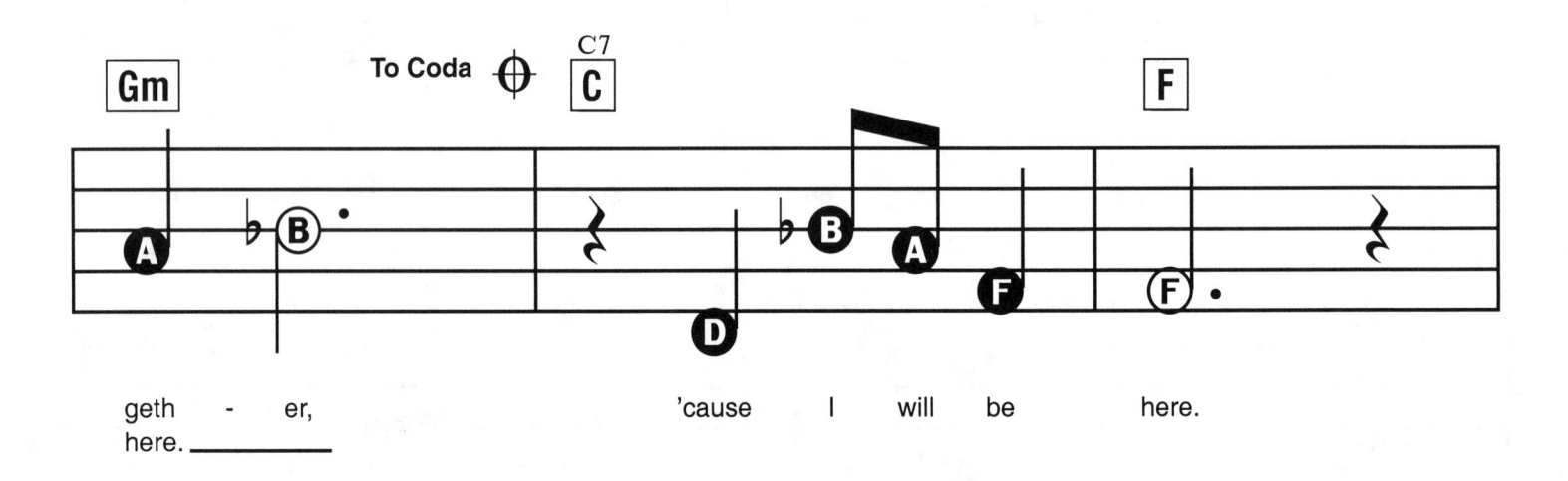

Dm	G7 / G		
here.	When the laugh-ter turns to		
here	to watch you grow in		

C	F	Bb	
cry-in' through the win-nin', los-in' and	try-in', we'll be to-		
beau-ty and tell you all the things you are	to me. I will be		

Gm	To Coda ⊕ C7 / C		F
geth - er,	'cause I will be here.		
here.			

D.C. al Coda
(Return to beginning
Play to ⊕ and
Skip to Coda)

Bb	F	Bb

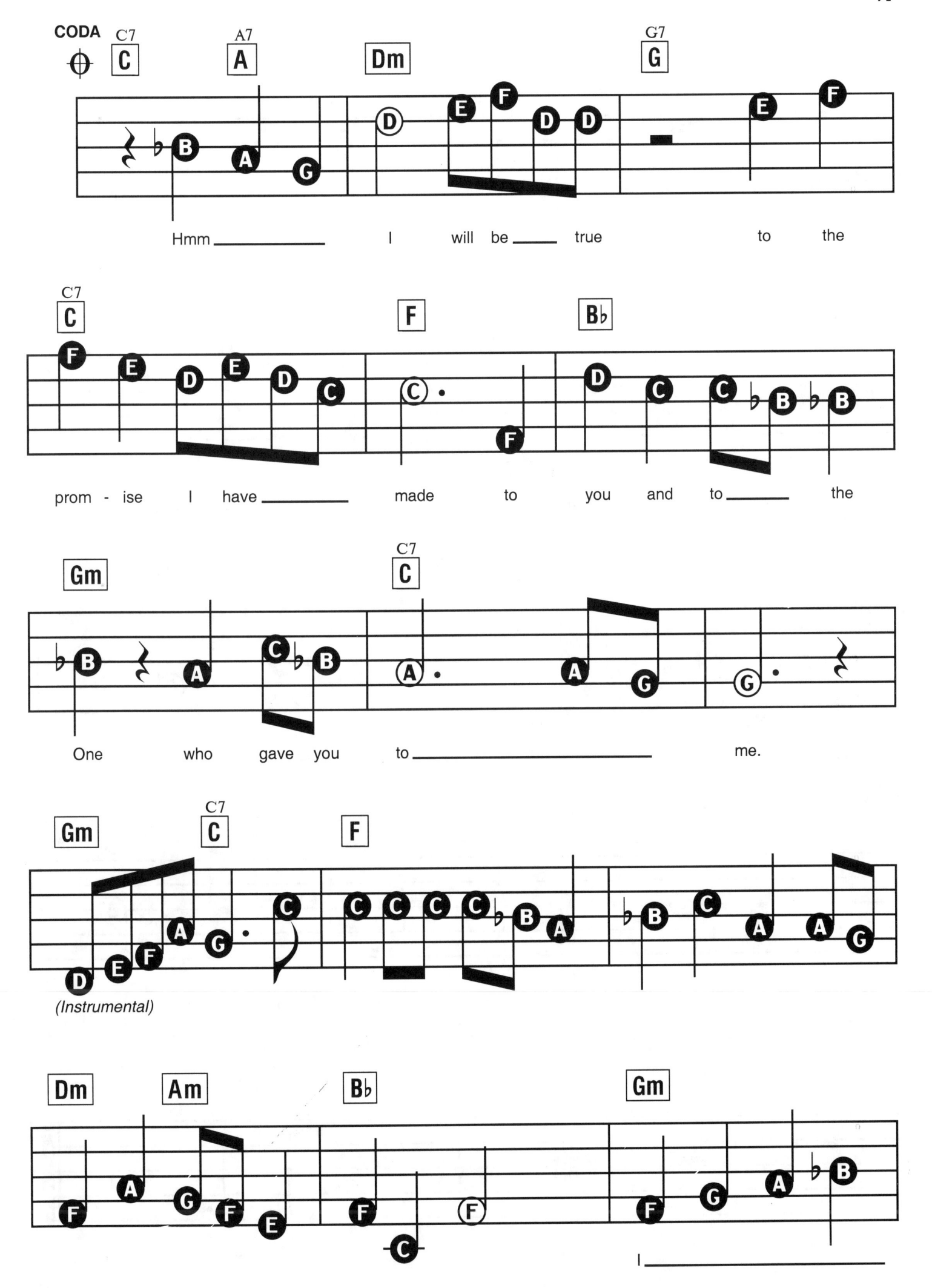

Hmm___ I will be ___ true to the prom-ise I have ___ made to you and to ___ the One who gave you to ___ me.

(Instrumental)

I ___

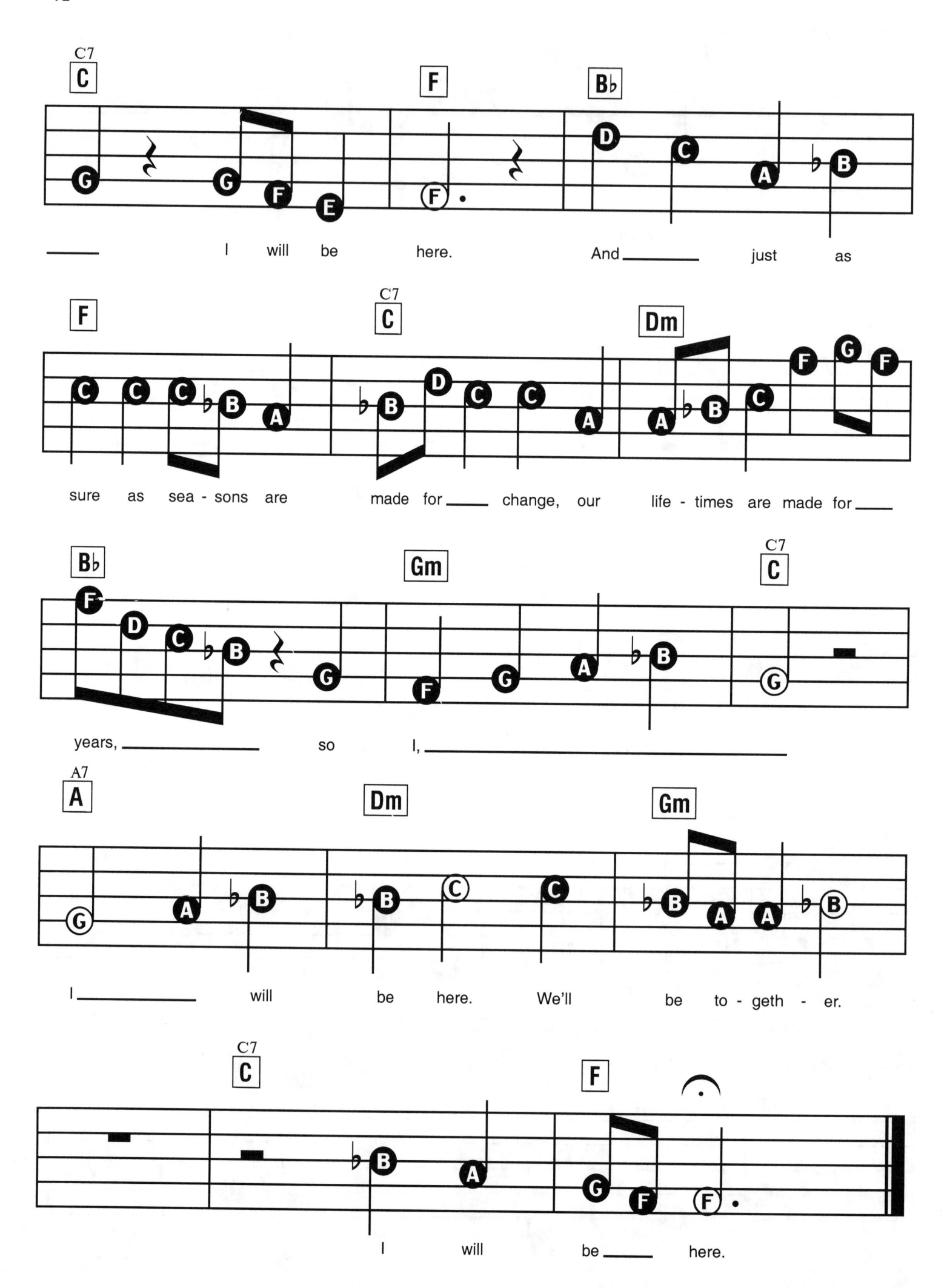

I will be here. And just as sure as seasons are made for change, our lifetimes are made for years, so I, I will be here. We'll be together. I will be here.

I'll Be

Registration 4
Rhythm: Waltz

Words and Music by
Edwin McCain

N.C. 𝄋 **C**   **F**

G E D C C A A F E D

The strands in your eyes ___ that col - or them
rain falls ___ an - gry on the

C   **G**

E E E E D C A C D D C

won - der - ful stop me ___ and steal my breath. ___
tin roof as we lie ___ a - wake in my bed. ___

F   **C**   **F**

G E D C C C F E D

And em - 'ralds from moun - tains thrust towards the
And you're my sur - viv - al, you're my liv - ing

C   **G**

E D E D C A C C D D C

sky, ___ nev - er re - veal - ing their depth. ___
proof ___ my love is a - live and not dead. ___

© 1997 EMI APRIL MUSIC INC. and HARRINGTON PUBLISHING
All Rights Controlled and Administered by EMI APRIL MUSIC INC.
All Rights Reserved   International Copyright Secured   Used by Permission

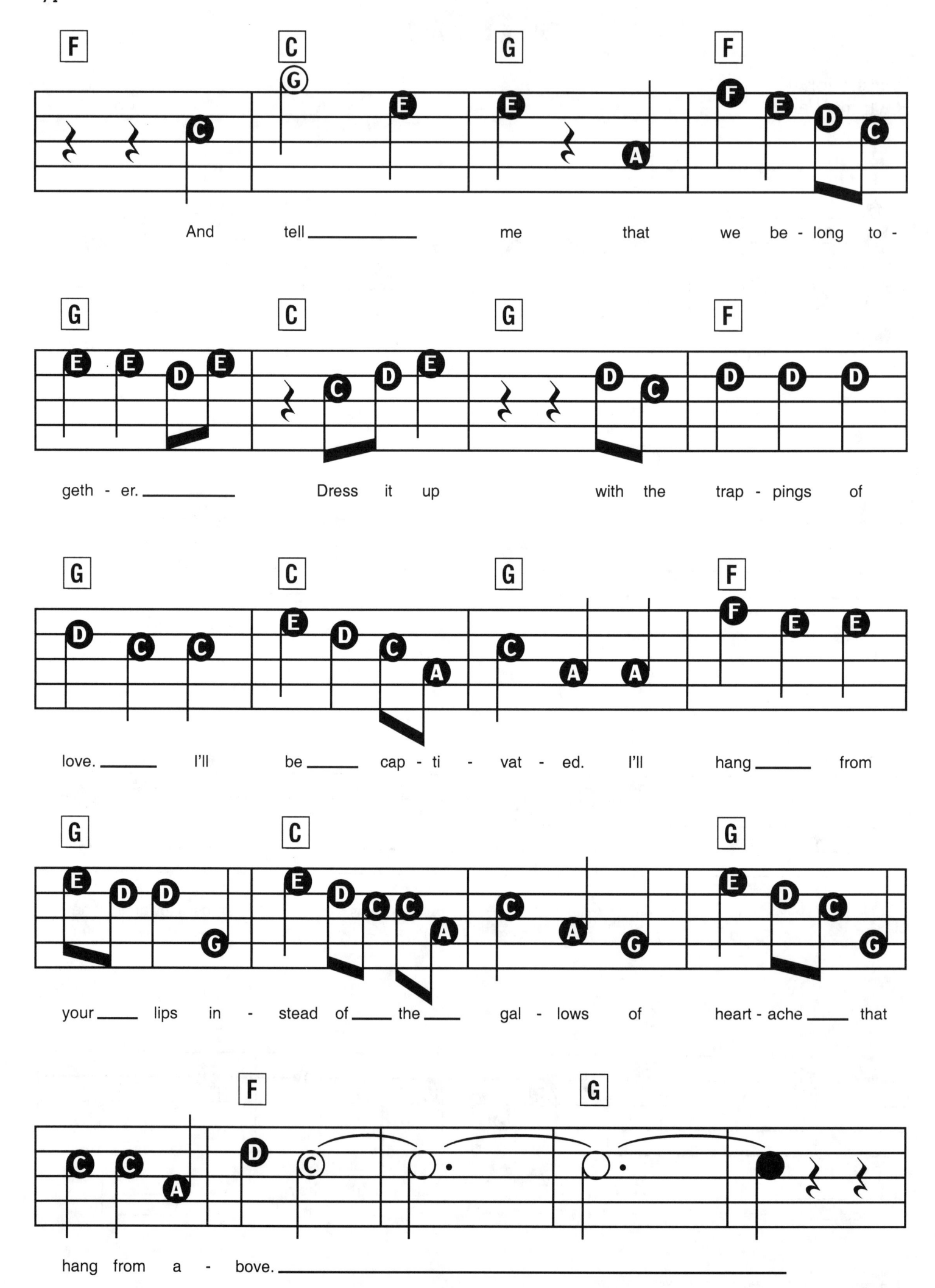

And tell _____ me that we be-long to-geth-er. _____ Dress it up with the trap-pings of love. _____ I'll be _____ cap-ti-vat-ed. I'll hang _____ from your _____ lips in-stead of _____ the _____ gal-lows of heart-ache _____ that hang from a-bove. _____

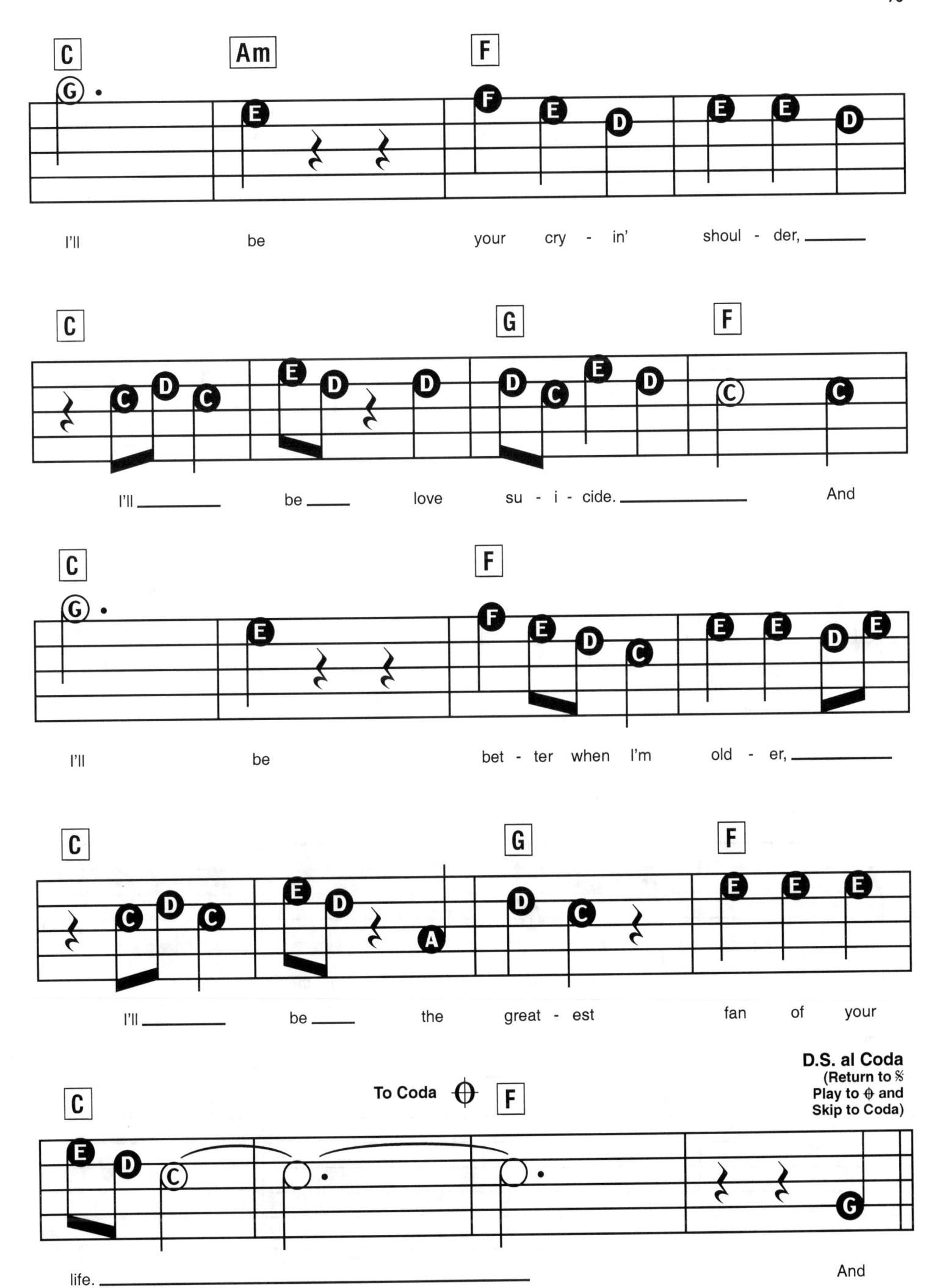

I'll be your cry-in' shoul-der, I'll be love su-i-cide. And I'll be bet-ter when I'm old-er, I'll be the great-est fan of your life. And

76

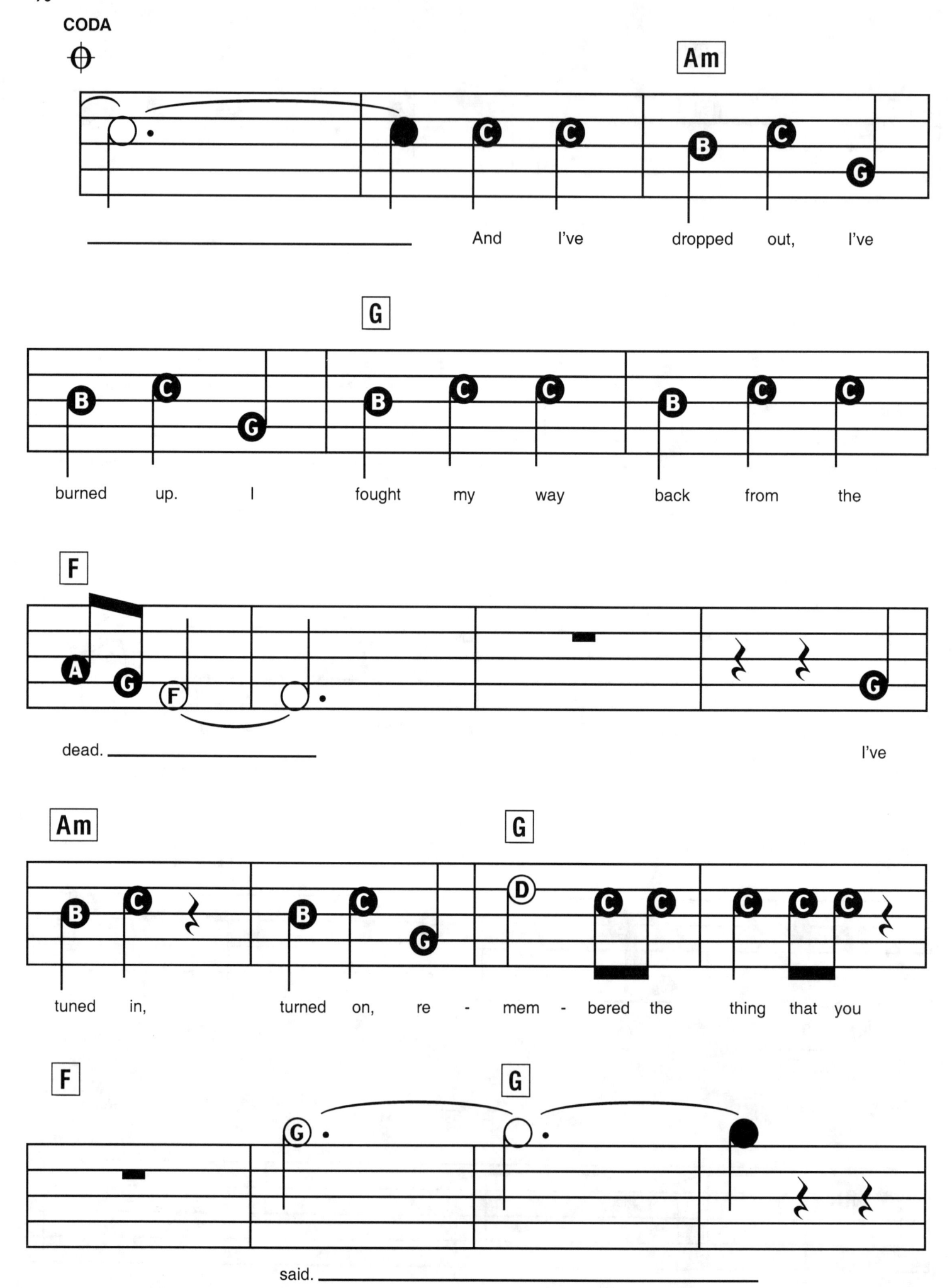

CODA

And I've dropped out, I've burned up. I fought my way back from the dead. I've tuned in, turned on, re-mem-bered the thing that you said.

I'll be your cryin' shoulder,

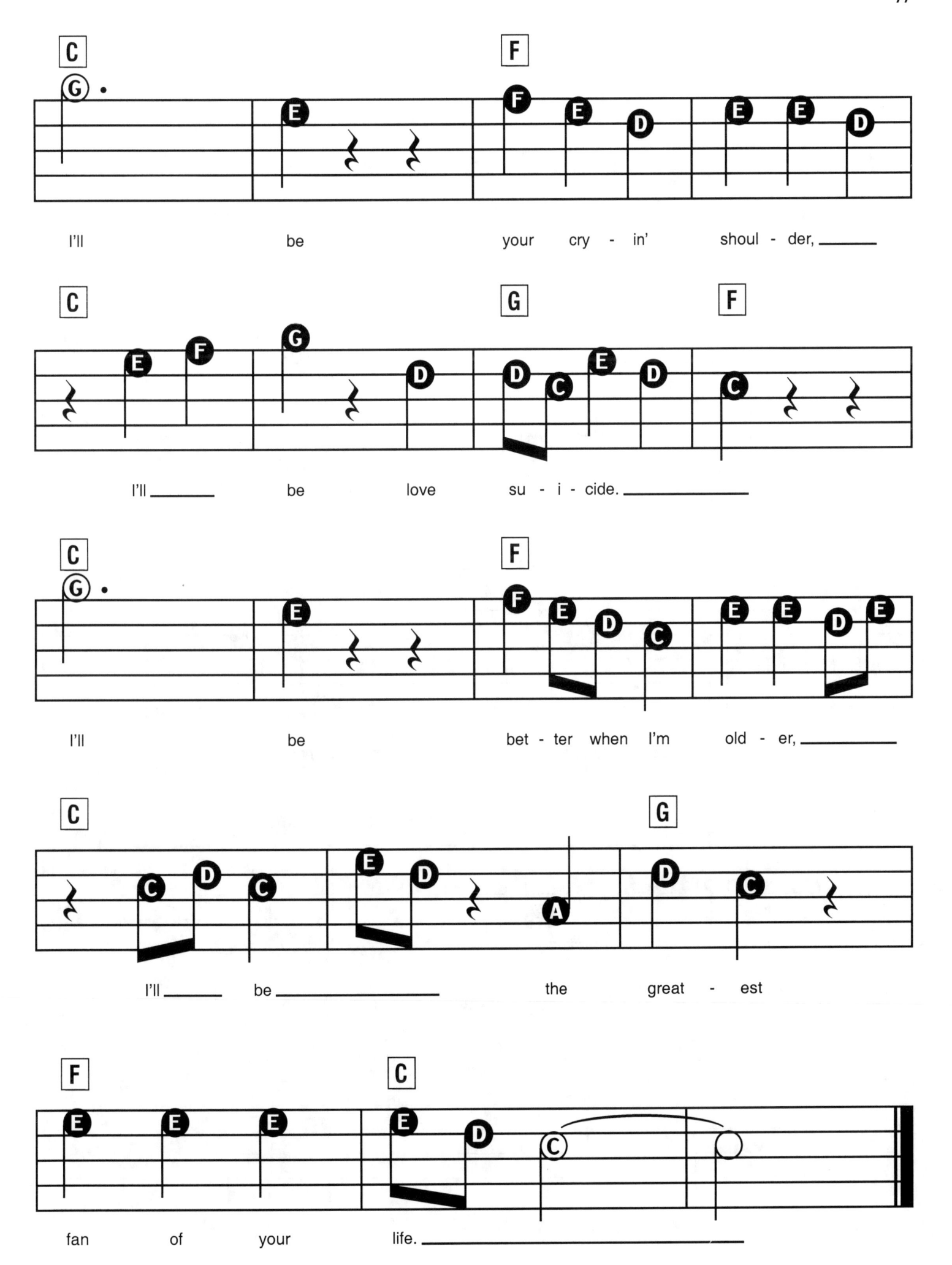

I'll be love suicide.

I'll be better when I'm older,

I'll be the greatest fan of your life.

If

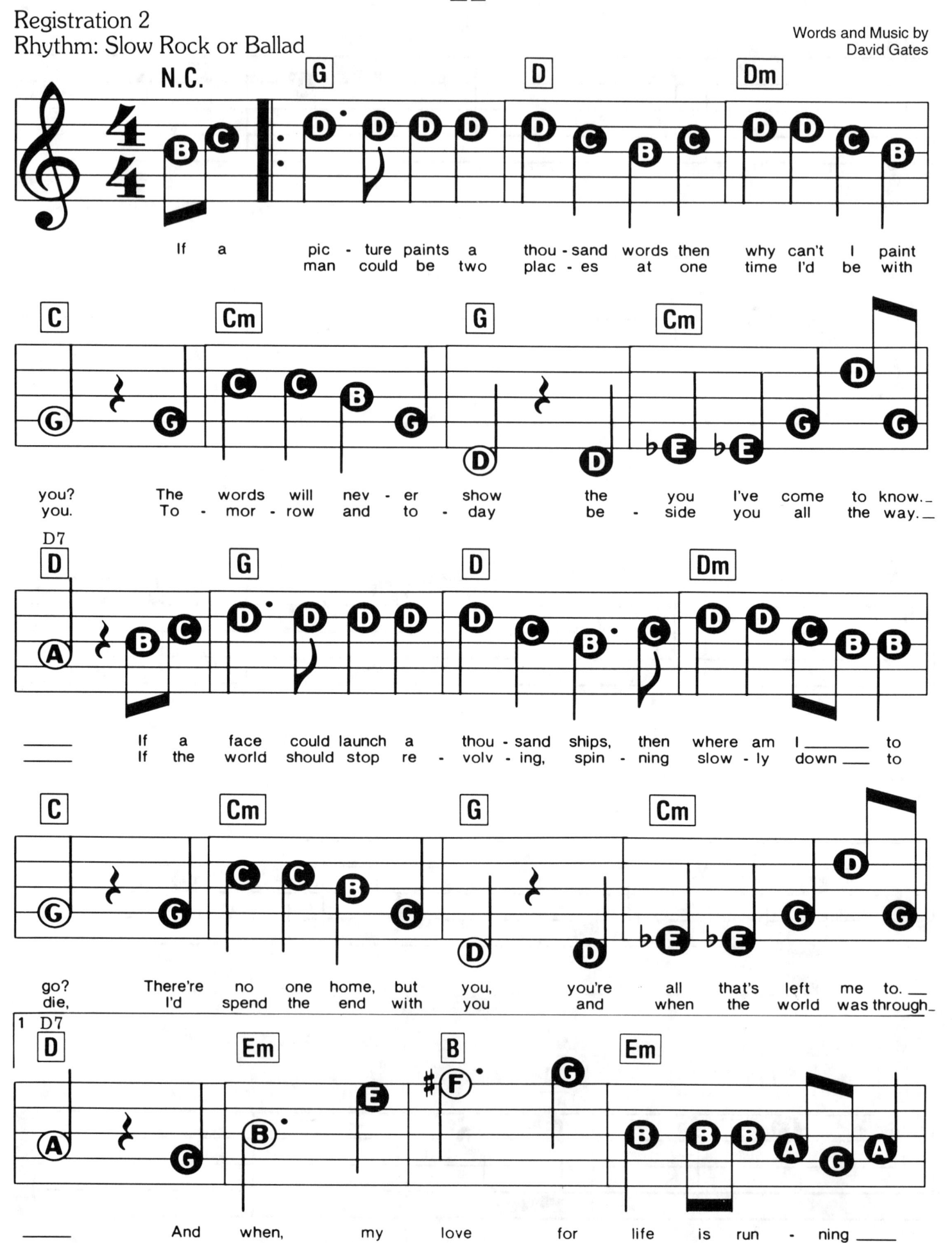

Registration 2
Rhythm: Slow Rock or Ballad

Words and Music by
David Gates

If a picture paints a thousand words then why can't I paint
man could be two places at one time I'd be with

you? The words will never show the you I've come to know.
you. Tomorrow and today beside you all the way.

If a face could launch a thousand ships, then where am I to
If the world should stop revolving, spinning slowly down to

go? There're no one home, but you, you're all that's left me to.
die, I'd spend the end with you and when the world was through

And when, my love for life is running

© 1971 (Renewed 1999) COLGEMS-EMI MUSIC INC.
All Rights Reserved International Copyright Secured Used by Permission

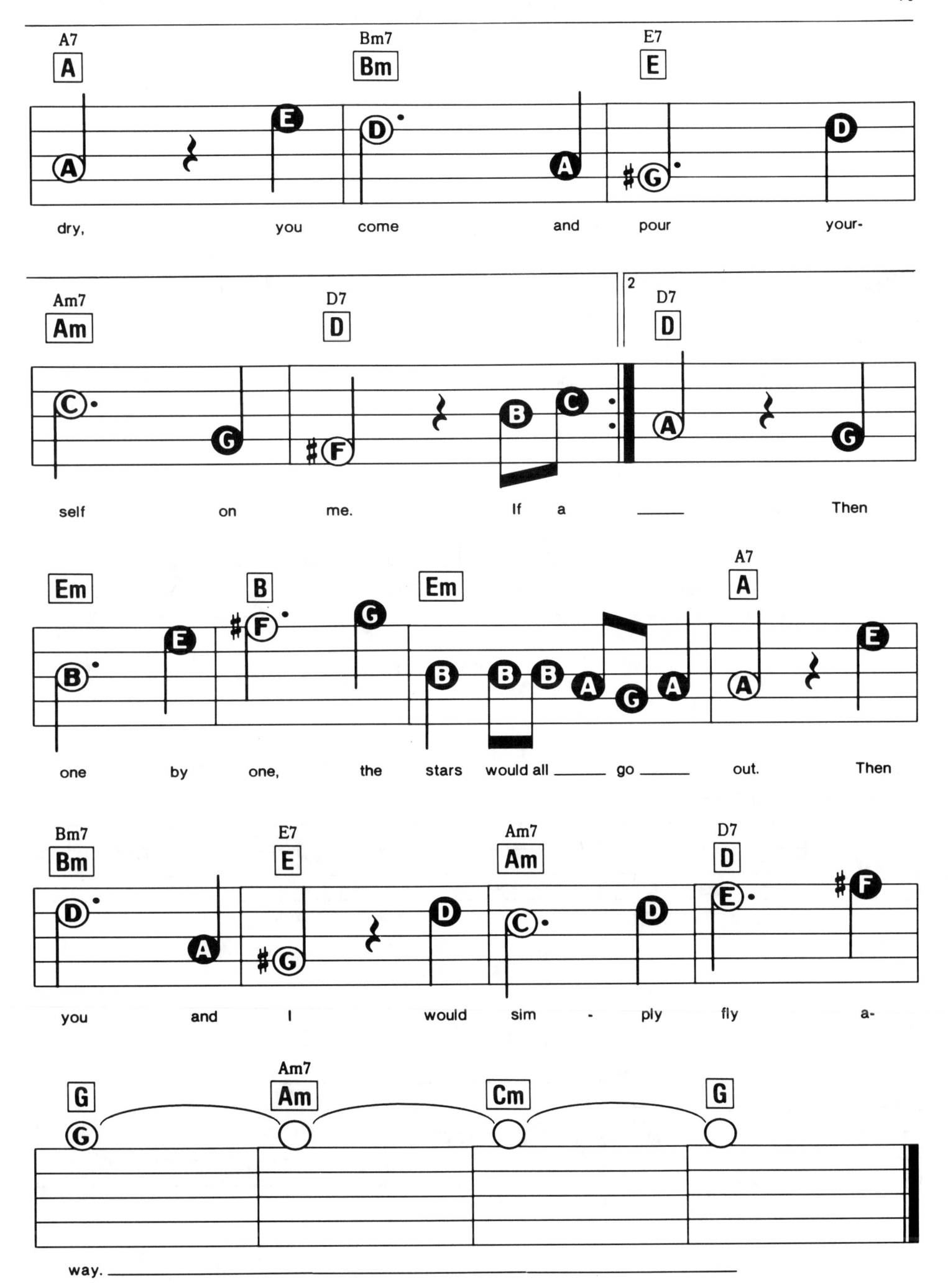

dry, you come and pour your-self on me. If a ____ Then one by one, the stars would all ____ go ____ out. Then you and I would sim-ply fly a-way. ____

It's Your Love

Registration 2
Rhythm: Ballad

Words and Music by
Stephony E. Smith

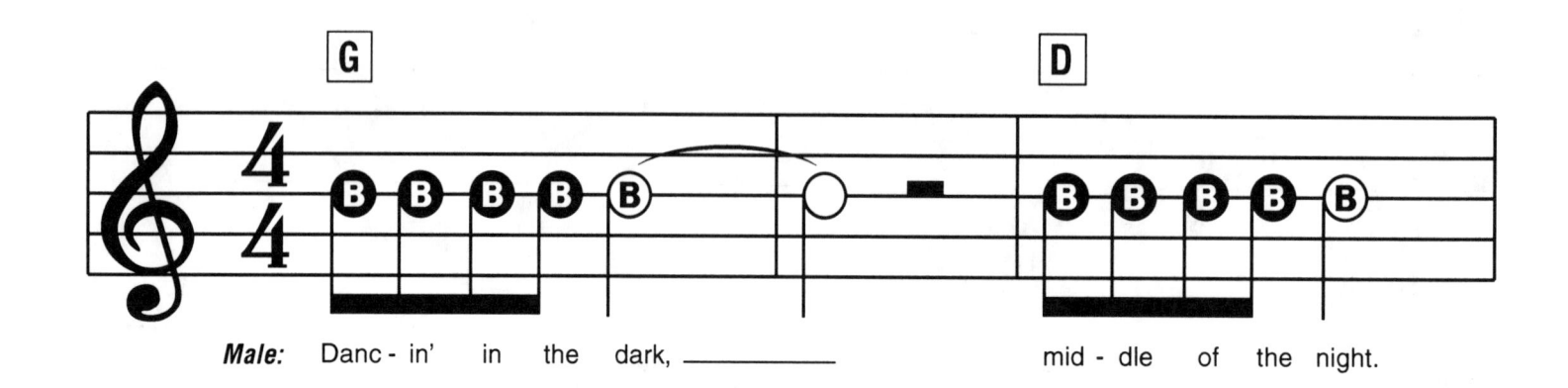

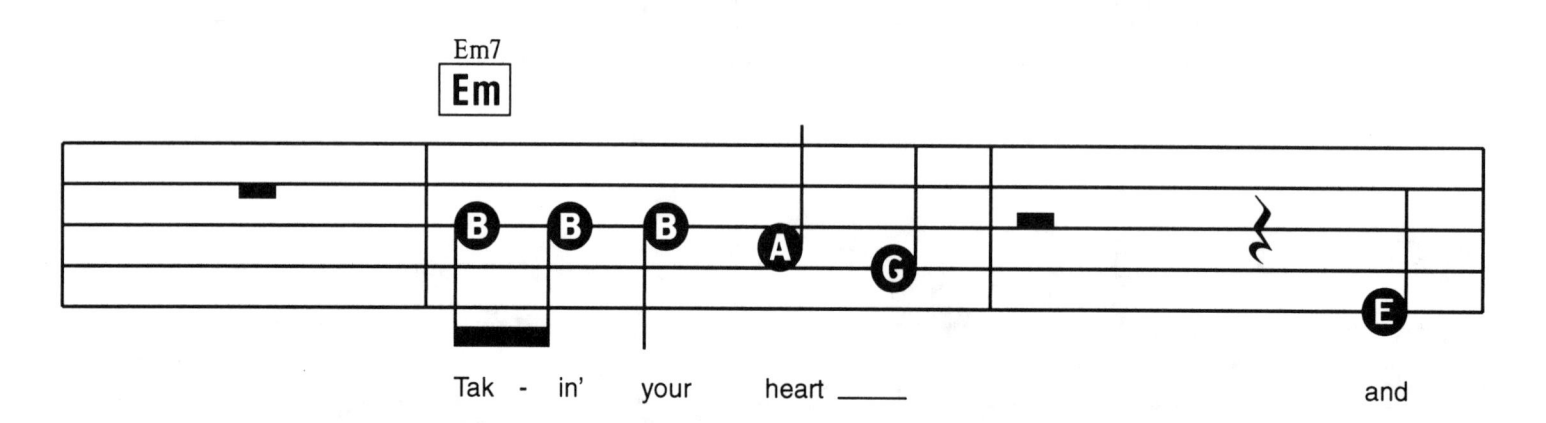

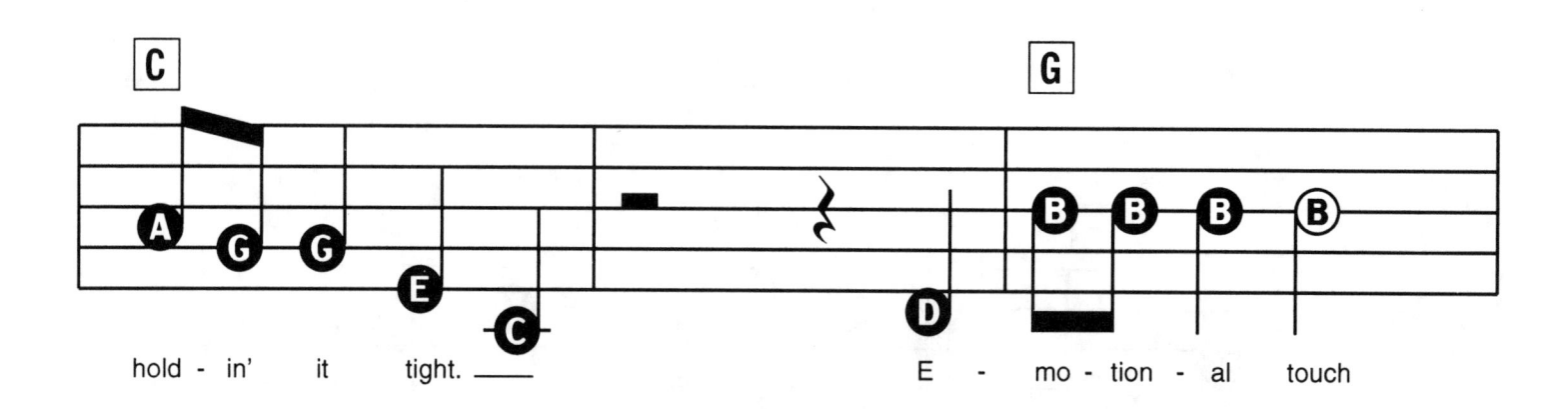

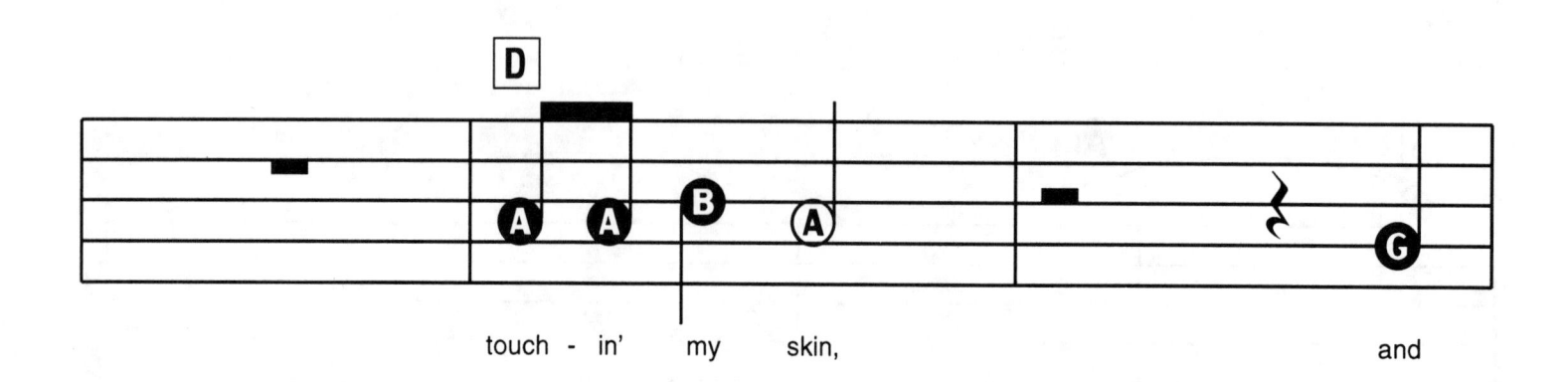

Male: Danc - in' in the dark, _____ mid - dle of the night.

Tak - in' your heart _____ and hold - in' it tight. _____ E - mo - tion - al touch touch - in' my skin, and askin' you to do what you've been doin' all over again.

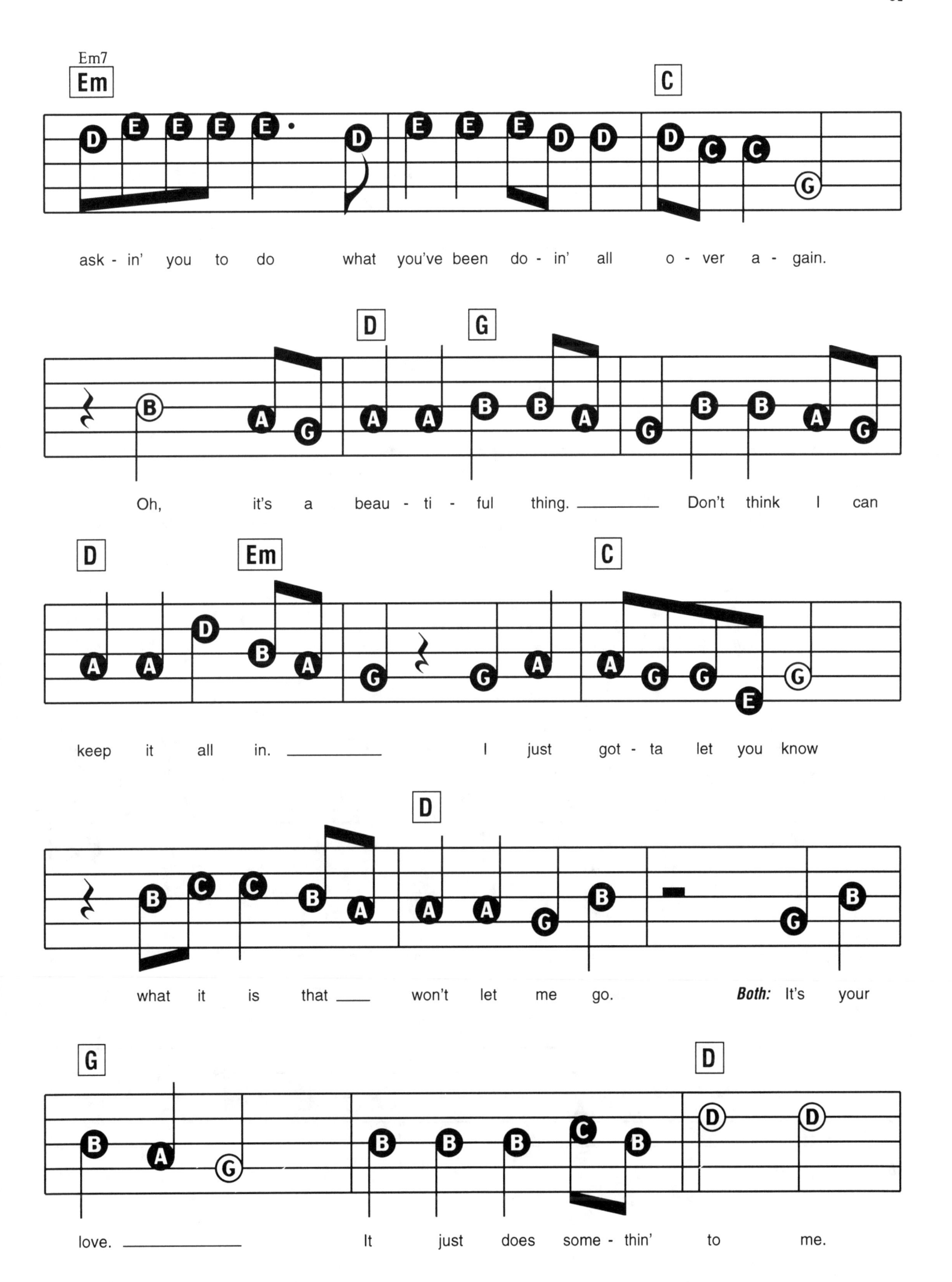

Oh, it's a beautiful thing. Don't think I can

keep it all in. I just gotta let you know

what it is that won't let me go. **Both:** It's your

love. It just does somethin' to me.

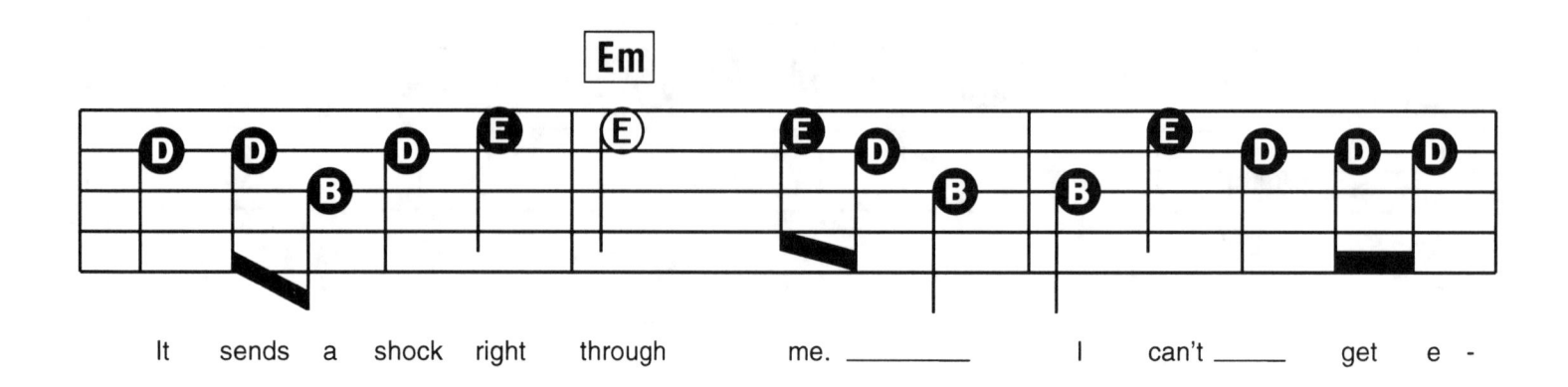

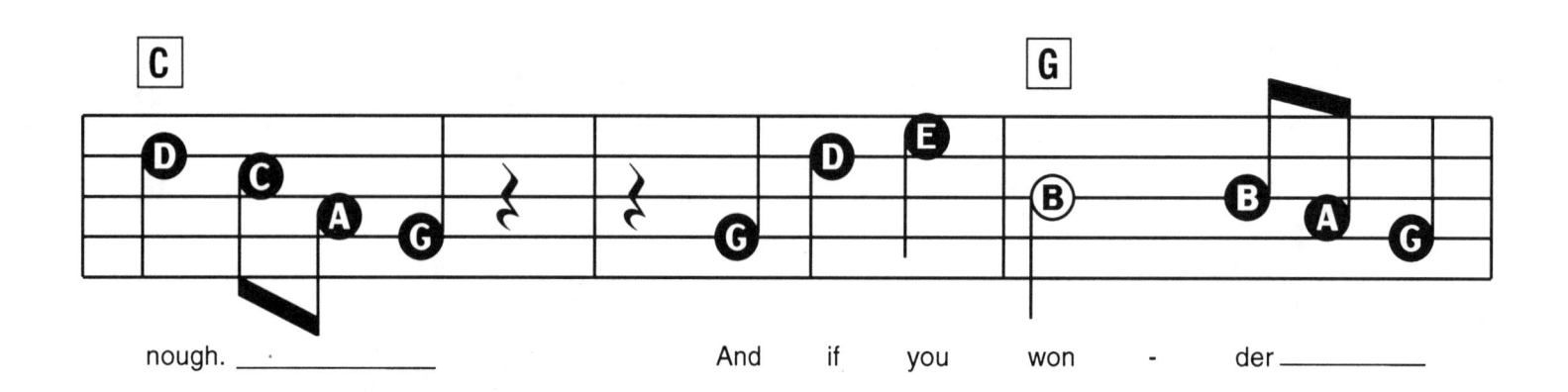

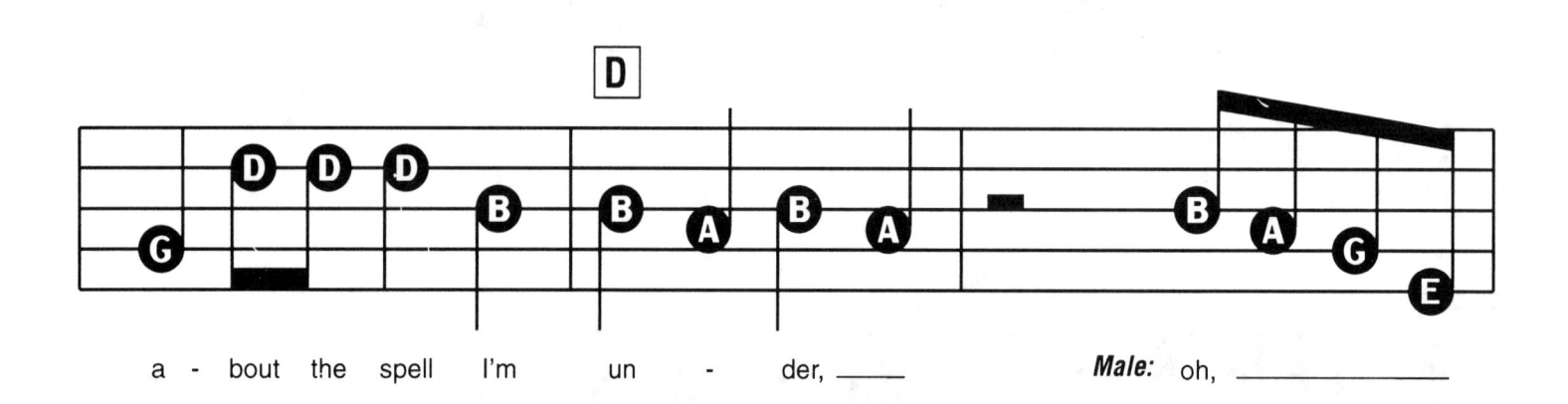

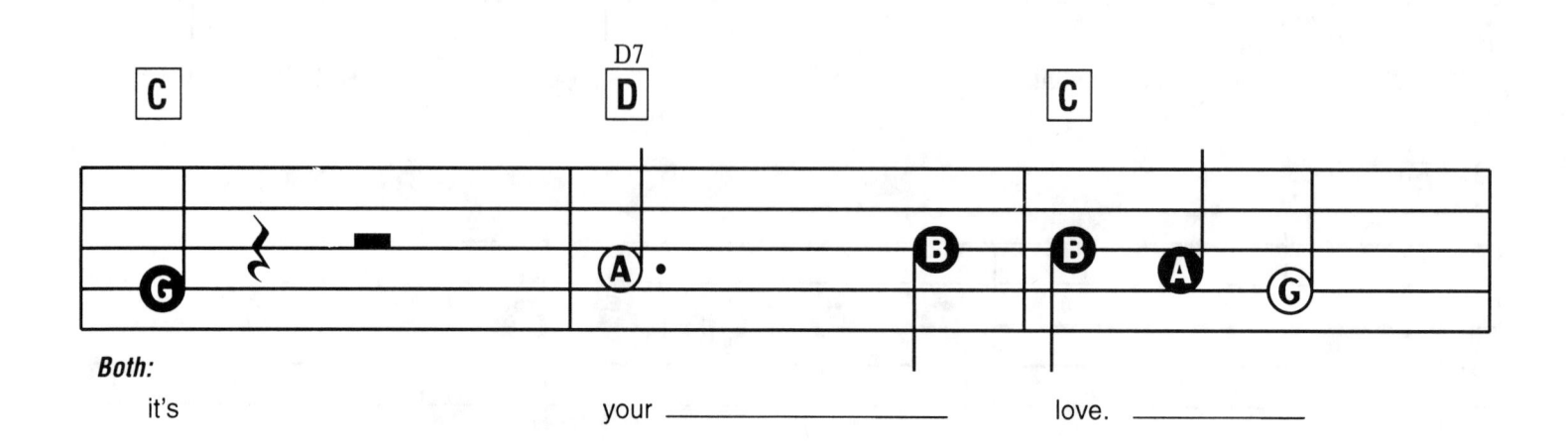

It sends a shock right through me. ____ I can't ____ get e-nough. ____ And if you won-der ____ a-bout the spell I'm un-der, ____ *Male:* oh, ____ *Both:* it's your ____ love. ____

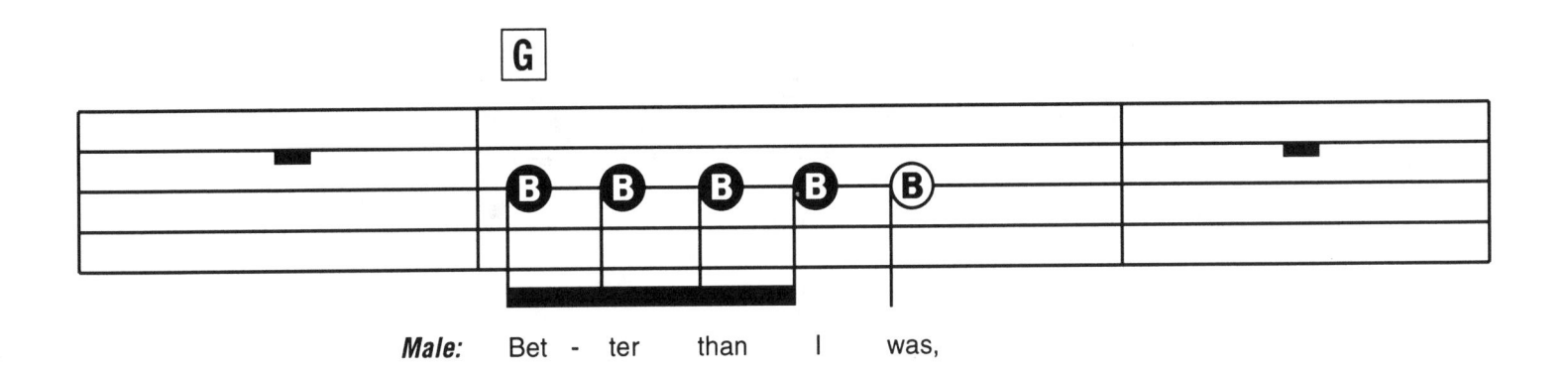

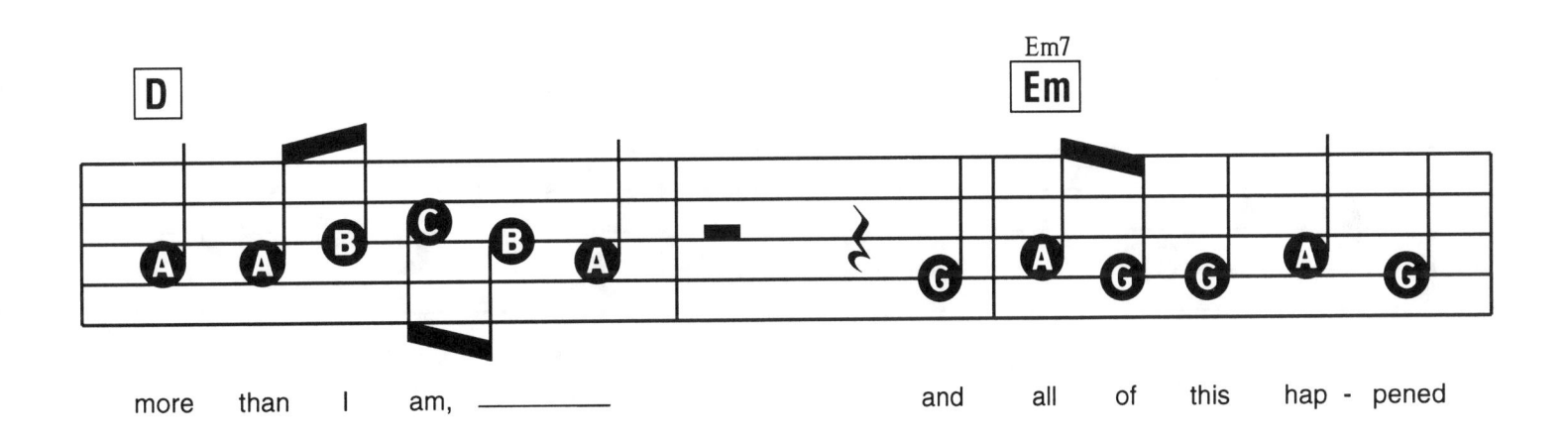

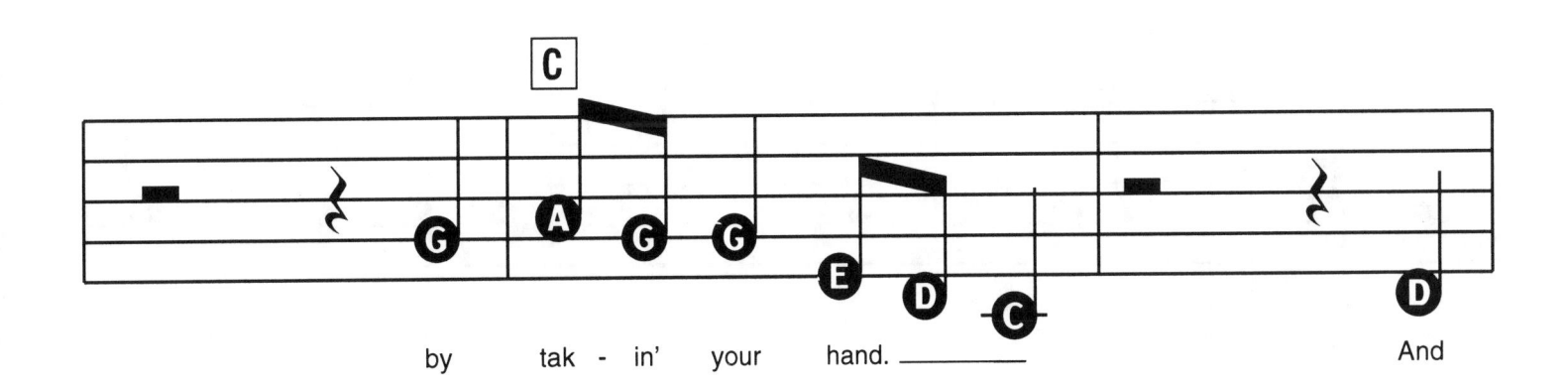

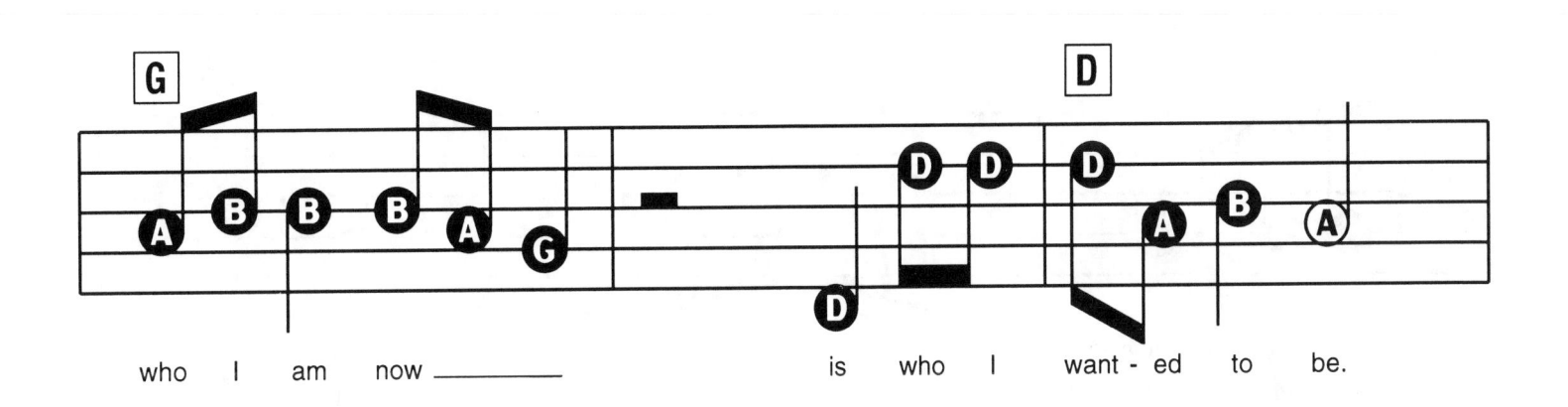

Male: Better than I was, more than I am, and all of this happened by takin' your hand. And who I am now is who I wanted to be.

84

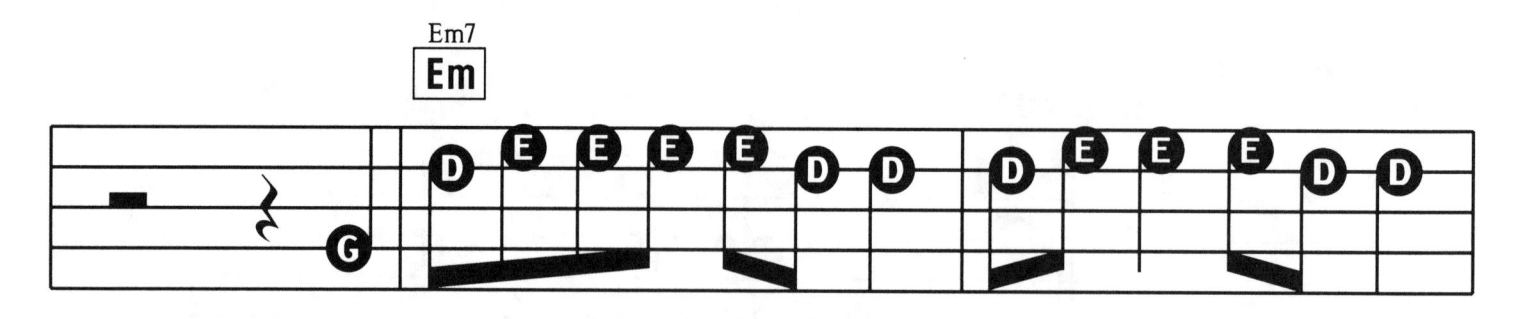

Both: And now that we're to-geth-er, I'm strong-er than ev-er. I'm hap-py and free. Oh, it's a beau-ti-ful thing. ____ Don't think I can keep it all in. ____

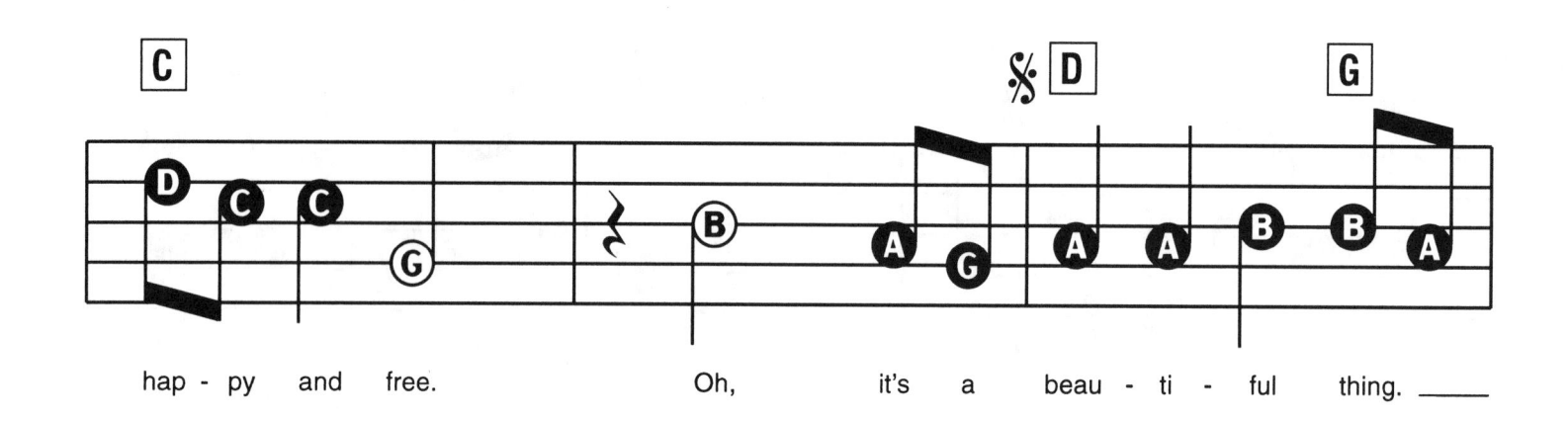

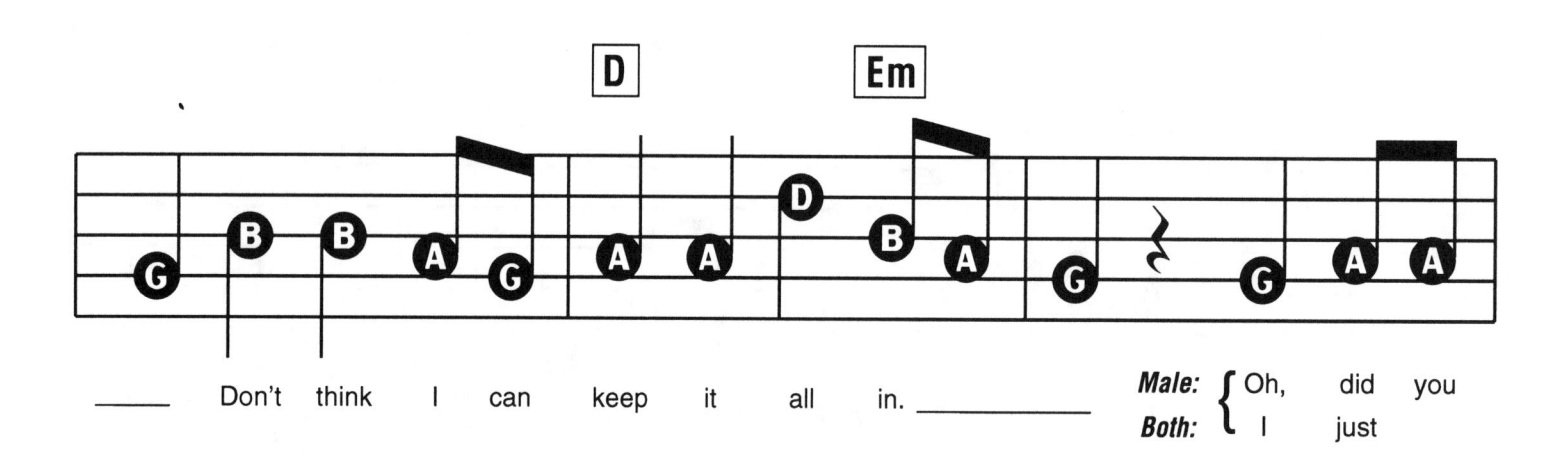

Male: Oh, did you ask me why I've changed? All I got-ta do is say your sweet name. ____
Both: I just got-ta let you know what it is ____ that ____ won't let me go.

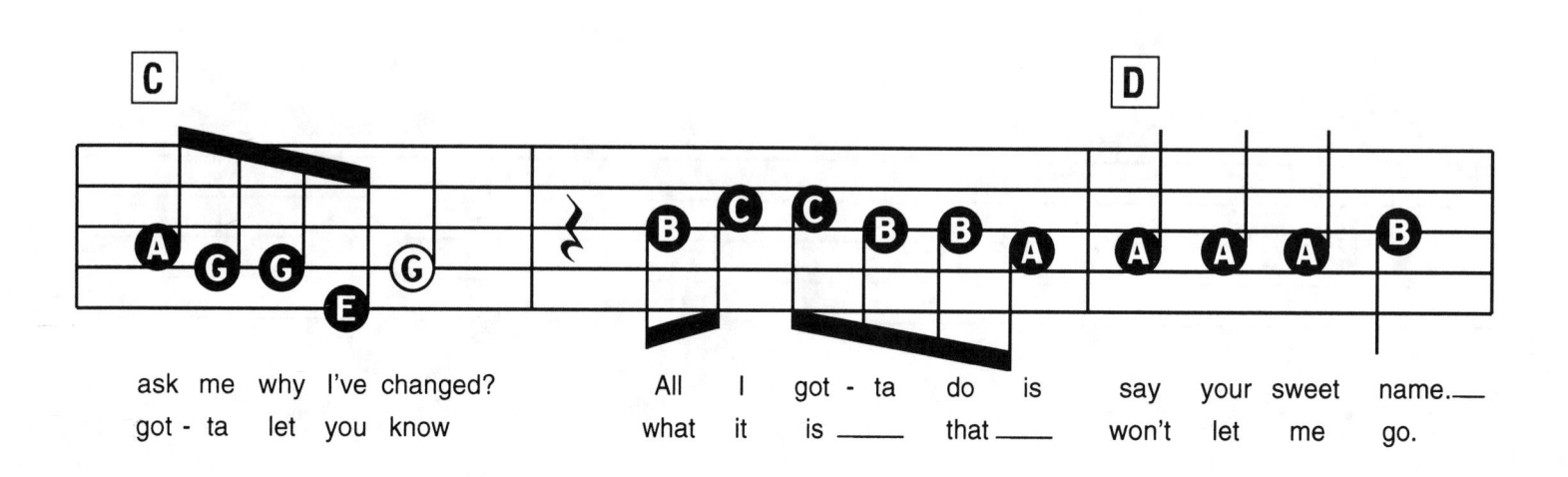

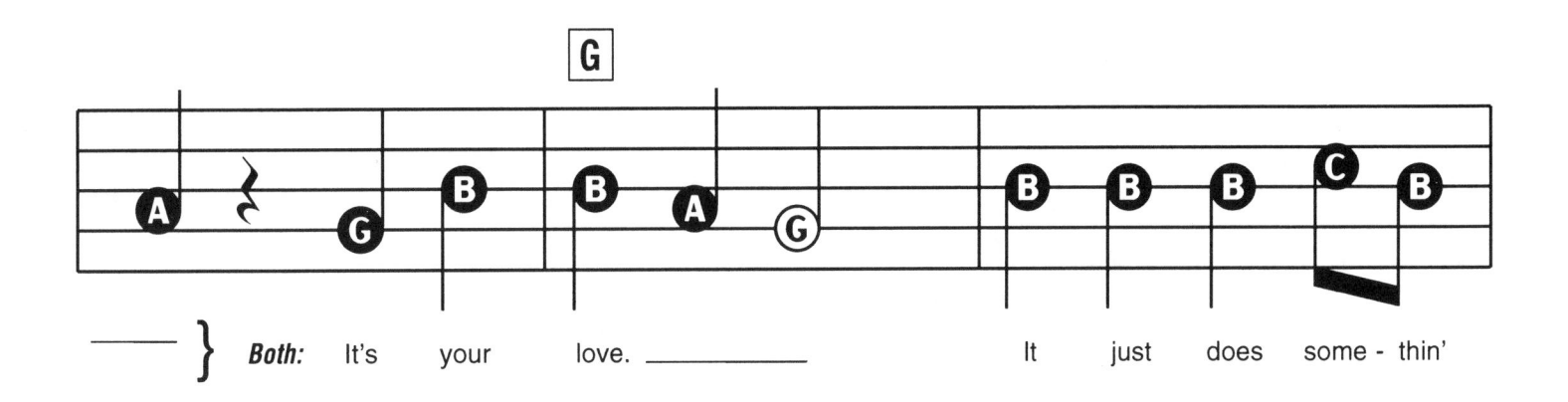

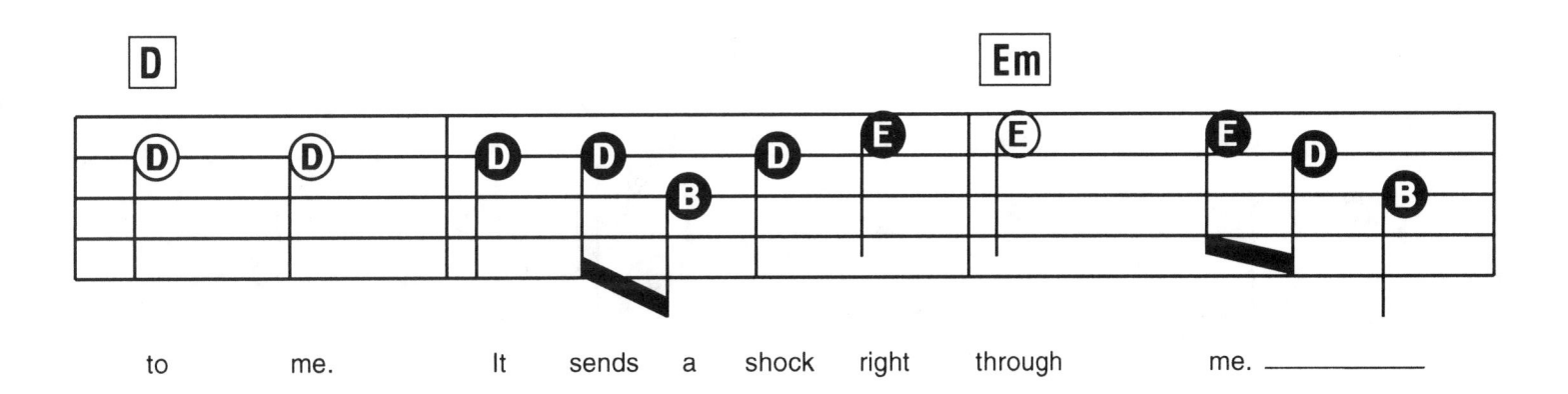

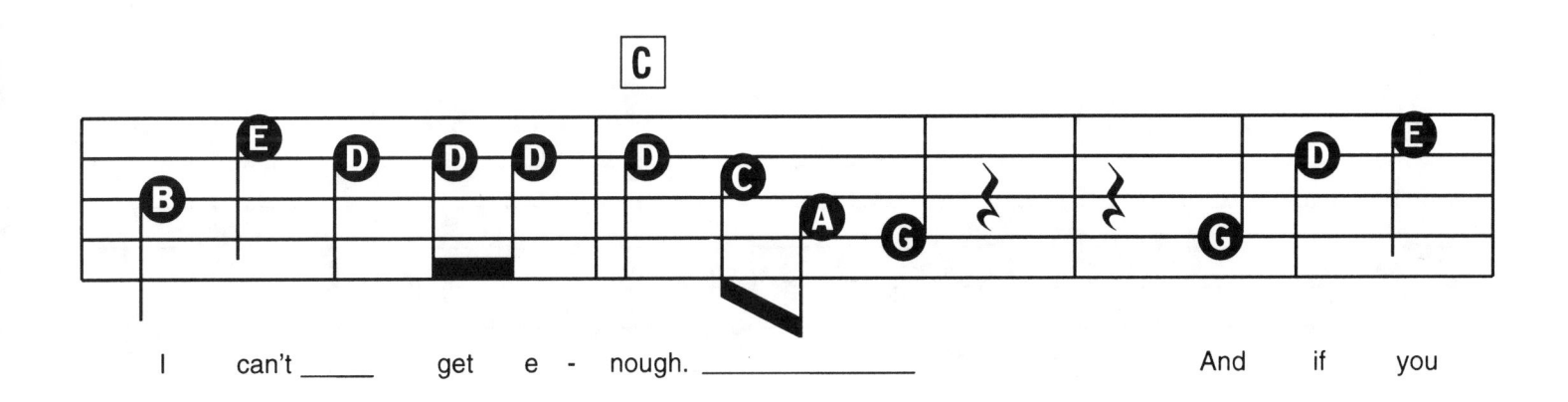

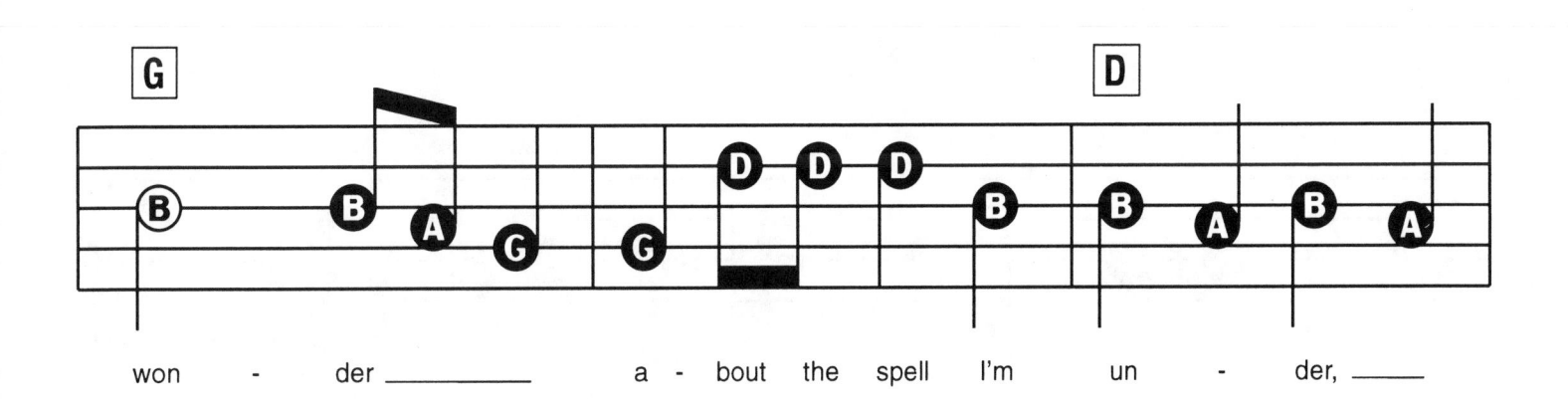

Both: It's your love. It just does some-thin' to me. It sends a shock right through me. I can't get e-nough. And if you won-der a-bout the spell I'm un-der,

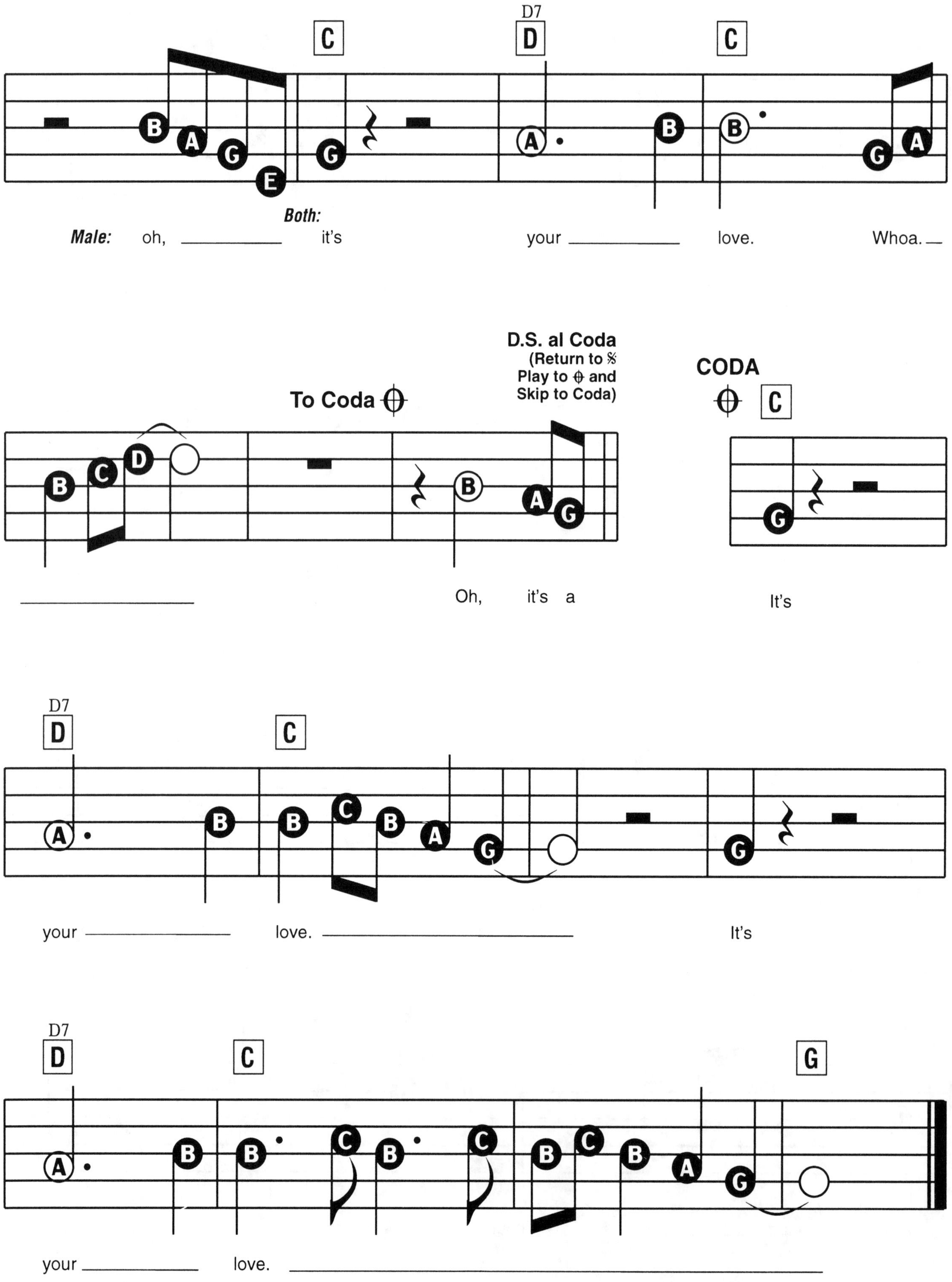
D7
Both:
Male: oh, it's your love. Whoa.
To Coda
D.S. al Coda
(Return to 𝄋
Play to ⊕ and
Skip to Coda)
CODA
Oh, it's a
It's
D7
your love.
It's
D7
your love.

Save the Best for Last

Registration 8
Rhythm: 8 Beat

Words and Music by Phil Galdston,
Jon Lind and Wendy Waldman

Some - times the snow comes down in June.
nights you came to me when
snow comes down in June.

Some - times the sun goes 'round the moon.
some sil - ly girl had set you free.
Some - times the sun goes 'round the moon.

I see the pas - sion in your eyes.
You won - dered how you'd make it through.
Just when I thought a chance had passed,

Some - times it's all a big sur -
I won - dered what was wrong with
you go and save the best for

© 1989 EMI VIRGIN SONGS, INC., BIG MYSTIQUE MUSIC, UNIVERSAL - POLYGRAM INTERNATIONAL PUBLISHING, INC.,
KAZZOOM MUSIC INC., WINDSWEPT PACIFIC ENTERTAINMENT CO. d/b/a LONGITUDE MUSIC CO. and MOON AND STARS MUSIC
All Rights for BIG MYSTIQUE MUSIC Controlled and Administered by EMI VIRGIN SONGS, INC.
All Rights Reserved   International Copyright Secured   Used by Permission

prise. 'Cause there was a time when all I did was wish you'd
you. 'Cause how could you give your love to some-one else and

tell me this was love. It's not the way I hoped or
share your dreams with me? Some-times the ver-y thing you're

how I planned, but some-how it's e-nough. And now we're
look-ing for is the one thing you can't see. But now we're

stand-ing face to face.
stand-ing face to face. } Is-n't this world a cra-zy

place? Just when I thought our chance had passed, you go and save the best for last. All of the last. Some-times the ver-y thing you're look-ing for is the one thing you can't see.

D.S. al Coda
(Return to 𝄋
Play to ⊕ and
Skip to Coda)

Some-times the last.

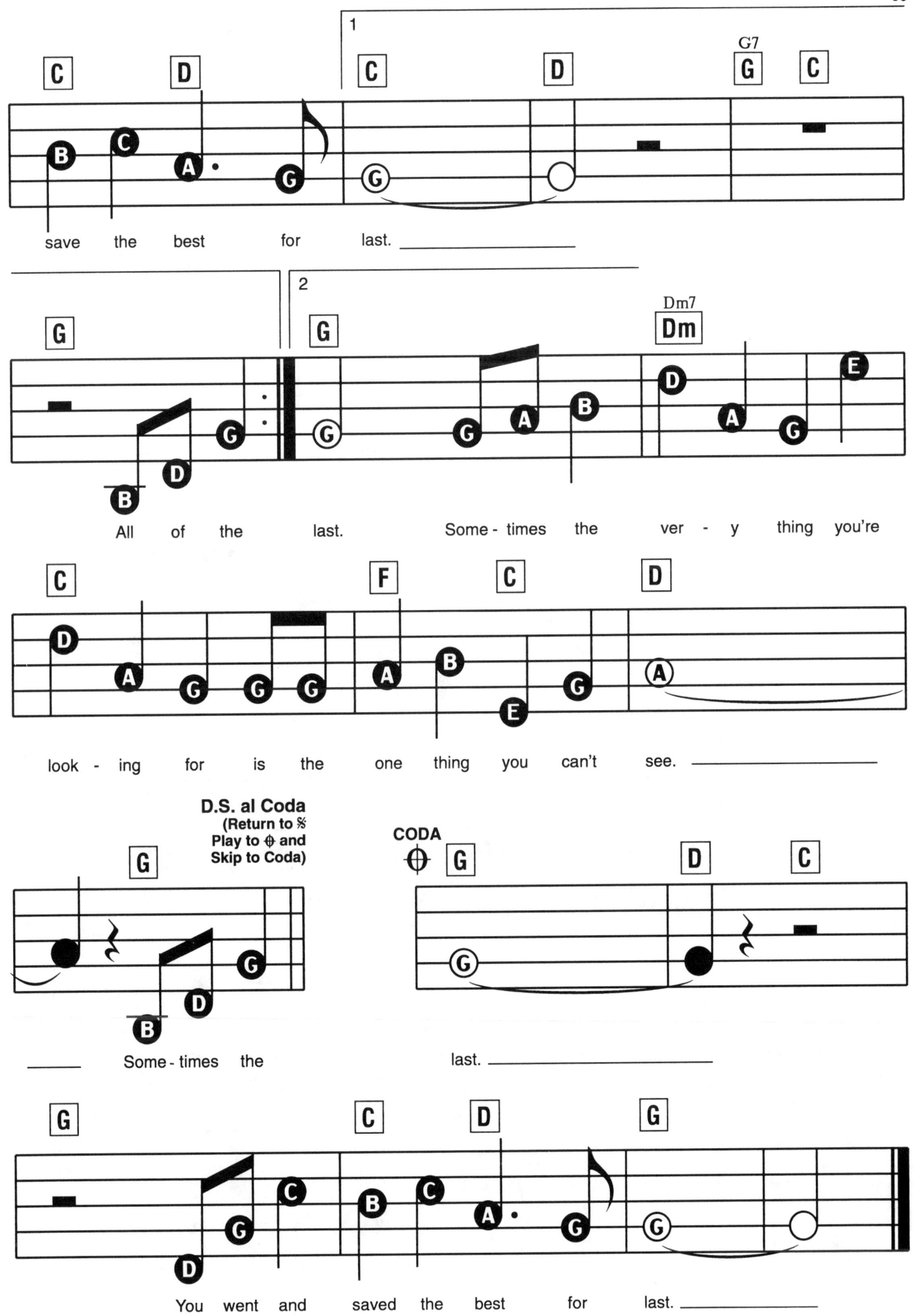

You went and saved the best for last.

Just the Way You Are

Registration 4
Rhythm: Rock or Jazz Rock

Words and Music by
Billy Joel

Don't go chang - ing to try and
Don't go try - ing to some___ new
said I love you and that's for -

please me you nev - er let me down be -
fash - ion don't change the col - or of your
ev - er and this I prom - ise from the

fore. Mm___ mm. Don't i -
hair. Mm___ mm. You always
heart. Mm___ mm. I could not

mag - ine you're too fa - mil - iar
have my un - spok - en pas - sion
love you an - y bet - ter

© 1977, 1978 IMPULSIVE MUSIC
All Rights Reserved   International Copyright Secured   Used by Permission

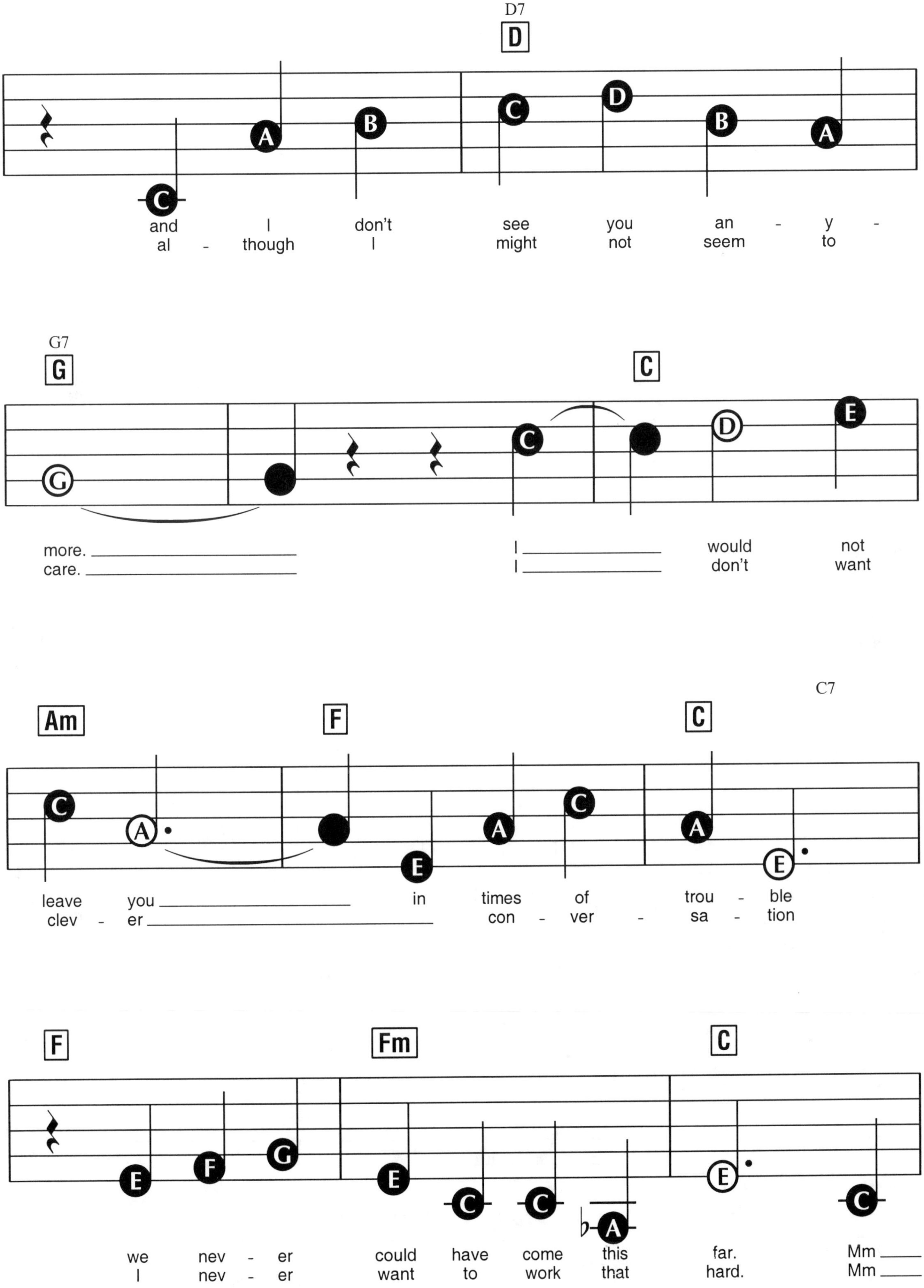
D7
D
and I don't see you an - y -
al - though I might not seem to
G7
G
C
more.
care.
I
I
would not
don't want
Am
F
C
C7
leave you in times of trou - ble
clev - er con - ver - sa - tion
F
Fm
C
we nev - er could have come this far.
I nev - er want to work that hard.
Mm
Mm

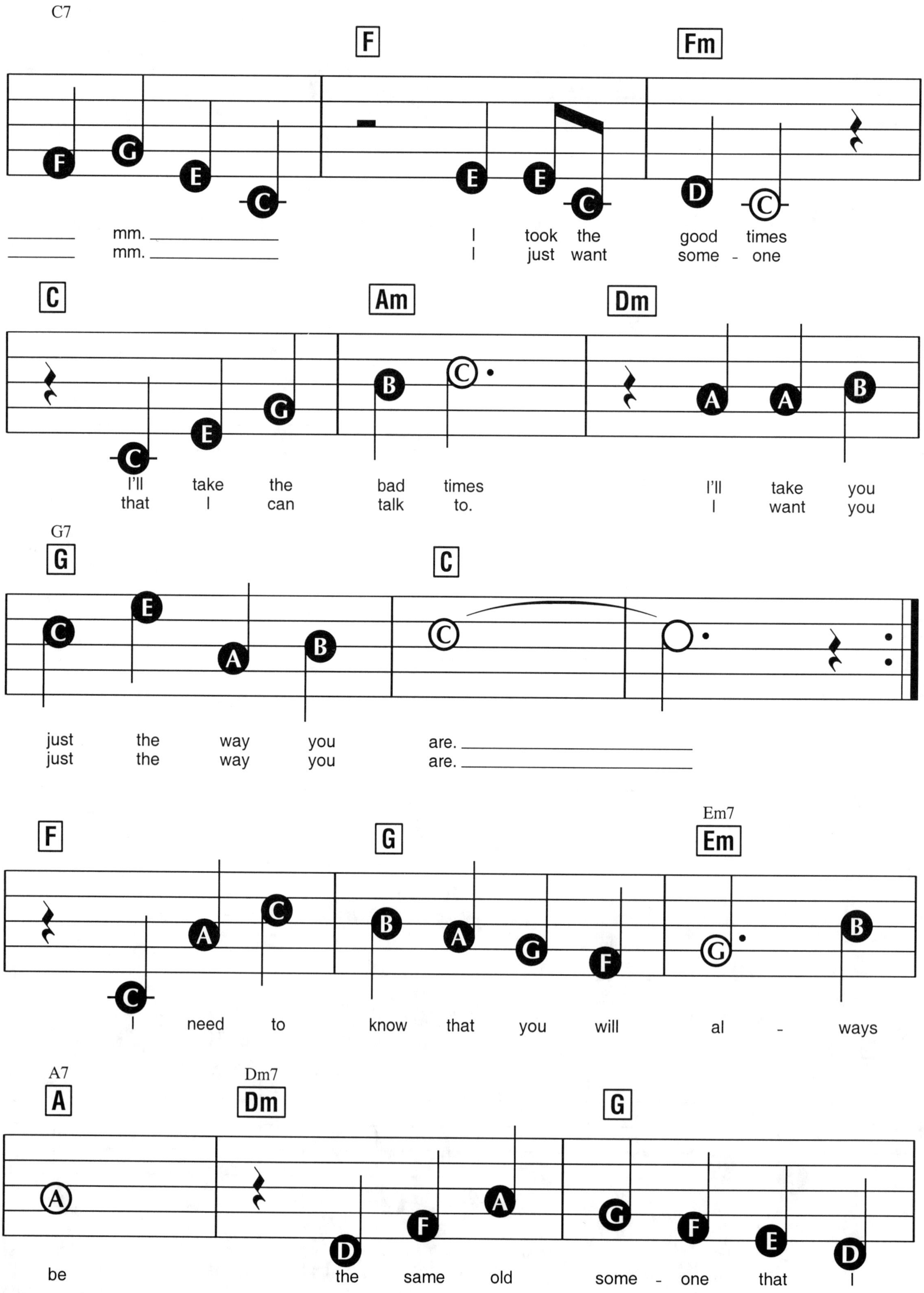
C7
F
Fm
mm. I took the good times
mm. I just want some - one
C
Am
Dm
I'll take the bad times I'll take you
that I can talk to. I want you
G7
G
C
just the way you are.
just the way you are.
F
G
Em7
Em
I need to know that you will al - ways
A7
A
Dm7
Dm
G
be the same old some - one that I

knew. Oh, what will it take till you be - lieve in me the way that I be - lieve in you. I love you just the way you are.

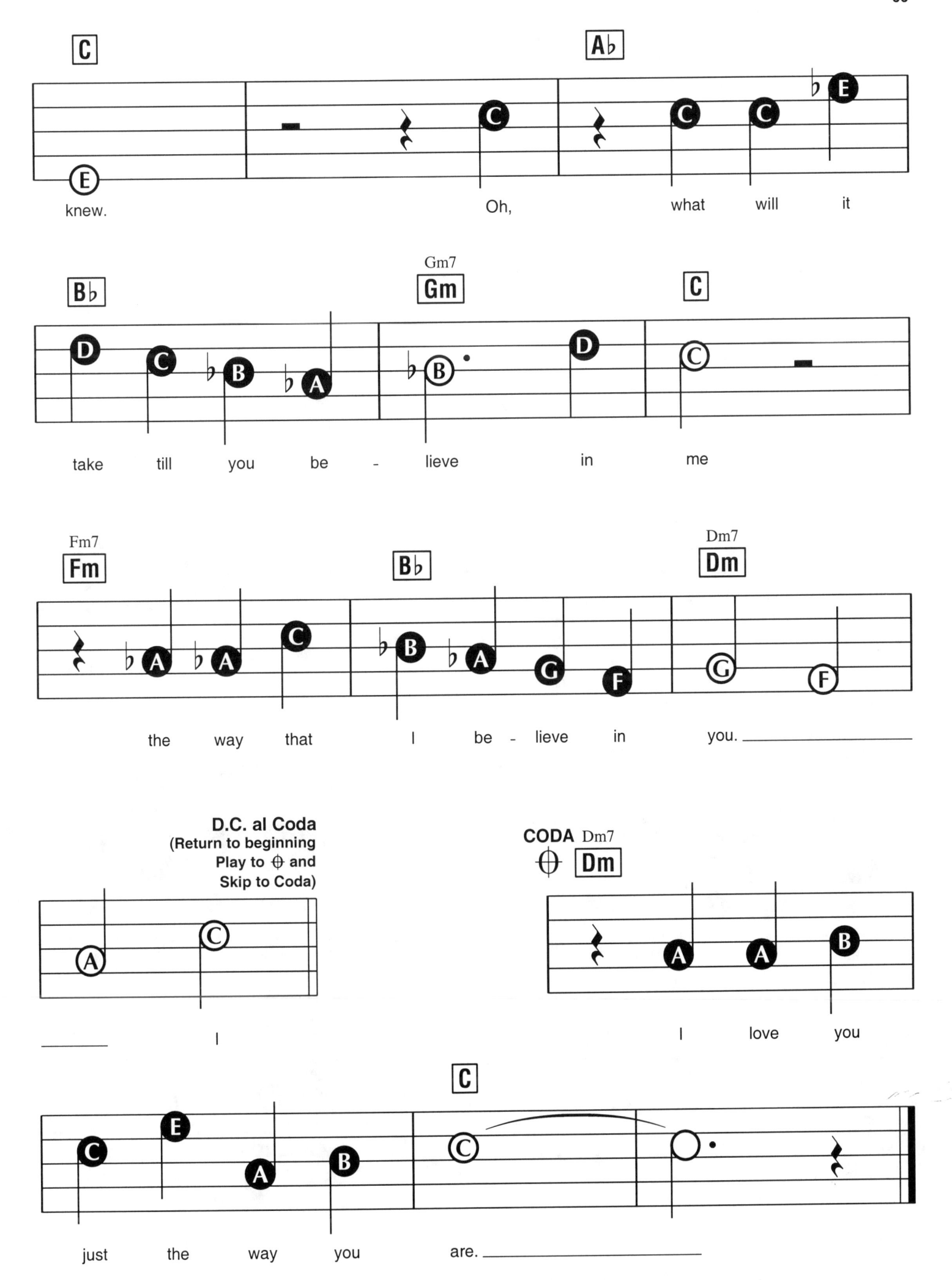

The Keeper of the Stars

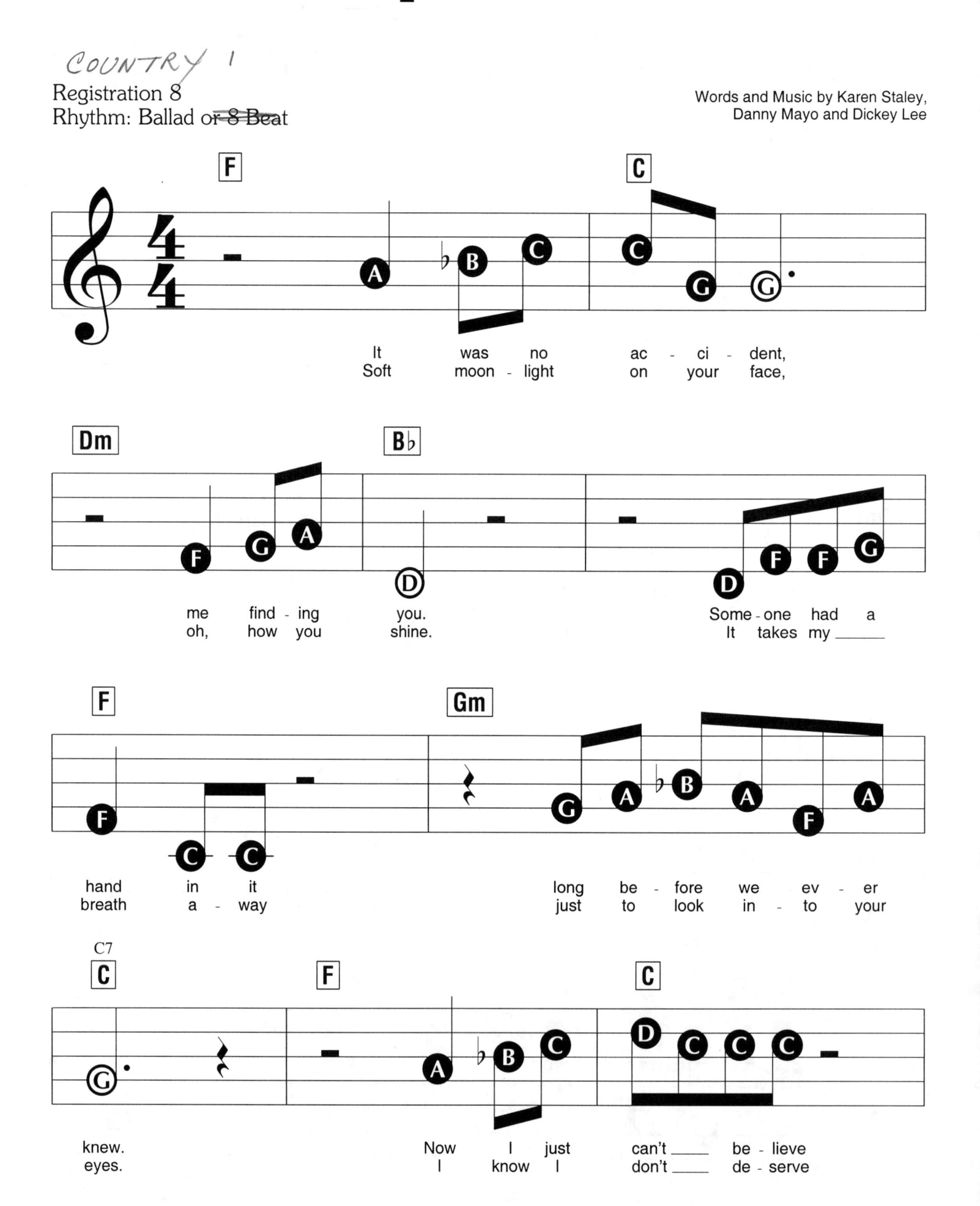

COUNTRY 1

Registration 8
Rhythm: Ballad or ~~8 Beat~~

Words and Music by Karen Staley,
Danny Mayo and Dickey Lee

It was no ac - ci - dent, me find - ing you.
Soft moon - light on your face, oh, how you shine.

Some - one had a hand in it long be - fore we ev - er knew.
It takes my breath a - way just to look in - to your eyes.

Now I just can't be - lieve
I know I don't de - serve

Copyright © 1994 by Careers-BMG Music Publishing, Inc., Sixteen Stars Music,
Murrah Music Corporation, Universal - Songs Of PolyGram International, Inc. and Pal Time Music
International Copyright Secured   All Rights Reserved

you're in my life. Heav-en's smil-in'
a treas-ure like you. There real-ly

down on me as I look at you to-
are no words to show my grat-i-

night. So, I tip my hat
tude. I tip my

to the Keep-er of the Stars.

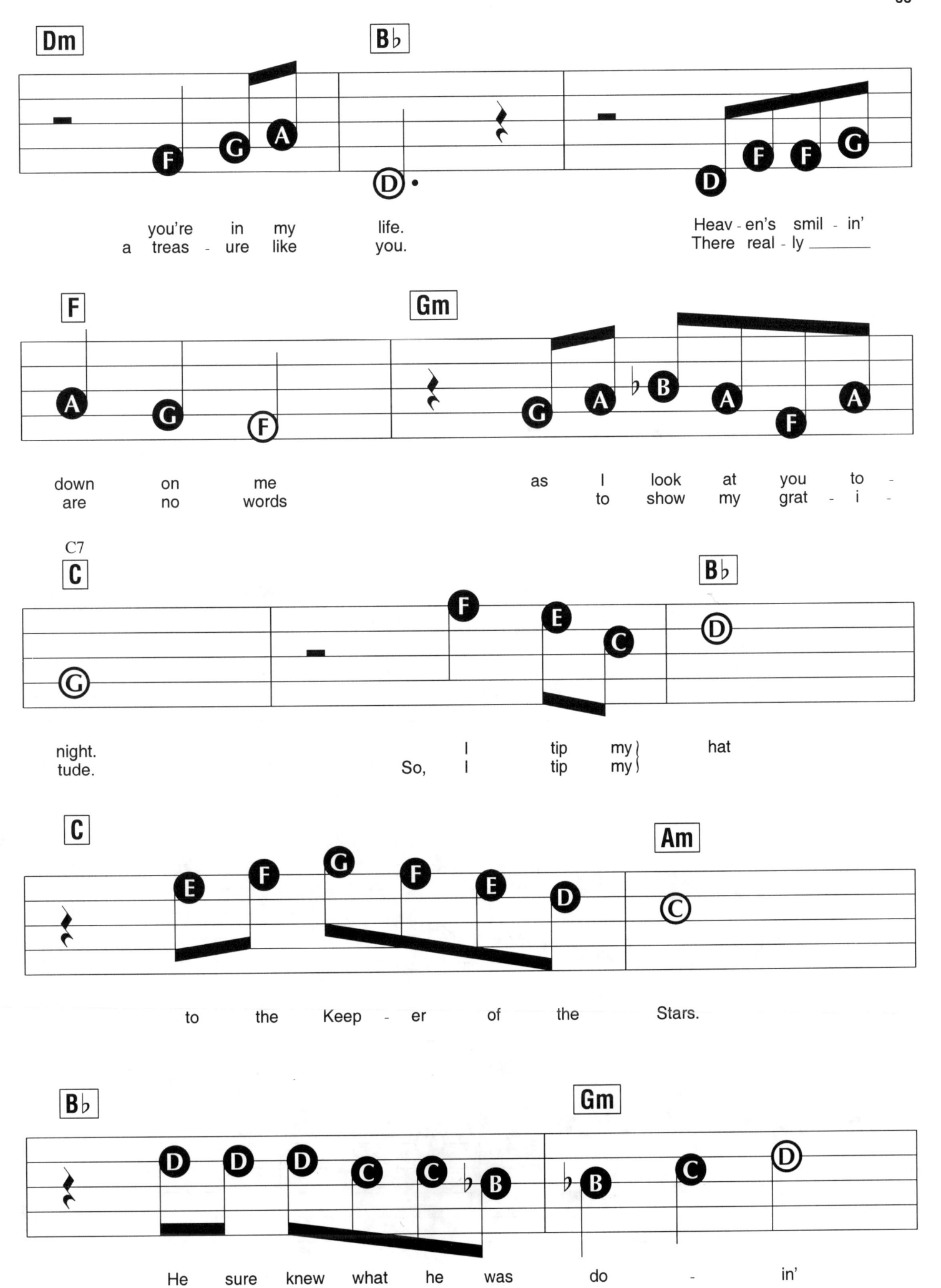

He sure knew what he was do - in'

when he joined these two hearts.

I hold ev - 'ry - thing

when I hold you in my arms.

I've got all I'll ev - er need,

thanks to the Keep - er of the Stars.

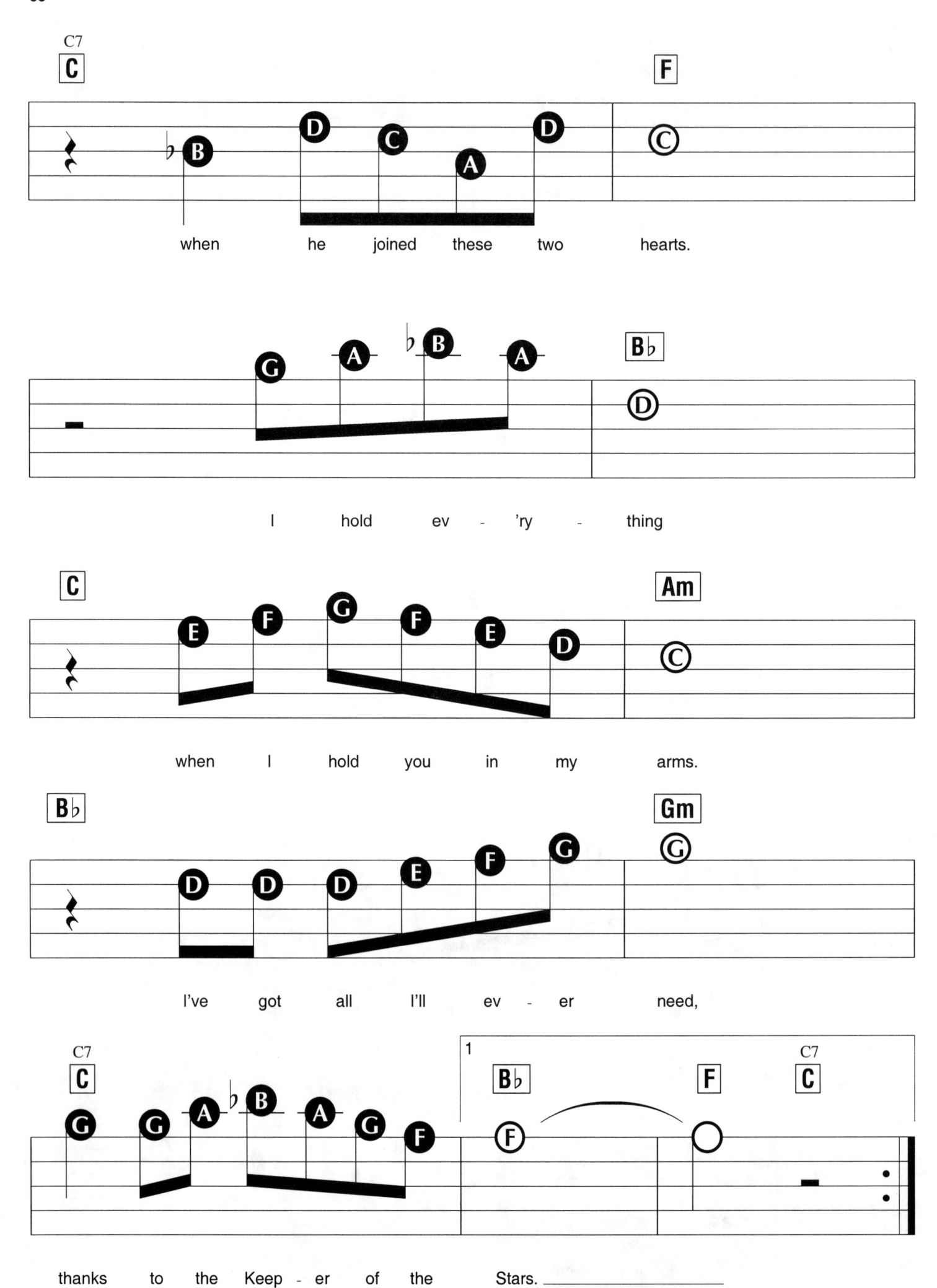

97

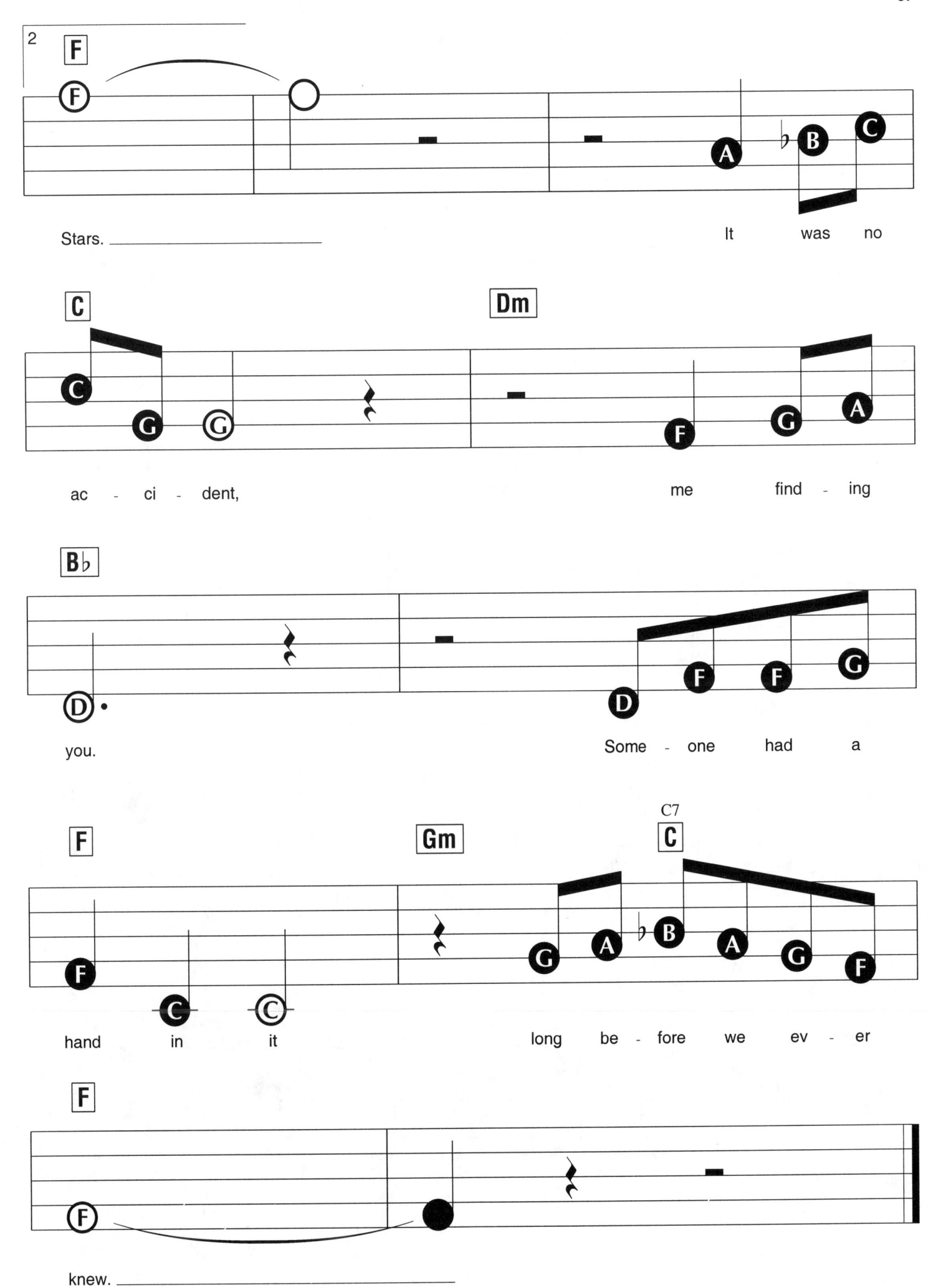

Stars. It was no ac-ci-dent, me find-ing you. Some-one had a hand in it long be-fore we ev-er knew.

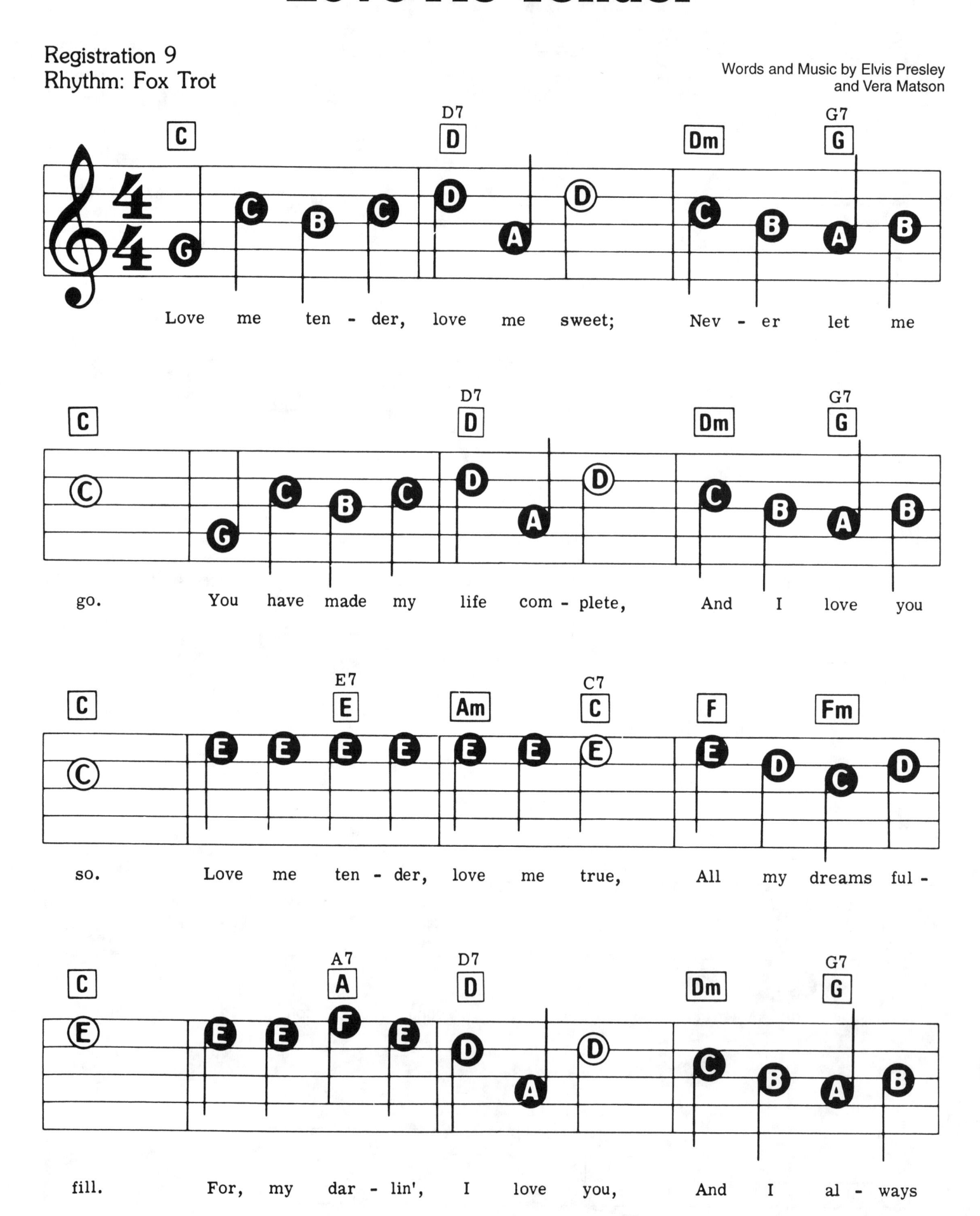

Love Me Tender

Registration 9
Rhythm: Fox Trot

Words and Music by Elvis Presley
and Vera Matson

Love me ten - der, love me sweet; Nev - er let me go. You have made my life com - plete, And I love you so. Love me ten - der, love me true, All my dreams ful - fill. For, my dar - lin', I love you, And I al - ways

Copyright © 1956 by Elvis Presley Music, Inc.
Copyright Renewed and Assigned to Elvis Presley Music (Administered by R&H Music)
International Copyright Secured   All Rights Reserved

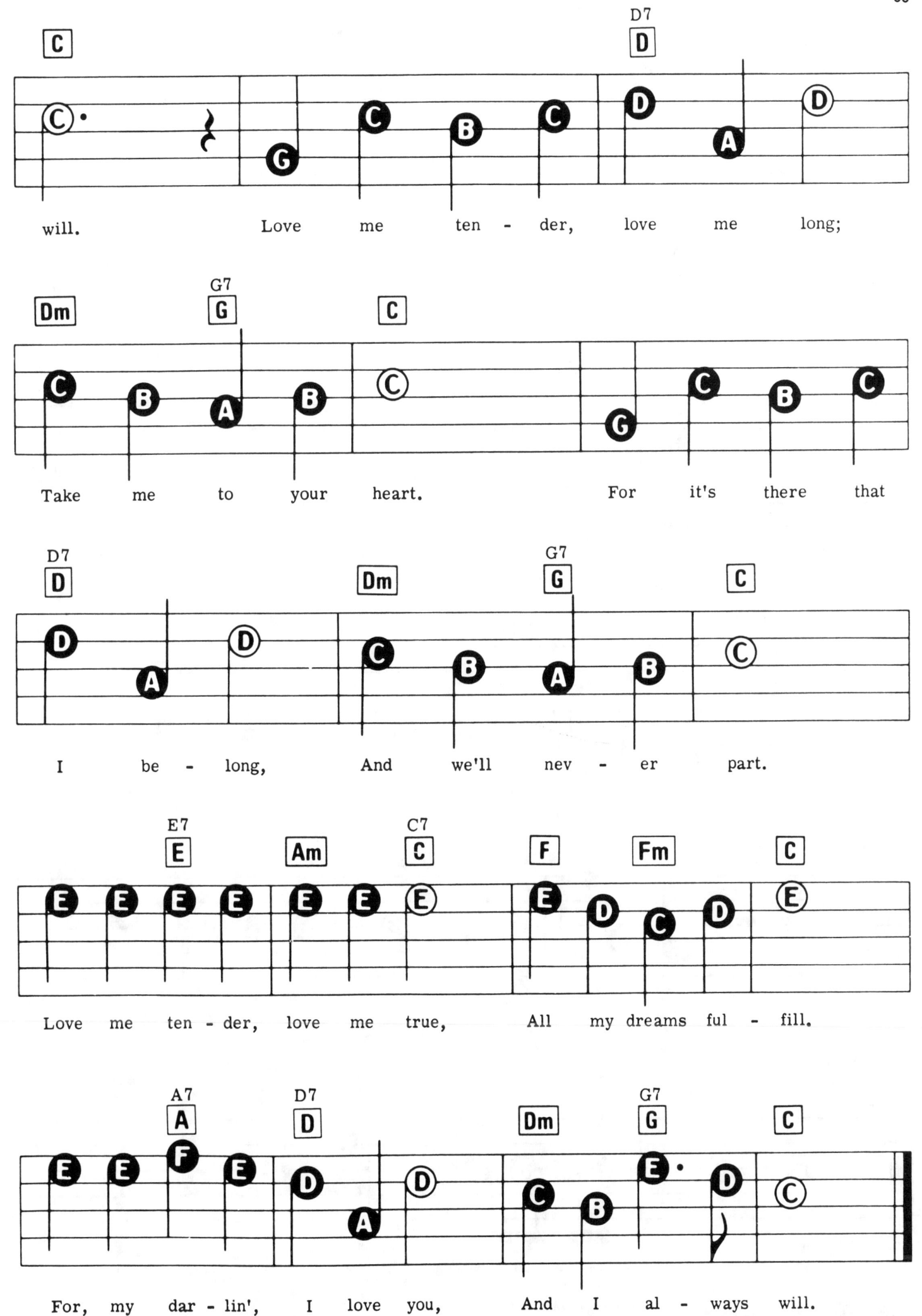

will. Love me ten - der, love me long; Take me to your heart. For it's there that I be - long, And we'll nev - er part. Love me ten - der, love me true, All my dreams ful - fill. For, my dar - lin', I love you, And I al - ways will.

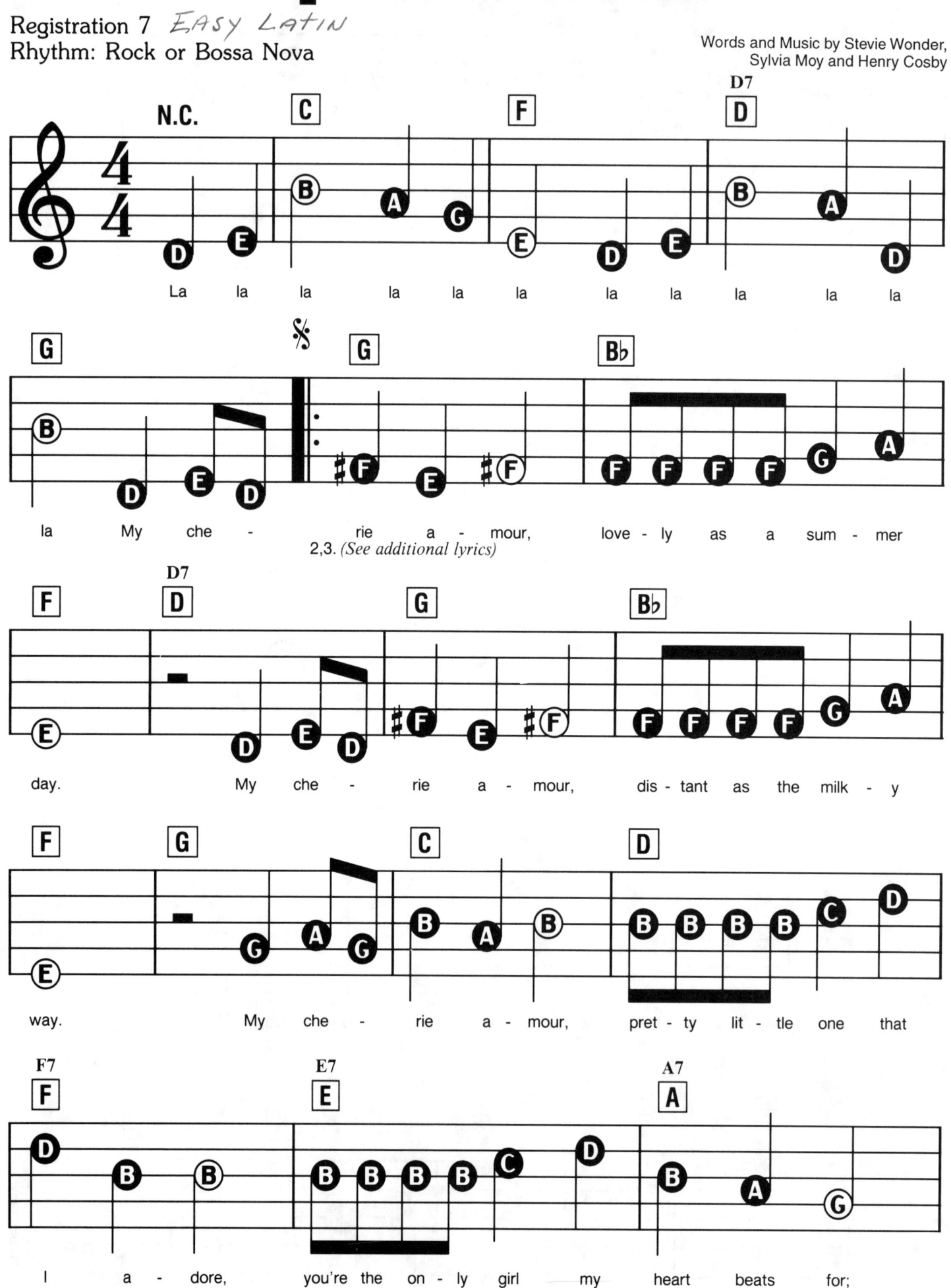

My Cherie Amour

Registration 7 *EASY LATIN*
Rhythm: Rock or Bossa Nova

Words and Music by Stevie Wonder,
Sylvia Moy and Henry Cosby

La la la la la la la la la la la la My cherie amour, lovely as a summer day. My cherie amour, distant as the milky way. My cherie amour, pretty little one that I adore, you're the only girl my heart beats for;

© 1968 (Renewed 1996) JOBETE MUSIC CO., INC., BLACK BULL MUSIC and SAWANDI MUSIC
c/o EMI APRIL MUSIC INC. and EMI BLACKWOOD MUSIC INC.
All Rights Reserved   International Copyright Secured   Used by Permission

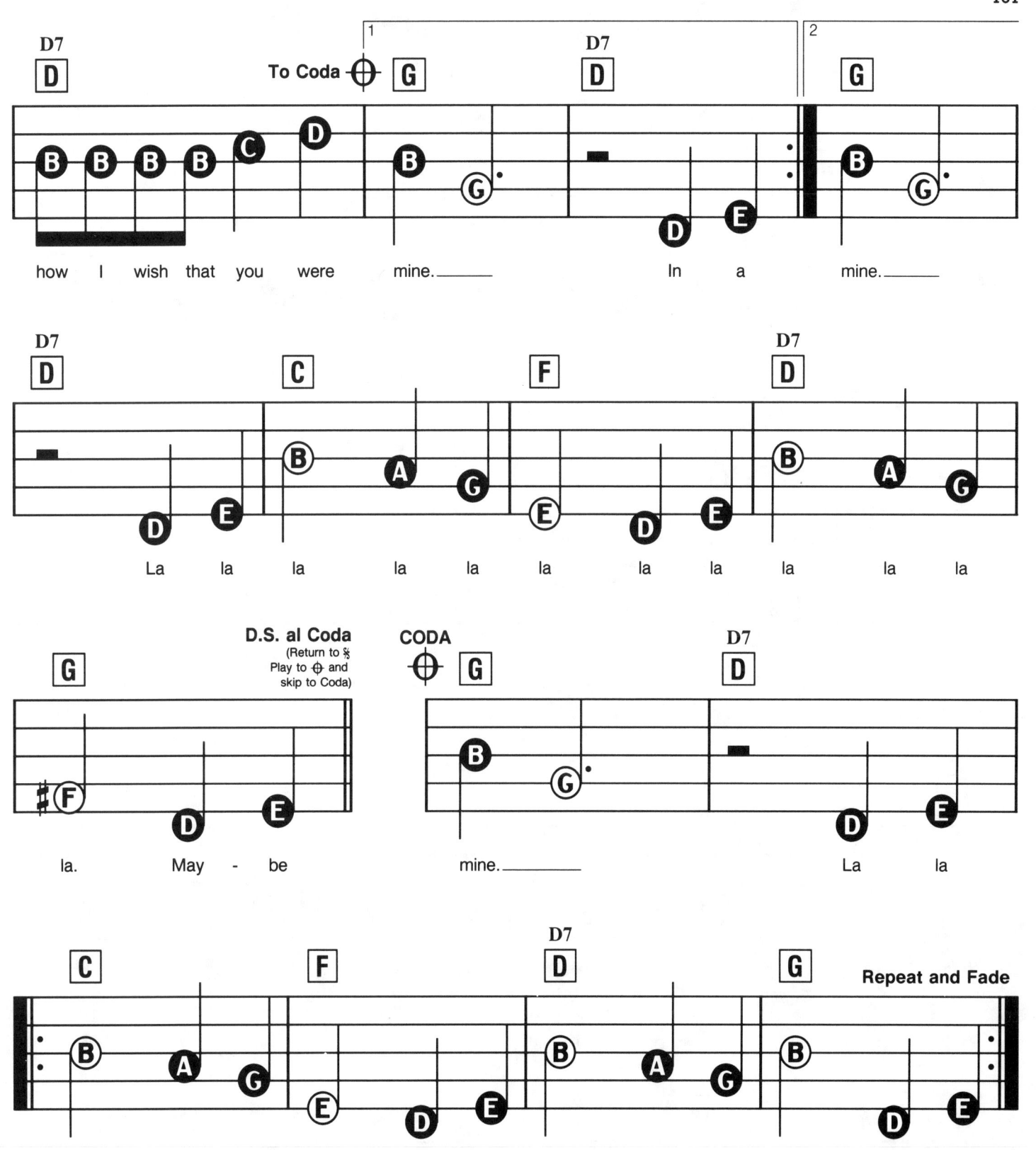

Additional Lyrics

2. In a cafe, or sometimes on a crowded street,
   I've been near you, but you never notice me.
   My cherie amour, won't you tell me how could you ignore,
   That behind that little smile I wore, how I wish that you were mine.

3. Maybe someday you'll see my face among the crowd;
   Maybe someday I'll share your little distant cloud.
   Oh, cherie amour, pretty little one that I adore,
   You're the only girl my heart beats for; how I wish that you were mine.

My Funny Valentine
from BABES IN ARMS

Registration 1
Rhythm: Ballad

Words by Lorenz Hart
Music by Richard Rodgers

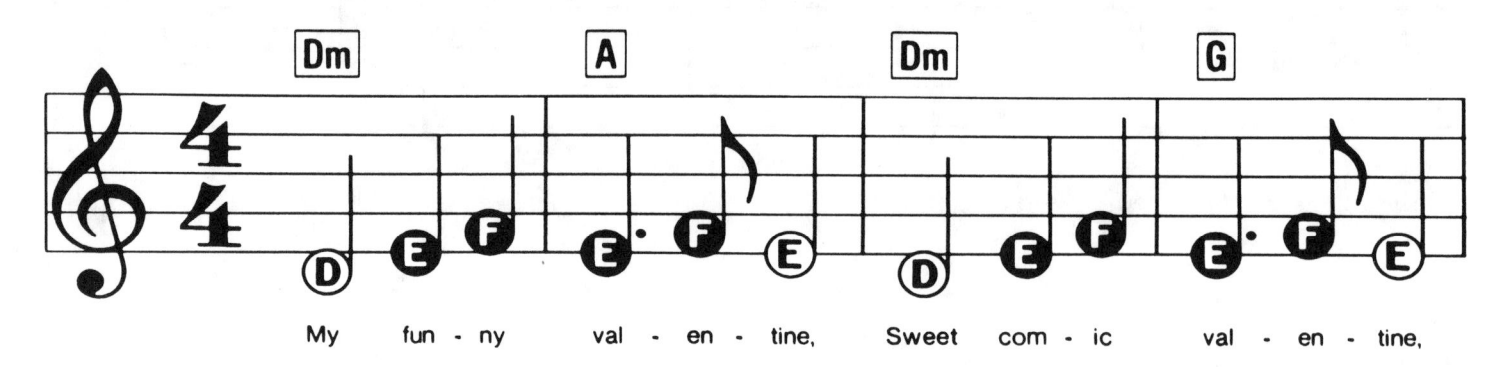

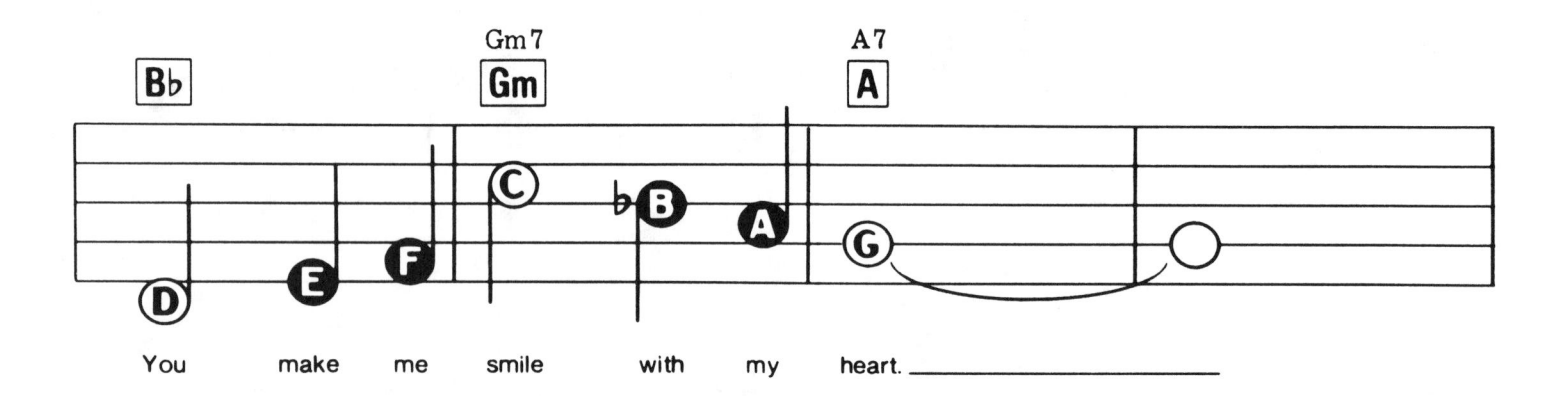

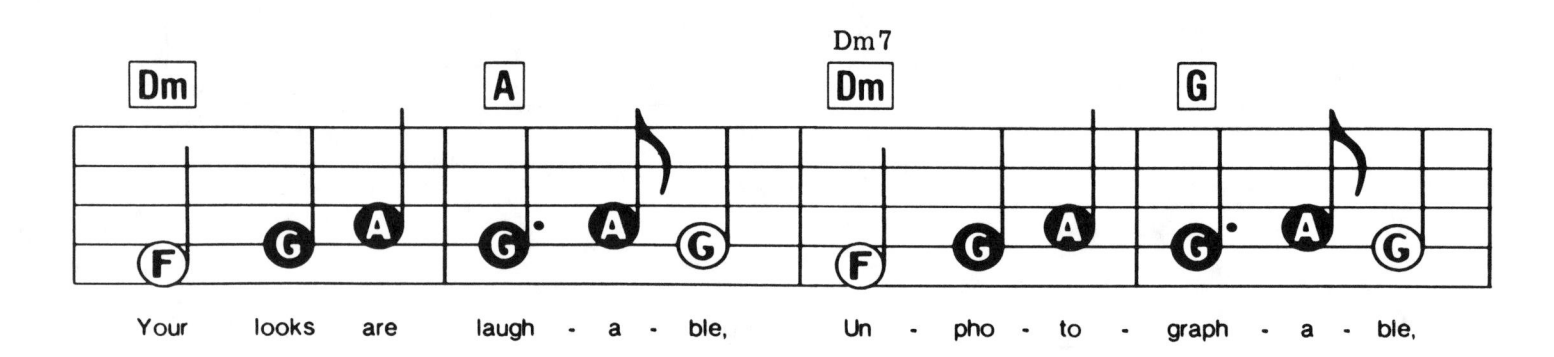

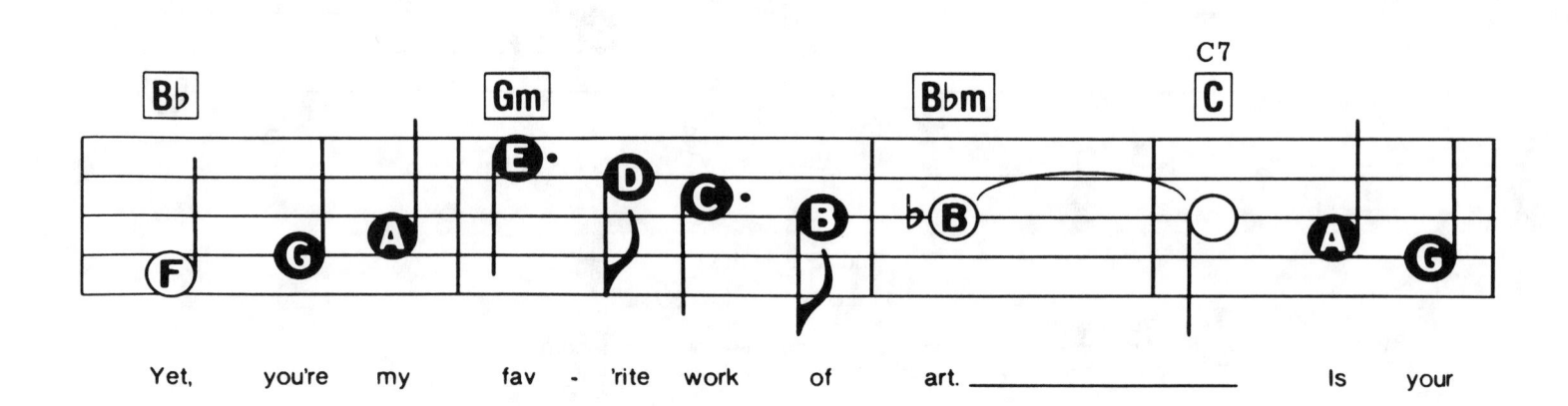

My fun-ny val-en-tine, Sweet com-ic val-en-tine,

You make me smile with my heart.

Your looks are laugh-a-ble, Un-pho-to-graph-a-ble,

Yet, you're my fav-'rite work of art. _____ Is your

Copyright © 1937 by Williamson Music and The Estate Of Lorenz Hart in the United States
Copyright Renewed
All Rights on behalf of The Estate Of Lorenz Hart Administered by WB Music Corp.
International Copyright Secured All Rights Reserved

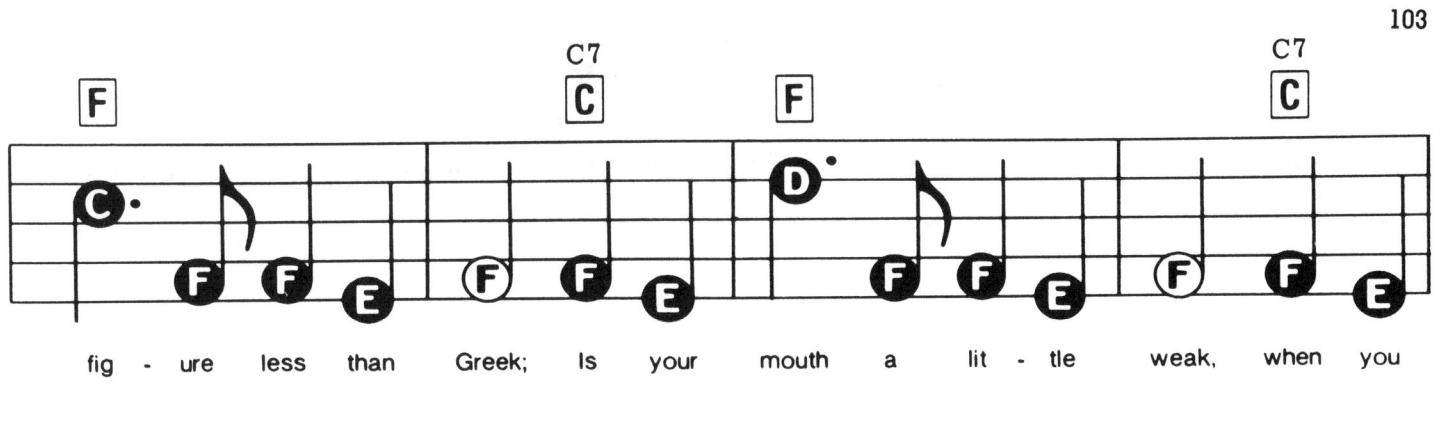

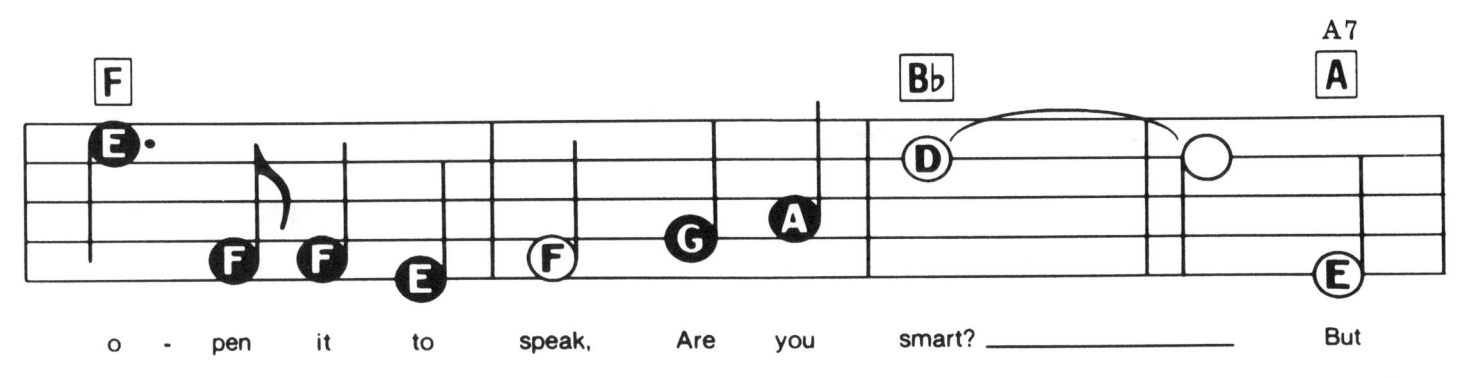

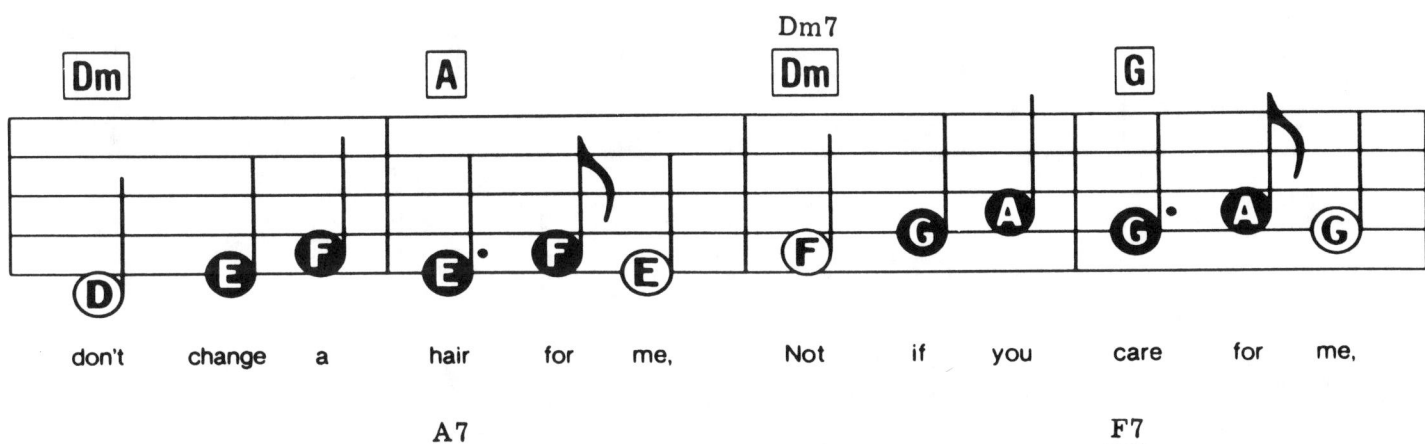

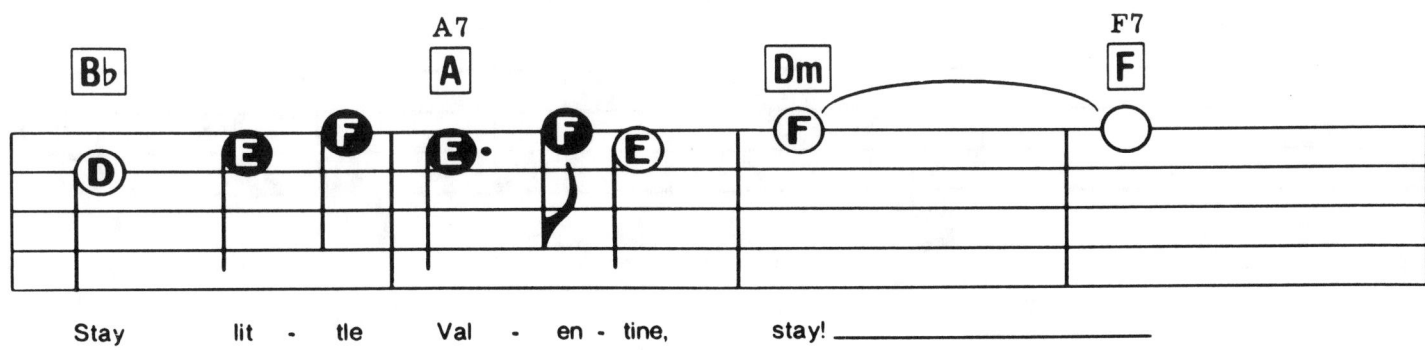

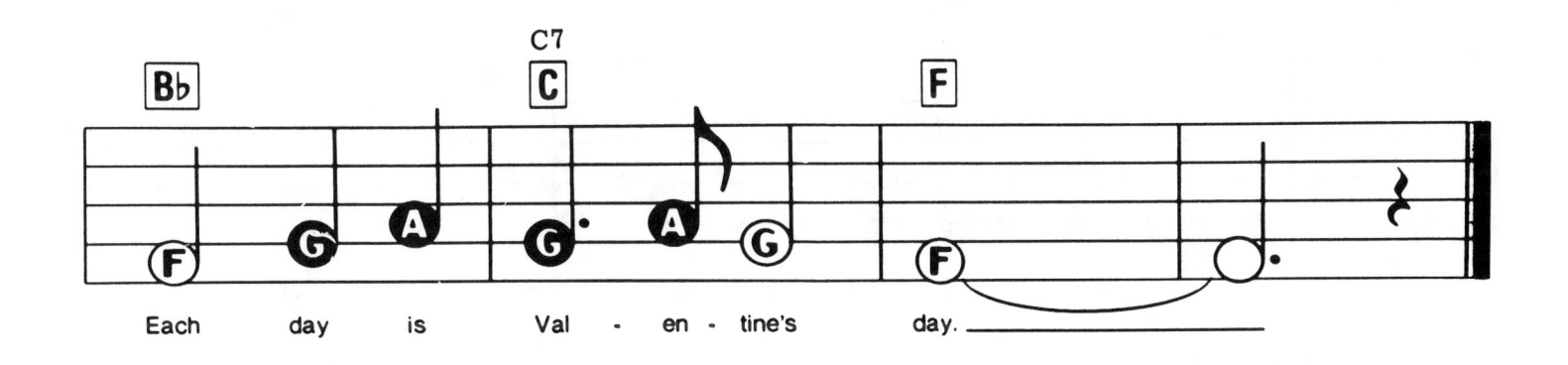

figure less than Greek; Is your mouth a lit-tle weak, when you o-pen it to speak, Are you smart? _____ But don't change a hair for me, Not if you care for me, Stay lit-tle Val-en-tine, stay! _____ Each day is Val-en-tine's day. _____

My Heart Will Go On
(Love Theme from 'Titanic')
from the Paramount and Twentieth Century Fox Motion Picture TITANIC

Registration 8
Rhythm: Ballad

Music by James Horner
Lyric by Will Jennings

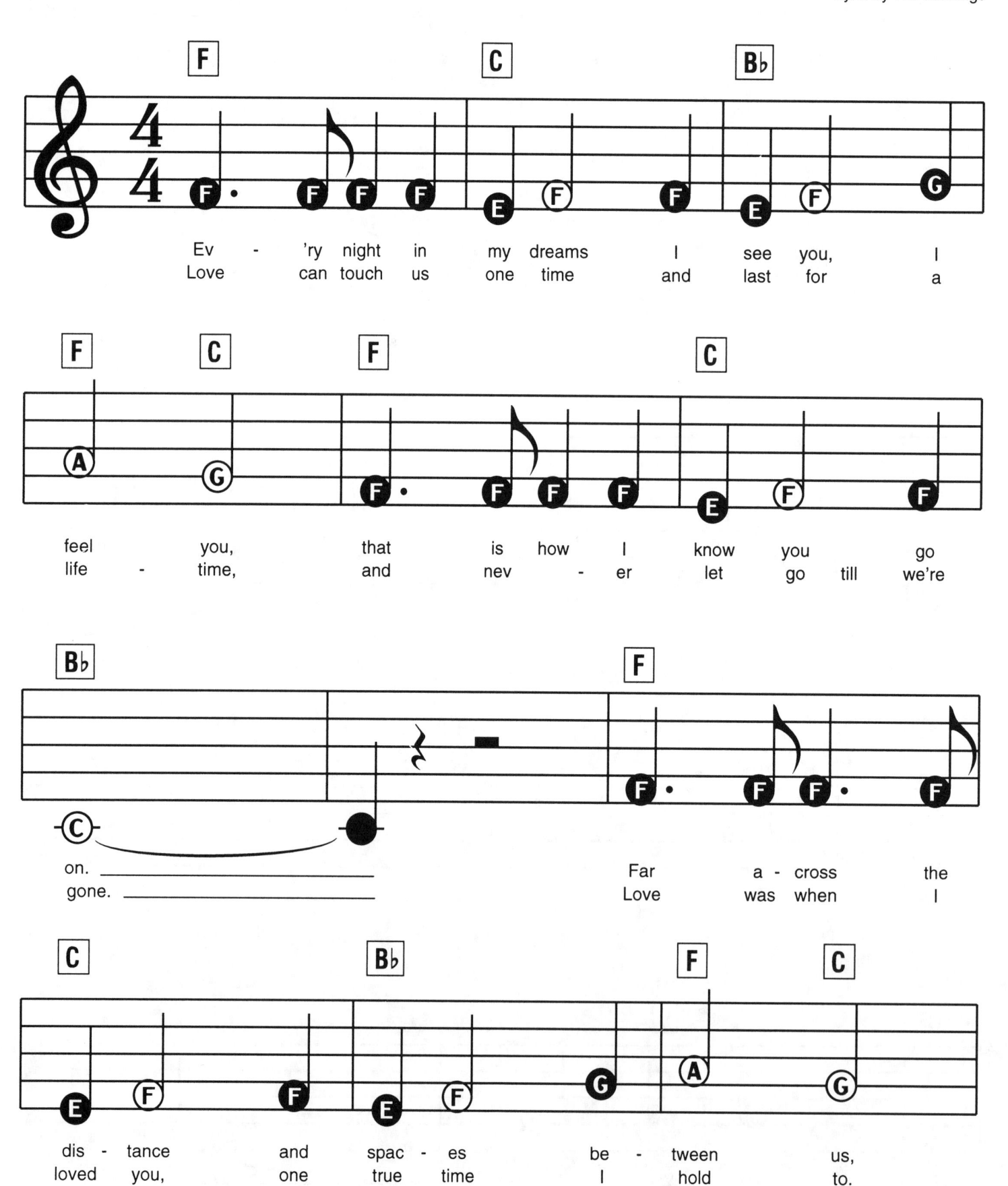

Ev - 'ry night in my dreams I see you, I
Love can touch us one time and last for a

feel you, that is how I know you go
life - time, and nev - er let you go till we're

on.
gone.

Far a - cross the
Love was when I

dis - tance and spac - es be - tween us,
loved you, one true time I hold to.

Copyright © 1997 by Famous Music Corporation, Ensign Music Corporation, TCF Music Publishing, Inc., Fox Film Music Corporation and Blue Sky Rider Songs
All Rights for Blue Sky Rider Songs Administered by Irving Music, Inc.
International Copyright Secured   All Rights Reserved

105

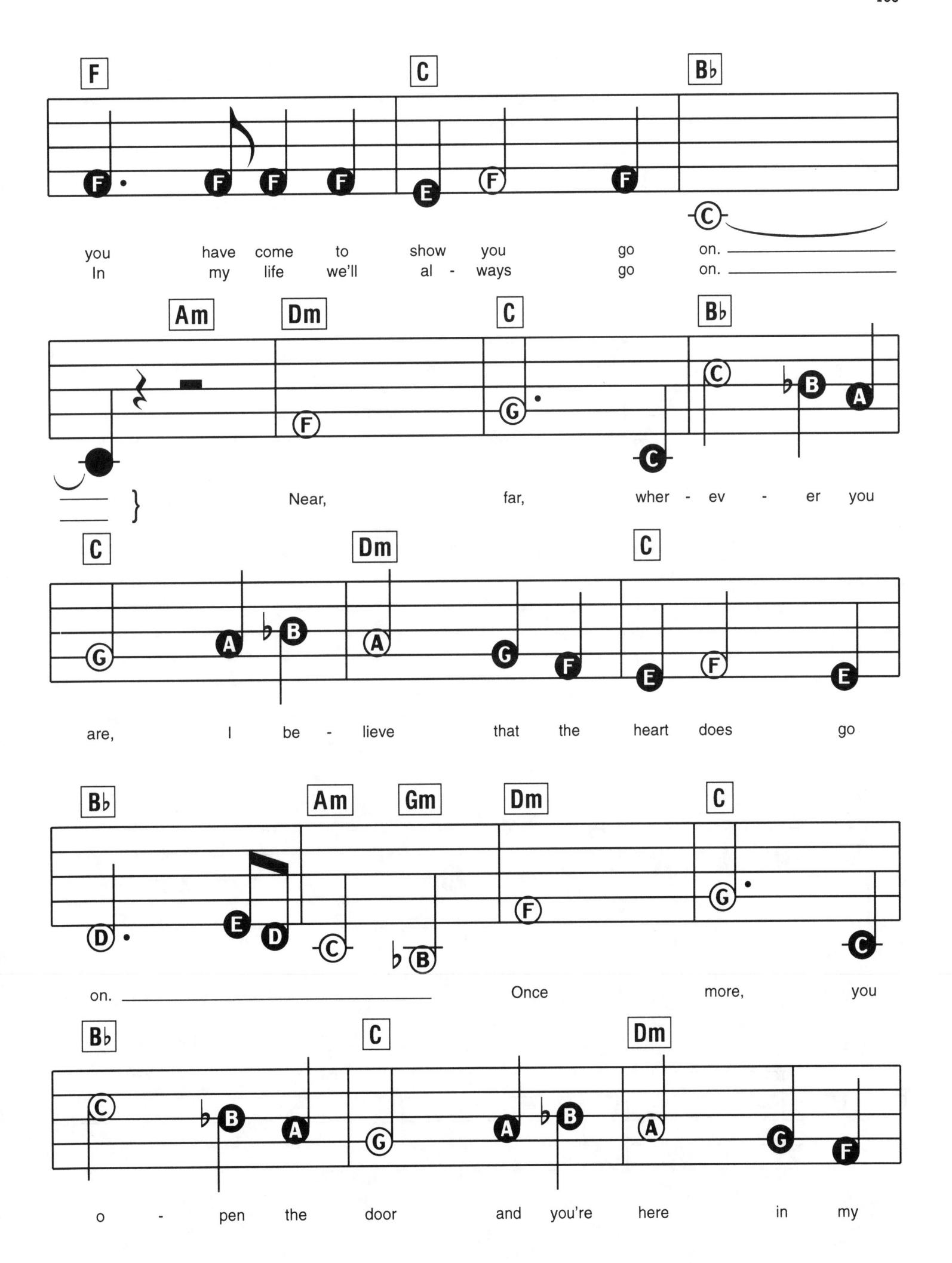

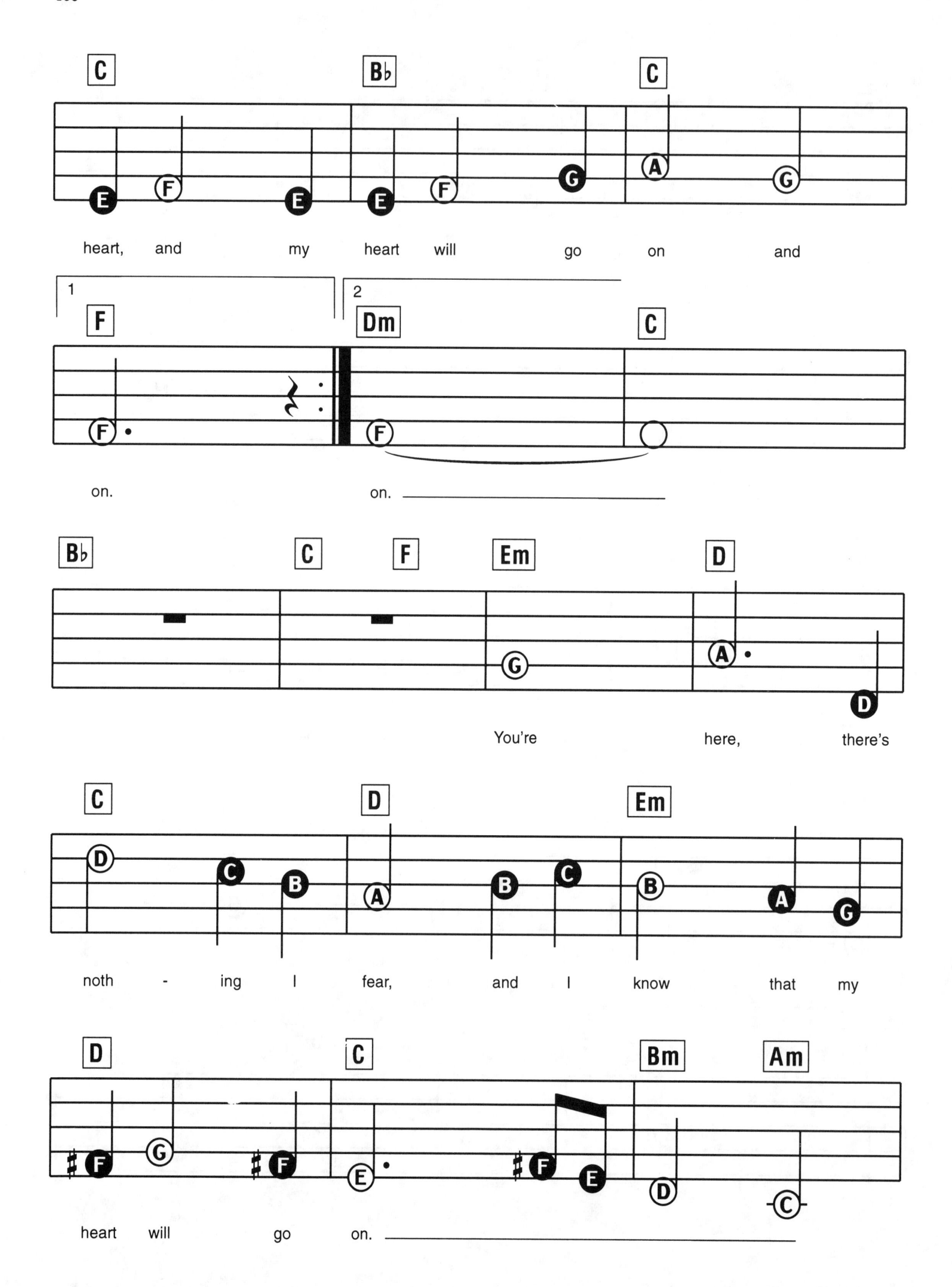

heart, and my heart will go on and

on. on.

You're here, there's

noth-ing I fear, and I know that my

heart will go on.

107

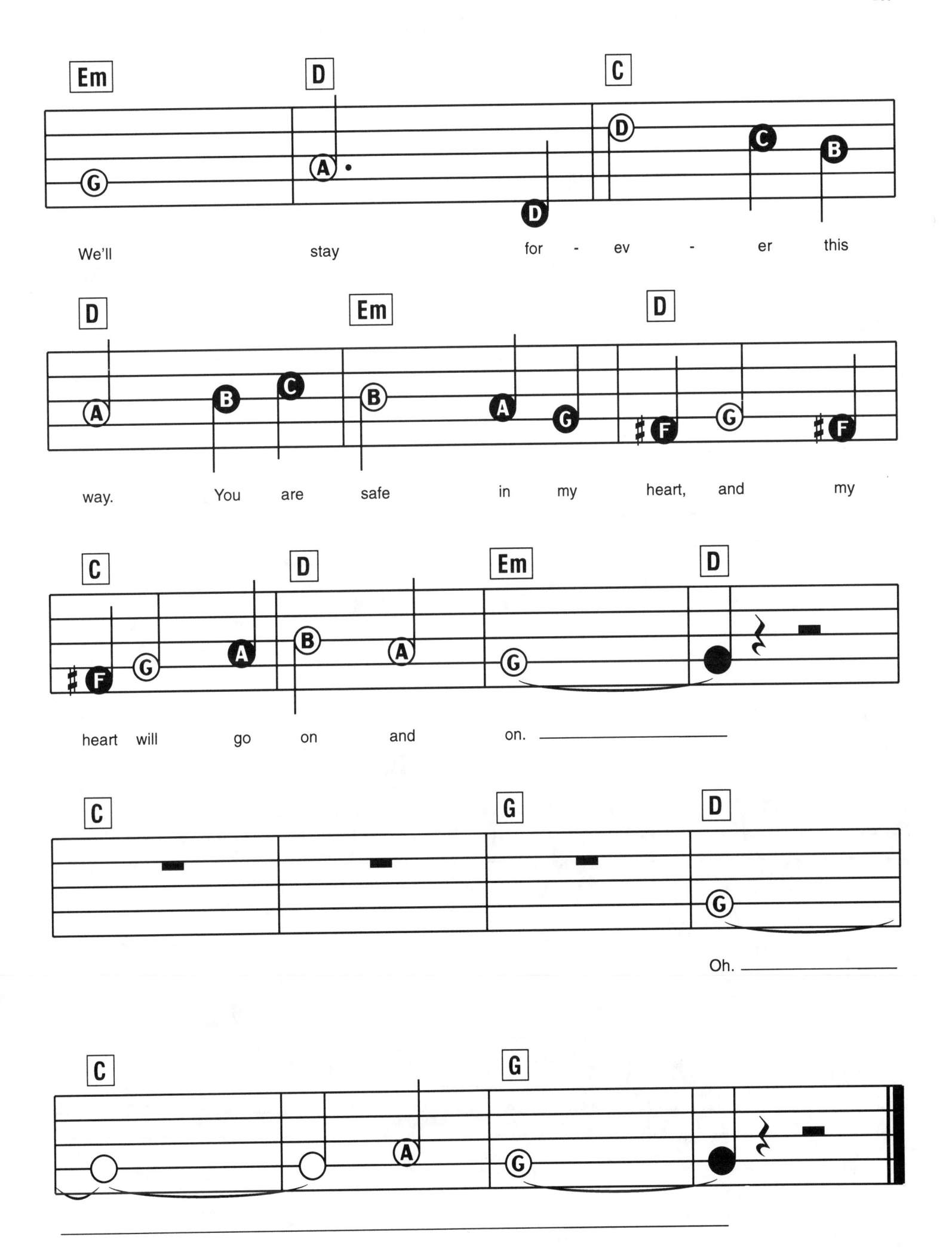

Ribbon in the Sky

Registration 2
Rhythm: 8 Beat or Rock

Words and Music by
Stevie Wonder

Oh, so long for this night I prayed that a
lowed, may I touch your hand, and if

star would guide you my way to share with me the
pleased may I once a-gain, so that you too will

spe - cial day where a rib - bon's in the sky for our
un - der - stand there's a

love. If al - rib - bon in the sky for our

© 1982 JOBETE MUSIC CO., INC. and BLACK BULL MUSIC
c/o EMI APRIL MUSIC INC.
All Rights Reserved International Copyright Secured Used by Permission

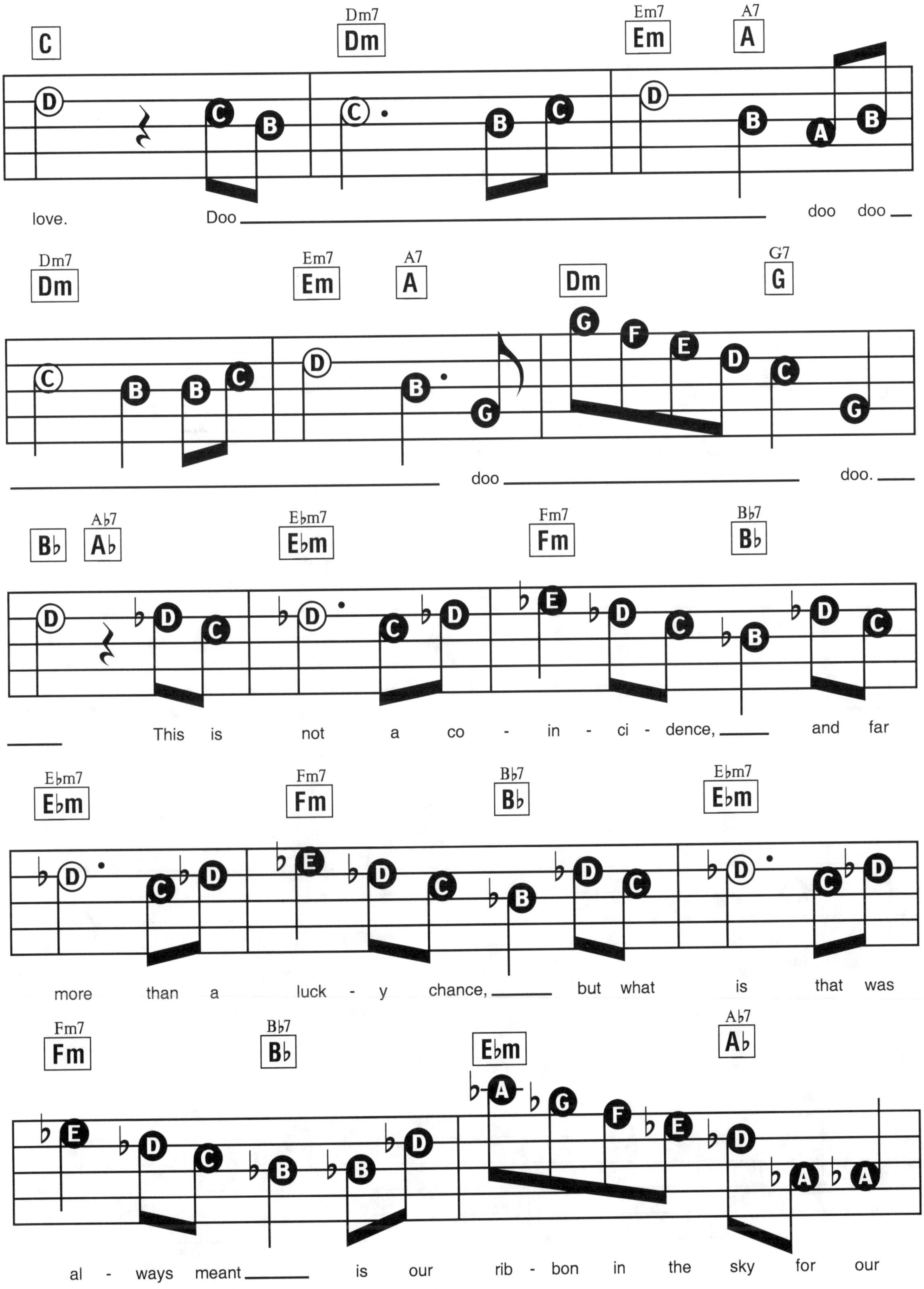
C Dm7 Dm Em7 Em A7 A
love. Doo doo doo
Dm7 Dm Em7 Em A7 A Dm G7 G
doo doo.
B♭ A♭7 A♭ E♭m7 E♭m Fm7 Fm B♭7 B♭
This is not a co - in - ci - dence, and far
E♭m7 E♭m Fm7 Fm B♭7 B♭ E♭m7 E♭m
more than a luck - y chance, but what is that was
Fm7 Fm B♭7 B♭ E♭m A♭7 A♭
al - ways meant is our rib - bon in the sky for our

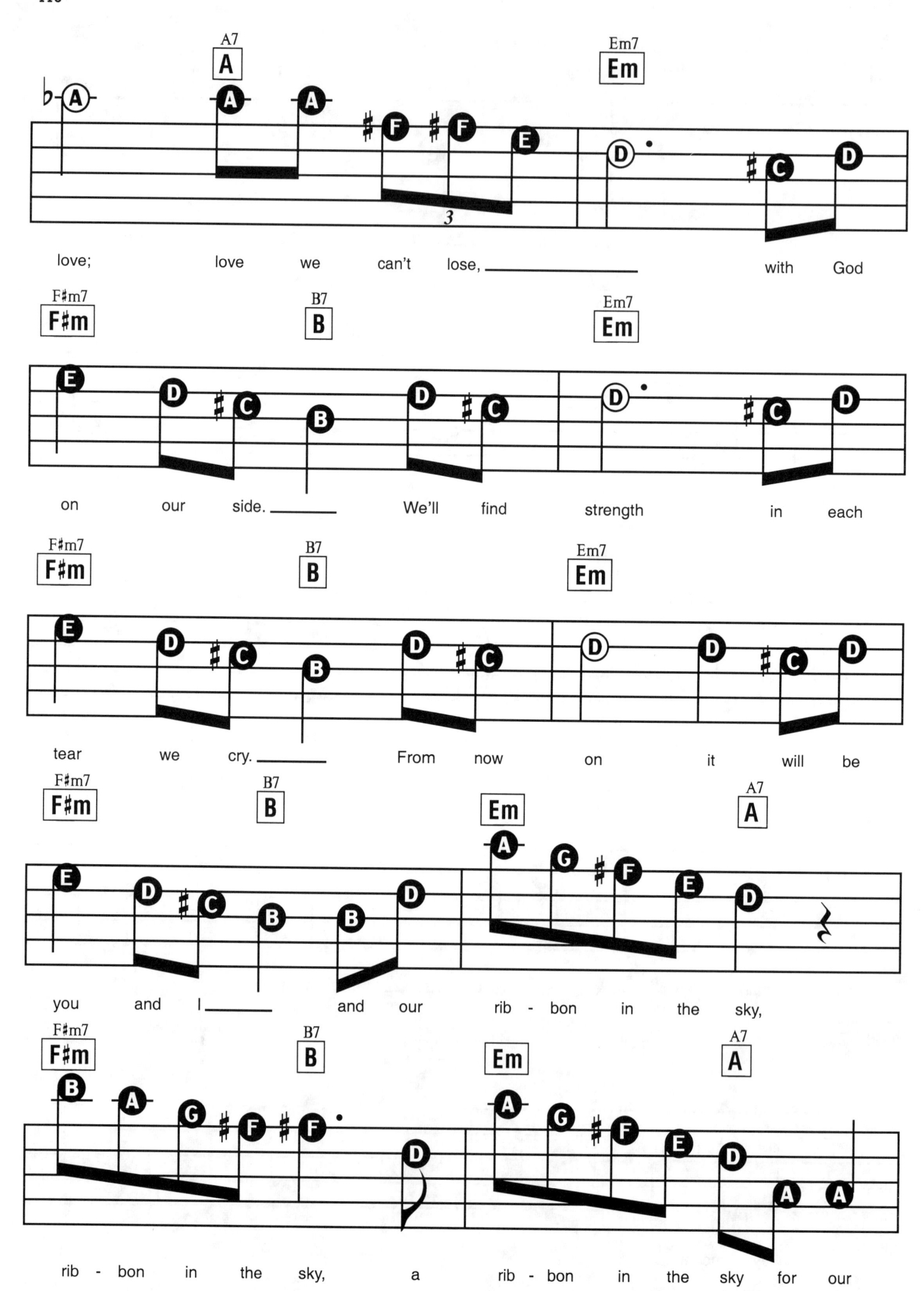

love; love we can't lose, _____ with God on our side. _____ We'll find strength in each tear we cry. _____ From now on it will be you and I _____ and our rib-bon in the sky, rib-bon in the sky, a rib-bon in the sky for our

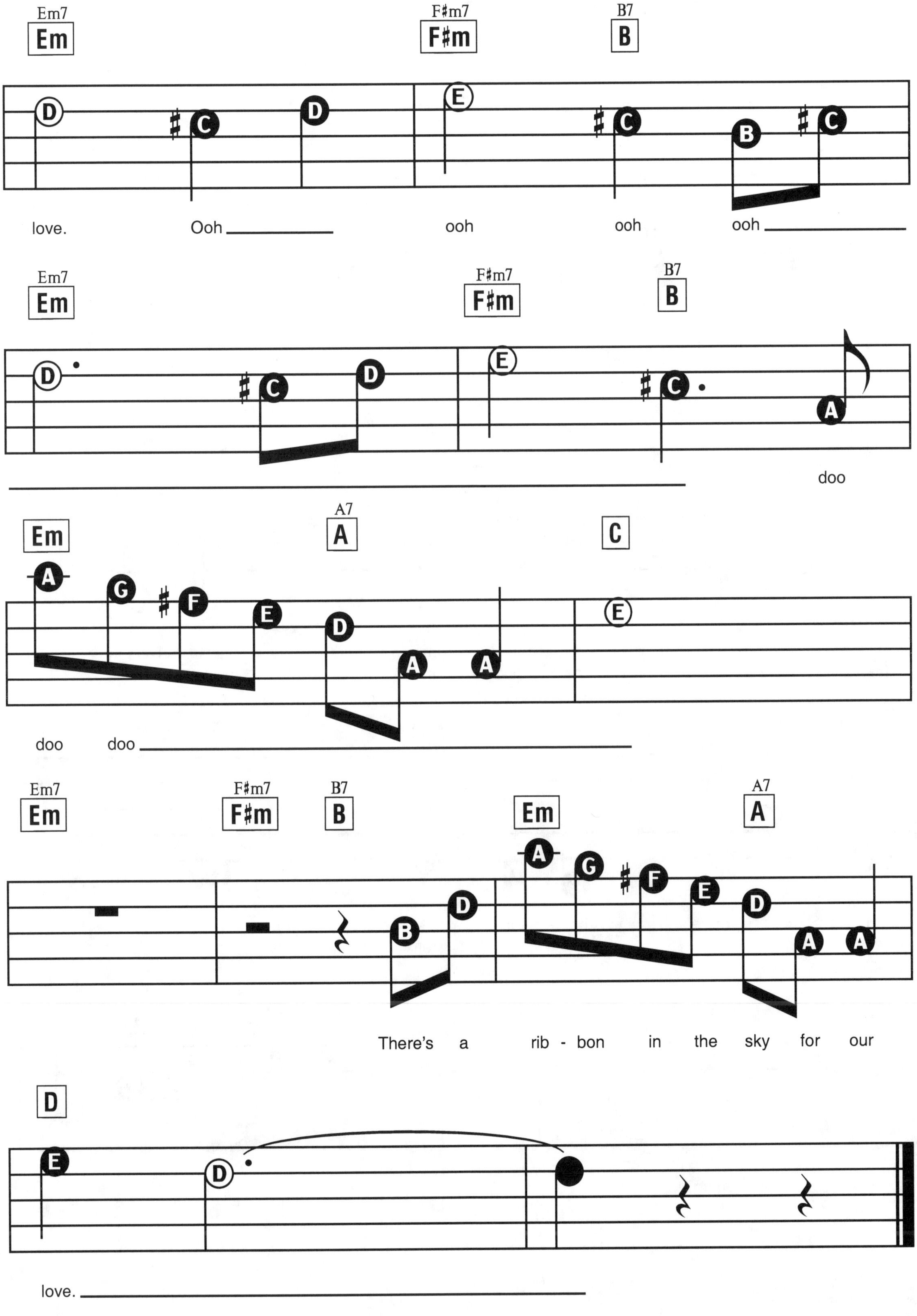
Em7
Em
F♯m7
F♯m
B7
B
love. Ooh
ooh ooh ooh
Em7
Em
F♯m7
F♯m
B7
B
doo
Em
A7
A
C
doo doo
Em7
Em
F♯m7
F♯m
B7
B
Em
A7
A
There's a rib - bon in the sky for our
D
love.

Saving All My Love for You

Registration 1
Rhythm: Rock or Slow Rock

Words by Gerry Goffin
Music by Michael Masser

A few sto-len mo-ments is all that we share.
not ver-y eas-y living all a-lone. My

You've got your fam-'ly and they need you there. Though I
friends try to tell me find a man of my own. But

try to re-sist, be-ing last on your list, but
each time I try, I just break down and cry. 'Cause I'd

no oth-er man's gon-na do,
rath-er be home feel-in' blue, } so I'm sav-ing all my love for

© 1978 SCREEN GEMS-EMI MUSIC INC., LAUREN-WESLEY MUSIC INC. and PRINCE STREET MUSIC
All Rights for LAUREN-WESLEY MUSIC INC. Controlled and Administered by SCREEN GEMS-EMI MUSIC INC.
All Rights Reserved   International Copyright Secured   Used by Permission

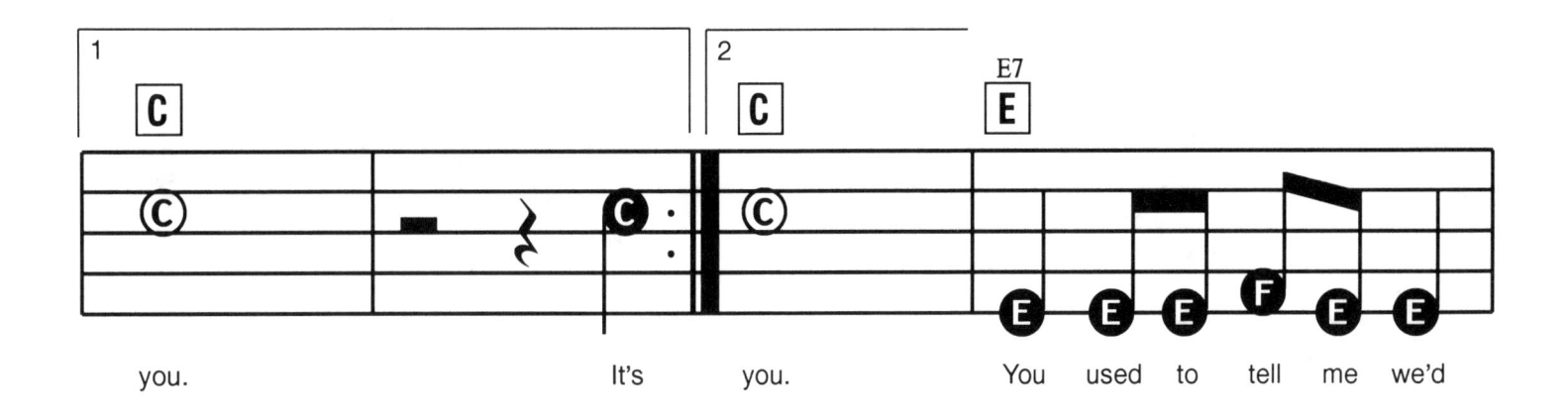

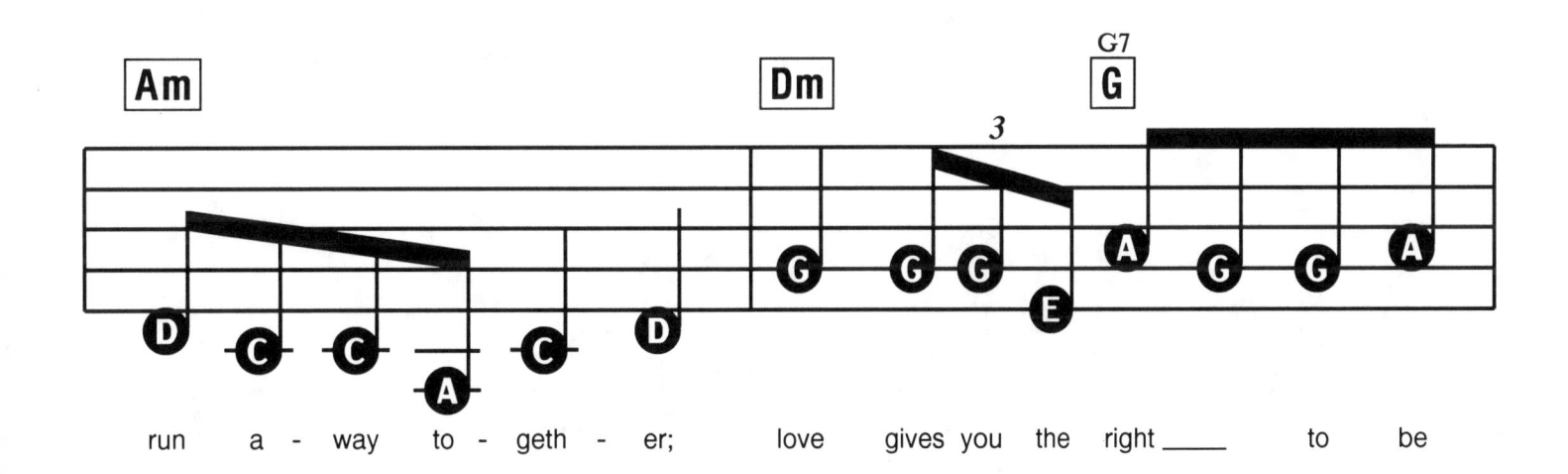

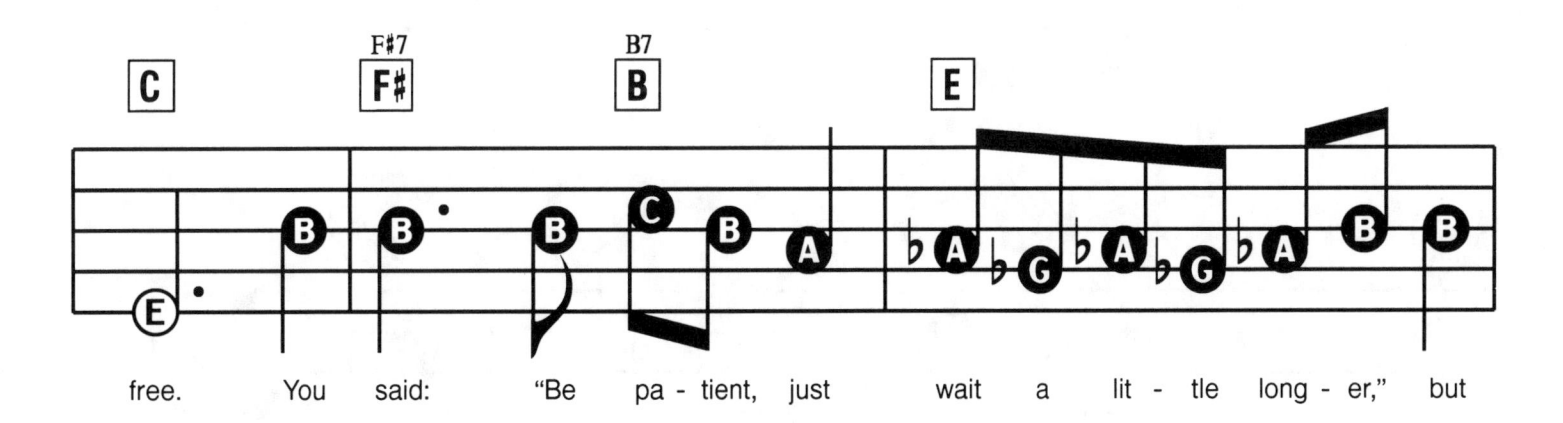

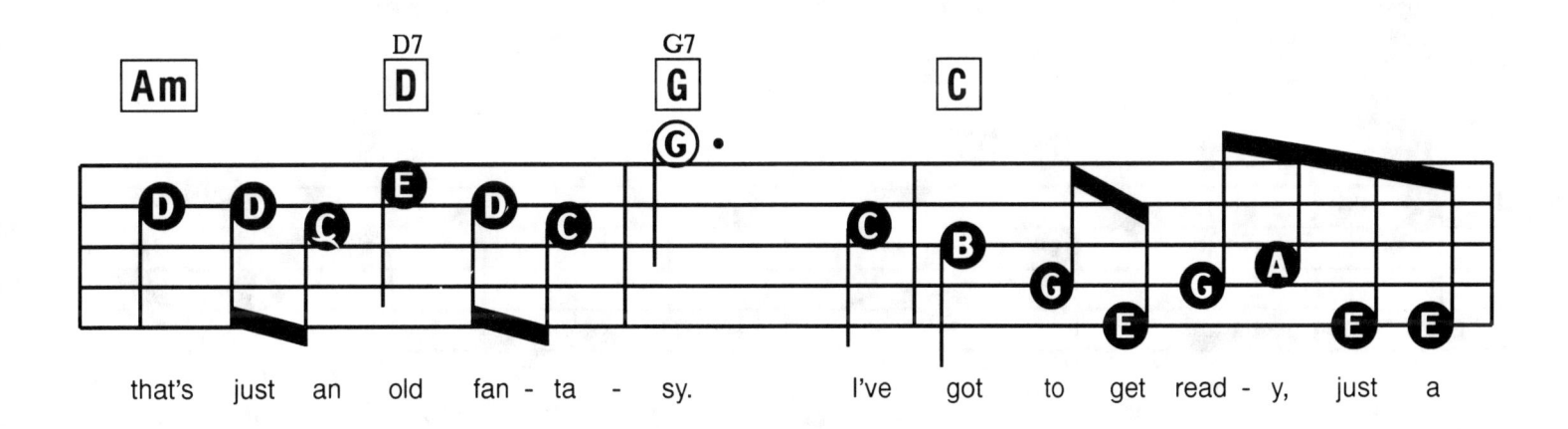

you. It's you. You used to tell me we'd

run a-way to-geth-er; love gives you the right ___ to be

free. You said: "Be pa-tient, just wait a lit-tle long-er," but

that's just an old fan-ta-sy. I've got to get read-y, just a few min - utes more. Gon - na get that old feel - ing when you walk through the door. 'Cause to - night is the night for feel - ing all right. We'll be mak - ing love the whole night through, so I'm sav - ing all my love, yes I'm sav - ing all my love, yes I'm sav - ing all my love for

you. _____ No oth-er wom-an is gon-na love you more. 'Cause to-night is the night that I'm feel-ing all right. We'll be mak-ing love the whole night _____ through; _____ so I'm sav-ing all my love, yes I'm sav-ing all my lov-ing, yes I'm sav-ing all my love for you. _____

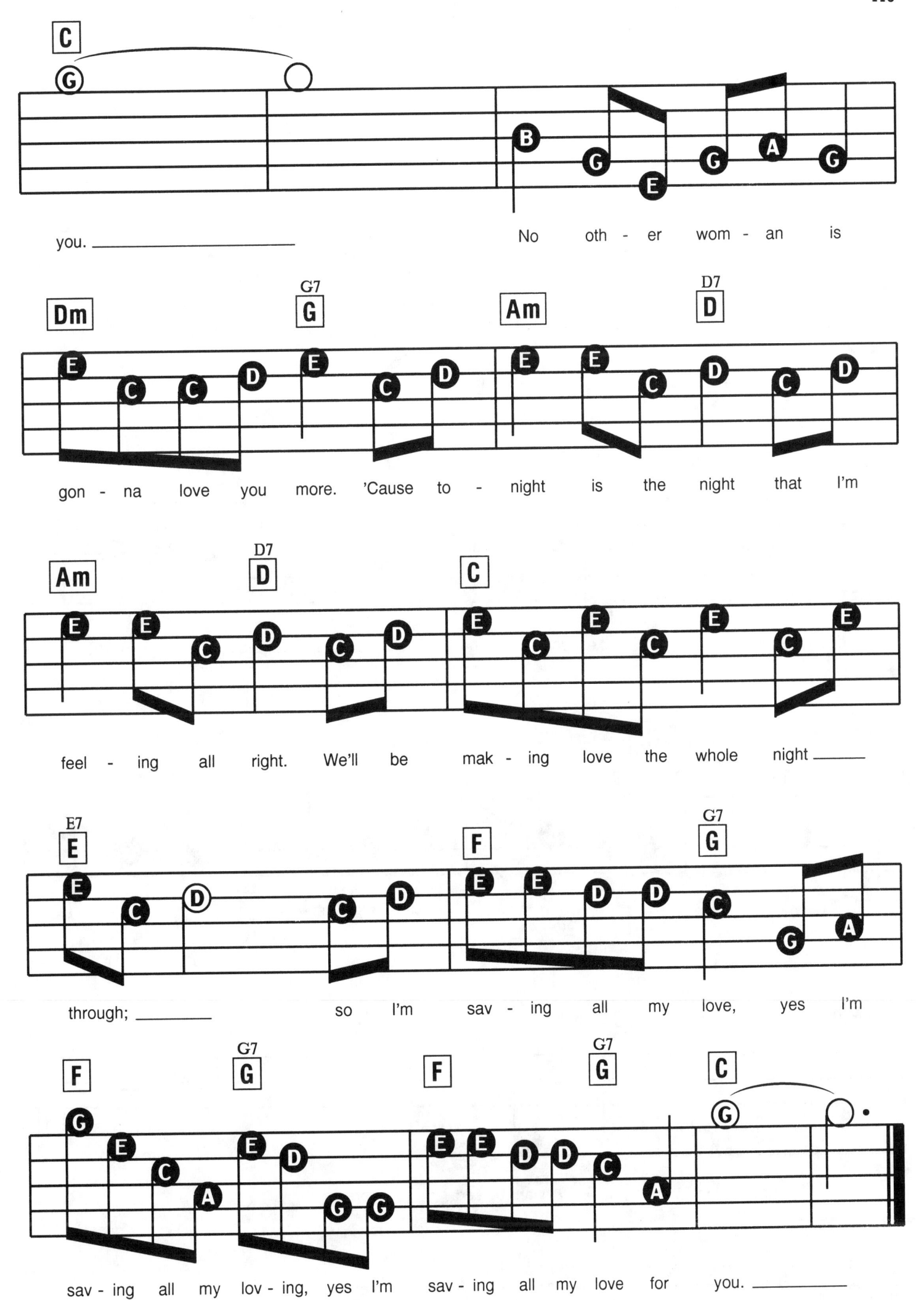

To Love You More

Registration 9
Rhythm: 8 Beat or Rock

Words and Music by David Foster
and Junior Miles

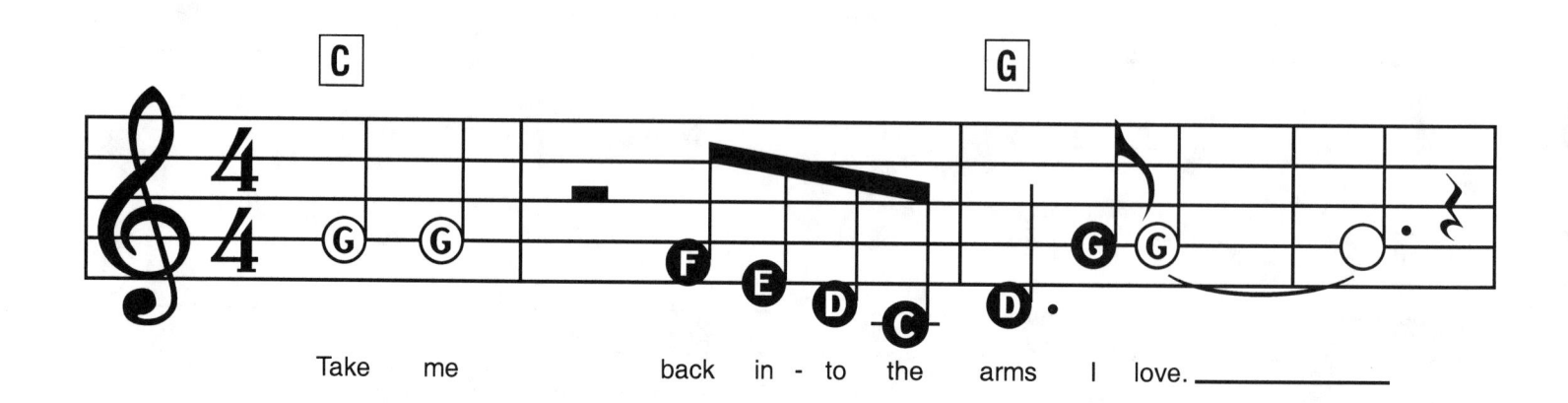

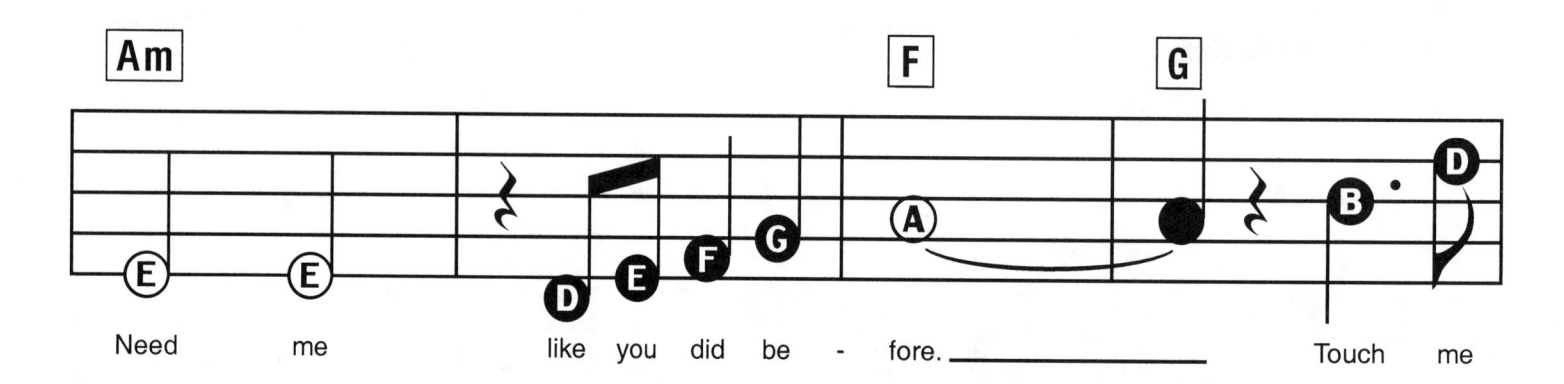

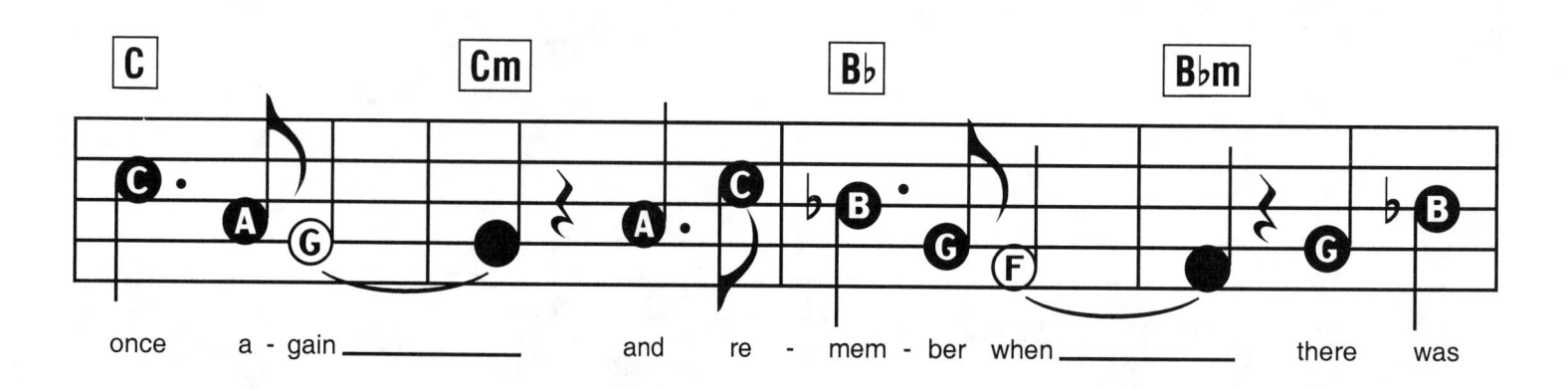

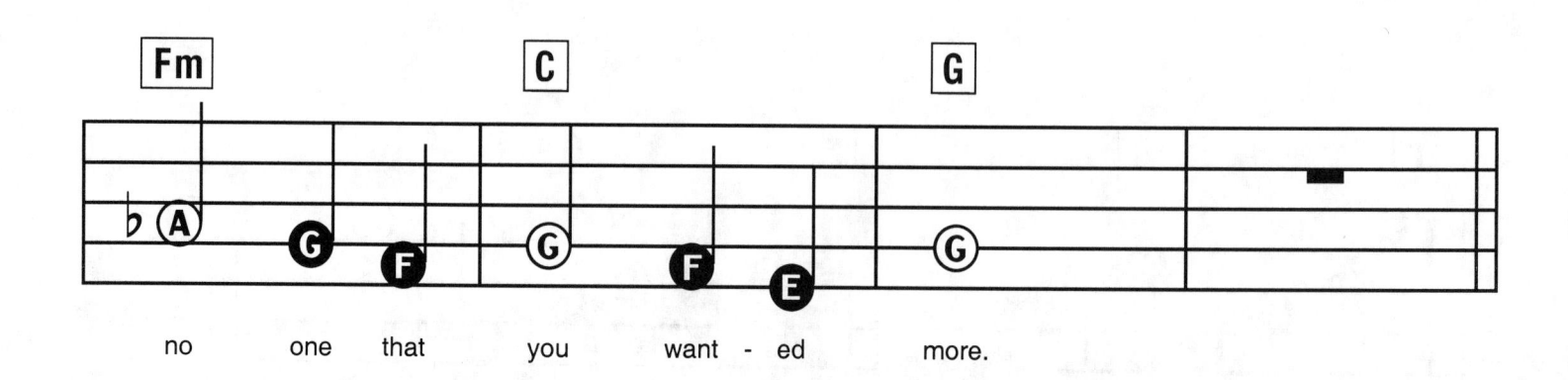

Take me back in-to the arms I love. Need me like you did be-fore. Touch me once a-gain and re-mem-ber when there was no one that you want-ed more.

Copyright © 1995 by One Four Three Music and Boozetunes
All Rights for One Four Three Music Administered by Peermusic Ltd.
All Rights for Boozetunes Controlled and Administered by Universal - MCA Music Publishing, A Division of Universal Studios, Inc.
International Copyright Secured   All Rights Reserved

C			G		

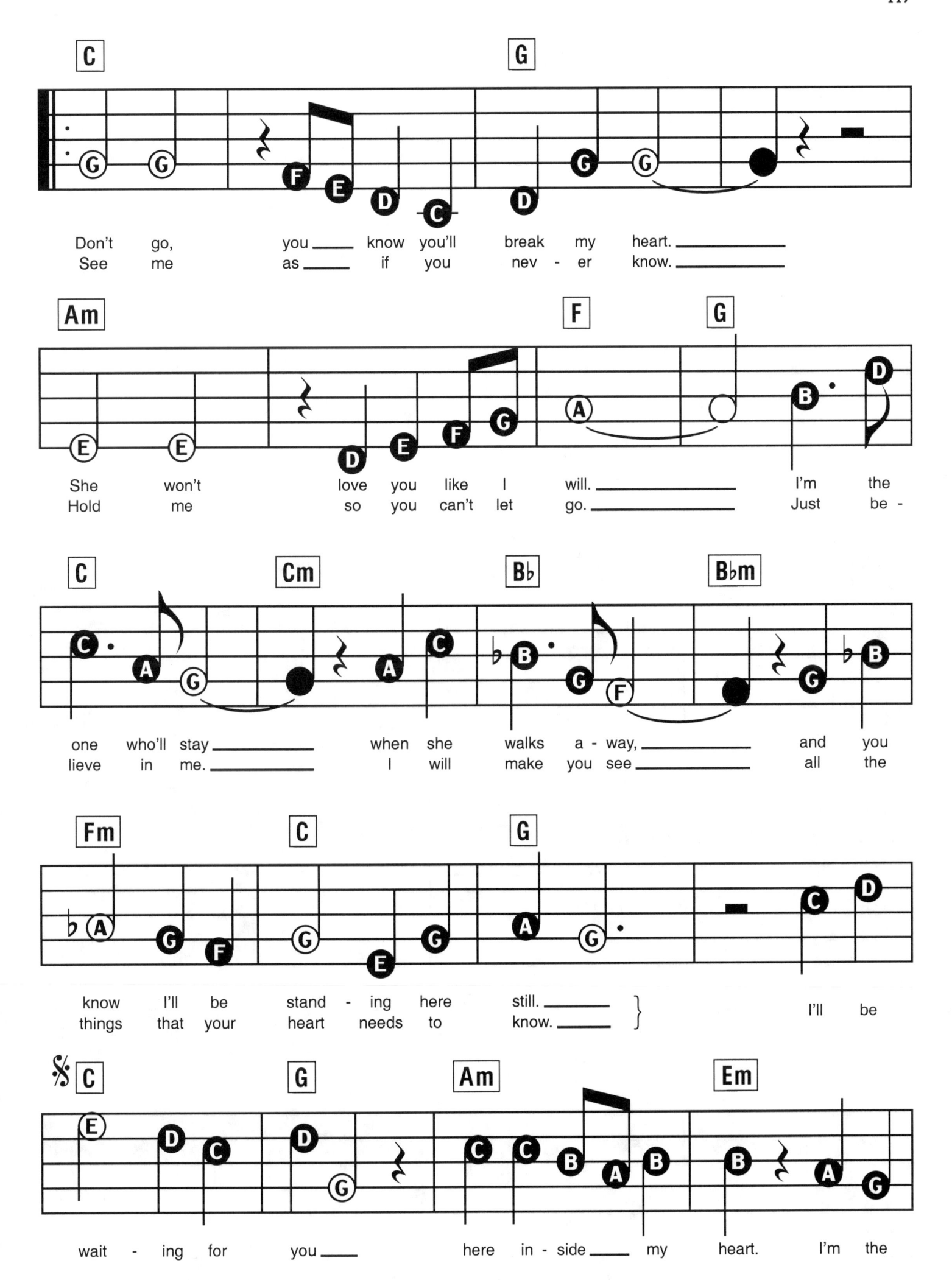

Don't go, you know you'll break my heart.
See me as if you nev-er know.

Am		F	G

She won't love you like I will. I'm the
Hold me so you can't let go. Just be-

C	Cm	Bb	Bbm

one who'll stay when she walks a-way, and you
lieve in me. I will make you see all the

Fm	C	G	

know I'll be stand-ing here still. ⎫ I'll be
things that your heart needs to know. ⎭

C	G	Am	Em

wait-ing for you here in-side my heart. I'm the

one who wants to love you _____ more.

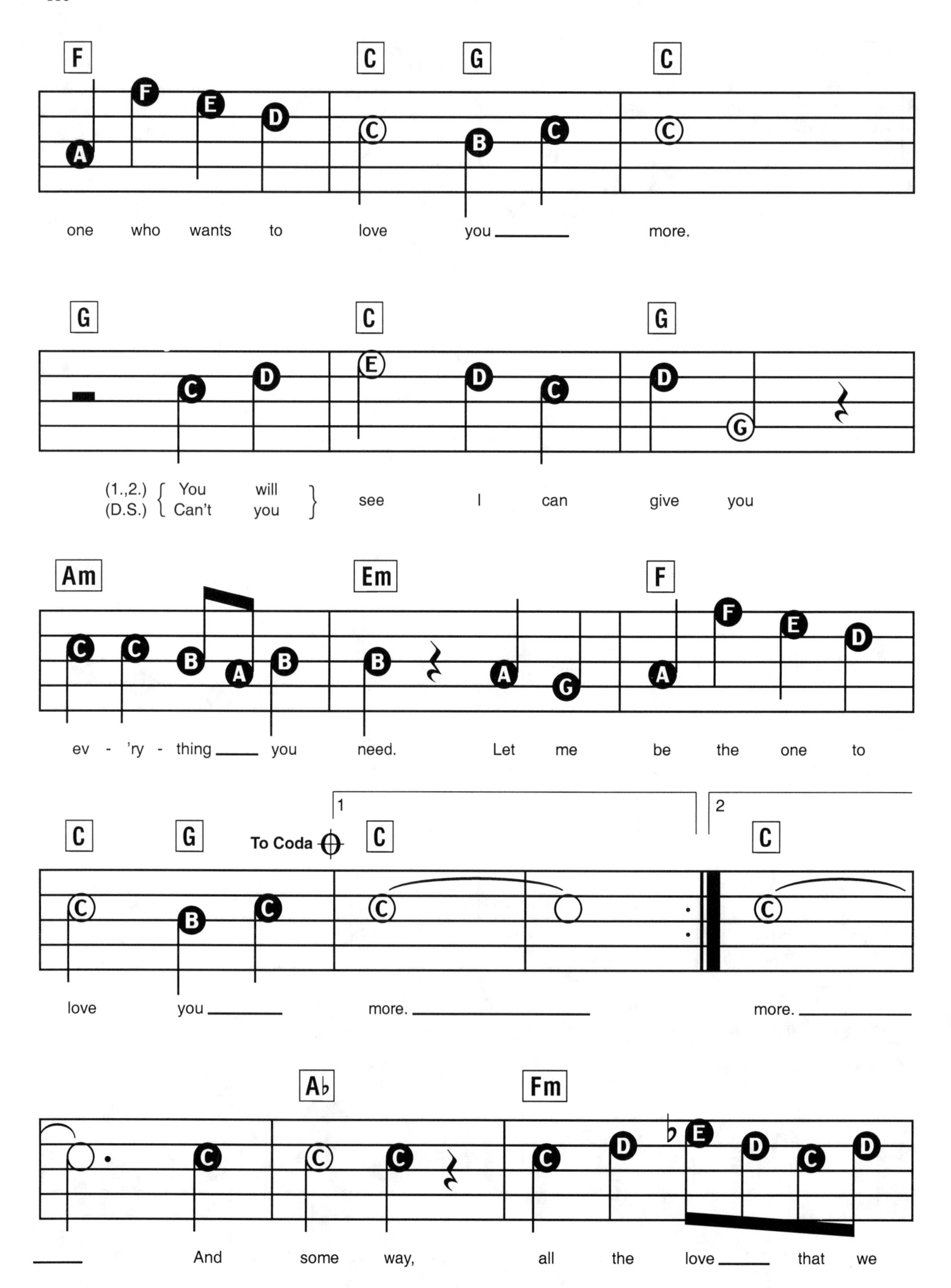

(1.,2.) You will
(D.S.) Can't you } see I can give you

ev - 'ry - thing _____ you need. Let me be the one to

love you _____ more. _____ more. _____

And some way, all the love _____ that we

| C | F | A♭ | Fm |

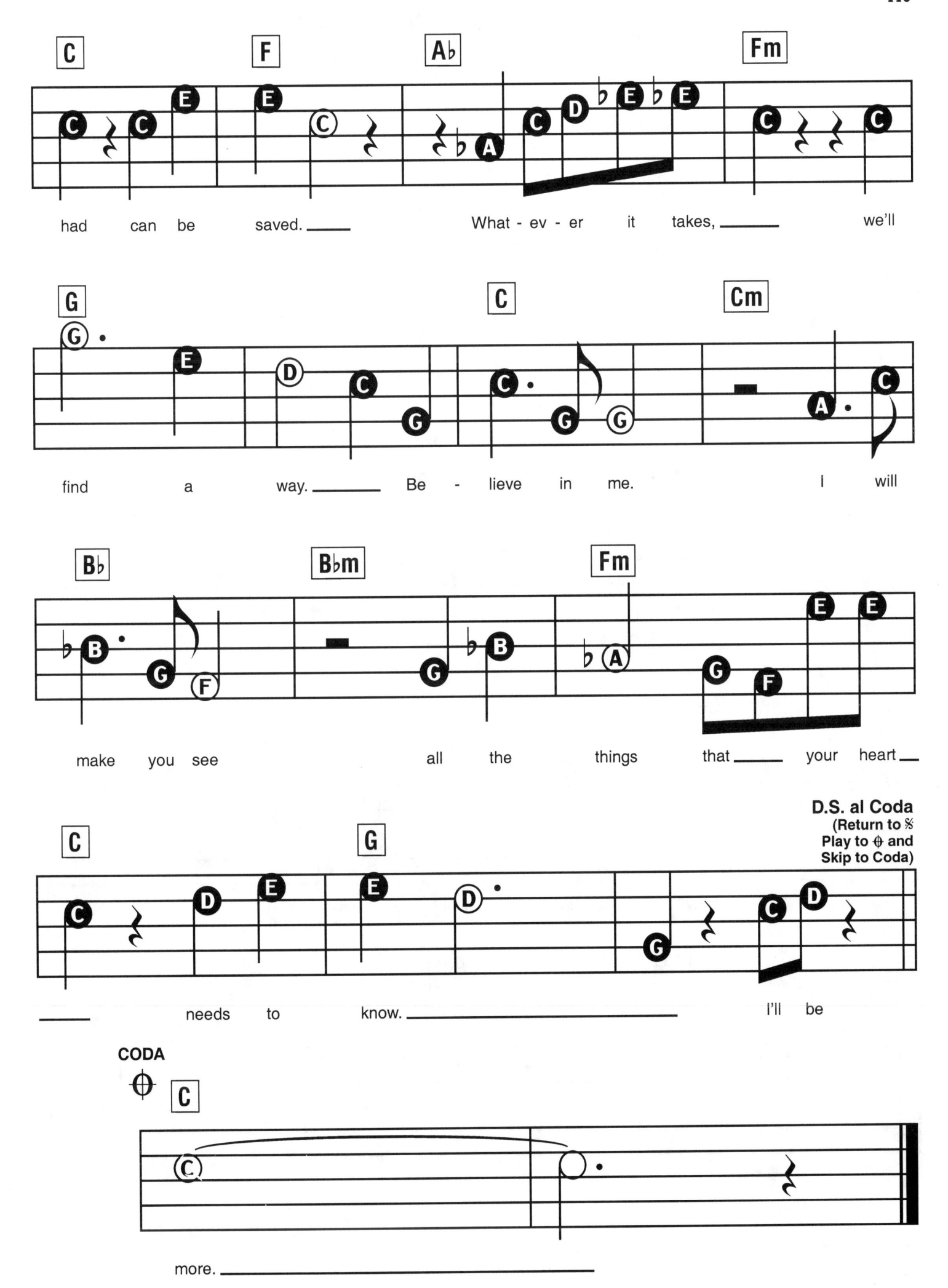

had can be saved. What-ev-er it takes, we'll

| G | C | Cm |

find a way. Be-lieve in me. I will

| B♭ | B♭m | Fm |

make you see all the things that your heart

D.S. al Coda
(Return to 𝄋
Play to ⊕ and
Skip to Coda)

| C | G |

needs to know. I'll be

CODA
⊕ | C |

more.

Unchained Melody
from the Motion Picture UNCHAINED

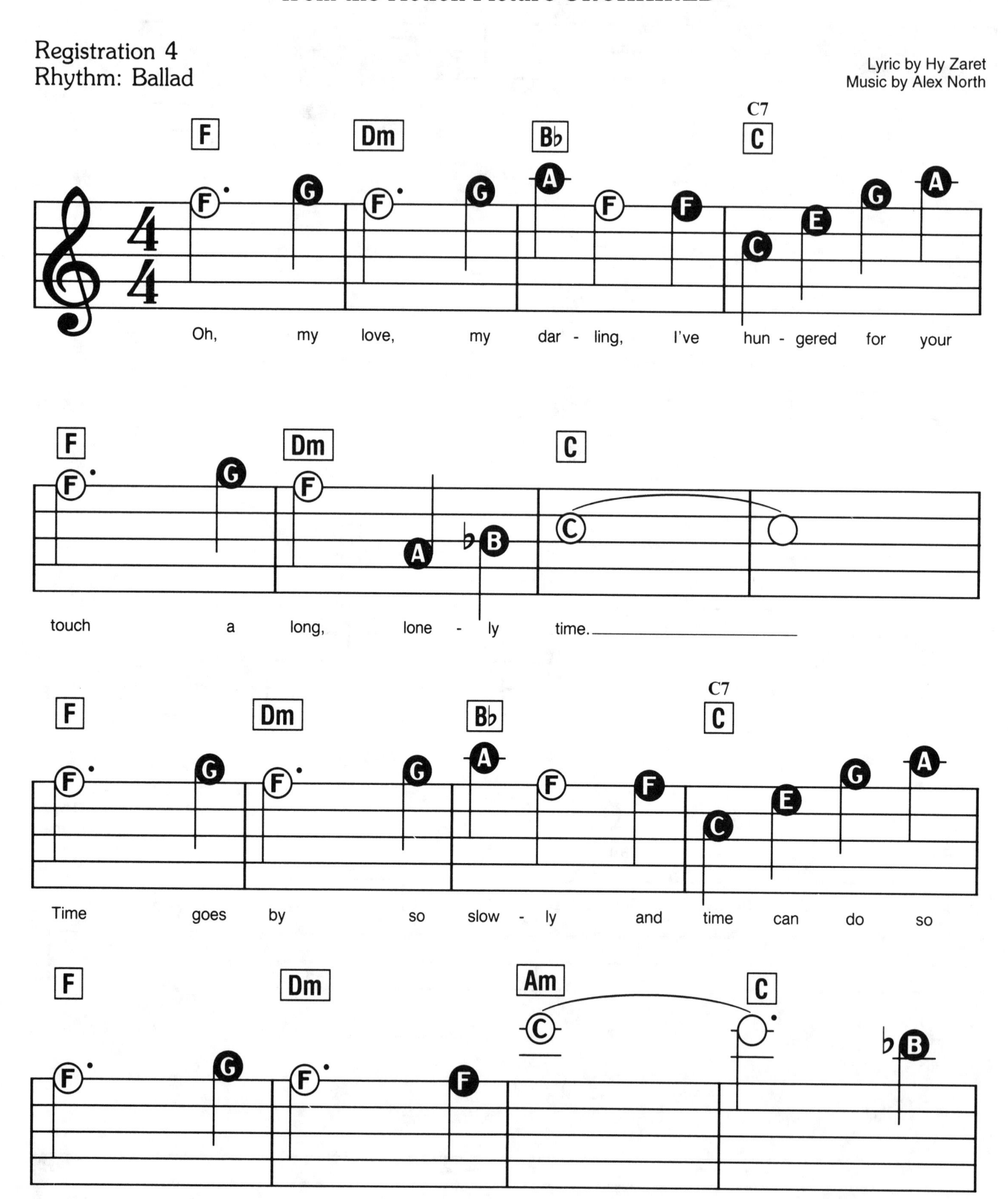

Registration 4
Rhythm: Ballad

Lyric by Hy Zaret
Music by Alex North

Oh, my love, my dar - ling, I've hun - gered for your touch a long, lone - ly time.

Time goes by so slow - ly and time can do so much, Are you still mine?

© 1955 (Renewed) FRANK MUSIC CORP.
All Rights Reserved

need your love. _____ I need your love. _____ God
speed your love _____ to me! _____

Lone - ly riv - ers flow to the sea, to the
Lone - ly riv - ers sigh, "Wait for me, wait for

sea. To the o - pen arms of the
me! I'll be com - ing home, wait for

sea. _____
me!" _____

D.C. al Fine
(Return to beginning
Play to Fine)

Valentine

Registration 8
Rhythm: Pops or Rock

Words and Music by Jack Kugell
and Jim Brickman

If there were no words, no way to speak,
All of my life, I have been wait-ing for

I would still hear you. If there were no
all you give to me. You've o-pened my

tears, no way to feel in-side, I'd still feel for you. And
eyes and shown me how to love un-self-ish-ly. I've

(1., D.S.) e - ven if the sun re - fused to
(2.) dreamed of this a thou - sand times be -

© 1996 EMI APRIL MUSIC INC., DOXIE MUSIC, MULTISONGS, INC., A Division of CAREERS-BMG MUSIC PUBLISHING, INC. and BRICKMAN ARRANGEMENT
All Rights for DOXIE MUSIC Controlled and Administered by EMI APRIL MUSIC INC.
All Rights for BRICKMAN ARRANGEMENT Administered by MULTISONGS, INC., A Division of CAREERS-BMG MUSIC PUBLISHING, INC.
All Rights Reserved   International Copyright Secured   Used by Permission

shine, e - ven if ro - mance ran out of rhyme,
fore, but in my dreams I could - n't love you more.

you would still have my heart un -
I will still give you my heart un -

til the end of time. You're all I need, my love,
til the end of time. 'Cause all I need is you,

1.
___ my val - en - tine.

2.
___ my val - en - tine.

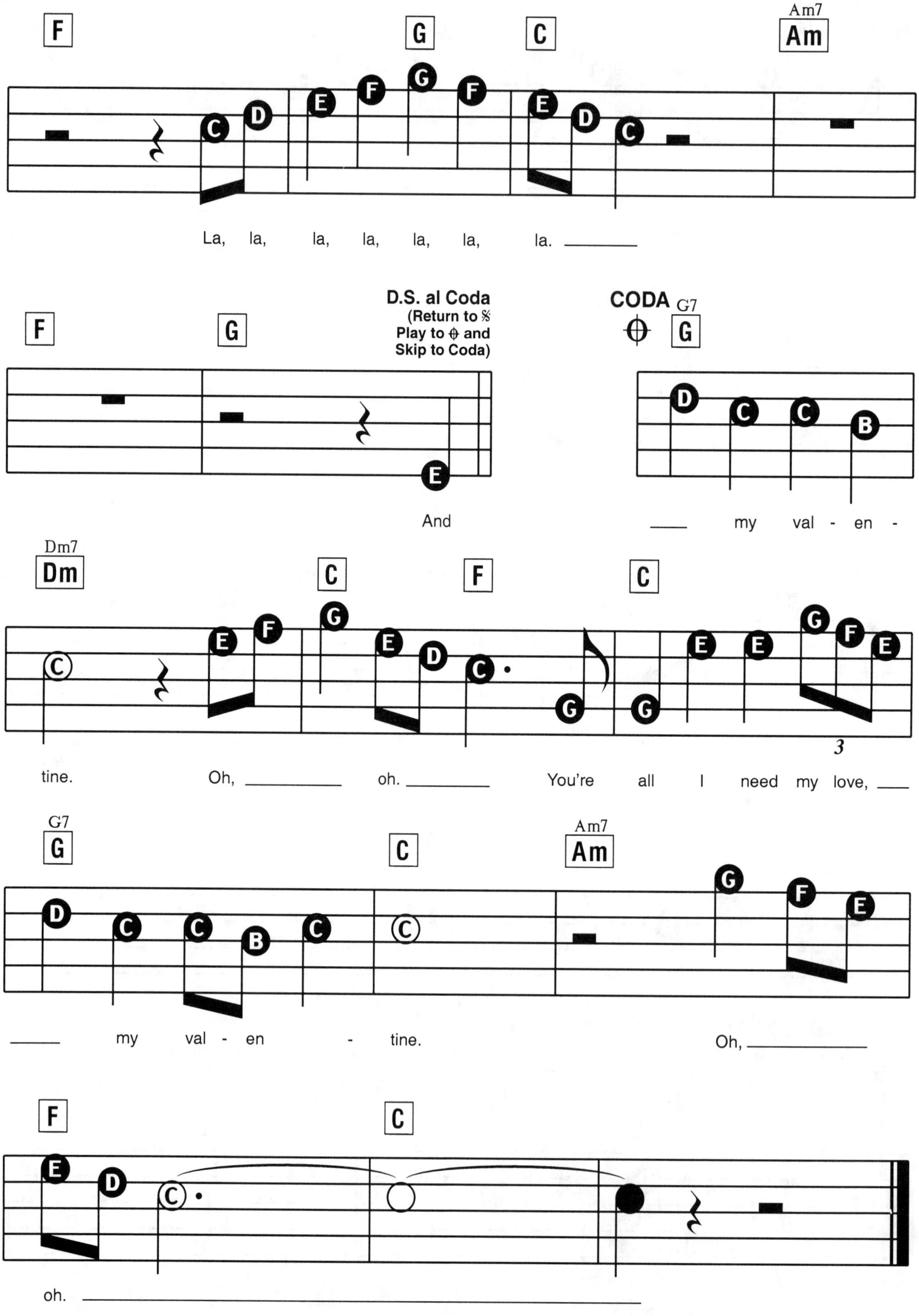
F G C Am7 Am
La, la, la, la, la, la, la.
F G
D.S. al Coda
(Return to 𝄋
Play to ⊕ and
Skip to Coda)
And
CODA G7 G
my val - en -
Dm7 Dm C F C
tine. Oh, oh. You're all I need my love,
3
G7 G C Am7 Am
my val - en - tine. Oh,
F C
oh.

A Whole New World
from Walt Disney's ALADDIN

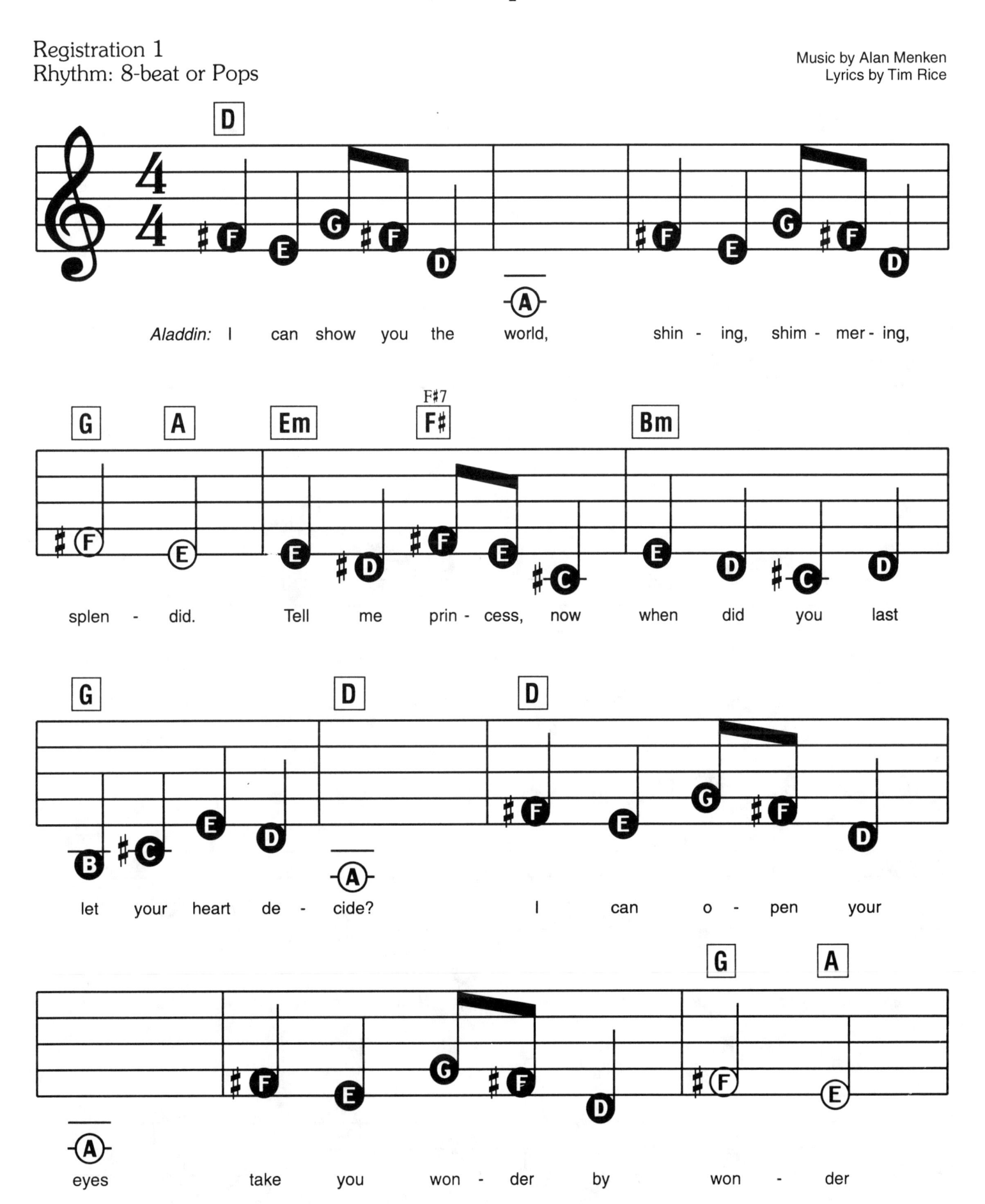

Registration 1
Rhythm: 8-beat or Pops

Music by Alan Menken
Lyrics by Tim Rice

Aladdin: I can show you the world, shin - ing, shim - mer - ing, splen - did. Tell me prin - cess, now when did you last let your heart de - cide? I can o - pen your eyes take you won - der by won - der

© 1992 Wonderland Music Company, Inc. and Walt Disney Music Company
All Rights Reserved Used by Permission

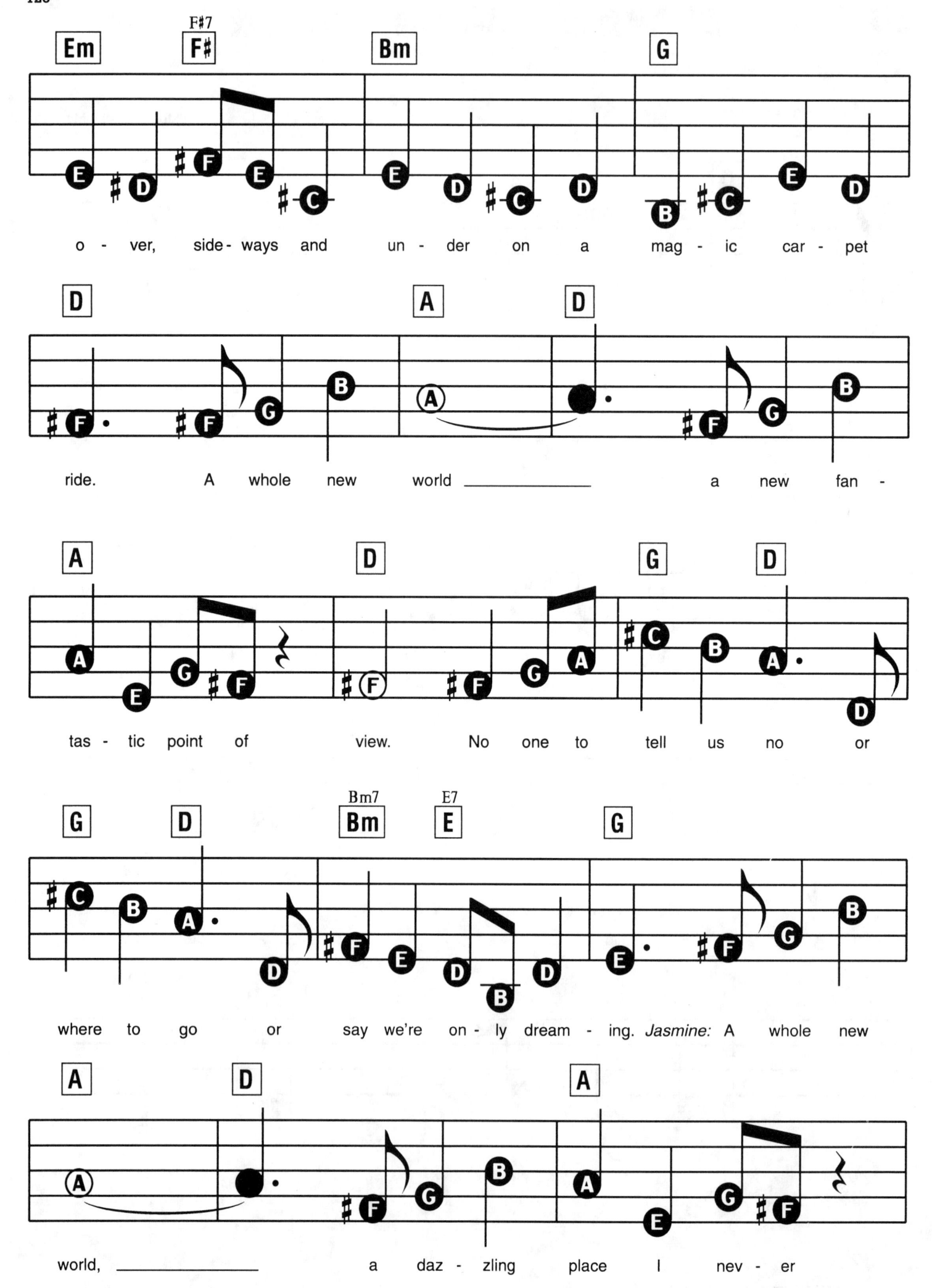

o - ver, side - ways and un - der on a mag - ic car - pet ride. A whole new world _____ a new fan - tas - tic point of view. No one to tell us no or where to go or say we're on - ly dream - ing. *Jasmine:* A whole new world, _____ a daz - zling place I nev - er

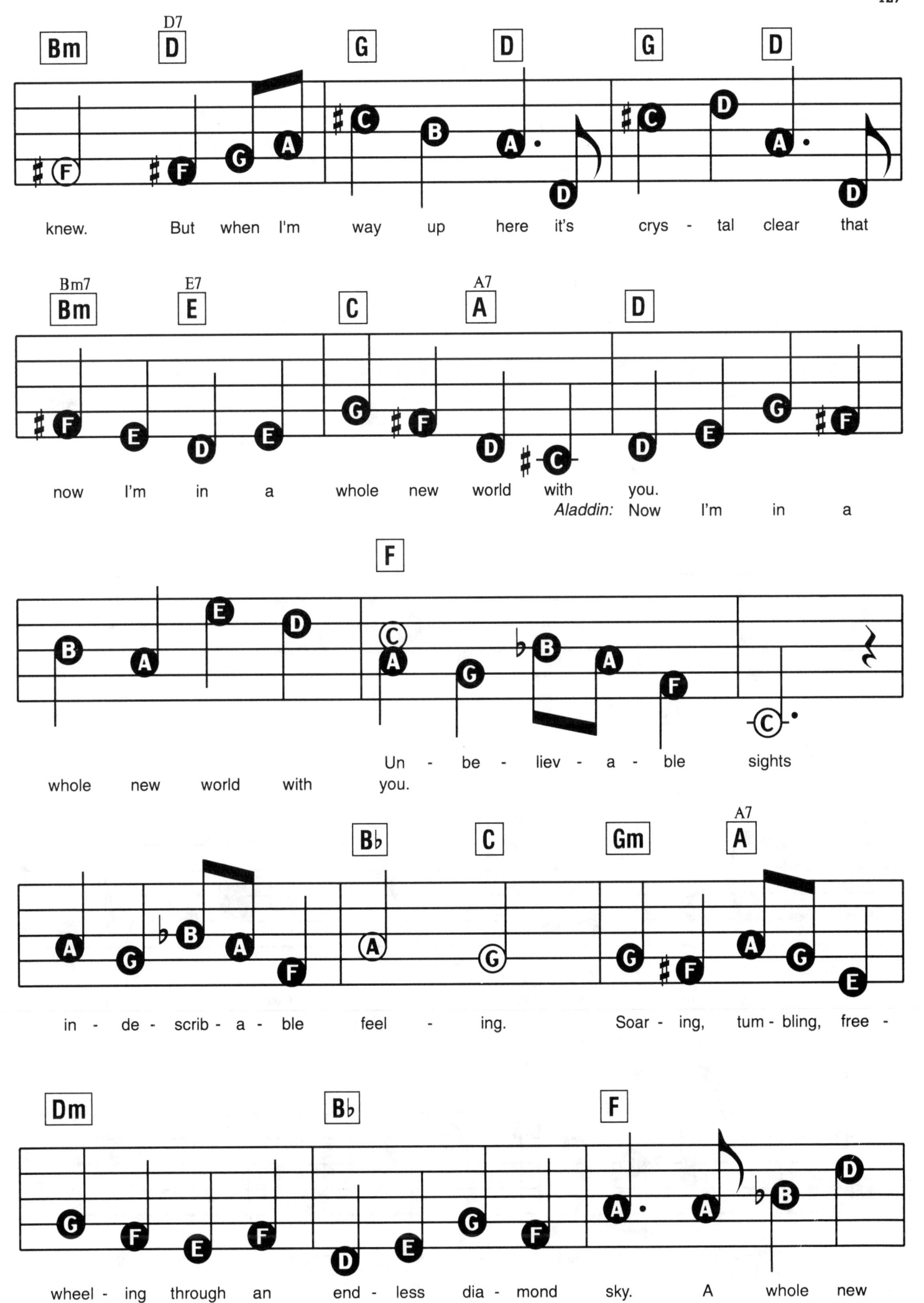

knew. But when I'm way up here it's crys - tal clear that now I'm in a whole new world with you. *Aladdin:* Now I'm in a whole new world with you. Un - be - liev - a - ble sights in - de - scrib - a - ble feel - ing. Soar - ing, tum - bling, free - wheel - ing through an end - less dia - mond sky. A whole new world, _____ a hun-dred thou-sand things to see. I'm like a shoot-ing star I've come so far I can't go back to where I used to be. Ev-'ry turn a sur-prise. Ev-'ry mo-ment red let-ter. I'll chase them an-y-where. There's time to spare.

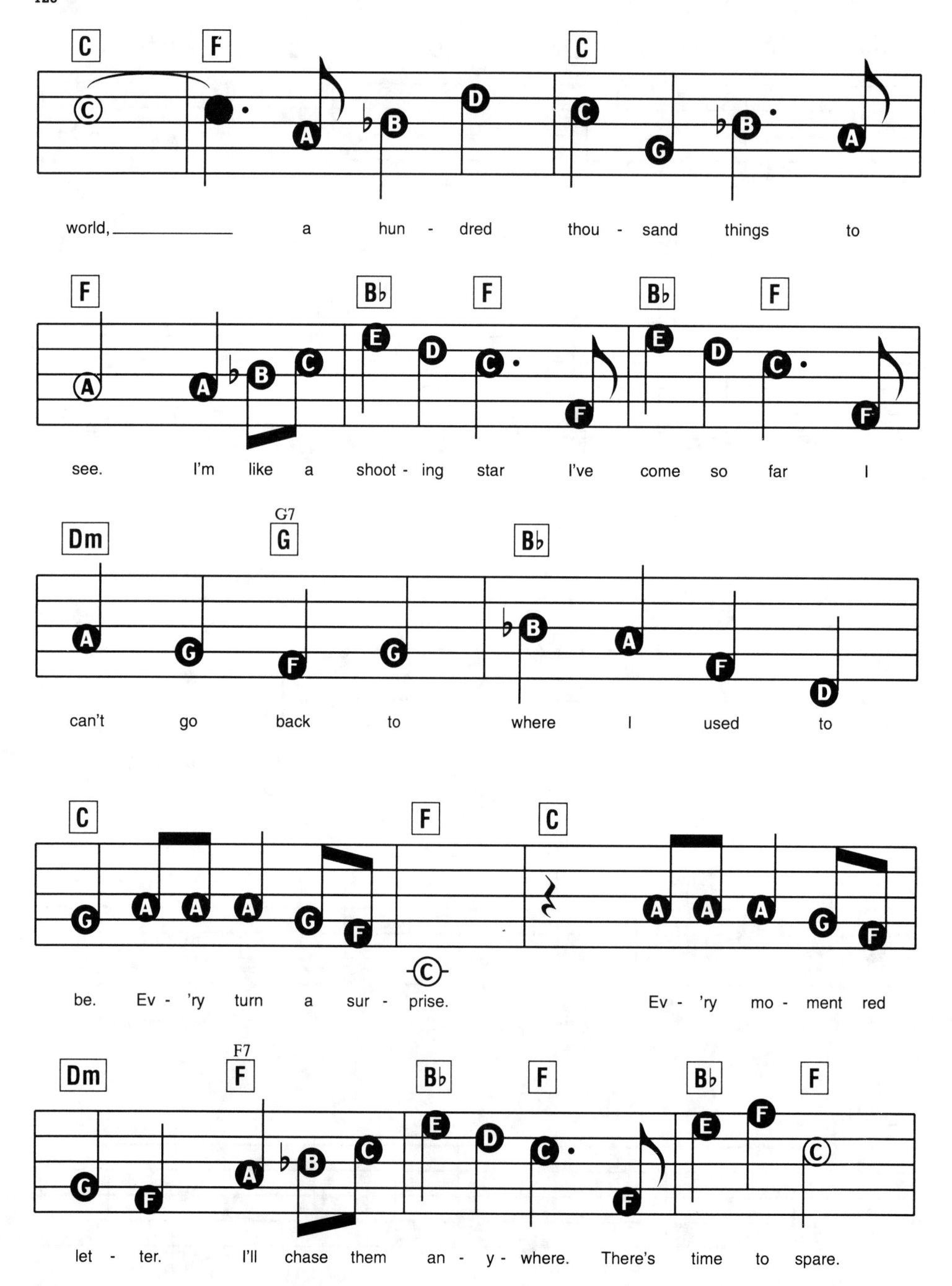

Let me share this whole new world with you.

A whole new world, A whole new world, that's where we'll

be. that's where we'll be. A thrill-ing

chase A won-d'rous place for you and
for you and

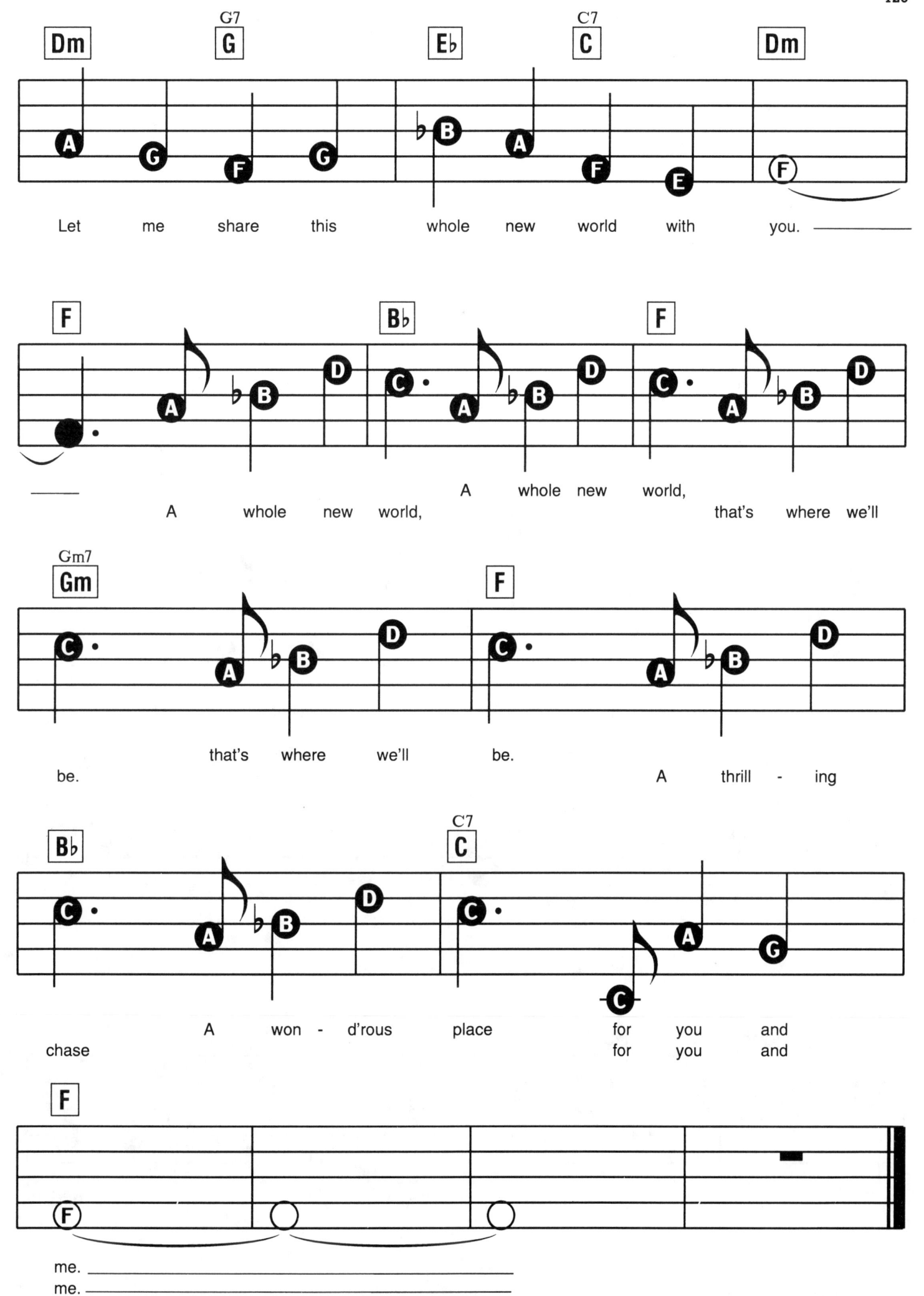

me.
me.

When I Fall In Love

featured in the TriStar Motion Picture SLEEPLESS IN SEATTLE

Registration 10
Rhythm: Fox Trot or Ballad

Words by Edward Heyman
Music by Victor Young

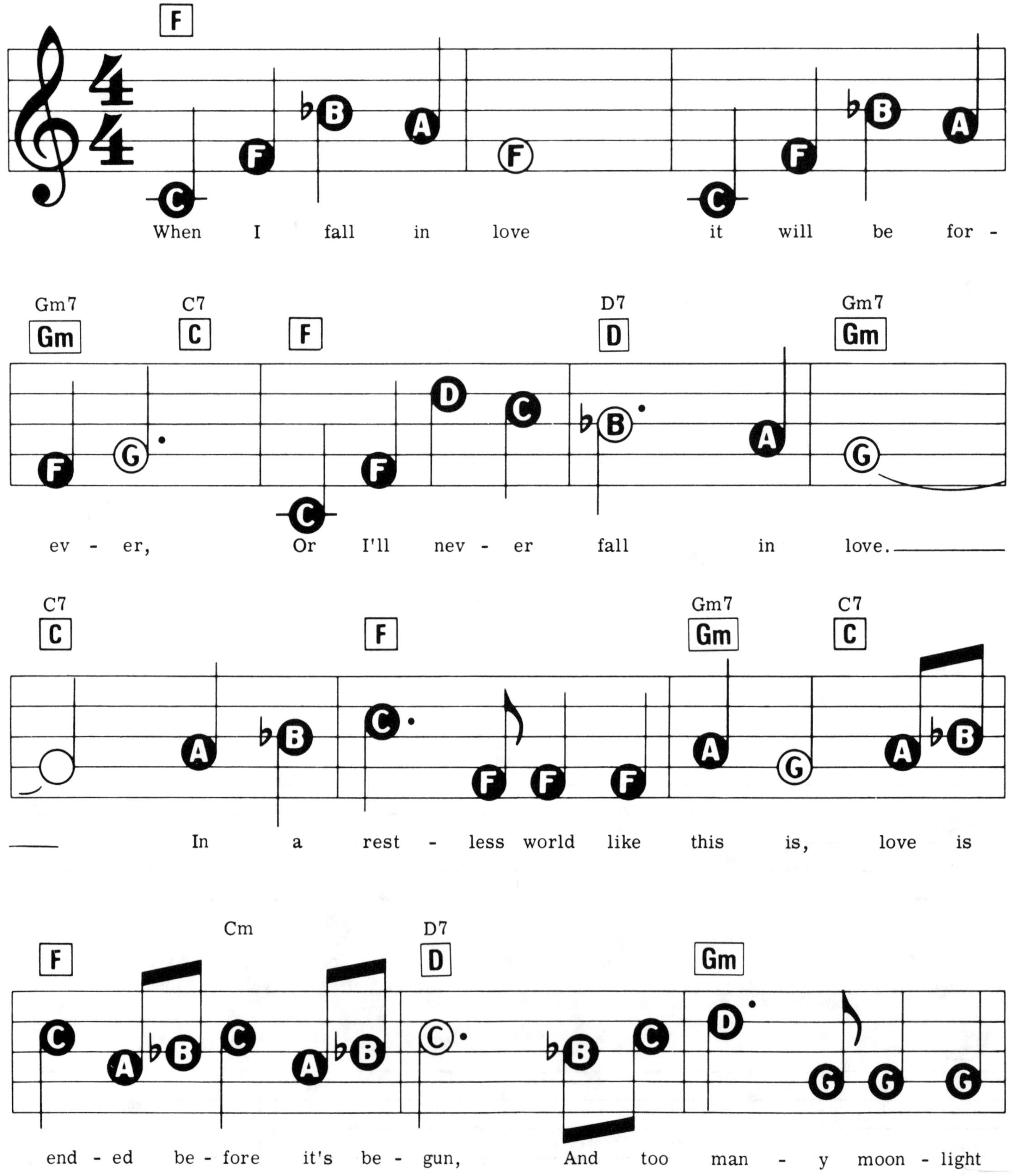

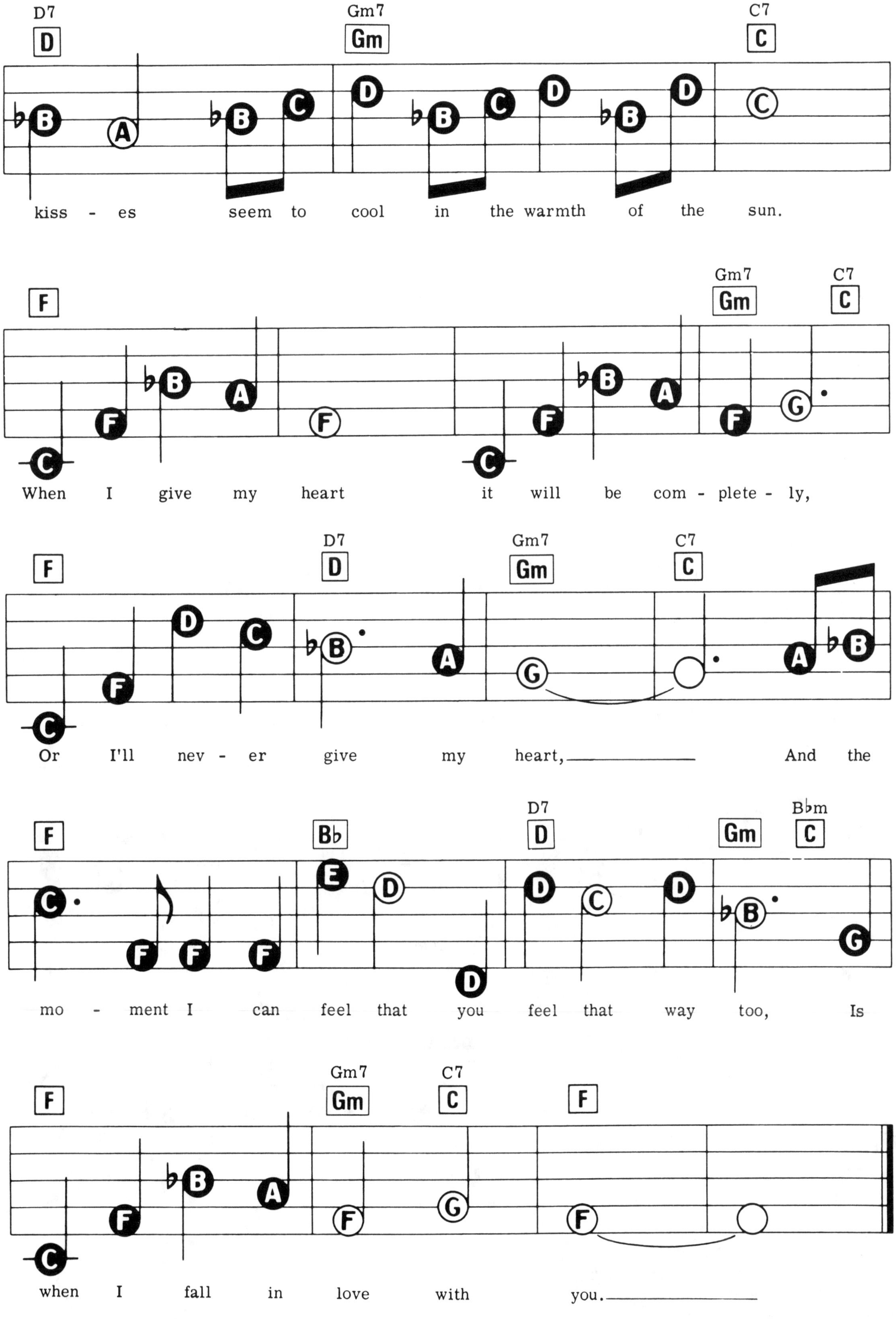
D7 D Gm7 Gm C7 C
kiss - es seem to cool in the warmth of the sun.
F Gm7 Gm C7 C
When I give my heart it will be com - plete - ly,
F D7 D Gm7 Gm C7 C
Or I'll nev - er give my heart, And the
F B♭ D7 D Gm B♭m C
mo - ment I can feel that you feel that way too, Is
F Gm7 Gm C7 C F
when I fall in love with you.

A Wink and a Smile

featured in the TriStar Motion Picture SLEEPLESS IN SEATTLE

Registration 1
Rhythm: Shuffle or Swing

Music by Marc Shaiman
Lyrics by Ramsey McLean

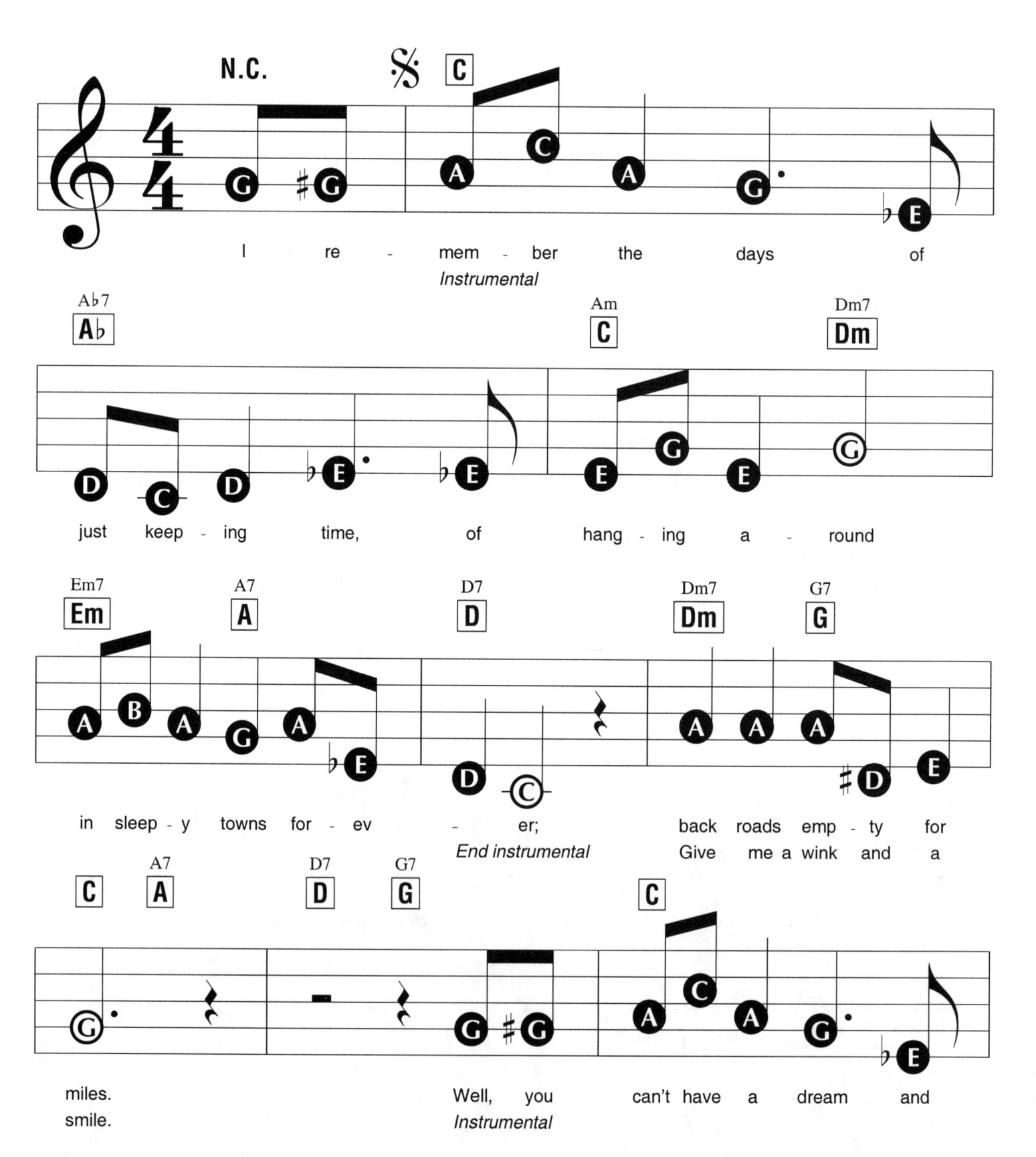

I re-mem-ber the days of
Instrumental
just keep-ing time, of hang-ing a-round
in sleep-y towns for-ev — -er; back roads emp-ty for
End instrumental Give me a wink and a
miles.
smile. Well, you can't have a dream and
Instrumental

Copyright © 1993 TSP Music, Inc., Triple Star Music, Inc.,
  Clean Con Music and Winding Brook Way Music
All Rights on behalf of TSP Music, Inc. and Triple Star Music, Inc. Administered by
  Sony/ATV Music Publishing, 8 Music Square West, Nashville, TN 37203
All Rights on behalf of Clean Con Music Administered by Warner-Tamerlane Publishing Corp.
All Rights on behalf of Winding Brook Way Music Administered by
  Sendroff & Associates, P.C., 1500 Broadway, New York, NY 10036
International Copyright Secured   All Rights Reserved

Ab7 / Ab		C	
D C D Eb· Eb		E G E G A	
cut it to fit,	but	when I saw you, I	

Em7 / Em	A7 / A	D7 / D	G7 / G
B	A G A Eb	D C	A G A G A
knew we'd	go to-geth	- er	like a wink and a
		End instrumental We'd go to-geth-er	like a wink and a

C	Ab7 / Ab	C / F	C
C·	—	C A C· C	E G
smile.		Leave your old ja - lop - y	
smile.		Now my heart hears mu - sic;	

F7 / F	C7 / C	Am	
C A C A	G·	A C A C C A	
by the rail - road	track.	We'll get a hip dou - ble	
such a sim - ple	song.	Sing it a - gain; the	

D7 / D	Ab7 / Ab	*To Coda* ⊕ G7 / G
C C A C	D D B G A	G
dip tip top - py	two - seat Cad - il - lac. ___	
notes nev - er end.	This is where I be - long. ___	

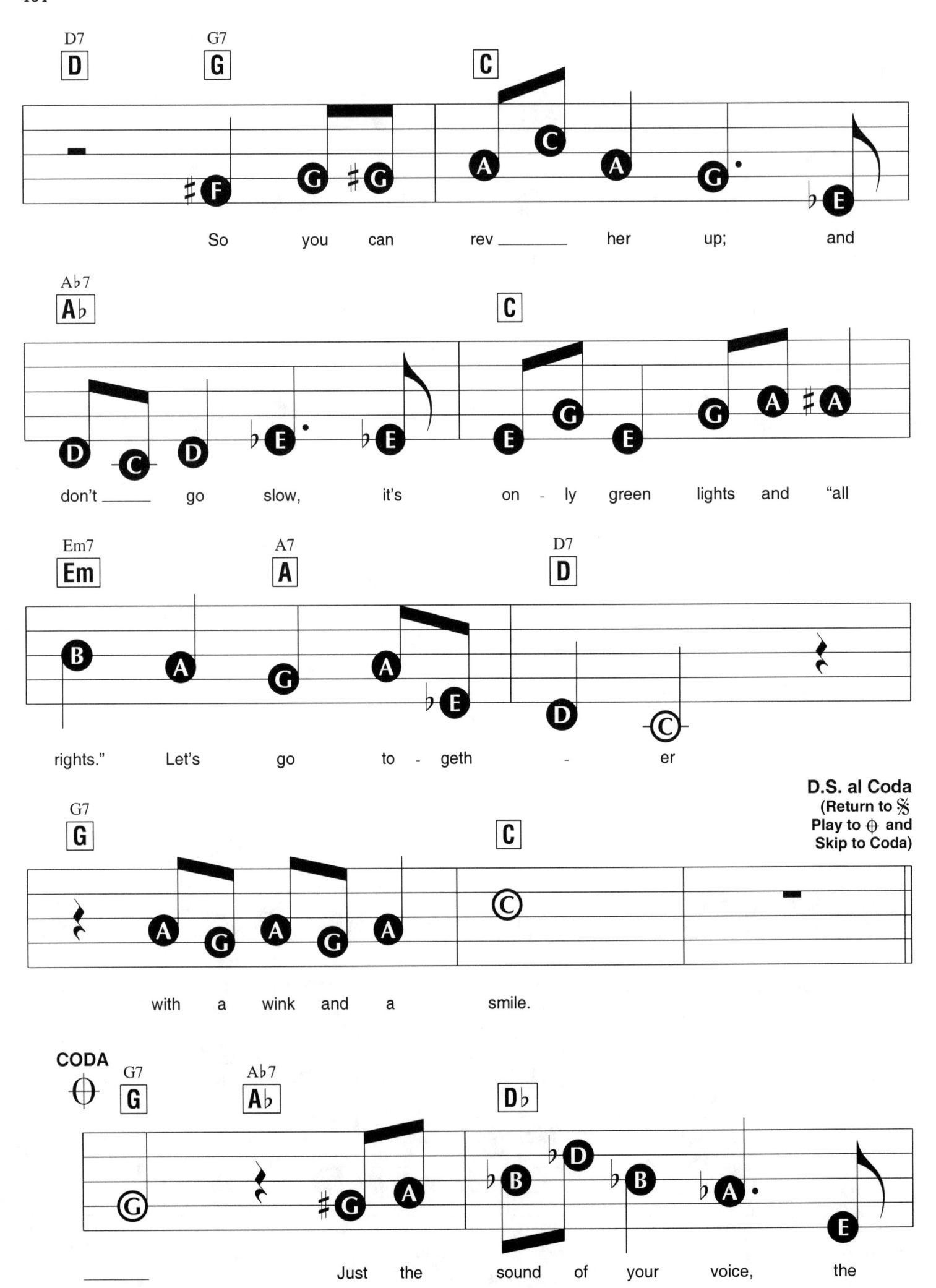

So you can rev ___ her up; and don't ___ go slow, it's on-ly green lights and "all rights." Let's go to-geth-er

D.S. al Coda
(Return to 𝄋
Play to ⊕ and
Skip to Coda)

with a wink and a smile.

CODA

Just the sound of your voice, the

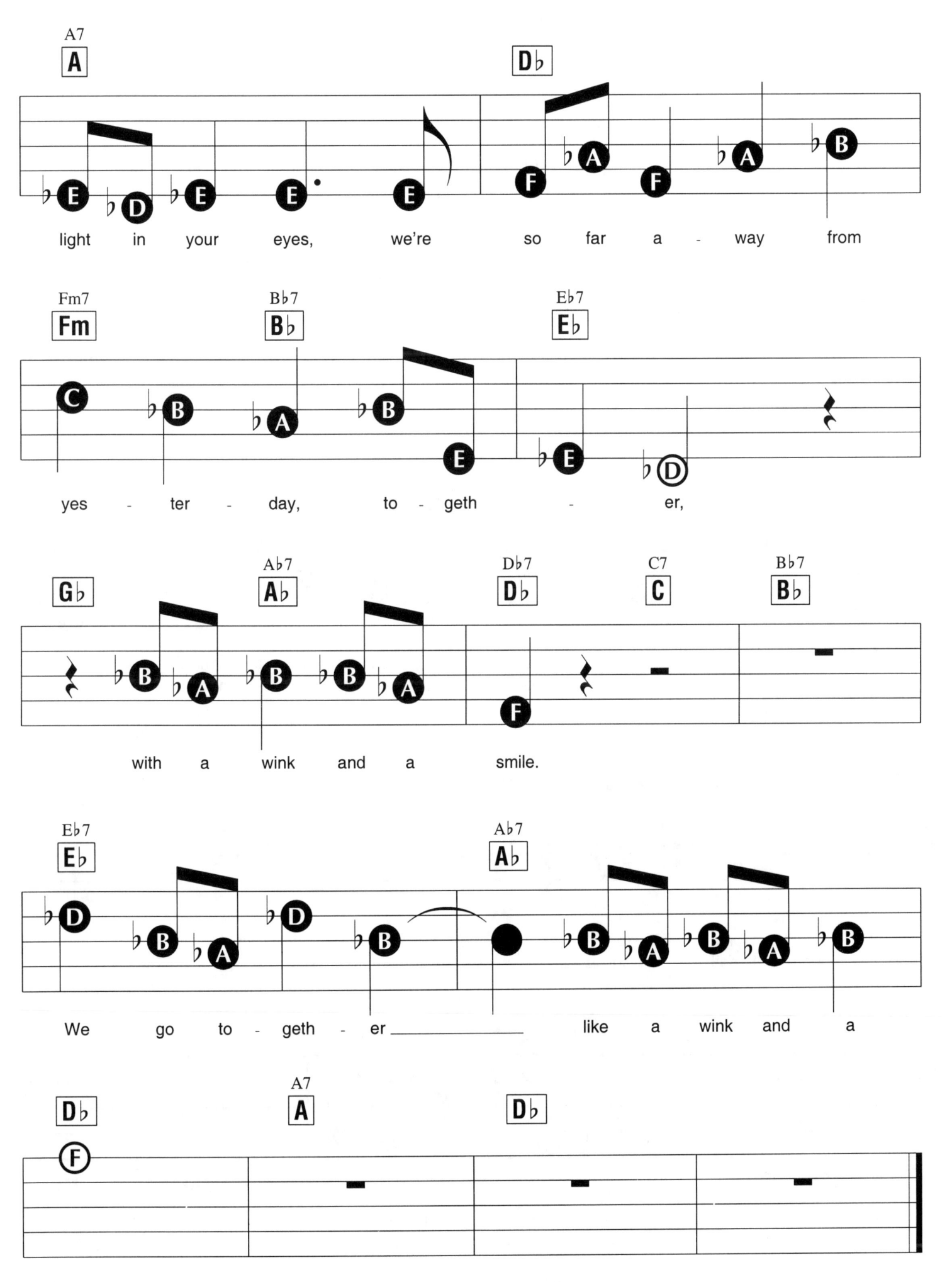

light in your eyes, we're so far a - way from
yes - ter - day, to - geth - er,
with a wink and a smile.
We go to - geth - er like a wink and a
smile.

You and I

Registration 3
Rhythm: 8 Beat or Rock

Words and Music by
Stevie Wonder

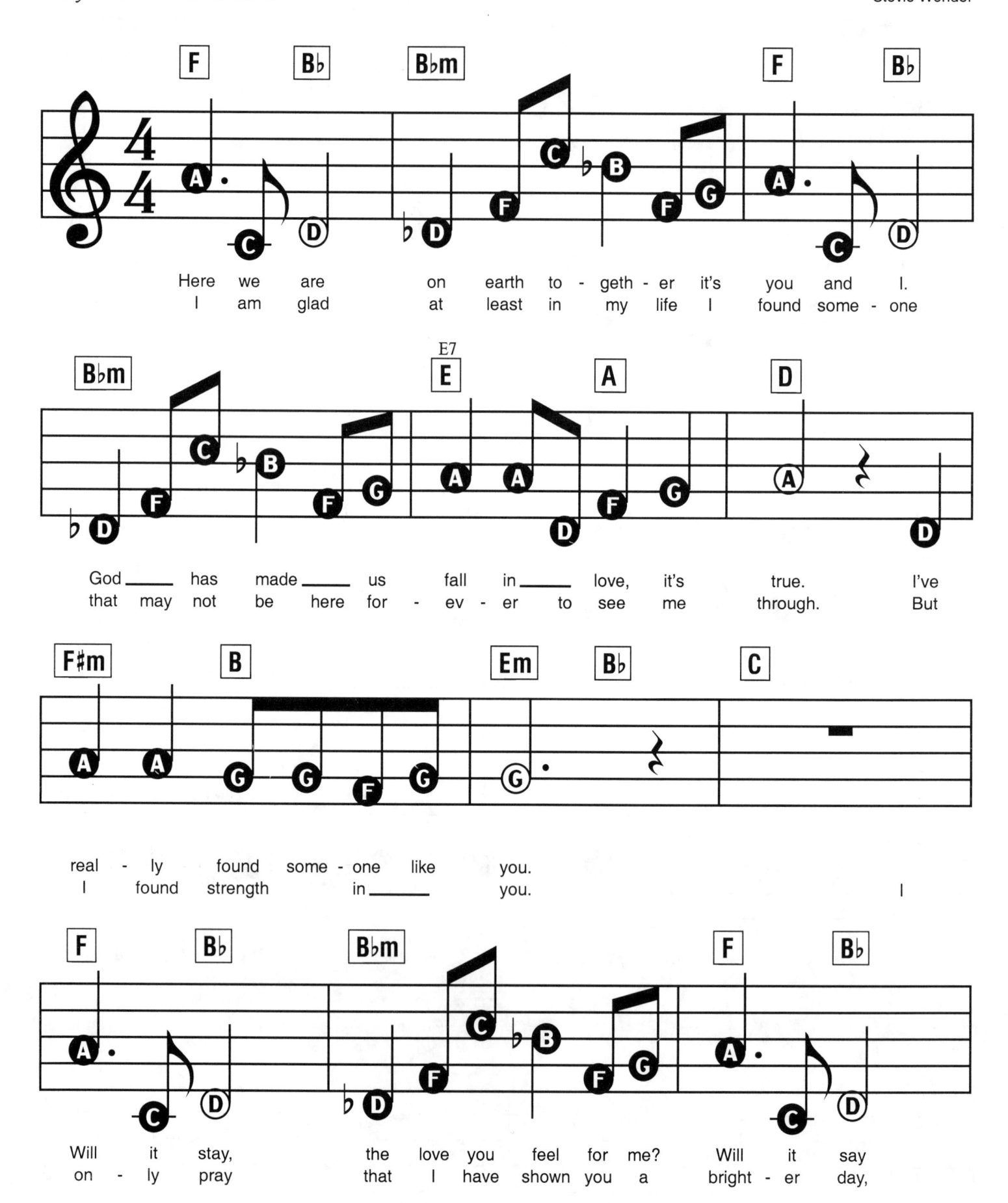

F | B♭ | B♭m | F | B♭

C A. C ♭B A. C
D ♭D F G D

Here we are on earth to-geth-er it's you and I.
I am glad at least in my life I found some-one

B♭m | E E7 | A | D

♭D F C ♭B F G A A F G A
D

God has made us fall in love, it's true. I've
that may not be here for-ev-er to see me through. But

F#m | B | Em B♭ | C

A A G G F G G.

real-ly found some-one like you.
I found strength in you.   I

F | B♭ | B♭m | F | B♭

A. C ♭B A. C
C D ♭D F G C D

Will it stay, the love you feel for me? Will it say
on-ly pray that I have shown you a bright-er day,

© 1972 JOBETE MUSIC CO., INC. and BLACK BULL MUSIC
c/o EMI APRIL MUSIC INC.
International Copyright Secured   All Rights Reserved   Used by Permission

137

You Are the Sunshine of My Life

EASY LATIN

Registration 7
Rhythm: 8 Beat or Bossa Nova

Words and Music by
Stevie Wonder

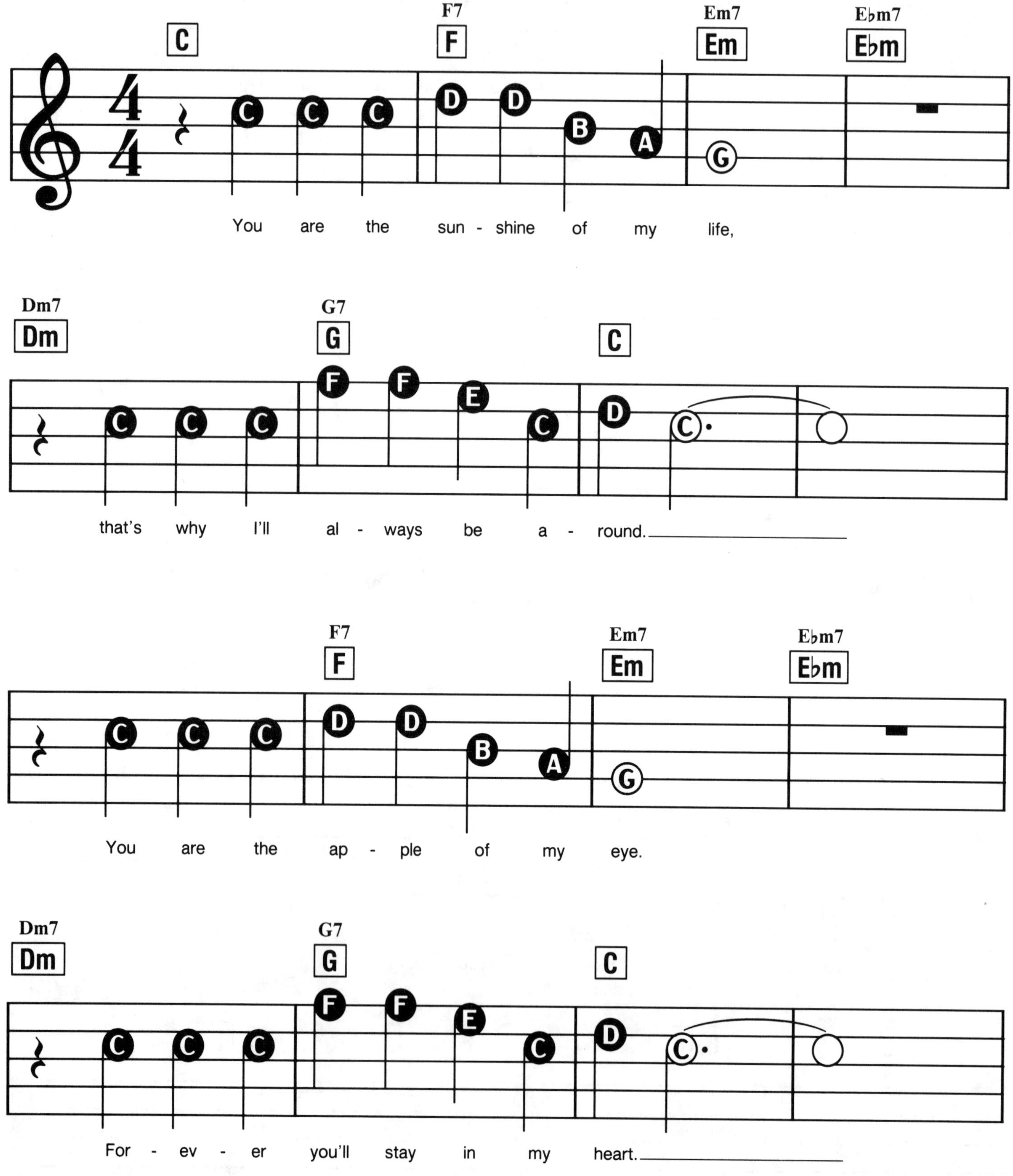

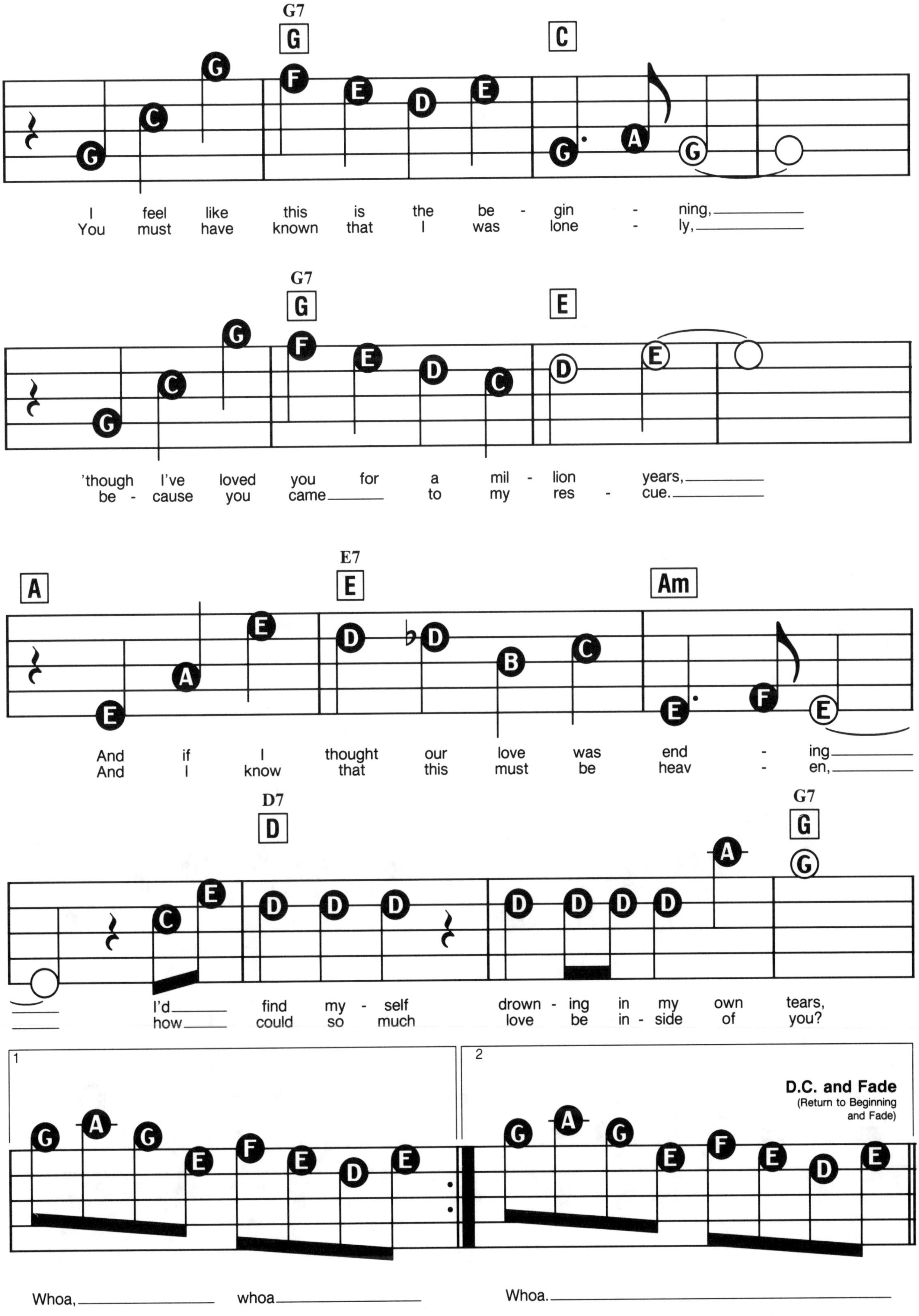
G7
C
I feel like this is the be - gin - ning,
You must have known that I was lone - ly,
G7
E
'though I've loved you for a mil - lion years,
be - cause you came to my res - cue.
A
E7
Am
And if I thought our love was end - ing
And I know that this must be heav - en,
D7
G7
I'd find my - self drown - ing in my own tears,
how could so much love be in - side of you?
1
2
D.C. and Fade
(Return to Beginning and Fade)
Whoa, whoa
Whoa.

You'll Be in My Heart

(Pop Version)
from Walt Disney Pictures' TARZAN™

Registration 1
Rhythm: Rock or Pops

Words and Music by
Phil Collins

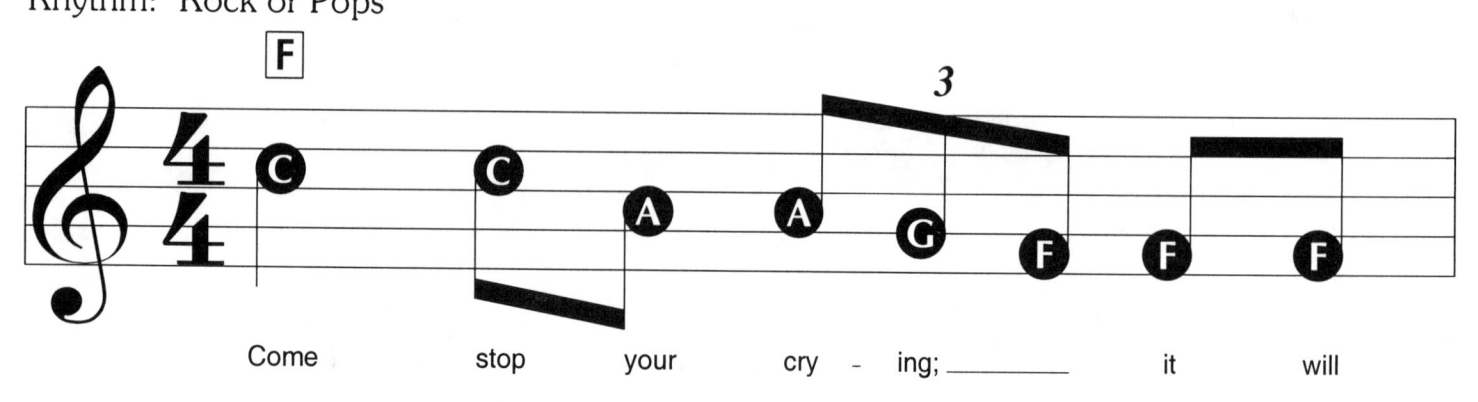

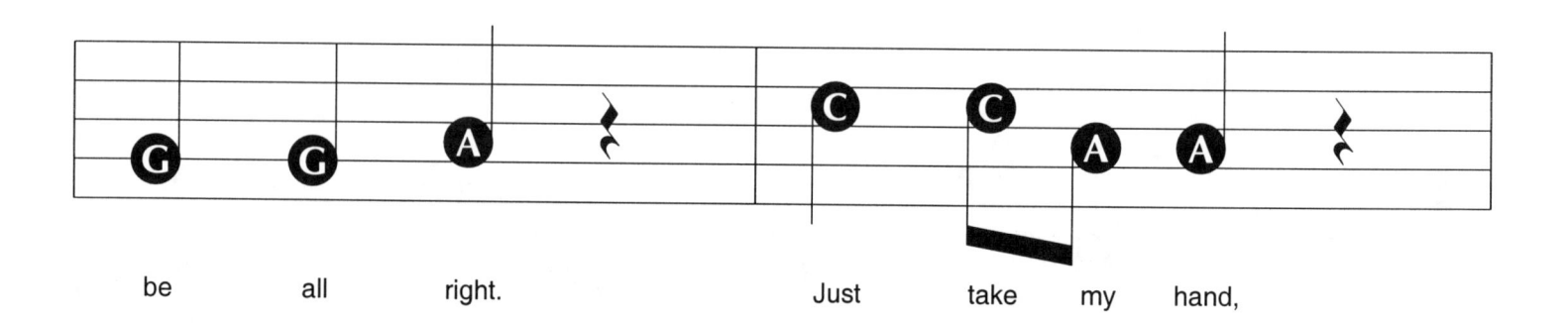

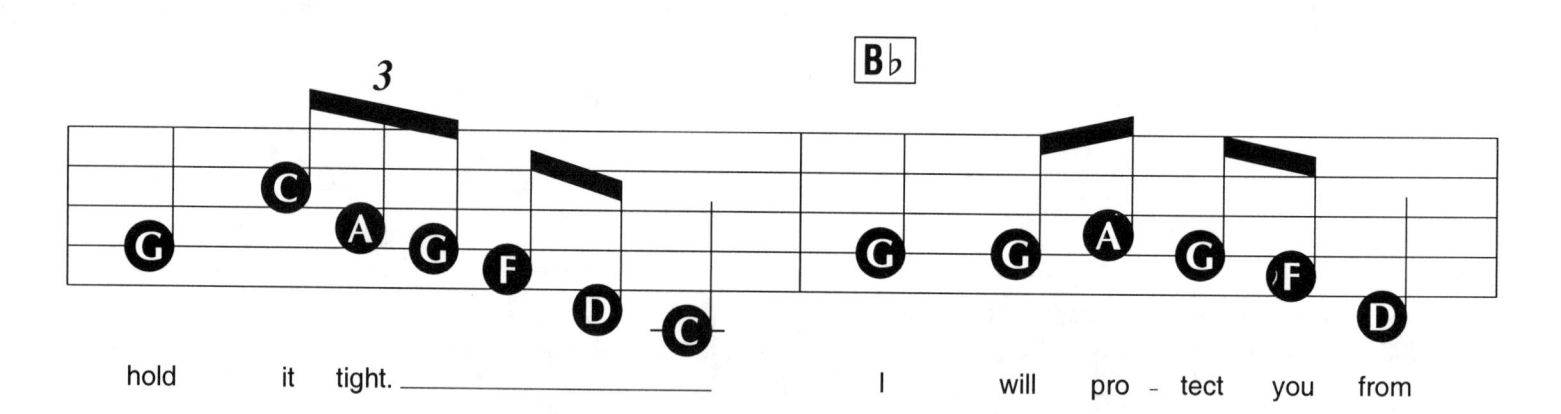

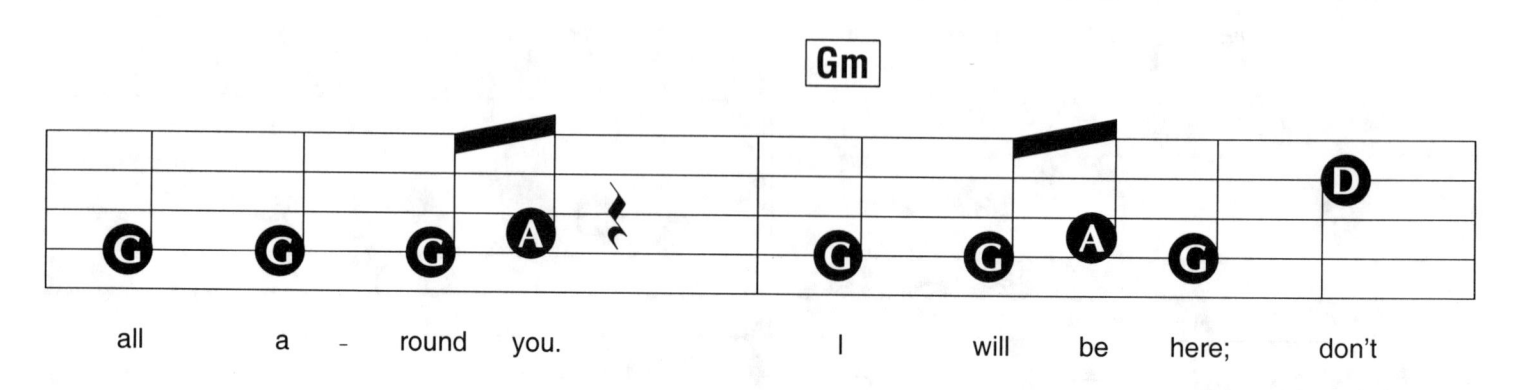

Come stop your cry-ing; it will be all right. Just take my hand, hold it tight. I will pro-tect you from all a-round you. I will be here; don't

© 1998 Edgar Rice Burroughs, Inc. and Walt Disney Music Company
All Rights Reserved Used by Permission

141

| C | F | C | F |

you cry. For one so small you seem so strong.
Why can't they un-der-stand the way we feel?

| | | C | F |

My arms will hold you, ___ keep you safe and warm. ___
They just just don't trust ___ what they can't ex-plain. ___

| Bb | | | |

This bond be-tween us can't be bro-ken.
I know we're dif-f'rent, but deep in-side us,

| G | | C | A |

I will be here; don't you cry. 'Cause
we're not that dif-fer-ent at all. ___ And

| D | | G | A |

you'll be in ___ my ___ heart, yes, you'll be in my ___

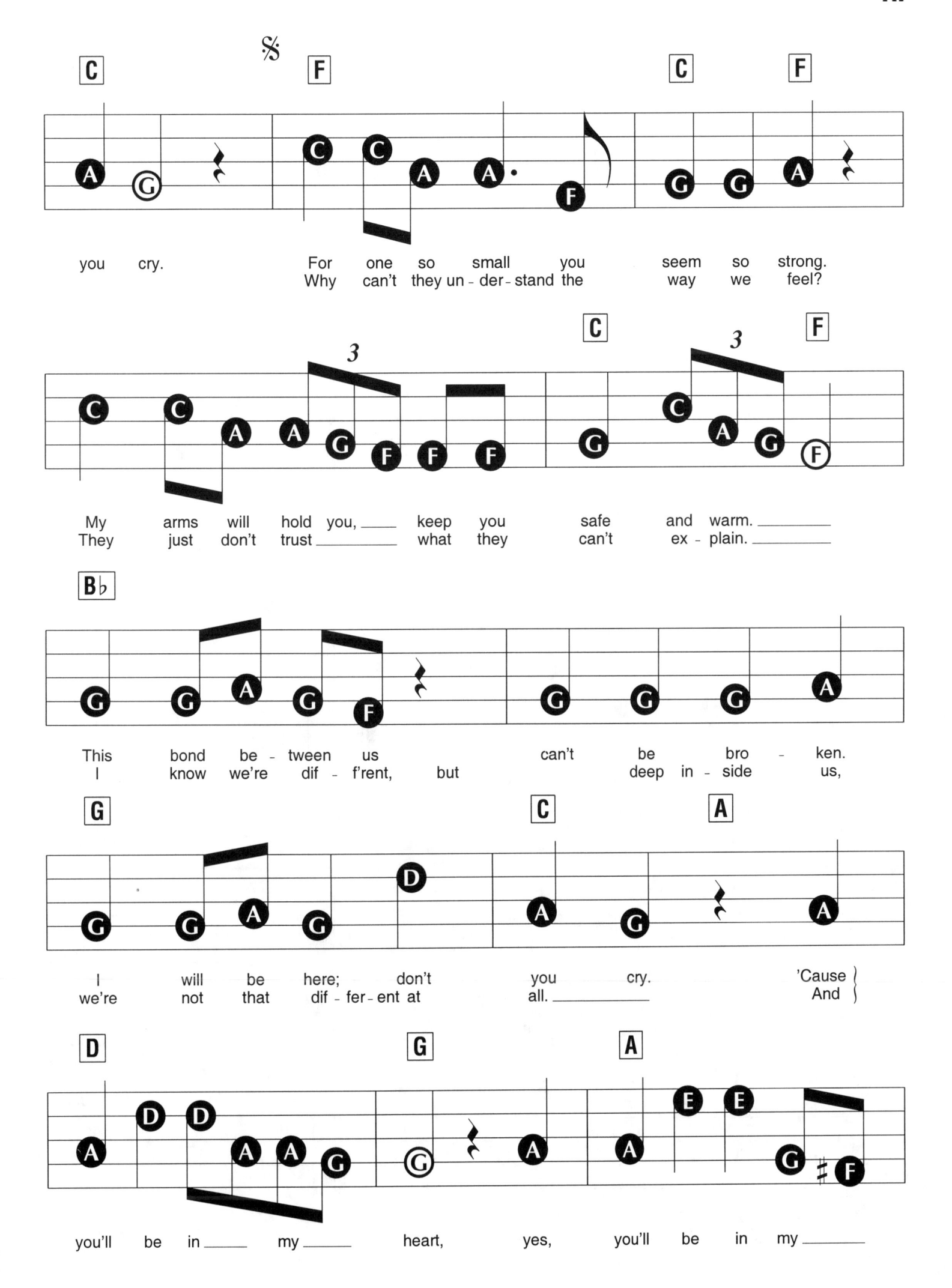

heart from this day on now and for - ev - er -

To Coda

more. You'll be in ____ my ____

heart no matter what they ____ say. You'll

be here in ____ my ____ heart

D.S. al Coda
(Return to 𝄋
Play to ⊕ and
Skip to Coda)

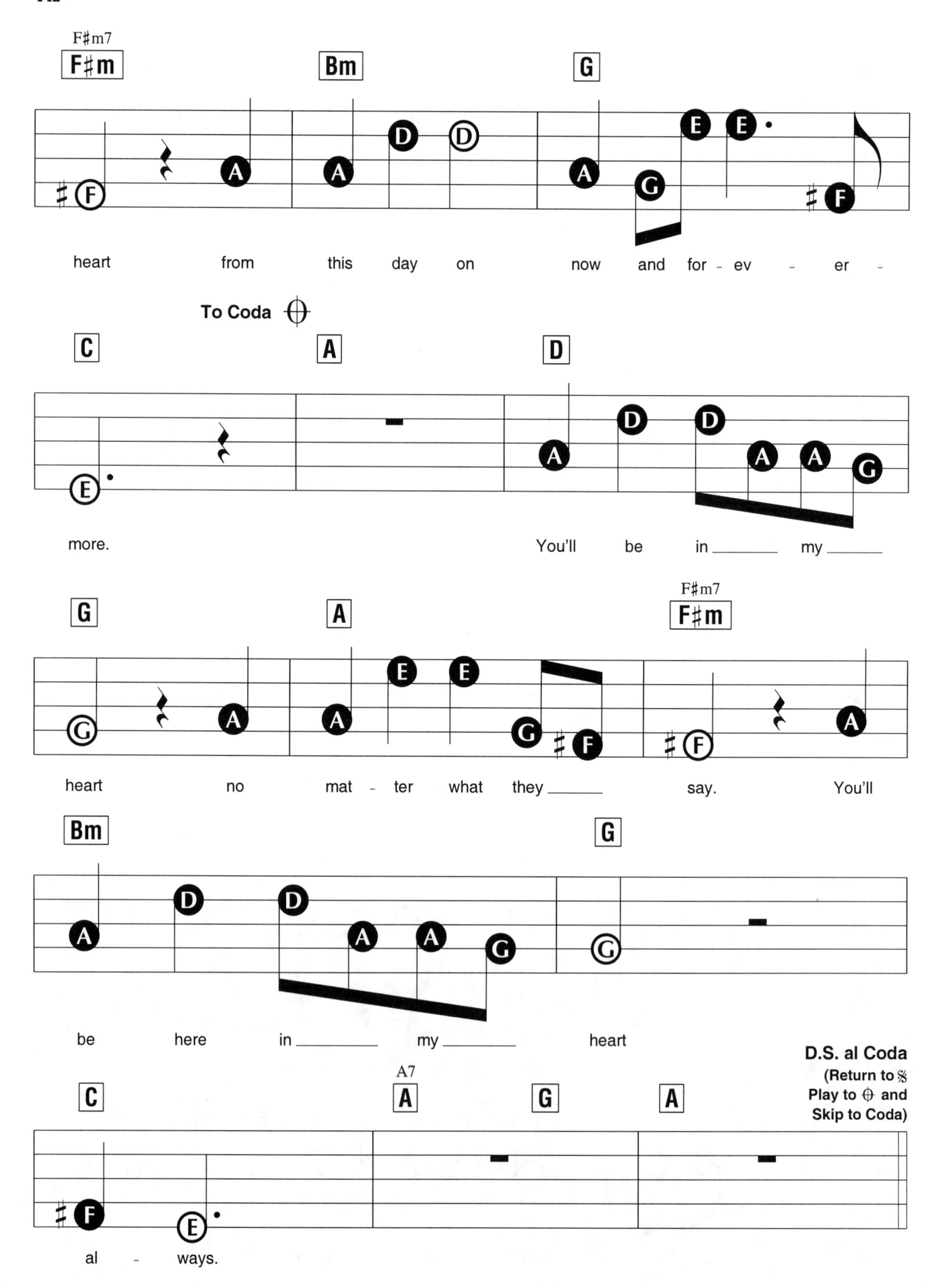

al - ways.

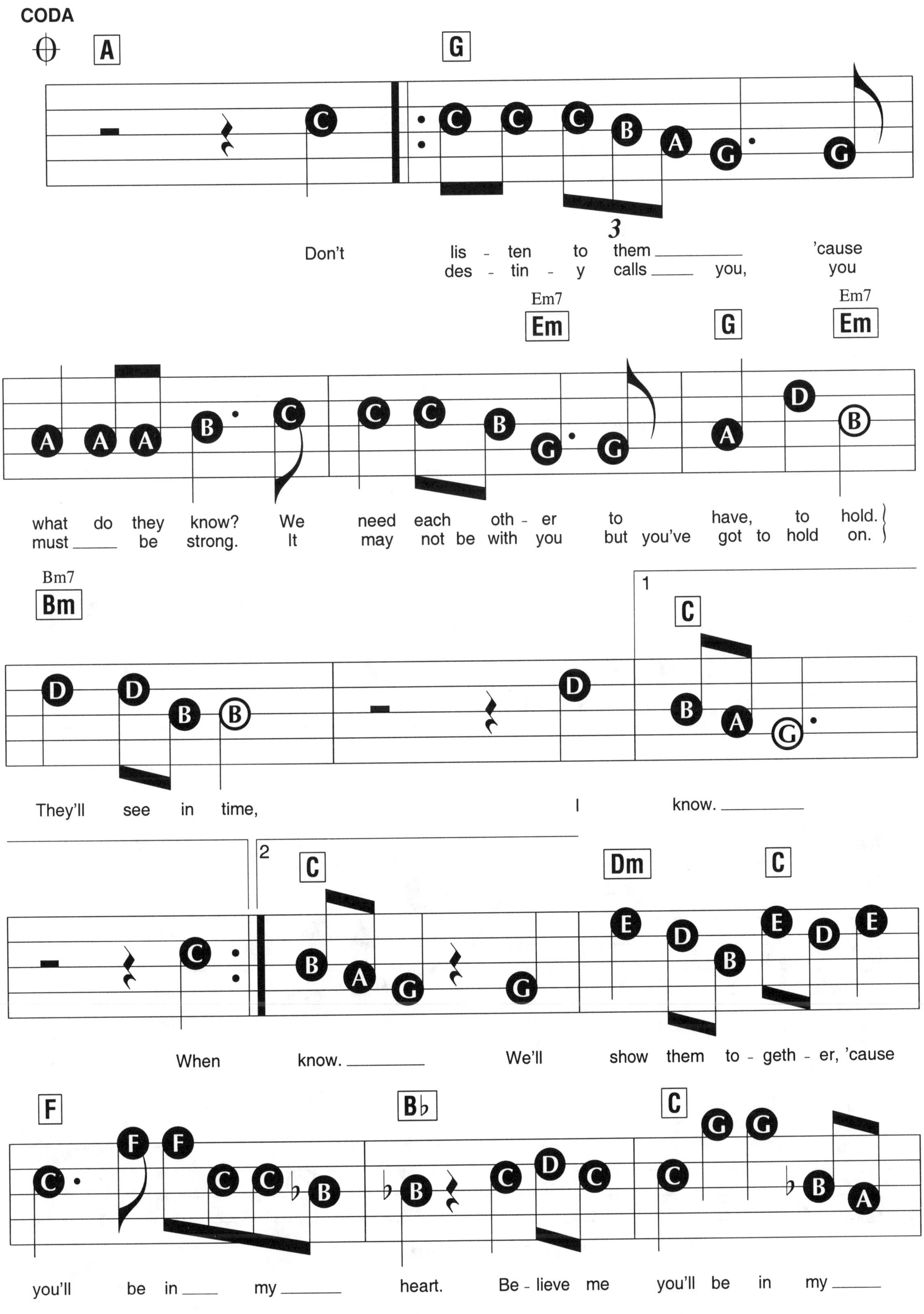
CODA
A
G
Don't lis - ten to them 'cause
des - tin - y calls you, you
Em7
Em
G
Em7
Em
what do they know? We need each oth - er to have, to hold.
must be strong. It may not be with you but you've got to hold on.
Bm7
Bm
1
C
They'll see in time, I know.
2
C
Dm
C
When know. We'll show them to - geth - er, 'cause
F
B♭
C
you'll be in my heart. Be - lieve me you'll be in my

Am7		Dm	
Am		**Dm**	
A — E E D C		C F F A G	
heart.	I'll be there from	this day on,	now

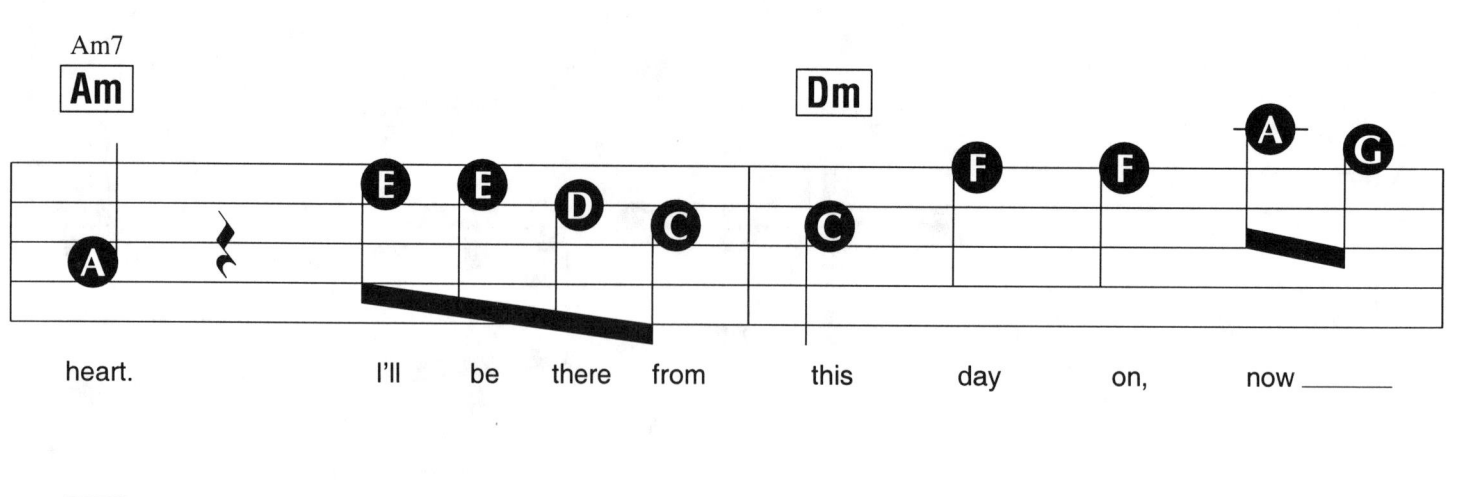

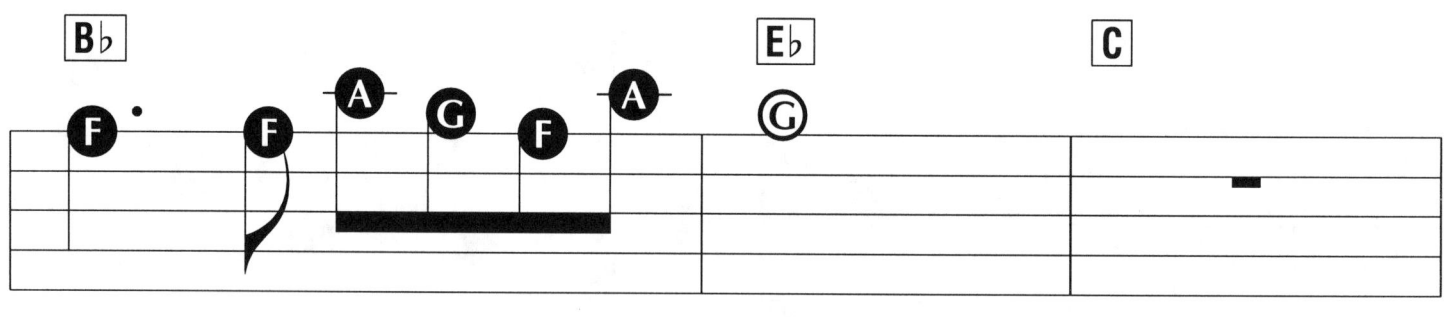

B♭		**E♭**	**C**
F. F A G F A		G	
and	for - ev - er - more.		

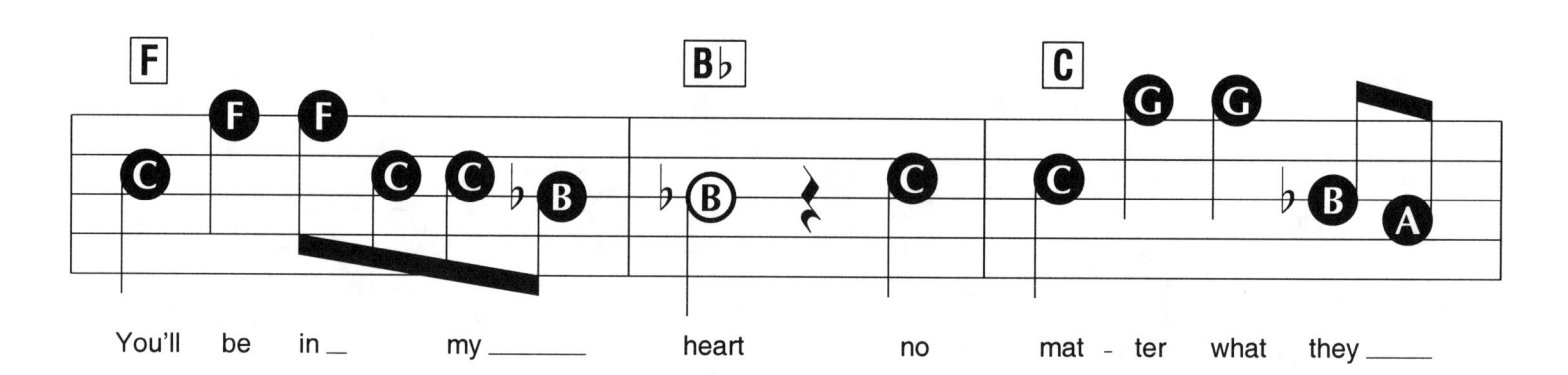

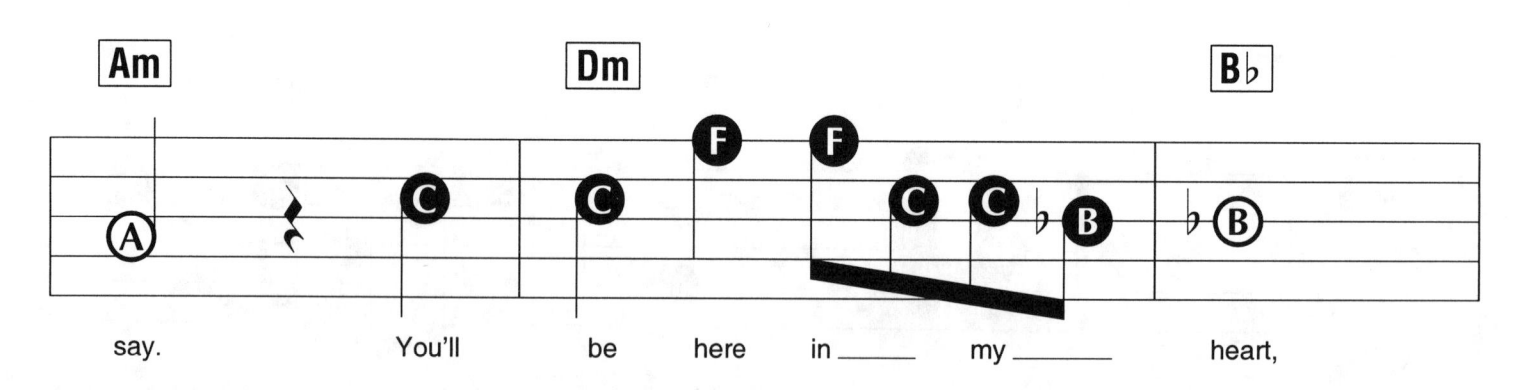

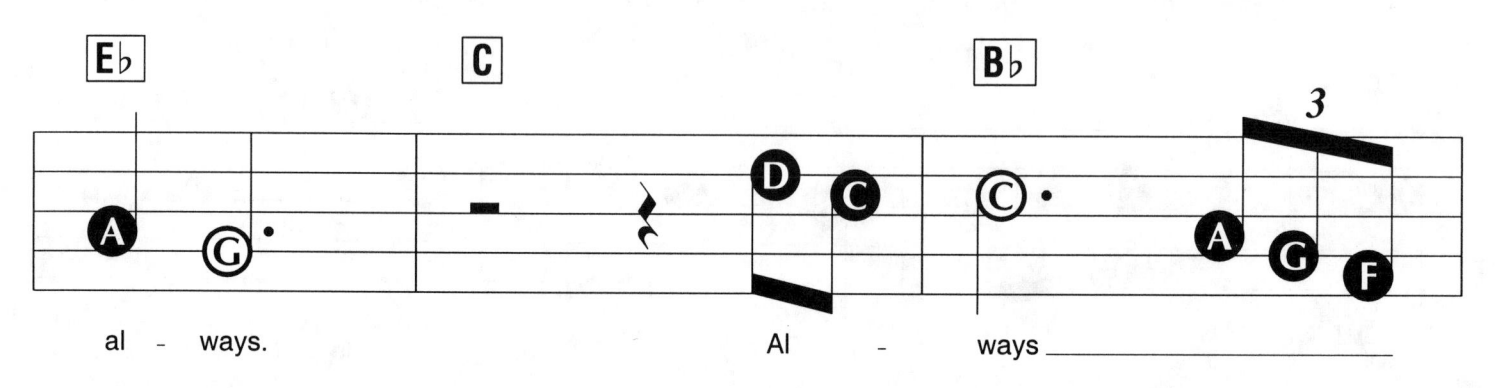

F		**B♭**	**C**
C F F C C B♭	B♭ C	C G G B♭ A	
You'll be in my	heart no	mat - ter what they	

Am		**Dm**	**B♭**
A	C C	F F C C B♭	B♭
say.	You'll be here in	my	heart,

E♭	**C**	**B♭**	
A G.	D C	C. A G F	
al - ways.	Al -	ways	

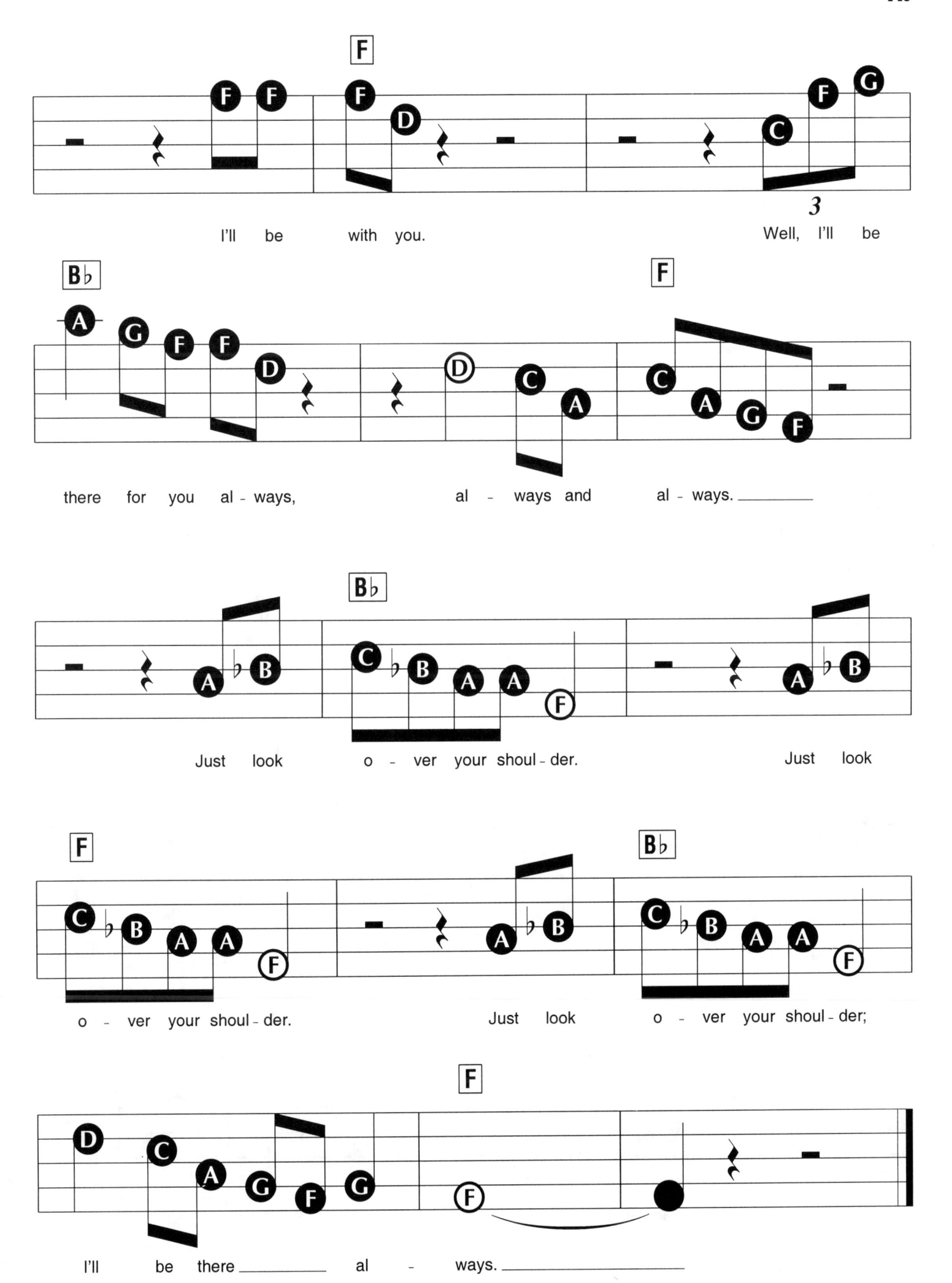

I'll be with you. Well, I'll be there for you al-ways, al-ways and al-ways. Just look o-ver your shoul-der. Just look o-ver your shoul-der. Just look o-ver your shoul-der; I'll be there al-ways.

Wonderful Tonight

Registration 4
Rhythm: Pops or Rock

Words and Music by
Eric Clapton

It's late in the eve - ning; she's won - d'ring what clothes to wear. She puts on her make - up and brush - es her long blonde hair. And then she asks me, "Do I look all

We go to a par - ty, and ev - 'ry - one turns to see this beau - ti - ful la - dy is walk - ing a - round with me. And then she asks me, "Do you feel all

It's time to go home now, and I've got an ach - ing head. So I give her the car keys and she helps me to bed. And then I tell her, as I turn out the

Copyright © 1977 by Eric Patrick Clapton
All Rights for the U.S. Administered by Unichappell Music Inc.
International Copyright Secured   All Rights Reserved

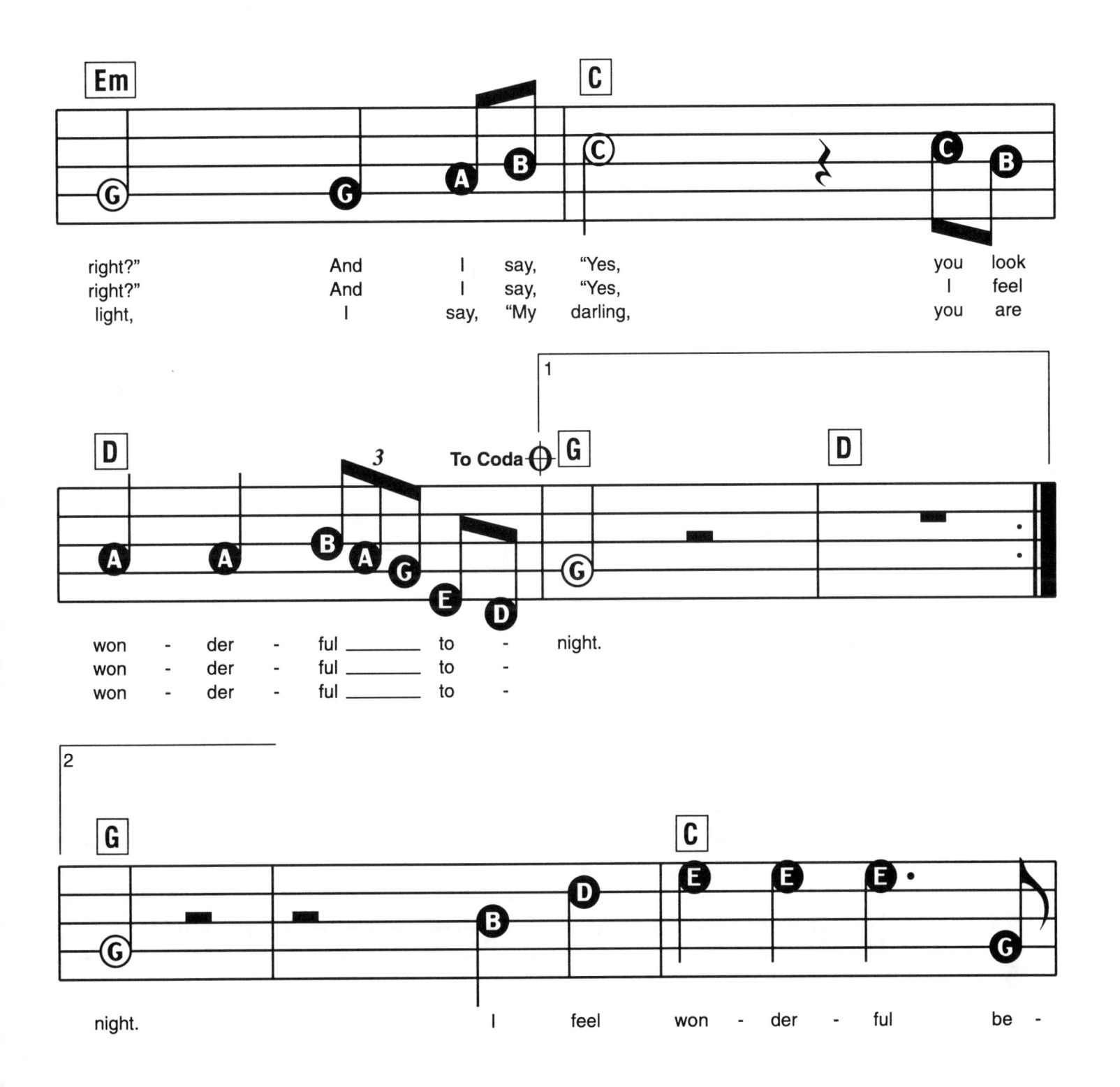

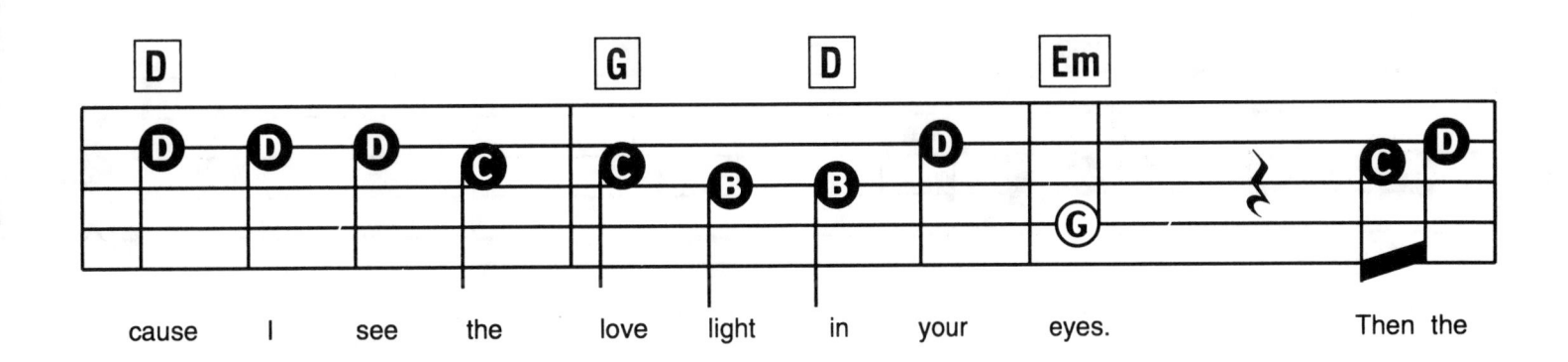

right?" And I say, "Yes, you look
right?" And I say, "Yes, I feel
light, I say, "My darling, you are

won - der - ful _____ to - night.
won - der - ful _____ to - night.
won - der - ful _____ to -

night. I feel won - der - ful be -

cause I see the love light in your eyes. Then the

won - der of it all is that you just don't re - al -

D.C. al Coda
(Return to beginning
Play to ⊕ and
Skip to Coda)

ize how much _____ I love you.

CODA

night. Oh, my dar - ling you are

won - der - ful _____ to - night." _____

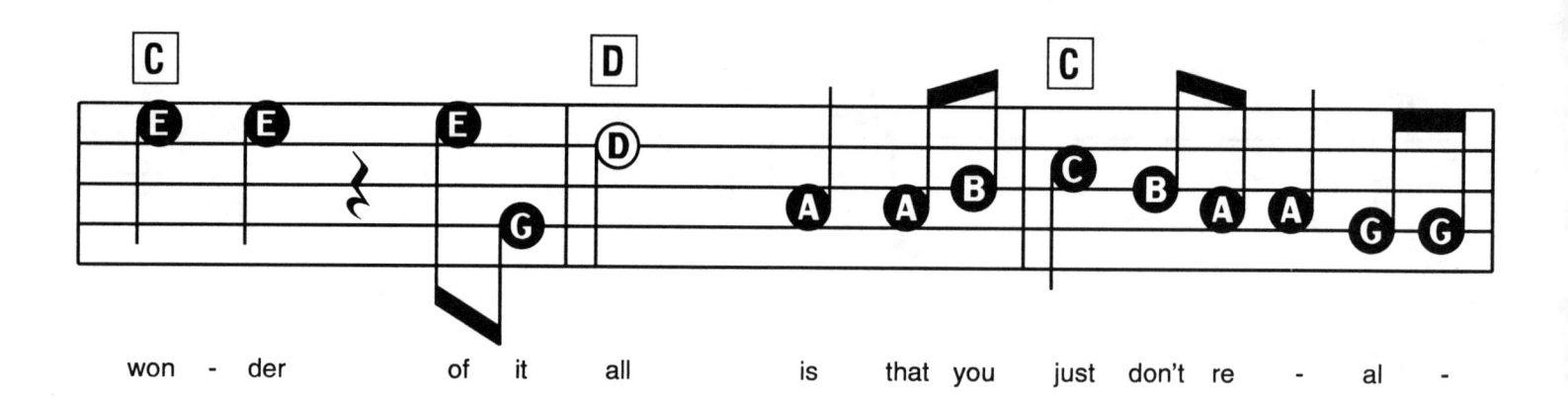

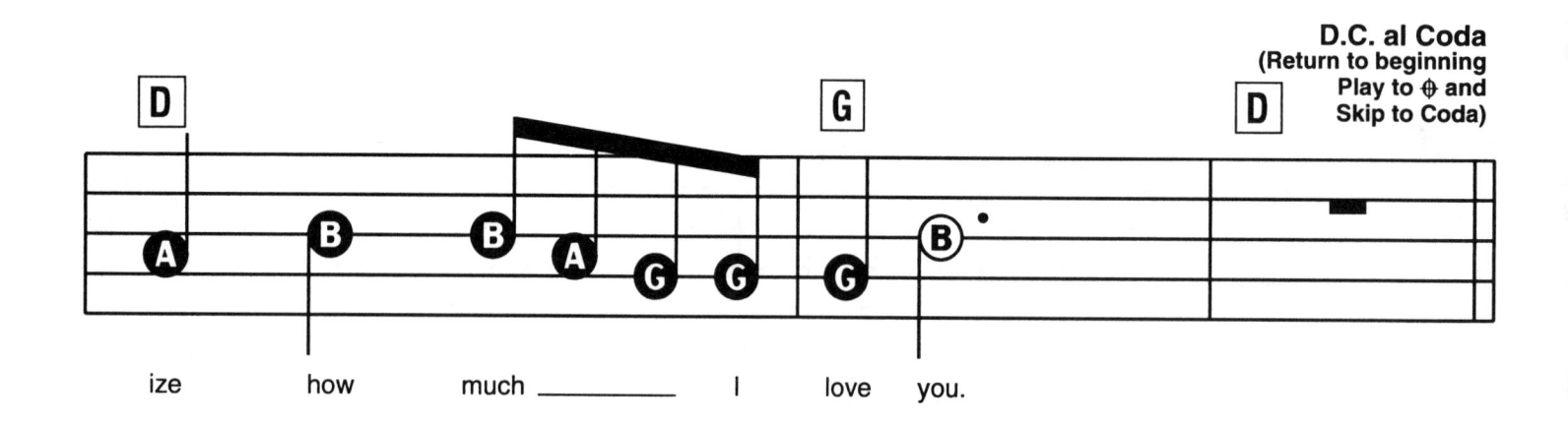

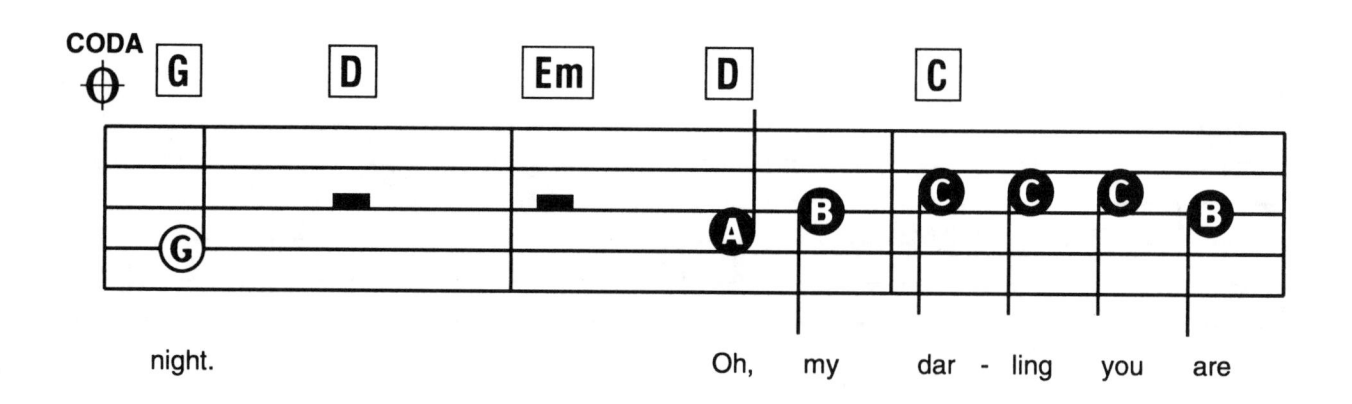

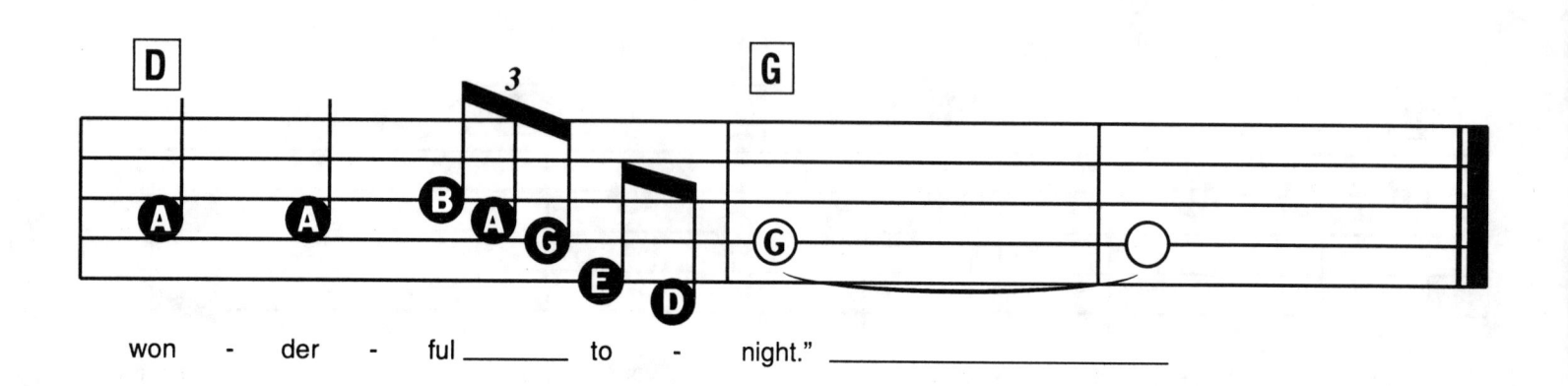

E-Z Play Today Registration Guide

- Match the Registration number on the song to the corresponding numbered category below. Select and activate an instrumental sound available on your instrument.
- Choose an automatic rhythm appropriate to the mood and style of the song. (Consult your Owner's Guide for proper operation of automatic rhythm features.)
- Adjust the tempo and volume controls to comfortable settings.

Registration

1	Flute, Pan Flute, Jazz Flute
2	Clarinet, Organ
3	Violin, Strings
4	Brass, Trumpet
5	Synth Ensemble, Accordion, Brass
6	Pipe Organ, Harpsichord
7	Jazz Organ, Vibraphone, Vibes, Electric Piano, Jazz Guitar
8	Piano, Electric Piano
9	Trumpet, Trombone, Clarinet, Saxophone, Oboe
10	Violin, Cello, Strings